## DATE DUE

|  |  |  |  |
|--|--|--|--|
|  |  |  |  |
|  |  |  |  |
|  |  |  |  |
|  |  |  |  |
|  |  |  |  |
|  |  |  |  |
|  |  |  |  |
|  |  |  |  |
|  |  |  |  |
|  |  |  |  |
|  |  |  |  |
|  |  |  |  |
|  |  |  |  |
|  |  |  |  |
|  |  |  |  |
|  |  |  |  |
|  |  |  |  |
|  |  |  |  |

DEMCO 38-296

# THE EMERGENCE
## OF A
# NEW LEBANON

# THE EMERGENCE OF A NEW LEBANON

## FANTASY OR REALITY?

EDWARD E. AZAR
PAUL A. JUREIDINI
R. D. McLAURIN
AUGUSTUS R. NORTON
ROBERT J. PRANGER
KATE SHNAYERSON
LEWIS W. SNIDER
JOYCE R. STARR

ɪ in Publication Data

ᴵⁿᶜˡᵘᵈᵉˢ ᶦⁿᵈᵉˣ.
   1. Lebanon—Politics and government—1975—Addresses,
essays, lectures. I. Azar, Edward E., 1938
DS87.E47 1984            956.92'044            84-15974
ISBN 0-03-070736-6 (alk. paper)

Published in 1984 by Praeger Publishers
CBS Educational and Professional Publishing
a Division of CBS Inc.
521 Fifth Avenue, New York, NY 10175 USA

© 1984 by Praeger Publishers

56789 052 98765432

Printed in the United States of America
on acid-free paper

# Preface

Long the most familiar of the Middle East countries to Americans, Lebanon has become something of an alien. Those who have only recently come to know the name associate Lebanon with extremism, bigotry, and violence. Their portrait is that of a poor, war-torn land not unlike other Third World states except in the savagery of its divisiveness. Those Americans who knew Lebanon in years past, and there were many, have tended to err just as grievously by assuming that the Lebanon whose shattered landscape they see on the front pages of their newspapers or in the more vivid images of television is the same Lebanon they once knew. Geography is more static than society.

Apart from the literature on the violence in Lebanon—which is largely one-sided material—there is no body of knowledge dealing with contemporary Lebanon. The conflicts in that country both resulted from and created numerous and far-reaching changes in Lebanese society. Let there be no mistake—whatever Lebanon will be in the future, we have passed a watershed. Lebanon is not the same country it was five, ten, or fifteen years ago; the political circumstances have fundamentally and irrevocably changed. This book is an attempt to begin to look at the nature of the changes that have taken place in Lebanon.

Dottie Breitbart, our editor at Praeger, has commented on our brashness in dealing with a topic so volatile. How can we write about the Lebanese Army, for example, when every day it is subject to powerful divisive tendencies? When, in fact, the political circumstances may condemn the institution and even eliminate it before this book is released?

This book makes no claim to be the definitive work on Lebanon, not on the new Lebanon any more than on the old. It is possible that Lebanon's political circumstances will stabilize; but it is at least possible—and the common assumption of all the coauthors of this book—that change will continue.

Still, treating the present as history is all the more important because we believe that the future of Lebanon will depend upon critical decisions and actions over the next few years. Because significant change has already occurred in Lebanon, an understanding of the processes that have accompanied those changes and of the nature of contemporary Lebanon is important to a realistic awareness of the Middle East; to an appreciation of the problems and prospects of conflict reduction and resolution; and to the construction of the necessary

v

foundation to support the critical decisions and actions ahead.

The book is organized in four sections. The first part describes the evolution of Lebanon from 1982, following the War of 1982, to 1983. There is a substantial literature on Lebanon up to 1982, but very little on the critical year that followed. This section does not discuss the substance of policies or politics, but rather is designed to serve as a backdrop for the rest of the book.

Part Two, Focus on Lebanon, incorporates four chapters. Chapter 2 discusses Lebanese political culture and how it has been affected by the recent years of turmoil. The recent key political and economic developments in Lebanon are analyzed in Chapters 3 and 4. The next chapter discusses the army, which was widely seen, until recently, as the key to the future stability of Lebanon and has been, since independence, the principal symbol of Lebanese sovereignty. All three chapters concentrate on issues and problems internal to Lebanon.

Part Three addresses the responses of two Lebanese communities to external threats. Modern Lebanon has been characterized by the active role of nongovernmental armed forces, usually called "militias." The tendency of outside observers has been to overlook the degree and direction of social change in the Christian and Shi'a communities since 1975, and to assimilate the Lebanese Forces and 'Amal to the general category of "militias," without recognizing that these paramilitary forces represented a phenomenon well beyond the traditional Lebanese militia experience.

The fourth section embraces more international perspectives. Chapter 8 is an analysis of how Lebanese policy options have been influenced by other regional countries, and the chapter suggests alternatives for the future. Chapter 9 traces the evolution of the Lebanese relationship with the United States, which is seen as the principal external supporter of the Lebanese government today.

# Acknowledgments

The authors individually and as a group owe a great deal to numerous organizations and persons both Lebanese and American. In particular, we are pleased to express our gratitude to L. Akoury, J. Basil, R. Basil, J. Burton, E. Charbin, R. Dekmejian, M. Hage, B. Jenkins, N. Maasry, A. Moon, R. Parker, A. Phillips, Gabe Phillips, George Phillips, S. Phillips, E. Saadi, J. Tamer, J. Waletzky, L. Waletzky, and S. Yamasaki; as well as to Abbott Associates, Inc., A.I.D., A.L.L., the Center for International Development (University of Maryland), the Center for Strategic and International Studies (Georgetown University), Claremont Graduate School, the Ford Foundation, the RAND Corporation, U.S.I.A., and the University of Maryland Foundation; and to the Embassy and Government of Lebanon which permitted a number of the authors to conduct interviews in Lebanon and the United States.

# Contents

## PART IV
## LEBANON AND THE WORLD

# PART I

# BACKGROUND

# 1
# Lebanon after the War of 1982

## Paul A. Jureidini and
## R. D. McLaurin

## INTRODUCTION

Over the years, a whole literature has been constructed on the society and polity of Lebanon.[1] Although some few English-language books have focussed on explaining the politics of Lebanon alone—the most well-known being Hudson's *The Precarious Republic*[2] and Binder's *Politics In Lebanon*[3]—none really touched the heart of Lebanon's unique way of life and politics.[4] The "consociational democracy" paradigm and others were constructed to deal with this singular case, but few who have been close to the functioning of the Lebanese system could really be satisfied with this or other extant models.

The absence of an isomorphic model creates a major problem for those who seek to understand Lebanon today, and no less a problem for those who would explain the state of the country. Without a model, the framework to identify, describe, and assess the elements of the system and how it is functioning is also lacking. The present chapter, which is an update on politics in Lebanon since the war of 1982, cannot and does not attempt to resolve these critical analytical and methodological problems. In order to overcome the framework difficulties they create, we leave to the reader the integrative and analytical burdens. We set for ourselves the goal of description, because even baseline data to understand the nature of contemporary Lebanese politics have been lacking.[5]

The process by which Lebanon, the only Arab state bordering Israel that did not actively participate in the Arab-Israeli conflict after 1949, became an Israeli-Syrian playground[6] is too long and complex for comprehensive treatment in this summary. Consequently, this

3

chapter will sketch the nature of Lebanon, summarize the processes that led to the conflict of 1982, describe the effects of the Israeli invasion, and discuss the course of political evolution since that time.

## NATURE OF LEBANON

Even more than most Middle East states, Lebanon is a complex of various religious and ethnic groups with only a very short tradition attached to present boundaries.[7] The historic basis of Lebanese identity is the Christian heartland of *Djebel Lubnan* (Mount Lebanon), which for centuries had a separate regime under Ottoman rule. However, the creation of a distinct Lebanon by the French after World War I was not based on the concept of a Christian state. Rather, several minorities—Shi'as,[8] Druzes,[9] and a wide array of different Christian communities—were politically grouped together with a large number of Sunnis. No single group was demographically dominant over the others, and the sum of Christian groups was approximately equal to the aggregate of the Muslim groups. To this new unit neither the Shi'as nor the Druzes took particular exception, since both communities had greater significance in a small country composed of all minorities than either would have had in a greater Syria in which they were but small minorities in a vast Sunni majority. Nor did the Christians interpose great objections to the new state, although many resented being incorporated into an entity in which Christians did not constitute a greater majority. In contrast, Sunnis were vehement in their opposition to the new creation.

The sectarian balance of Lebanon being both the essence of its creation and the most divisive element of its existence, a unique political system was developed based upon confessional (i.e., sectarian) representation not only in the House of Deputies (parliament), but also in the distribution of key political offices. This so-called confessional political system worked relatively well for several decades on the surface, but was characterized by significant weaknesses inherent in the system:

1. Distribution of political goods was based upon the census of 1932, whose validity was questioned by many. As such, the system was overly rigid and did not allow for demographic change, because the communities' leaders at the time of the National Pact could only agree on a system for 1943, not on one for the future. No Sunni was prepared to reject the possibility that Lebanon and Syria would eventually unite. No Christian was prepared to establish a system

that might eventually subordinate the Christian community in a Muslim state.

2. The confessional system perpetuated the salience of sectarian differences at the heart of the society. Since the distribution of goods was based on confession, religion remained the essence of one's identity. The unintended effect was to confessionalize all problems that otherwise might be administrative, economic, or political in nature.

Yet, ultimately, the confessional system might have worked in the Lebanese environment, which is dominated by a pluralist cultural outlook uncommon in the Middle East. However, no country lives in a vacuum, and Lebanon bordered on Palestine. Thus, the war of 1948–1949 necessarily involved Lebanon, even if briefly and unimportantly from a military point of view. The impact on Lebanon of the first Palestine War was felt in the sudden influx of large numbers of Palestinian refugees, most of them Muslim. Given the sectarian balance and its criticality in the Lebanese political system, there was never any way of addressing the problem of the refugees in Lebanon. Even leaving aside the political repercussions of absorption, the potential total collapse of the confessional balance in Lebanon prevented any serious consideration of the absorption of Palestinians by proffering nationality.

The June War of 1967 further complicated the problem of the Palestinians in Lebanon by adding to their number, by substantially heightening their national consciousness, and, in a real sense, by breathing new life into the transnational Palestinian movement. After 1967, and especially after 1970 as a result of the influx of Palestinian refugees of the civil war in Jordan, the phenomenon of Palestinians arming in Lebanon gathered great momentum, pushing some Christian groups into a reactive arming process of their own.[10]

Moreover, from 1969 to 1976 the Syrian regime supported active subversion of the Lebanese government by infiltrating both Palestinians and Syrians-cum-Palestinians from Syria, sometimes directly fighting Lebanese Army units. During the crises of 1969, 1971, and 1973, these trends accelerated, with two results—the turning of Lebanon into a vast, armed camp; and the rapid increase of serious tensions between the Christian community as a whole,[11] on the one hand, and the Palestinians, on the other. The paralysis of the Lebanese government and its inability to manage these crises, or to allow the Lebanese Army to reassert the supremacy of the Lebanese state within the territory of Lebanon,[12] assured that an eventual explosion would occur.

The Israeli invasion of 1982 materially altered a number of factors in the Lebanese equation. First, PLO forces were compelled to withdraw from Beirut and all areas under Israeli occupation. Second, Bashir Gemayel was elected president. Next, the United States was drawn into the negotiations over Lebanon and the overall Arab-Israeli settlement issue once again from a different angle. Lastly, the Lebanese government was offered a chance to reassert Lebanese sovereignty.

Since the Syrian intervention in June 1976, Syria and Israel have used Lebanon as an arena to destabilize the Middle East and to un-track any peace or other initiatives unacceptable to either of them. Syria's army was in Lebanon as an "Arab Deterrent Force" nominal-ly, but had become an army of occupation by 1978. The Israeli inva-sion six years later threatened to end Syria's role, as Israel clearly in-tended to force the Syrian Army out of Lebanon—or wipe out the equivalent of three to five divisions of its personnel there. Consequent-ly, Syria decided to remove its military through negotiations that would also lead to an Israeli withdrawal. However, as a result of a combination of the Reagan initiative, the assassination of Bashir Gemayel, and pressure on Israel by the United States, Syrian forces were not withdrawn. Their continued presence permitted the PLO to reinforce its own important presence in both the Beqa'a Valley and around Tripoli. It is clear that both Israel and Syria saw Lebanon as the best burial ground for the overall Reagan initiative.[13]

## ACTORS AND RESOURCES

### Internal Dispositions

In the years after the large-scale internal conflict in Lebanon began, that country experienced a social and political revolution that is little understood either domestically or outside. As a result of this transformation, the political forces bear little resemblance to those that characterized the Lebanese landscape in 1975 and earlier, even if the physiognomy of the actors appears the same. The domestic actors in Lebanon today operate under a wholly different set of parameters from those in place before. The most important of these actors are: (1) the Government of Lebanon, (2) the Lebanese Forces, (3) the Christian community, (4) the Shi'a community, (5) the Sunnis, and (6) the Druzes.

There is no question that Lebanese society can be disaggregated in many alternative ways. It would be as much a mistake to look at the

Lebanese social mosaic in purely sectarian terms as it would be to conceive of the last eight years of violence in a strictly religious perspective. Yet, at the present time the Lebanese social forces on the scene and able to act are most clearly those part of, or associated with, religious communities. Moreover, political, economic, and security considerations today cluster very closely around confessional identities.

The religious communities of Lebanon tend to live in relatively identifiable geographic areas. That is, each has areas of predominance and areas shared with other sects. In the case of the Christian, Mount Lebanon is an historically Christian area, and in fact has a discrete history of government. Christians also enjoy some isolated areas of predominance in the Beqa'a Valley, the Shuf, and southern Lebanon. However, the Beqa'a and the south are generally inhabited principally by the Shi'as, while the Shuf is a predominantly Druze area. Northern Lebanon is a complex amalgam of Christian, Sunni, and Shi'a, without any clear-cut dominant group. Unlike the other communities, Lebanon's Sunnis do not have any hinterland of their own. They are traditionally the majority in the three coastal cities of Tripoli, Beirut, and Sidon, but approximately 40,000 'Alawis have recently moved into the Tripoli area, Beirut has long been "shared," and the future of Sidon must await the restoration of Lebanese government authority to become clear.

## Government of Lebanon

The Government of Lebanon today controls very little territory—practically speaking, only marginally more than Beirut itself. Nor can the government lay claim to many resources, since it does not have the power to access them. As far as those resources already subject to the government—the personnel and equipment that belong to the government and the other resources that do lie within the area controlled by the government—are concerned, most are either qualitatively or quantitatively inadequate to enable the Government of Lebanon to carry out its responsibilities.

The Lebanese Army has had few major military end-items. It has only recently received M-48 tanks from the United States, for example. Moreover, although its personnel are well educated and very qualified by Middle East standards, the command has been somewhat politicized as a result of the last several years' internal problems, the mission of the army remains ambiguous, and the operational experience of field-grade officers is virtually nil.[14] Given a chance to establish itself, the army would perform well militarily against any foe except Israel, and would certainly assist in reestablishing the legitimacy of the Lebanese government as a whole. However, the problems of the army must first be resolved, and the resolution of these problems may well depend upon tacit cooperation of Israeli, Palestinian, and Syrian forces, a cooperation that has not been in evidence to date.

The rest of the Lebanese government resources are even less dependable. The bureaucracy, never very efficient, is believed to have eroded significantly in its motivation and willingness to work.[15] The private sector has never had a close relationship to the government, and, in fact, continues to view the problems of Lebanon and options open to its government largely in terms of narrow personal interests. Much talent has left the country, and its willingness to return is very clearly conditioned upon the course of political events.

Finally, there is the president. Amin Gemayel was elected almost unanimously following the assassination of his brother, Bashir. However, as Bashir had imposed himself on, first, the Lebanese Maronites, then upon the Christian community as a whole, and later upon the other communities—all as a result of the judicious threat and application of force—he entered the scene as president-elect in a position of power. He controlled what was, in September 1982, the most significant Lebanese military force in Lebanon. And he represented himself to the Muslim communities—accurately—as perhaps the only Lebanese politician powerful in his own right who could negotiate successfully with Israel for the withdrawal of Israel forces and the return of Muslim Lebanese land to the Muslims. Clearly, Amin Gemayel did not bring the same assets to the presidency. His relationship to the Lebanese Forces is weak; his appeal to the Christian community is conditional at best; his ability to persuade Israel to withdraw is more questionable, and therefore his value to the Druze and Shi'a communities less clear. By contrast, it is true that the president is generally more popular among Sunnis (and to some extent all Muslims) than was his brother. Certainly, he was accepted by the other Arab governments more readily.

## The Lebanese Forces[16]

The Lebanese Forces, even without Bashir Gemayel, remains an important political, as well as military, force. It represents an activist, nationalist, reformist, and youth oriented (in the gerontocratic Lebanese environment) social movement, catalyzed by Bashir, that will not easily be blunted. The leadership of the Lebanese Forces split to some extent following the death of Bashir. Some returned to their Kata'eb identity. Others, particularly in intelligence and senior military command positions, remained closely linked to Israel. Some supported the new president, while others did not. Sheikh Pierre Gemayel became the single most important figure in influencing the thinking of the Lebanese Forces by virtue of his control over the Kata'eb elements.

From a purely military standpoint, the Lebanese Forces consists of about 6,000 regulars, but can quickly mobilize to a fighting force of over 20,000 men. The command of the Lebanese Forces is relatively well organized by regional standards, and personnel are experienced in low-intensity conflict and highly motivated. The Lebanese Forces has a relatively good supply of equipment, including heavy weapons (armor, artillery, and the like), and the training of regulars has been excellent. It is not clear how well reserves, which constitute the bulk of the force, are trained.

It is a capital mistake to perceive the Lebanese Forces as principally a military force, however. It is true that its importance in Lebanon today lies partly in its ability to bring impressive force to bear to support the realization of its objectives. At the same time, without its independent social and political identity the Lebanese Forces would certainly not be the critical actor that it is. The command of the Labanese Forces was established in effect as a shadow government, embracing most of the functions of any other government, from sanitation and health to transportation, youth affairs, and labor. Moreover, from the outset the Lebanese Forces was heavily oriented toward planning and policy formation in all of these areas. The death of Bashir has not altered the existence or vitality of this discrete sociopolitical actor, and the Lebanese Forces continues to render its own judgments as to the future course of events and the role Lebanon should pursue with respect to them.

## The Christian Community

The Lebanese Forces is widely seen as the "Christian militia." In fact, this is only partially true. Certainly, the Lebanese Forces is composed primarily of Christians and is built at this time on the Christian community. However, it represents, in terms of genesis, history, ideology, composition, and activity, a relatively small portion of even the Maronite community in Lebanon. At present, the Lebanese Forces serves as the catalyst of Christian unity, the defender of all of the Christian heartland (but not the southern Christian strongholds), and the symbol of Lebanese independence. Still, to the extent that it remains associated in the public mind with the Kata'eb party, the Lebanese Forces cannot be seen as representative of the Christian community as a whole.

Christians constitute slightly less than half of the total Lebanese population, according to the most informed accounts. (Lebanon has not had a census since 1932.) Although the Christians are divided into numerous sects, Maronites comprise a majority of the Christian community and approximately a quarter of the total Lebanese population. The Greek Orthodox faith represents slightly less than half the Maronite total. There are also large numbers of Greek Catholics and Gregorians.

Although they represent a minority in a country of minorities, Christians have clearly been the dominant group in Lebanon. The history of the country since its creation under the French mandate has revolved in large part around the Christian community, and the community's financiers, entrepreneurs, traders, and educators continue to play a role both in Lebanon and in the region as a whole out of all proportion to their numbers.

By themselves, the Christians as a community looked to the Lebanese Forces to provide the firepower to defend the community and to protect its interests, for most of their other militias have long since been integrated into the Forces or have disappeared. However, in recent years, a tacit and somewhat intermittent alliance between the Christian community and Israel emerged as well. While neither member of this partnership proved reliable, there are many shared interests at the tactical level. The threat of potential Israeli intervention was a major defensive weapon of the Christian community for over five years.

## The Shi'a Community

Traditionally left out of the process of development and modernization, left out of the essence of the Lebanese economy, and kept outside the corridors of social and political power as well, the Shi'a community, which is the largest sect in Lebanon today, underwent a rapid process of mobilization under the leadership of Imam Musa Sadr just before and especially during the conflict period. The Shi'as have had an extremely high birthrate, but another reason for the extraordinary growth of the Shi'a community is the return to Lebanon of large numbers of Lebanese Shi'as, many quite wealthy, from overseas (especially from West Africa). 'Amal, the Shi'a militia, and short for *Harakat 'Amal* ("movement of hope"), was established by the imam while he was still the spiritual—and temporal—leader of the community and before his mysterious disappearance on a trip to Libya. By 1980, 'Amal clearly represented, both symbolically and physically, the Shi'a community.[17] One of 'Amal's major problems after the imam's disappearance was competition for power at the top of the organization. Following the Israeli invasion and occupation of most of those 'Amal strongholds not occupied by Syria, 'Amal's leadership picture became even more confused with at least four different groups claiming or competing for the mantle.

When Syria entered Lebanon in June 1976, 'Amal parted company with the National Movement to align itself with Syria. From 1976 to the present, 'Amal has largely sided with Syria, not because of religious affinity so much as because of the geographical propinquity of some Shi'a areas of Lebanon (notably, the Beqa'a) and Syria. However, following the Israeli invasion of 1982, the Shi'a community was caught in something of a vise, because its southern lands were occupied by Israel and its surrogate, Sa'ad Haddad, while the Beqa'a remained under Syrian and Palestinian occupation. To the extent that Israel and Syria enjoy parallel interests and pursue parallel policies, the Shi'a community directly or indirectly acts to support these policies. However, where Israeli and Syrian approaches conflict, the Shi'a community faces serious problems in arriving at a feasible strategy. Although in 1982 and early 1983 the Shi'as—probably reflecting the greater importance of the south to the community as a whole—quietly and indirectly responded to Israel, Syrian-controlled elements were more vociferous, and pro-Khomeini groups like that of Hussein Moussavi, with Syrian encouragement, garnered attention out of all proportion to their size.

The Shi'a community as a whole had not spoken with violence against, but only in support of, Lebanon through 1982. As Syria encourged fundamentalist Shi'as in the cast, so Israel encouraged the formation of small, private Shi'a militias in the south. Neither of these phenomena was representative of the bulk of the Shi'a population, however, which continued to identify with the mainstream of 'Amal. The real strength of the Shi'a community was its size and its physical domination and control—should foreign forces withdraw—of substantial territory. Thus, the power of the Shi'as is that in the event the country should reassert itself and either build a national state based on a new national pact or follow a more decentralized policy, the Shi'as, as the plurality, pose a direct threat to the traditional Sunni position.

## The Sunni Community

Most adversely affected by the events of the past few years has been the Sunni community. The return of large numbers of Shi'as from Africa and elsewhere and their higher birthrate have made them a plurality in Lebanon, while the Sunnis have traditionally claimed the second-ranking position (after the Maronites). More important, the superimposition of Palestinian dominance over the Sunni community perverted the course of Sunni politics such that the community was forced to support Palestinian positions irrespective of Sunni interests which frequently conflicted with those of the Palestinians. In the process of suppressing the articulation of Lebanese Sunni views, the Palestinians also prevented the emergence of new Sunni elites, with the result that there is today no means of ascertaining Sunni perceptions. The Sunni community continues to be officially represented by a number of traditional leaders such as Sa'eb Salaam. Whether he or other Sunni deputies reflect the true views of the Sunni community is unknown. Moreover, a younger generation of Sunni leaders that began to emerge during the conflict in Lebanon was not the only political casualty of the violence. In addition, the Sunni merchant class of Beirut acquired a more separate, identifiable set of political attitudes that is underrepresented by the traditional leaders of the community as a whole.

We have already indicated the geographic isolation of the Sunni community in what, for all practical purposes, are three city enclaves. This isolation has had additional important implications, however. Whereas other communities had sufficient territorial contiguity to maintain internal contact, the Sunni did not enjoy this advantage. On the contrary, they were isolated from each other, which prevented a communal leadership, embracing all the country, from arising. Currently, Beirut Sunni support for the president is a reflection of this situation. There is a clear realization that the traditional position of the Sunni community in Lebanon is threatened by the Shi'as. It was a Sunni imperative to prevent the legitimization or concretization of this change. Consequently, the Sunni community has consistently supported the government. Indeed, greater dissent from government policy has been heard among Christian than among Sunnis.

While a number of militias were partly or wholly based on Sunni participation during the years of internal conflict, virtually all of these were incapacitated during 1982. In some cases, weapons were hidden, but all heavy firepower and most equipment above the light arms level were eliminated. Consequently, the Sunni community has no real organic firepower in a country where political influence has tended in the last few years to come from the barrel of a gun. However, Lebanese Sunni still maintain their number-two position in the Lebanese government, a position that in itself confers considerable power. Moreover, the Sunni community maintains ties with the surrounding Arab world which also provides it with a certain degree of indirect influence. Sunni links, particularly to Saudi Arabia, were considered important by Amin Gemayel prior to his turn toward Syria in 1984.

## The Druze Community

The Druzes are the smallest major sect in Lebanon. There are fewer Druzes than Shi'as, Maronites, Sunnis, Greek Orthodox, or even Melkites (Greek Catholics). The Jumblatts—Kamal and then, following his assassination, his son, Walid—were at one time the principal leaders of the Lebanese Druze community. However, the Jumblatts had several roles in Lebanese politics, and their direction of the Progressive Socialist Party (PSP) and its militia, and leadership of the National Movement were quite distinct from their role within their own community. Indeed, many Lebanese Druzes resented what appeared to be the Jumblatt concentration on Lebanese leftist politics at the expense of dedicated protection of Druze interests.

The Israeli invasion in 1982 altered Druze politics considerably. The occupation of Druze lands by Israeli and Israeli-supported forces created a strong incentive (as in the Shi'a case) to support Bashir Gemayel, since it was believed that he alone could effect an early liberation of Druze lands. Consequently, the role of Walid Jumblatt receded in favor of other Druze leaders, notably the late Amir Majid Arslan. The death of Bashir Gemayel very seriously complicated the perspectives of the Druze community, however, because Israel began to exploit and exacerbate Druze–Christian differences[18] in order to demonstrate to Amin Gemayel Israel's ability to prevent the extension of central government authority—and of peace and security to Lebanon—without Israel's directly intervening. In this strategy, Israel very wisely exploited the continuing ties of its own Druze community with the Druzes of Lebanon.

However, the history of the Druzes is clear on one point: the community avoids fighting on the losing side whenever possible. No Druzes contested IDF entry into the Shuf, for example. Israeli leaders therefore felt they had the Druzes in a good position, a position where the community could not act against Israeli interests. This was also true of the Lebanese Forces. Consequently, Israel was unwilling to allow either party to suffer a clear-cut defeat at the hands of the other in the Shuf.

The Druzes of Lebanon anticipated an Israeli withdrawal from their territory, but not at the expense of the loss of their lands to other interlopers. Therefore, many Druzes were prepared to cooperate with Israel if necessary to prevent, for example, the imposition of an oppressive or growing Lebanese Forces presence in Druze areas.

Although the PSP was, in fact, a virtual noncombatant during the Lebanese internal conflict of 1975–1982, the Druzes as a community were relatively well armed only in terms of light weapons. The PSP militia was only partially disarmed by the Israelis in their invasion, and elements of the Druze community were rearmed by Israel in the fall of 1982 in order to constrain both the Lebanese government and the Lebanese Forces.

Druze control over an important area, and one shared with many Christians, constitutes their principal claim to power in Lebanon. Given the very small size of the community, this is an important asset. Like the other communities, the Druze as a minority also wield influence as a result of their potential alliance with one or more of the other communities in Lebanon or with their coreligionists in Israel or Syria.

## EXTERNAL

### Israel

By January 1, 1983, Israel effectively occupied most of Lebanon south of Beirut-Jennin. Israeli leaders believed this occupation could be translated into a permanent Israeli interest and role in Lebanon. Israel and Lebanon agreed upon a security arrangement that would "safeguard" northern Israel, a kind of "security belt" extending well into Lebanon. While the Israeli presence in Lebanon was not particularly popular in Israel, public support for some arrangement of this type was widespread.

Israel has several different types of assets in Lebanon. The first and most obvious at present is the IDF deployment in the country. Since Israel is by far the most powerful country in the Middle East, the IDF occupation is symbolic of the presence of that military power even though only a small part of it is actually in Lebanon currently. Second, Israeli territorial contiguity and the political repercussions of the Israeli presence are a very potent political influence in their own right. A third asset is the close association of Israel with a number of domestic actors in Lebanon. Fourth, the common interests of Israel and Syria constitute a considerable resource in the hands of both. Let us consider each of these factors individually.

• The Israeli military presence in Lebanon is a constraint on several actors in the country's complex political drama. The IDF prevents Syrian freedom of action and reoccupation of parts of Lebanon taken over by the Israeli forces. It prevents, as well, the reassertion of PLO power and presence in those areas. By contrast, Israel's military superiority ensures complete Israeli freedom of action within zones occupied by the IDF, and denies effective control to the central government of Lebanon, local ethnic and religious groups, or United Nations forces deployed in the south. Moreover, the presence of the IDF atop the ridges surrounding the Beqa'a constitutes an implicit threat to Syria, since it permits Israel to circumvent Syria's formidable defenses in the Golan Heights.

• The fact that Lebanon borders Israel is an important consideration in the planning of both countries' governments. To Israel, Lebanese internal order is a matter of concern, since northern Israel has, at times, been attacked by hostile forces based in Lebanon but not subject to the effective control of the Lebanese government. Although the magnitude of this threat is and has always been quite limited—it is more of a domestic Israeli political issue than a serious security threat—the determination of the Israeli government to guard against a return to the previous conditions is clear and understandable. Nor is the Lebanese government immune to the implications of Israeli contiguity. In considering the future course of Lebanese foreign policy, Lebanese leaders are not likely to forget that the legacy of the past will necessarily live with them in the future. They are intensely aware of Israeli concerns, and they know, too, that the precedents of Israeli retaliatory attacks against Lebanese territory over the years and of invasions in 1978 and 1982 have legitimized—at least to Israeli leaders—a certain pattern of behavior that must be recognized. Thus, Israeli attention to Lebanon is assured for the foreseeable future, and the Lebanese government can be expected to anticipate this continued Israeli concern in its own policy planning. Of all the external powers active in Lebanon today, the Lebanese realize that Israel is the most likely to be able to exert at least a denial influence. Its government is stable, its army strong, its propinquity perpetual.

• Nor does Israel necessarily limit itself to the role of an *external* actor. Over the years, the Israelis have developed a number of allies within the Lebanese body politic, even though the quality of their actual relationship with each may vary over time. Some allies are or have been: (1) the Lebanese Forces, (2) various individual Christian leaders, (3) some southern Shi'as and a portion of the Shi'a leadership, (4) some Druzes and a number of Druze leaders, and (5) the "militia" of the late Sa'ad Haddad.

• Finally, there is the question of Israeli-Syrian common interests. It is clear that the two countries constitute something of a security threat to each other so long as both are in Lebanon. It is also clear that their long-term objectives are diametrically opposed, most notably with respect to the future of the Golan Heights. However, leaving these differences aside, Israel and Syria share many interests, especially tactical. Both opposed, for example, the Reagan peace initiative, even if for very different reasons. Thus, both saw Lebanon as the way to kill the initiative, first by bogging down U.S. diplomats in a time-consuming effort to secure Israeli, PLO, and Syrian withdrawal, and then, if necessary, by intermittently raising the threat of Israeli-Syrian conflict in Lebanon's Beqa'a Valley. However, to keep open this last option it was necessary to prevent the effective withdrawal of either party from Lebanon.

Consequently, the Lebanese government is correct when it sees Israel as a powerful actor in Lebanon for the foreseeable future. These assets essentially checkmated the more limited advantages of Syria and the PLO as long as the IDF was deployed along the maximal Beirut-Jennin line, and also offset to a large extent the leverage of the United States. The Israelis were not in a position to create the Lebanon they wanted, but they *were* in a position to prevent the realization of others' objectives there. Indeed, they could relatively easily ensure the disappearance of Lebanon as it has existed in favor either of a cantonal/confederated state or of the emergence of several small ministates.

## The PLO

The PLO was compelled to abandon its independent role in most of Lebanon as a result of the outcome of the Israeli invasion of 1982. Since the forced evacuation of Palestinian leaders from Beirut, PLO forces have been limited to those areas in which they could hide behind Syria's more formidable military presence. Thus, PLO personnel operated in the north, especially around Tripoli, and in the Beqa'a Valley. As a major military force, however, the PLO was essentially finished in Lebanon, for it became an arm of the Syrians there. This development was consolidated in 1983, as the Syrian government sponsored a rebellion against the traditional PLO leadership of Yasser Arafat, whose forces were primarily limited to the Tripoli area.

This is not to say that the PLO had no residual political power in Lebanon beyond its military face, however. There remained several hundred thousand Palestinians in Lebanon, most of whom were presumed to support the PLO. Moreover, the links between the Sunni community and a number of Arab states, including Saudi Arabia and Syria, were clearly influenced by the relationships of those states with the PLO. Thus, the Palestinians and the PLO had some influence on Lebanese developments both as a result of the magnitude of the refugee problem (which constrains the government) and as a function of the Lebanese Sunni community. It is, however, clear that the aggregate influence wielded by the PLO and by the Palestinian community in Lebanon was severely reduced as a result of the events of 1982.

## Syria

Syria's position, too, suffered a major setback as an outcome of the Israeli invasion. From 1976, when Syria intervened in Lebanon, until 1982, the Syrian occupation force gave Syria virtual dominion over most of the country. Although there were limits on what Syria could achieve with its partial control, it is still true that Syria dictated to a very considerable degree the course of many of the events in Lebanon over the past half-dozen years.

After the war of 1982, Syria still occupied the Beqa'a and northern Lebanon. Its control over these areas continued to provide tangible political benefits, since without being able to extend its control there the central government could not create a stable, united Lebanon. Syria does not, in any case, want such a Lebanon, since it has long seen Lebanon as both a part of Syria in some sense, and yet a threat to Syria as well. It is true that Syrian expatriates in Lebanon have plotted many coups against their former country. Syria, then, like Israel, was in a position to block more options than it could pursue.

Occupation also permitted Syria to control the PLO combat remnants, keep them out of Syria, and yet maintain the thesis that would be a "front" against Israel. The takeover of most of those elements in the Beqa'a in 1983 put Syria within striking distance of its longtime objective of control over the PLO.

However, Syrian assets were not limited to those conferred by its military occupation of the north and east. In addition, many Syrians have long had very close ties to Lebanese elements. Syrian political parties and movements have always found powerful reflections in Lebanon, and families, religious communities, and ethnic groups are only arbitrarily divided by the national boundary between the two countries. Moreover, the 'Alawi community in Lebanon has received an infusion of people of a very substantial magnitude during the last years of Syrian occupation, so that it is now thought to be something approaching 40,000 strong, residing almost totally in and near Tripoli.[19]

## Saudi Arabia

Saudi Arabia has never been among the most active participants in Lebanese politics, but it has maintained ties with a number of parties, especially after the Saudi role in regional affairs began to grow following the Arab oil embargo of 1973–74. Currently, Saudi Arabia entertains direct or indirect contacts with most of the principal parties in the Lebanese quagmire, now including—though very indirectly—Israel.

Saudi influence in Lebanon is based upon five factors:

(1) Its quiet but important linkages within the Sunni community, primarily among the traditional leadership elites rather than the young, aspiring leaders;

(2) Its wealth, which is deemed a potential resource for Lebanese reconstruction and an actual base of the financial role of Lebanon in the region and the world;

(3) Its financial support of Syria, which is often believed to have some influence over Syrian policy in Lebanon;

(4) Its particularly close relationship with the United States;

(5) Its role in the Arab and Muslim worlds which could help facilitate the legitimization of various Lebanese policy courses in those arenas.

## The United States

The United States inserted itself forcefully into the Lebanese situation following the introduction of Syrian surface-to-air missiles into the Beqa'a Valley in 1981. Although its attention to Lebanese crises can be seen as intermittent at best since that time, the deep involvement of the U.S. government in the attempt to resolve the so-called "missile crisis" certainly led to much more visible activity in Washington during the period following the Israeli invasion a year later.

The United States does not enjoy many of the advantages of the other domestic and external actors discussed above. It is not geographically contiguous with, or even close to, Lebanon. There are few shared bonds of history, family, or ethnicity involved. While it is certainly true that Lebanon's role as regional banker brought about the interaction of the two countries in a financial sense, this relationship was not particularly significant from the American point of view.

In spite of the absence of many of the assets others enjoy in Lebanon, the United States is a superpower and does maintain close relations with several of the countries involved in Lebanon—particularly Israel and Saudi Arabia. Moreover, the problem of Lebanon over the last few years has several times posed major threats to American regional policy. In addition, the Reagan administration was searching for a Middle East role in 1982, and the juxtaposition of this search with Lebanon's search for a protector should not go unnoticed. The presumed American influence over Israel (at a time when Israel occupied large areas of Lebanon) was also significant. Too, many Lebanese, especially in the Christian community, have for years looked to the United States for leadership, friendship, protection, and cooperation. (It is difficult to explain this appeal, based as it is on a largely one-sided feeling that may have originated with the seminal role of the American University of Beirut, the prominent activity of Americans in the Beirut of the 1950s, and the American intervention in 1958.)[20] Finally, the relative wealth of the United States in terms of human resources, as well as economic and material goods, was seen by many Lebanese as the reservoir from which Lebanon had to draw, not only to reconstruct the country following the years of violence and destruction, but also to reorient the country in terms of its intellectual and functional directions.

More specifically, the United States was expected to be very forthcoming in economic and military assistance to Lebanon over the succeeding years. Lebanon was looking to the United States to rebuild—and in many ways to build—its armed forces, to cooperate in the planning of its reconstruction, to support the improvement in the effectiveness of government, and to facilitate the institutional foundation for greater Lebanese integration. Recognizing the capital role the United States was expected to play, its influence on Lebanese policy decisions was considerable. At the same time, the United States dealt most comfortably at the government-to-government level, and this constituted something of a handicap in Lebanon where many of the principal actors were not governments.

## POLITICAL DEVELOPMENTS AFTER 1982

The election of Bashir Gemayel appeared to mark a clear departure in Lebanese history. With the strong support of the army, the Lebanese Forces, the Christian, Shi'a, and Druze communities, and the United States, he approached administration with the kind of base and power that enabled him to promise fundamental change and to confront the basic issues in Lebanon, most particularly the National Pact.

The National Pact, the social contract underlying the polity, was formulated for the 1940s, and is clearly in need of very substantial revision. The events of 1969, 1973, 1975–76, and since suggest strongly that any attempt to reconstitute Lebanon without a change in the National Pact faces intimidating realities. Demographic, attitudinal, and political changes have both separated communities, on the one hand, and underlined the value to each of the unity of Lebanon, on the other. Yet, as the National Pact of 1943 was designed to ensure the survival and security of each community in the face of threats it perceived at that time, the same Pact today accentuates and perpetuates new threats to each, and insecurity for all. One possible reaction to these threats is a new pact, or a revision to the original Pact, perhaps recognizing a form of devolution. There is extensive support for change, but opposition is likely to be strong in the Sunni community which fears that any opening of the question of a new National Pact may lead to a new allocation of power that will legitimize the presumed numerical superiority of the Shi'as within the Muslim community or will, at least, increase the Shi'a role at Sunni expense.

The momentum of a Lebanese renaissance, symbolized in the 1982 election, was centered in the image of Bashir Gemayel. Whatever the elements, violent and otherwise,[21] that had catapulted him to the fore, Gemayel was responsible for the fact that Lebanon in September 1982 saw in itself a new beginning. Few realized the degree to which that rebirth was tied to Bashir Gemayel. American support was strong—built on his confidence.[22] Reconciliation was underway—engineered by his nationalist fervor.[23] Unity was reborn—the progeny of his strength. Hope was in bloom—the seed of his activism.

Thus, the Syrian-engineered[24] assassination of the president-elect did more than end the life of a young, determined, and charismatic leader. It also endangered the newfound essence of Lebanon reborn. Amin Gemayel was elected overwhelmingly by parliament in the aftermath of his brother's death, but Amin Gemayel had not planned for the presidency; Amin Gemayel had no political base; and Amin Gemayel had no firepower.[25]

From the outset, then, Amin reemphasized the Sunni community, and looked to it to secure Saudi support. In this direction he immediately aroused distrust in the Christian community, which tended to see such practices as the return of the discredited old system. Moreover, whereas Bashir's attraction to the Druzes and Shi'as had arisen from his strength and his supposed influence on Israel, Amin's weakness and quick reassertion of Arabism rapidly cost him leverage over both groups. In effect, the president's strongest support came from among Lebanon's weakest major sect, the Sunnis.

Lacking the time for planning or the base for an independent policy, the Lebanese government committed itself to following the American approach. Yet, the United States had little appreciation for the subtleties of Lebanese politics, and believed that Syria and Israel were both willing to withdraw from Lebanon in exchange for relatively minor concessions. In fact, this was not the case.

Syria might have withdrawn in exchange for the best deal it could get had Bashir Gemayel lived. Many Syrians believed that sooner or later the Syrian Army would withdraw or be forced out by the IDF through the collusion of Bashir and Israel. However, Amin Gemayel's turn toward the Arab world, on the one hand, and Israeli public sentiment against future military action following the massacres in Sabra and Shatila, on the other, effectively assured Syria that it would not be forced out.

In the case of Israel, the Begin government sought a much higher price than anticipated, and this was for two reasons. First, Amin Gemayel's embrace of the Arab world, and his early comments, immediately persuaded Israeli leaders that Israel's security was not a principal concern of Amin Gemayel. Since the president did not control the Lebanese Forces, and since there was little indication he would exercise effective control of the south with only conditional Christian and Shi'a support, the Israelis felt they required much greater freedom of action in the south. Second, the Israeli government wished to show a clear and tangible result from the investment in Israeli lives during the summer. Israeli leaders sought a peace treaty, but the Gemayel government was not prepared to go that far.

In many respects, the pincers of Israeli and Syrian occupation and the significance of the withdrawal of foreign forces dominated domestic politics. Negotiations between Israel and Lebanon, with the United States as an active participant, were complex and confusing. At times, the United States braked agreement between the parties; at other times, poor internal communication on the Lebanese team seemed to prevent forward movement. Only Israel seemed to have a clear conception of objectives and priorities. The United States protected Lebanon in some cases from overcommitments, while prodding the Lebanese in other instances.

Yet, the net effect of caution in the negotiations was to consume time. The product, an agreement acceptable to all three parties, was not welcomed in the Arab world and was rejected by Syria. Concessions to Israel in the south—some of which were expected to be terminated when, within three years, Lebanon signed a full peace—were very substantial. Lebanese understood that such concessions were necessary to secure Israeli withdrawal in the absence of a peace treaty, and the agreement was overwhelmingly approved by the Chamber of Deputies. However, separate accords between Israel and the United States ensured the agreement was also contingent upon Syrian withdrawal.

The Syrians had no intention of leaving Lebanon. Although they insisted to Lebanese officials they would withdraw when requested or when the IDF withdrew, there was no longer any significant cost to the presence in Lebanon. Indeed, the payoff was just beginning. With the PLO reduced to territory under Syrian control, Syria could finally impose its fiat on the organization. Moreover, since Israel insisted it would not withdraw without Syrian withdrawal, Assad held in his hands the ability to control IDF deployments and restrict the Lebanese government to Beirut. In addition, occupying the Beqa'a, Syria held half the Shi'a territories; occupying the north, Syria held important Christian territories and Sunni Tripoli.

The government of Amin Gemayel, determined to represent all Lebanese, endeavored from the outset to rally all segments of the population. Thus, Amin approached Shi'a leaders affiliated with 'Amal, Suleiman Frangieh, the Druzes, and remained close to the Sunnis. However, the government could offer no protection to Frangieh in the north, and the traditional Shi'a establishment blocked any effective rapprochement with Nabih Berri of 'Amal. The Druze were involved with other parties.

Among the Druzes, several phenomena occurred simultaneously. The Arslan clan, which had supported both Gemayel brothers, was weakening politically, although many Arslanis remained in the Druze irregular forces. Walid Jumblatt was the principal Druze leader, but he could not control the community as a whole. More important, perhaps, Israel was pushing many young Druzes, especially in the militia, toward a more independent role. In effect, Israel was sponsoring the same kind of new, young leadership that had earlier given rise to Bashir from the Christian militias. Jumblatt, aware of this developing challenge to his leadership, sought the recognition of the government as the principal Druze leader. However, when challenged to put an end to Israeli-tolerated Druze shelling of Beirut, Jumblatt was unable to stop the attacks. The Beirut government became convinced Jumblatt no longer "called the shots" in the Shuf.

For different reasons, then, Suleiman Frangieh, Nabih Berri, and Walid Jumblatt all found themselves in league with Syria. Rashid Karame, who often supported Syria and Syrian 'Alawis in Tripoli against the Sunni community, had long since become a primary Syrian ally. The signature of the Lebanese-Israeli withdrawal accord gave Assad compelling reasons to play his hand. Under no circumstances could Syria withdraw now, because the Syrians were convinced that such an action, which would lead to Israeli withdrawal, would also establish a strong U.S.-Lebanese alliance; contribute to a full Lebanese-Israeli peace treaty and a tacit triangular entente involving

Lebanon, Israel, and the United States; and would completely isolate Syria. However, the private agreement between the United States and Israel that the IDF withdrawal would not be effected until Syria withdrew gave him veto power.

Israeli leaders appear to have concluded that Lebanon required a new Israeli strategy. Believing Gemayel was implacably hostile to Israel, convinced by the summer of 1983 that, in fact, no peace treaty would emerge, and with a new leadership in the defense ministry, Israeli leaders opted to pull back their forces to reduce the cost of the policy in Lebanon and to show Amin Gemayel the error of his ways. The IDF would withdraw south of the Awwali River, and would evacuate most of the Shuf against a promise by the Druze community to prevent Palestinian attacks from that area.[26] (The threatened retaliation was believed enough to hold the Druzes to their promise.) The Israelis saw a new game in Lebanon: the country would be *de facto* partitioned, with Syria holding the north and northeast, Israel the south. The Druzes would constitute a buffer state, autonomous for all practical purposes, but would continue to cooperate, as during occupation, with Israel. The area under control of the Lebanese government (and Lebanese Forces) would constitute a Christian ministate. Most Israelis believed this ministate would eventually come to realize that its interests lay with Israel, but in the interim at least it would not trust its fate to the tender mercies of Syria.

Although neither Beirut nor Washington approved of the Israeli policy, and although neither liked the assumptions on which it was based, these assumptions seemed to be the reluctant conclusions there, too. The "game" had certain rules, however, and Syrian behavior demonstrated decisively that Syrian leaders were playing a different game. With Israel politically paralyzed, Syria had only to secure American withdrawal to force the Gemayel government to its knees, administer the final blow, and thereby control all of Lebanon north of the IDF northernmost line.

It was at this stage, therefore, that Syria embarked on a new offensive designed to force the United States out of the picture and destroy the Gemayel government. The tools—Lebanese political figures—were readily available, and Syrian assets included the PLO, now under Syrian domination in the Beqa'a, a very small Khomeini movement, and the Druzes. Syrian Druze "volunteers" and Syrian "Palestinians" (PLA or Saiqa) could also be employed. The timing was made perfect by Israeli determination to withdraw from the Shuf and by a sudden paralysis of the Israeli government brought about by the decision of Menachem Begin to resign.

A crisis was clearly on the horizon. Thus, Robert McFarland, the president's new envoy, met with Walid Jumblatt and an aide to Gemayel in Paris. Negotiations proceeded surprisingly well, and an accord was reached not only with Jumblatt, but also on behalf of other members of the dissident group, particularly Frangieh. However, on the eve of the Israeli withdrawal, Syria was not about to permit such an accord, and rejected it out of hand. Fighting erupted between elements of 'Amal and the Lebanese Army and between various other Syrian-controlled groups, such as the S.S.N.P. and Mourabitoun,[27] and the army. The two LAF brigades en route to the Shuf had to be diverted to Beirut, where, although they distinguished themselves in difficult urban fighting, they were tied down.[28] Thus, as Israel withdrew, no LAF units were available for deployment to the Shuf.

Immediately, the Druze began a general offensive. Even earlier, during the Beirut operations, Syrian 130mm artillery, firing from the upper Metn, had harrassed the LAF. Now, Syrian support was open, as the Syrians provided armor, artillery, logistic and communications support, and intelligence to the Druzes. Damascus also mobilized PLO resources on behalf of the Druzes.

Syria sponsored the Druze attack. However, as the combat intensified, more and more Druzes concluded that the survival of their community was at stake, and so, many fought on this basis. The truth was clear. Syria ignited the conflagration and could extinguish it at will. Negotiations demonstrated this reality, as Syrian leaders time and again rejected cease-fire accords. The combatants, whatever their public postures, understood where the real power lay. When, on September 23, it became clear that the U.S. Congress would support an 18-month extension to the Marine presence in Lebanon, Syria rapidly approved a cease-fire whose basic terms had been agreed to by the other parties much earlier.

How had the Gemayel government and Israel responded to this evolving situation? Never fully supported by the Christian community, Gemayel's flirtation with the Arab world and resistance to collaborating with Israel—which in fact reflected U.S. policy—particularly rankled the Lebanese Forces. Indeed, it is likely that either the Lebanese Forces or the community as a whole would have taken action against Amin, but they were neutralized by the presence of Sheikh Pierre Gemayel at the head of the Kata'eb party, still a major influence on the Lebanese Forces, and by the absence of an alternative to Amin. At every turn, the president went as far as he could to accommodate the Druzes, the Sunnis, the Shi'as, and the Syrians, but the fact that the Syrians were determined to cripple the government, and the willingness of Lebanese political leaders to allow themselves to be used by foreign powers, predictably condemned Gemayel's efforts.

The bare facts of the period after the May 1983 agreement are that the government of Lebanon was unable to effect any change in the occupation and that, despite very fruitful reconciliation talks in Geneva in November 1983, confidence in the government's ability to deal with the crisis and in U.S. will to remain involved was eroding.

Increasing attacks on the multinational force units culminated in coincidental suicide truck bomb assaults at the Marine compound (in which 241 Marines were killed) and the French MNF compound (56 killed). For the first time, Americans realized the cost of the commitment in Lebanon was already high. After this attack, carried out by Iranian and Syrian agents,[29] the U.S. government was paralyzed by uncertainty over its course in Lebanon. The Marines were portrayed as a political force in the United States where they constituted a military activity, and as a military force in Lebanon where they were a political activity. With an election on the horizon—a horizon much closer than any conceivable settlement—the Marines were withdrawn in February 1984.

Meanwhile, the principal Lebanese factions met in Geneva to discuss national reconciliation in November 1983. Contrary to their public postures, they encountered few internal Lebanese impediments to accord. The principal sticking point was *not* internal reforms; rather it was the May 17 agreement with Israel (presumably because this was the major issue raised by Syria, which backed the opposition to the government). Yet, neither Israel nor the United States was prepared to accept cancellation of the accord, which in fact had never been fully ratified by Lebanon. Since Lebanon depended on the United States for economic and military aid, and needed Israeli withdrawal, the impasse was complete.[30]

The level of violence increased through late 1983 and into early 1984. In the first week of February, under pressure from both 'Amal and the PSP, one army brigade (the sixth in West Beirut) returned to its barracks and another was betrayed by several of its commanders, who defected. Army forces under the direction of the government controlled only East Beirut, although the sixth Brigade in West Beirut still considered itself loyal. The situation appeared very similar to that of 1976. It was not.

In order to understand the course of events after May 1983, it is necessary once again to consider the different groups and regions of Lebanon. Three of the major communities took little part in developments. The Sunnis remained largely powerless (despite the movement of extensive arms into Beirut in early 1984), divided and isolated in their three cities, and directionless. Faced with the possible loss of community power to the Shi'as, there were some indications by late 1983 of a rise in Sunni fundamentalism. The Greek Orthodox had lost their Kura base in 1976, and lost their presence in the Shuf in 1983. They, too, along with the Greek Catholics, maintained a low profile.

### The Christians

By late 1983, Amin Gemayel had lost the popular support of the Christian community as a whole, even including most members of the Kata'eb. However, the more desperate the situation became, the less easy it was to consider alternatives. The military setbacks inflicted on the Lebanese Forces, and the divisions in the army created by the larger political problems Lebanon faced, reduced the power of these two hotbeds of Lebanese nationalist feeling.

Nor was this the only problem besetting the Lebanese Forces. Only Bashir Gemayel had been able to channel the activism of the Forces in one direction. Without him, the divergent trends took a heavy toll on the organization's effectiveness. One group inside the Lebanese Forces pursued a Bashirist, ultranationalist posture; another returned to its Kata'eb roots; another remained close to Israel; yet another supported the government irrespective of its policies.[31] (These groups were not mutually exclusive. Most Lebanese Forces personnel probably fitted in two or more categories.)

The Christian community feared for its survival, particularly after the events of early February 1984 when both Druze and Shi'a militias seized all of the areas under nominal government control except the Christian heartland and a few Lebanese Army outposts overlooking Beirut.

### The Shi'as

In the year after June 1982, the Shi'as' evolution was rapid. However, like the Sunnis, the Shi'a community geographical divisions began to take their inevitable toll. The east, under Syrian occupation, was arrested in its social development, and the weight of Syrian control as well as the intrusion of other foreign elements confounded analysis. Israeli occupation in south Lebanon, by contrast, accelerated the mobilization of the community. While many, if not most, Shi'as had welcomed Israeli intervention in June 1982 to remove the PLO, they certainly did not welcome Israel's prolonged stay. Political and social mobilization in the south was catalyzed by the occupation, and in late 1983 took on an increasingly radical, fundamentalist hue.[32]

The principal impact of the Shi'as on Lebanese government originated in Beirut's southern areas, since the south and east were occupied. The Amal organization, though splintered, continued to exert a moderating influence on the Shi'a community, supporting government policy for the most part. Shi'a deserters were returned to the army. But here, too, the moderates—including the secular Amal leader, Nabih Berri, and Sheikh Mohammed Mehdi Shamseddin of the Higher (Shi'a) Islamic Council—were in a sense falling behind the growing militancy of their community. When, in the events of February 1984 Berri was compelled to ask army soldiers to refuse to fire on their Shi'a coreligionists, the clock had run out on Lebanese Army support for Gemayel. Before, he might have turned to the Shi'as on his own; now it was too late.

## The Druzes

If Walid Jumblatt had been losing his base of power in 1982 and 1983,[33] the victories in 1983 and 1984 gave him momentum. The PSP by late 1983 was purely Druze, Christian residents of the Shuf having been expelled irrespective of sect or partisan affiliation, and the PSP was now fighting for Druze interests. In the euphoria of victory, few seemed to consider the cost. For the Shuf was heavily damaged, and its economic base, which depended on Christian–Druze interdependence, was destroyed for the foreseeable future. Moreover, neither the Israeli nor the Syrian backers of the Druze were likely to help them convert military victories to political power in the aftermath of hostilities. Having served their purpose, the Druze were likely to be discarded.

## FROM PAX SYRIANA TO PAX SYRIANA: A REPRISE

Irrespective of its purposes, the 1982 Israeli intervention in Lebanon established conditions that might have led to the restoration of Lebanese sovereignty. Instead, within 18 months it was Syrian domination of Lebanon that was restored, a substantial level of destruction and heavy toll in human lives added to the already awesome tally of the 1975–1982 period, and both the United States and Israel were dealt serious setbacks for their involvement. What happened?

On the American side there were major miscalculations concerning Israel, Lebanon, and Syria. American policymakers underestimated Syrian determination to remain in and dominate Lebanon

north of the Israeli lines. They also underestimated Israeli determination to achieve a full peace immediately. And they overestimated the
Lebanese nationalist impulse. Both Israel and Syria saw Lebanon as a
zero sum game. Syrian leaders recognized early that their forces
would be able to remain in Lebanon, since it was apparent by early
1983 that neither Israel nor the United States was prepared to compel
withdrawal. For Syria, the major challenge was to remove the
Americans, which is to say the MNF, since its presence was the independence lifeline of the Lebanese government. Israeli leaders
sought a peace treaty which would justify the human cost of the 1982
intervention. Persuaded by the United States to accept less than a full
peace, their price was higher—concessions Syria perceived as a threat
not to its military security, but to its political interests.

American objectives and those of Syria in Lebanon were completely incompatible. Each country's goals could only be achieved if
the other withdrew. Consequently, Washington had two choices and
only two—to increase its level of commitment to ensure Syrian departure, which could only be effected through the use of military force; or
to remove its commitment and the symbol thereof, the Marines. The
decision to pursue a nonexistent third option, slightly increased commitment, should have made it clear to everyone that ultimately the
United States would be forced to opt for the second alternative.

Because the United States was not prepared to compel foreign
forces to withdraw, Lebanon, too, had two options—to turn toward
Israel or to realign with Syria. Like Washington, Beirut perceived a
nonexistent third option, the American ally. The delay in selecting
between the real options only increased the cost of the final
choice—for both the United States, which lost substantial regional
credibility at a critical time, and Lebanon.

The legacy of Israel's venture was even more serious. As a result
of the nature of the war of 1982, the massacres, the cost in human
lives, the outcome, and the continuing costs of the aftermath, as well
as the fact that Israeli forces were now tied down occupying and
alienating a newly hostile Lebanese people, Israel underwent an experience similar to the American Vietnam trauma. The impact of the
divisions thus spawned in Israeli society was felt on government policy
which was both neutralized and diluted. Indeed, by mid-1983 there
were several mutually incompatible policies being pursued concurrently in Lebanon. The Israeli Druze had their agenda; the Ariel Sharon
clique continued to seek its own ends; Defense Minister Arens had a
different approach; Mossad and Military Intelligence each had its own
ideas; and so forth. Thus, while some Israelis tried to restrain the
Druze, others armed the PSP. While some were talking with moderate

Shi'as, others armed Shi'a hoods and tried to co-opt them as village militias, others concluded the Shi'as were impossible to work with, and still others, in trying to bring order in south Lebanon, alienated the Shi'as. Some continued to work with the Lebanese Forces, others endeavored to reduce the Israeli tie there. Some came to believe that an independent Gemayel government was important to Israeli interests, but most preferred to undermine Gemayel for not turning to Israel. Some saw Syria as the enemy in Lebanon, others believed the two could accommodate each other's needs, still others believed the Syrian presence in Lebanon was very much in Israel's interest.

On March 1 and 2, 1984, Amin Gemayel travelled to Syria, symbolically surrendering to Syrian policy. The MNF had left (except for the French who had indicated they would soon depart as well). Although some American military personnel (most of them involved with the army training program) remained, U.S. support had evaporated. Israel was too divided to decide to support the Gemayel government, particularly since additional military commitments would be required. In any case, Gemayel was unable and unwilling to pay the Israeli price for support.

## A NEW LEBANON—BUT WHAT KIND?

A number of Lebanese had spoken hopefully in 1982 of a "new Lebanon."[34] There were many varying ideas about the nature of this "new Lebanon," but the words represented the commitment of Lebanese nationalists to restore a sovereign Lebanon, unified, free, democratic, and pluralist in nature. Whether such a dream was capable of accomplishment under different circumstances may be debated. Certainly, the "new Lebanon" envisaged by those using the slogan has not materialized.

It is no less clear that a new era for Lebanon has dawned. If the new Lebanon they spoke of was the dream of Lebanese nationalists, then the new Lebanon that has emerged was surely their nightmare. For the new Lebanon will not be independent; will not be unified; will not be free; will not be democratic; and will not be pluralist. What it will be is less clear, but what it will not be is clear enough.

### Lebanese Dependency

Lebanon will not be independent. At least until either a change in regime in Syria or an Israeli-Syrian war, Syria will dominate Lebanon. Lebanese sovereignty has been a sham for years. Under the new circumstances, Syria will completely control the east and most of the north; will dominate Beirut and environs; and will have paramount influence in the Shi'a areas south to Israeli lines. Syria will also have some influence in the Shuf, but will necessarily share this influence with Israel.

Syria will make a concentrated effort to finally establish its control over, or else to demolish, the Lebanese Army, the premier symbol of Lebanese independence. Syria has been unable to control the army in the past, but the events of the spring of 1984 provide new opportunities to penetrate, dilute, and destroy the army's historic resistance to Syria.

## Lebanese Disunity

The future nature of Lebanon is unclear. The fiction of national unity will likely be maintained for some period. Lebanon has not been unified since 1975, or arguably earlier. The occupation by Israel and Syria shows no sign of ending soon, and Israel is likely to use surrogate forces in any areas from which its army decides to disengage. This is the face of disunity.

The reality is more serious yet. The excesses committed during the combat in the Shuf in 1983 as well as the expulsion of all of the Shuf's large Christian community have increased intercommunity distrust and hatred to levels unknown for at least a century. The settlement of 'Alawis around Tripoli and the introduction of militant Iranian Shi'as around Baalbek have injected new and unassimilable elements into the equation. Finally, the radicalization of the Shi'as in the south, a process that has been exacerbated and accelerated by the Israeli occupation, is producing a society that will not easily be reincorporated into a multireligious state.

More and more, the issue of partition is being considered. The Druze are moving toward full-scale autonomy, and the Christian community (rather than just its extremist elements) is giving cantonization much more serious consideration. Shi'as have opposed this in the past, but the growing gulf between the Shi'as of the east, those of the south, and those in the southern suburbs may also move them toward such an approach.

## Lebanese Subjugation

For the immediate future, most Lebanese will continue to live in a state occupied or dominated by either Israel or Syria. Apart from the issue of sovereignty, the freedoms the Lebanese had known and sought certainly now appear to be fantasies. Syria is a police state, and Syrian occupation of Lebanon has been heavy-handed, relying on terror and brutality to ensure a minimum of order and a maximum of compliance with Syrian policy. Israeli polices in the south, if not quite so heavy-handed, have been even more efficient in the past. (Israel's southern allies have, however, been quite as ruthless as the Syrians.) The challenge of fundamentalist revolutionism, which is increasingly confronting the Israeli occupation in the south, may engender Syrian-style heavy-handedness. It has already provoked several catastrophic errors (such as the IDF armed entry into Nabatiyyeh during the Shi'a festival of Ashura), which have added fuel to the revolutionary fire.

Whether at the hands of their occupiers, or the occupiers' puppets, or at their own hands, the Lebanese will no longer savor the individual liberty of the past. Many have argued that that freedom was one of the principal problems that led to the conflict of 1975, but it is doubtful that historians will place much credence in this hypothesis. In any case, the combination of Lebanese sectarian consciousness, Syrian oppression, and Israeli nationalist paranoia is not an appealing recipe to bring out the flavor of liberty.

## Lebanese Undemocratic Intolerance

One of the ironies of the 1983–84 period is that many of those who criticized the Lebanese government for resistance to reforms also urged it to turn toward Syria, a country not well known for its dedication to democratic methods or for its religious tolerance. In 1976, the Lebanese president (Suleiman Frangieh) and his Syrian counterpart agreed on an historic "constitutional document" which incorporated some reforms of limited scope but left intact the traditional leadership position of the Christians, including the Maronite presidency. (The reforms were blocked by Kamal Jumblatt's rejection.) Until the balance of power in Lebanon altered dramatically in early February 1984, every indication suggested that the Syrian government intended to reinforce the principal institutions of Lebanon, rejected substantial reforms but preferred to control Lebanon by penetrating and neutralizing its traditional system and by dominating (and propping up) its traditional leadership families.

Internal Lebanese reforms were readily agreed to by all parties in bilateral and multipartite talks, and reforms responsive to Lebanese needs were more likely to evolve in a context free from the pressures of Israeli or Syrian occupation. However, the dramatic weakening of the national government in February 1984 may lead to a Syrian move for substantive and responsive changes in order to broaden the base of Syrian control.

A major problem confronting reforms is the nature of demographic, geographic, and political power in Lebanon. The 1984 victories of the Druze, for example, may give what amounts to about six percent of the population a critical voice, while Sunni impotence and isolation may reduce to almost nil a community several times as large. With the declining levels of intercommunal trust, decentralization appears to be the only hope to retain any representative government, but foreign occupation and domination (even where occupation is not a factor) are more effective with less power in Beirut.

The levels of intolerance in Lebanon are unprecedented. Those who point to a history of massacres misread the theme of Lebanese history which is one of cooperation much more than conflict. The pattern of habitation shows an evolving concept of communal cooperation, but between selected communities and in specific areas. However, this evolution has been abruptly altered by recent history.

The last decade of sordid violence has, however, taken a heavy toll on tolerance, the sine qua non for pluralism. Moreover, the emergence of fundamentalist militancy among both Shi'a and Sunni Muslims, when combined with the militancy of some Christian groups, does not bode well for the future. Democratic pluralism is another, perhaps the greatest, casualty of the war.

## LEBANON: FANTASY OR HISTORY

These fundamental threats, not just to the existence of Lebanon, but also to its reasons for existence, cannot be lightly put aside. It would be premature to publish an obituary for the state of Lebanon, but it may be time to consider drafting one for the Lebanese idea. Syrian domination of most of Lebanon and Israeli domination of parts; massive human resettlement problems; a reconstruction unlikely to be adequately financed; and greater militancy on the part of all communities making up the country—these are not the foundations for confidence. Emigration of much of its youth, especially in the Christian community, will further sap Lebanon of the hope and dynamism needed to overcome recent tragedies. Finally, if Syrian-Israeli control endures more than five years, the north, east, and south of Lebanon may become politically, socially, and economically difficult to reintegrate into the state.

The hopeful sign is that, even as this is written, adversity has augumented rather than diminished the value of Lebanon as a country, Lebanon as a society, and Lebanon as an idea, in the Middle East.

## NOTES

1. This literature has been very substantially expanded by numerous volumes on the internal conflicts between 1975 and 1982.

2. Michael C. Hudson, *The Precarious Republic: Political Modernization in Lebanon* (New York: Random House, 1968).

3. Leonard Binder, *Politics in Lebanon* (New York: Wiley, 1966).

4. Other notable books: Michael W. Suleiman, *Political Parties in Lebanon* (Ithaca: Cornell University Press, 1967); Elie Salem, *Modernization without Revolution: Lebanon's Experience*; and in French, Charles Rizk, *Le Régime politique libanais* (Paris: Pichon et Durand-Auzias, 1966). Recent additions include David C. Gordon's two books, *Lebanon: The Fragmented Nation* (Stanford: Hoover Institution, 1980), and *The Republic of Lebanon: Nation in Jeopardy* (Boulder: Westview, 1983), and Edward E. Azar et al., *Lebanon and the World in the 1980s* (College Park, MD: University of Maryland, 1983).

5. The most useful sources, both for bibliographic and data purposes, are *Fiches du Monde Arabe* and *Panorama of Events* (or *Panorama de l'actualité*), edited by CEDRE, both published in Beirut.

6. See Annie Laurent and Antoine Basbous, *Une Proie pour deux fauves: Le Liban entre le lion de Juda et le lion de Syrie* (Beirut: Da'irat, 1983).

7. See R. D. McLaurin, ed., *The Political Role of Minority Groups in the Middle East* (New York: Praeger, 1979), especially chapters 2, 5, and 7, for discussions of the groups and their positions in Lebanon, and any of several standard histories of Lebanon, such as Philip K. Hitti, *Lebanon in History from the Earliest Times to the Present* (London: Macmillan, 1967), or Kamal Salibi, *The Modern History of Lebanon* (London: Weidenfeld, 1965).

8. Shi'ism is a minority Islamic sect that departs from "Sunnism," often described as the "orthodox Islam," in both dogma and social customs.

9. The Druzes are seen as Islamic by Christians, and by themselves and some Muslims. However, fundamentalists and many others, including most Muslims, see the Druze faith as essentially separate from Islam.

10. Some Christian militias were formed as early as the 1930s, and the quasifeudal structure of Lebanese society supported private armed units even earlier. But the quantitative change after 1969 was so great as to be a qualitative departure.

11. In 1975, the eruption of civil war did not find the Christians united against the Muslims, the Left against the Right, or the Lebanese against the Palestinians. However, the violence that grew out of the extremely complex fighting of 1975 forced most of the Christian community into at least tacit support of what later became the Lebanese Front. Certainly, by 1980 and 1981, the Christian community as a whole saw its existence threatened by the role and activities of the Palestinians and their allies. Even today *individual* Christians participate in the National Movement, but the community as a whole has become much more unified than ever before and identified with the Lebanese Front.

12. See Chapter 5.

13. Israel opposed and, in fact, quickly rejected the initiative because it envisaged the creation of a Palestinian polity in the West Bank. Syria opposed and rejected the initiative because Syrian leaders did not believe it was likely to help them recover the Golan Heights.

14. See Chapter 5 and Paul A. Jureidini and R. D. McLaurin, "Army and State in Lebanon," *Middle East Insight, III*, 2 (August-October 1983), 28–34. Cf. Adel A. Freiha, *L'Armée et l'état au Liban* (Paris: Librairie générale du droit et de la jurisprudence, 1980), and Fuad Lahoud, *Ma'sat al-jaish al-lubnani* (Beirut: 1977).

15. See "Perspectives on Lebanon's Economy: Reconstruction and Development," in Azar et al., *Lebanon*.

16. See Chapter 6.

17. See Chapter 7.

18. It is not correct to suggest that these problems were *caused* by Israel, however. The Shuf has been an area of Christian-Druze joint control, and the Chamoun base in the Shuf represented *Christian* rather than Maronite leadership. In a major sense, the Christian-Druze fighting in the Shuf is a reflection of changes within the Christian community.

19. The question of Tripoli may prove extremely troublesome, more than the Shuf or the south. How to manage the now-substantial 'Alawi community, the conflicting claims within a very divided Sunni community, Syria's interest in the port, and Lebanon's own interests may be a problem too complex to answer or resolve.

20. See R. D. McLaurin, "Lebanon and the United States," in Edward E. Azar et al., *Lebanon*.

21. Jonathan C. Randal, *Going All the Way* (New York: Viking, 1983), paints a very harsh portrait of Bashir Gemayel, but also provides more information on him than is readily available in other single sources. Robert J. Pranger points out that the national leader emerging from a bloody conflict is frequently he who demonstrated leadership *during* that conflict, and that Gemayel, personifying the antithesis of "business-as-usual," was a singularly appropriate leader for a 1982 Lebanon that recognized the necessity of fundamental change. ("Perspectives on Lebanon's Political Future," in Azar et al., *Lebanon*, Chapter 2.)

22. President Reagan symbolized the confidence of the U.S. administration in Bashir Gemayel when he said, "He was the light of hope."

23. See David Ignatius, "How to Rebuild Lebanon," *Foreign Affairs*, LXI, 5 (Summer 1983), 1147, and Randal, *Going*.

24. Bob Woodward, Richard Harwood, and Christian Williams, "Track in Killing of Gemayel Kin Leads to Syria," *The Washington Post*, February 8, 1984, A1.

25. When Amin was elected the Lebanese Army had not a single tank; no place to house its personnel; and no senior command structure considered "legitimate" by military personnel. The Lebanese Forces did not transfer its loyalty to Amin, and, in fact, dissatisfaction was evident from the outset.

26. See David Ignatius, "Partial Israeli Withdrawal in Lebanon Shows Change in Intelligence Thinking," *The Wall Street Journal*, August 25, 1983, 23.

27. We are not arguing that these groups have always been Syrian-controlled, only that they are *now* Syrian-controlled. The Syrian Social Nationalist Party was at one time quite independent of the Syrian government. During the conflict in Lebanon between 1975 and 1982 the party split, and today it is controlled by Damascus. The Mourabitoun ceased to exist as a coherent fighting force after the Israeli invasion of 1982. Since, it has depended upon Syria.

28. See Jureidini and McLaurin, "Army and State." With most of its personnel tied down in Beirut, the LAF was only able to deploy one understrength brigade to the Shuf, and this *after* the IDF withdrew. This unit had no secure LOC, limited organic firepower, and was effectively surrounded. Artillery support was vital to sustain the unit, and naval gunfire was also used. Air support appears to have been of more psychological than physical importance. Under these extremely harrowing conditions, and fighting in a relatively built-up area (at Suq el-Gharb), the LAF performed extraordinarily well.

29. Bob Woodward, Richard Harwood, and Christian Williams, "Beirut Bombing: Political Warriors Used Man Who Craved Death," *The Washington Post*, February 1, 1984, A1ff.

30. Cf. Joseph Maila, "Liban: la tragédie de la 'paix,' " *Etudes*, February 1984, 149–59.

31. There has been little dispassionate coverage of the internal divisions of any Lebanese community in world media. A reasonable discussion, though one still characterized by numerous errors, of these division within the Lebanese Forces is David B. Ottaway, "Christian Chiefs Weigh Abandoning Gemayel," *The Washington Post*, February 26, 1984, A16.

32. See, e.g., Judith Miller, "Israeli Assumes Driver of Truck Was a Shiite," *The New York Times*, November 15, 1983, 7; Judith Miller, "Israel to Cut Reliance on Haddad Troops," ibid., November 6, 1983, 14; Lynda Schuster, "Delight at Israeli Army's Ouster of PLO Is Turning to Anger in Southern Lebanon," *The Wall Street Journal*, December 2, 1983, 33; David B. Ottaway, "Israeli Security Steps in S. Lebanon Curb Economy, Spur Opposition," *The Washington Post*, December 3, 1983, A25; and Ottaway, "Islamic Fundamentalism Surges," ibid., December 13, 1983, A1.

33. See note 32 above.

34. E.g., Elie Salem, "Prospects for a New Lebanon," *AEI Special Analyses* (Washington, D.C.: American Enterprise Institute, 1982).

# PART II

# FOCUS ON LEBANON

# 2

# Lebanon and Its Political Culture: Conflict and Integration in Lebanon[1]

## Edward E. Azar

## INTRODUCTION

Over the past several years, a number of general and specific hypotheses have been advanced to explain the scope, intensity, and level of protracted violence in Lebanon. Very few of these hypotheses have attributed the problem to purely domestic sociopolitical structures and some have traced the root causes to external variables alone. The overwhelming body of studies assert that instability in Lebanon is a function of the linkages between that country's domestic and international environments.

In this chapter, I will argue that the recurrence of violence during the past decade is determined, to a great extent, by the overt and covert intervention and the pursuance of Syrian, Israeli and PLO policy objectives in Lebanon. Not all interventions were motivated by external forces alone—some have been encouraged by several Lebanese communities who found it necessary to recruit regional and international allies in accomplishing their communal objectives. At times, regional and international conflicts, such as the Palestinian-Israeli one, make their way into Lebanon and precipitate destruction and destabilization. In fact, Lebanese national integration and stability have *never* had a chance to flourish due to the blatant external intervention in Lebanese sociopolitical affairs and the exploitation of intercommunal fears.

Why Lebanon? Why do Lebanon's neighbors feel free to intervene in Lebanese affairs, carry out their proxy wars, conduct their own military campaigns, or destabilize Lebanon without much concern for sanctions, cost, etc.? Why do some Lebanese groups express greater loyalties to non-Lebanese entities and precepts than they do for

Lebanon? What have the Lebanese done about these social deformities in their country?

To try to answer these questions, one needs to examine the following:

1. Anxiety, fear and the lack of national integration in Lebanon.
2. The National Pact of 1943 and the system of governance derived from it.
3. Regional and international events and their impact on Lebanon.

## COMMUNAL ANXIETIES AND THE DILEMMA OF NATIONAL INTEGRATION

Lebanon is composed of diverse cultural and religious minorities, allowing only minimal social and political integration at the national level. Social relations across some religious communities are very rare. While economic exchange and transactions are widespread, there appears to be no proportional spillover into other types of societal and intercommunal relations. Thus, national loyalty among some Lebanese communities is low and national institutions have rarely succeeded in forging voluntary intercommunal bonds. Of course, the size and strength of each of Lebanon's communities add to the problem of achieving viable sociopolitical integration. Lebanon is composed of several religious communities, none of which is strong enough to dominate and shape a national destiny in its communal image, and yet none is so weak as to be effectively subdued.

The history of trust among the various Lebanese minorities is very poor. The roots of fear go back to the nineteenth century and earlier—fears of massacres, subjugation, or marginalization and control. Obviously, the events of the recent past have not reduced the level or scope of fear and anxiety among the minorities in Lebanon or elsewhere in the Middle East. Present-day trends in attitudes towards religious or cultural minorities in countries like Iran, Libya, and others in the Middle East do not inspire much confidence in the future of intercommunal relations. Baha'is, for example, are being subjected to extermination in Iran. Christian Arabs cannot acquire Saudi citizenship even if they are qualified by every other conceivable criterion simply because they profess a faith different than Islam. Christians in most Arab states cannot achieve top leadership posts simply because of their religious identity.

Members of Christian minorities in Lebanon and elsewhere in the Middle East fear the rise of Islamic fundamentalism in the region and worry about the return of the Ottoman-type treatment where, not long ago, Christians were used as scapegoats, excluded from certain public offices, not permitted to build new churches, wear green, carry a gun, ride a horse, etc. Whether there is a realistic basis for these fears in today's world or not is not the issue. Memories do not simply go away and those who have been victims of racism and segregation do not forget as fast as the external analyst or mere observer does. What matters is that these anxieties provide inertia and engender resistance to change or capitulation. Much of the present-day Khomeini or Qaddafi rhetoric translates into observable worry and concern within Lebanon.[2]

Of course, several attempts to reduce the level of fear and distrust have been taken (e.g., the 1943 National Pact) but with very limited success. Why?

The Lebanese political pact and system of 1943 contained positive features aimed at reducing intercommunal fears. Had the system been allowed to take root and grow, the situation might have been different than it has been so far. For example, the 1943 National Pact established in Lebanon an open political system and a structure which responds to the need for preserving the religious identity of its population. Compared with the rest of the states in the Arab League, Lebanon can boast a liberal parliamentary democracy with consociational characteristics and strong achievement-oriented communities. These features should be a source of strength for most multiethnic and multiracial societies. In Lebanon however, political democracy and the lack of a strong police force have made it easy for external forces, in collaboration with their Lebanese clients, to exploit the system and destabilize it.

Is the lack of national integration unique to Lebanon or to the Middle East? The answer is no. The Lebanese dilemma is familiar to countries made up of several religious, racial, and cultural communities which have had histories of competition and protracted crisis. In multiethnic and pluralist societies, stability and the reduction of *threat* require addressing the following concerns:[3]

1. Issues of *security* and anxiety about the future;
2. Approaches to rewarding intercommunal modes of *interaction*;
3. *Acceptance* of diversity, and solving the problem of minority–majority integration.

Lebanon has not been able to deal effectively with the above issues because it continues to fall prey to the intrigues and machinations of its stronger, conflictive, or often unstable neighbors—these neighbors continue (both directly and indirectly) to inflame religious anxieties and distrust and they have rarely shown much respect for Lebanese independence. Most recently, the actors have been Syria, the PLO, Israel, and their local or regional clients and allies. In the past the roster has included Egypt and the USSR, among others.

Has the National Pact of 1943 been a useful instrument for national integration in Lebanon? My reply is: *unfortunately, not as much as it should have been.* While the National Pact of 1943 represented a major social invention at managing political compromise and protecting religious and political identities, it also engendered some unreasonable costs and consequences. At the time it was concluded, the Pact promised an opportunity for greater national integration and independence, but as the events of the Middle East began to unfold after World War II, these positive expectations began to fade away. And as the intentions and behavior of Syria and its Lebanese allies (primarily the Moslem Sunnis) became apparent and threatening, the Lebanese Christian community (primarily the Maronites) became disenchanted and anxiety-ridden. Intercommunal stability in Lebanon began to require total conformity to the will of Syria and its increasingly radicalized allies of the Arab League states. Thus, when the government of Lebanon took an active and relatively independent role in regional or international affairs, and when this meant choosing options which differ from those of the Arab League countries, especially Syria, then Lebanon had to pay the price in terms of instability and domestic upheaval. During the past forty years, therefore, Lebanon was able to choose either political emasculation and sterility or destabilization and violence. This ugly choice has never been made more explicit as in the past decade of war and violence, and it has been dramatized by recent Syrian and other Arab states' reaction to Lebanon's agreement with Israel on May 17, 1983.

The developments and the events of the recent past have created their counterforce. Many Lebanese citizens, particularly Christian nationalists who resist the Syrian dominance of Lebanon, have become convinced that at the regional and international levels their country has to reassess and redefine the modalities of its goals and domain of relations. They have discovered that during the past four decades, instead of improving, the situation has continued to deteriorate. These Lebanese make projections of present-day demographic and ideological trends in Lebanon and the Middle East and discover that if these trends were to continue, Christians in Lebanon will become marginal and irrelevant to the social and political life of their country—a status familiar to minorities in Arab Moslem states. They fear being reduced to a mere cultural community and to second-class citizens.

Because religious identity is an important source of personal security and a locus for political ideas and action in Lebanon, the Lebanese have taken to defending their confessional system at a cost to national integration.[4] Lebanese nationalists, especially those of the Christian faith, feel that to barter away the system of confessionalism for something less predictable would be a tragic mistake. Thus, resisting major alterations to the status quo and the familiar has become a popular value.

## ORIGINS OF CONFESSIONALISM IN LEBANESE POLITICS

Prior to 1922, "Lebanon" referred only to Mount Lebanon proper, an Ottoman province covering an area about one third the size of the modern country. The area came under Ottoman rule in 1516, when Sultan Selim I (the Grim) conquered it from the Mamluks. For three centuries between 1516 and 1831, Mount Lebanon was a relatively calm area populated predominantly by Druze and Christians. The area was governed by local *emirs* who ruled according to a complex and carefully elaborated code of protocol along feudal lines. "Intersectarian strife" per se was a rare phenomenon in the area until 1831, largely because feudal norms placed a premium on loyalty between ruler and subject—regardless of faith—and because of the nature of Ottoman rule in what is now Lebanon.[5]

The year 1831 marked a turning point in this state of affairs, as the Pasha of Egypt laid siege to Mount Lebanon for ten years, using religious strife in the area as a mechanism to keep himself in control.

Vastly complicating the situation was the entry, in the same period, of outside international rivalries onto the Lebanese scene.[6] Napoleon's earlier occupation of Egypt and Palestine had alerted the British to the vulnerability of their trade routes to India and made them particularly anxious about French intentions. They therefore bolstered their links with the Ottoman Empire and attempted to insulate the French who sought other allies to promote their interests. In time, the British became increasingly involved, and even developed links with the Druze to compensate for the special relationship that existed between France and the Maronite Christians of Mount Lebanon.

In 1840, a military force composed of British, Austrian, and Turkish troops, joined by important Lebanese Maronites and Druze who had themselves become alarmed at the Egyptian incursions into their territory, ousted the Egyptian Pasha and deposed the local leader who, for his own reasons, had facilitated the Pasha's seizure of power. For the next two years the Great Powers, rejoined by France in 1841, wrestled with the question of how Lebanon could be administered to the satisfaction of all parties. The Ottoman Government tried to avert the possibility of Lebanese autonomy by unilaterally installing an Ottoman official as governor.[7] Once again, Druze, Maronites, and the Great Powers united against this attempt, and a critical meeting was held in May 1842, at the ministry of foreign affairs of the Sultan during which the administrative independence of Mount Lebanon was established. Thus, regional and international manipulation of internal Lebanese disputes and competition for increased spheres of influence in the area as among the various Lebanese subcultures was officially sanctioned. In addition, a precedent was also established permitting appeals for external intervention in an effort to tip the delicate internal balance. It was a pattern that was to prevail for over a century.

As a result of a series of compromises, the Great Powers finally agreed in 1842 to establish two separate districts, one Maronite and one Druze, which would each be run by a subgovernor. They also agreed to an administrative council to represent the six major sects in the country. Subsequent disputes arose in both districts where minority sects felt unrepresented. Some modifications were introduced, but the structure of the government was destined to increase rather than reduce tensions, because demographic divisions were not as neat and clear as the division and allocation of political responsibilities. An uneasy truce with sporadic eruptions prevailed until 1860.

The massacre of thousands of Christians in various parts of Lebanon and in Damascus in 1860 revealed that the system did not work. After much deliberation and bargaining, a new administrative structure was introduced which diverged from its predecessor in that it provided for reunification of the country under one ruler who was to be a Christian appointee of the Ottoman Porte (subject, of course, to European approval). The central Administrative Council of twelve members representing the six major sects was charged with matters of taxation and government spending, in addition to advising the Governor. This system—a product of lengthy deliberations and numerous compromises—was the precursor of the modern Lebanese governmental system. It survived in the same form until the advent of the French mandate in 1920.

France received the mandate over Syria and Lebanon in April, 1920, a couple of years after the defeat of the Ottoman Empire. In August, 1920, France expanded the borders of Lebanon to include the former Ottoman zones of Beirut, Tripoli, Sidon, Tyre, and the Beqa'a valley. This move necessitated revising the old system to accommodate the larger number of Sunni and Shi'a Moslems. The Maronite Christians no longer held an absolute majority in the country, although the various Christian groups combined slightly outnumbered the various Moslem groups. The French action had enormous significance for Lebanon, because the country became one of minorities, no one strong enough to ever oppose the French mandatory government or dominate the rest of the Lebanese state. There was opposition to this French action, but this was kept in check. In 1943, the French transferred sovereignty to the Lebanese who established the 1943 National Pact.[8] The principles embedded in this Pact were basically the same as those established in the nineteenth century agreement.

## THE NATIONAL PACT OF 1943

The modern Lebanese system evolved out of a unique historical experience. Fully aware of this situation, two Lebanese leaders, Bishara al-Khoury (a Maronite Christian) and Riyad al-Sulh (a Sunni Moslem) drafted the National Pact of 1943 with the British help.[9] The Pact formally addressed two thorny problems that the new state faced: *internal* distribution of power, and national character with respect to *external* relations.

The National Pact institutionalized a distribution of political power along confessional lines, based on each group's proportional size in the census of 1932 which found Christians to be a majority and Muslims a minority.[10] Thus the President would always be a Maronite Christian, the Prime Minister a Sunni Muslim, the Speaker of the Chamber of Deputies a Shi'a Muslim, and the deputy speaker a Greek Orthodox Christian. The Ministry of Foreign Affairs went to a Greek Orthodox and the Ministry of Defense to a Druze. Similarly, representation in the Parliament and in the Cabinet was allocated along confessional lines—six Christians for every five Muslims.[11] (This proportion would change to a one-to-one ratio if the Geneva 1983 national dialogue succeeds.)

The system was designed, in large part, to alleviate Christian fears that their *regional* minority status would somehow impinge on their historical *national* majority status in Lebanon. In return for some advantages in internal affairs, the Christians agreed to membership in the Arab community with special reservations.

This formula had positive and negative repercussions. On the domestic side, the parliamentary and presidential elections tended to produce very able politicians who had cross-communal appeal. While the President has ample constitutional powers available to him, his success had to be measured by his ability to work with the Sunni prime minister (the head of the cabinet) and the highly independent parliament and its Shi'a speaker. Certain laws require a two-thirds majority approval, and their passage requires legislative compromise. The country's electoral districts encompass multicommunal electorates, so each candidate had to campaign among Lebanese from all groups in order to win a parliamentary seat, and needed to be responsive to the demands of his district's residents and not only to members of his own sect or community.[12] This in turn created a natural mechanism that promoted the election of able leaders (often well-tested ones) possessing special competence in the art of compromise and consensus-building.

The major flaw of the 1943 National Pact was that it did not consider, whether intentionally or otherwise, what should be done in the event of a change in the proportional balance in the country. Of the two premises on which the Pact was based, which should take precedence?

Would *demographic* change determine the distribution of power? Would Christian fears about *minority* status in a Muslim region be decisive if demography was mooted? These questions have been so sensitive that no official census has been taken since 1932 and no doctrine has been developed to address the matter of this Christian fear.

Related to these issues is the problem of "representativeness." Does the president represent his nation or his religious community? Does the prime minister represent the Sunni interests or those of the whole country, including the Maronites and Druze?

And what about members of Parliament—how do they vote when an issue hurts their community but serves the national interests? The conflict between serving as a representative of one's religious group and serving as a representative of one's national district, combined with the high priority placed on the preservation of a government by consensus, has had paralyzing effects.[13]

While these problems are not unusual in democratic societies, in Lebanon the tendency toward paralysis is compounded by *mahsubbiya*—a tradition of loyalty to leading figures and families in the country which has been an important force in the area since feudal times.

Theoretically, confessionalism, if administered well, institutionalizes channels of cooperation, places high national value on accommodation and unity, and promotes moderation rather than extremism. Because Lebanese confessionalism recognizes the religious identity of communities and guarantees multiple channels of access to the national leadership, it can be a stabilizing and integrative force. But, political, ideological, and strategic polarization in the Middle East produced turbulence in the area which found its way, in one form or another, into Lebanon and consequently made a mockery of confessionalism and breached the second half of the National Pact repeatedly.

It is to a very brief history of these external relations that we now turn.

## THE NATIONAL PACT AND REGIONAL AND INTERNATIONAL EVENTS

The provisions in the National Pact that pertained to Lebanon's foreign relations were as pivotal—if not more so—as those which specified internal arrangements. In exchange for constitutional recognition of their majority status in the country, the Christians agreed to the preservation of a neutral stance in regional affairs. The Arab nationalists—notably the Sunni population, which preferred merger with Syria to the post-1920 status quo, acquiesced to the idea that Lebanon would have an "Arab face" but maintain its sovereignty and independence.[14]

Lebanon's internal stability and domestic politics were greatly affected by, and closely linked to, the course of events outside its borders. That this obtained even in the early years when Arab disarray precluded the dreams of unity and conservatism prevailed did not augur well for the future when pan-Arabism and radicalism would sweep the Arab world. Perhaps the fear of just such an eventuality propelled the Lebanese delegation at the first Arab Unity Conference in 1944 to insist upon "respect for the independence and sovereignty of Lebanon within its present frontiers." This clause was subsequently incorporated into the Arab League pact under Article 8 where all signatories agreed to respect one another's "system of government" and "abstain from any action calculated to change these systems." Article 9 specifically reserved the choice of initiating "closer cooperation and stronger bonds" to the respective states themselves. Lebanon acquired a neutral identity, and the Arab world pledged to respect that neutrality.

The establishment of the state of Israel in 1948 brought approximately 140,000 Palestinian refugees to Lebanon. As 95 percent of these were Muslims, their entry posed a considerable dilemma for the fledgling government. On the one hand, to give them citizenship would have meant destroying the carefully planned balance that had been written into the National Pact. From an Arab nationalist point of view, it would also represent admission of an Arab defeat and the permanent loss of Palestine. Thus both Arab and Lebanese nationalists were in agreement on the issue of keeping the Palestinian refugees unincorporated into Lebanon. Of course, Palestinian refugees in Lebanon took part in the economic life of the state and experienced in Lebanon a level of political and social freedom rarely known anywhere in the Arab world.

The explosive entry of Nasser of Egypt onto the world scene renewed the energies of the Arab nationalists in Lebanon, notably of the Sunni Muslims. Since independence, the Arab nationalists had strongly advocated the merger of all or part of Lebanon with Syria. Although they had accepted the 1943 National Pact, many still believed that merger with Syria would eventually come to pass. Nasser's ideas and rhetoric reignited that spark among Arab nationalists in Lebanon. Many of them began to look to Cairo for guidance and inspiration. Nasser himself encouraged this by appealing directly to the Lebanese populace.

Nasser's impact on internal Lebanese politics quickly became evident. The tendency of the opposition Arab nationalists to gravitate towards Cairo inspired grave concern among the country's Christian population. They feared that the pan-Arabist passions of the time might lead to the dissolution of Lebanon, or its merger with Syria or several Arab states together. They therefore turned to their traditional protectors—the West—as a counterweight to the fervor that swept through the region. Both the Arab nationalists and President Chamoun's government accused each other of deviating from the National Pact. Both groups felt that the other's excessive dependence on an external supporter required a response in kind.

The formation of the Baghdad Pact in 1955 rigidly polarized the Arab world. To complicate matters, Nasser made his first arms deal with the Soviet Union in 1955 and set in motion all sorts of destabilizing actions and reactions in the region. To the conservative American administration, this represented another example of Soviet penetration that had to be confronted and halted. Thus, the United States, for its own reasons, devised a means of strengthening its Lebanese connection which widened the distance between the camps—pro-United States and pro-Soviet Union—in the region.

The increasing polarization of regional and international relations had such a strong impact on the Lebanese government that in 1956 representatives of both groups appeared to be conducting foreign policy independently of one another. The Suez War of 1956 brought the tension to a breaking point. Lebanon had split along lines which mirrored the global dichotomy.

By March 1957 when the Eisenhower Doctrine was announced, the situation had indeed become grave. Waves of unrest swept throughout the Middle East. Given the state of affairs inside Lebanon, it was not surprising that the government had endorsed the Doctrine within a month of its inauguration and gave it the strongest support of any Middle East country.

In this situation, so pregnant with tension, the announcement in February 1958 that Egypt and Syria intended to merge and to establish the United Arab Republic (UAR) burst like a bombshell. It suddenly seemed that many regimes would soon topple under the weight of pan-Arabism.

This prediction was perceived as perilously accurate when violence and civil war erupted in Lebanon in May 1958, and the Iraqi regime was overthrown in July 1958 by a pro-Nasserite government. The UAR, though short-lived, actively fostered the internal Lebanese conflict and encouraged the destabilization of Chamoun's government.[15]

The fundamental principles of the National Pact had, in one way or another, been violated, as the Middle Eastern turmoil spread into Lebanon. Nasser's instigations on behalf of one group prompted the other half of the population to seek external support to reassert the internal balance. But externalization of the balance (directing it outward) did not prove feasible, as the parties whose assistance was sought were not, in turn, equal themselves.

## Post-1958

For about a decade, Lebanon made a feeble attempt to liquidate the consequences of the 1958 crisis. After implementing a few administrative changes which were intended to fine-tune the old system, and convinced that they had the system on course, the Lebanese turned their attention to what they knew best—finances, trade, and services, primarily in the Persian Gulf states of Saudi Arabia, Kuwait, and the United Arab Emirates.

The Lebanese elites immersed themselves in economic pursuits and the needs of the Persian Gulf states to the detriment of their own social and communal affairs. Whether this situation was necessary as a psychological escape from the anxieties of war and instability of yesteryear, or whether it represented a rekindling of the Lebanese self-image, namely that Lebanon is best at being the economic and commercial highway for the West and the Middle East, is not an issue to be addressed here. For a decade after 1958, though, the Lebanese set aside the contradictions inherent in their National Pact and dismissed the significance of the matter of war and peace in the Middle East. Eventually, of course, it was the issue of regional war and peace which led to the demise of Lebanese national authority and the large-scale destruction of lives and resources.

In the post-1958 period, business interests began to devour the Lebanese and to dominate all aspects of their individual and collective lives. Wealth and its accumulation had always been personal objectives without much concern for the political and social consequences of this preoccupation; the impact of this trait was almost incomprehensible for a society that had been founded on very delicate social and political imperatives.

During the decade of the 1960s and after, national income increased substantially, but attention to national and social integration were all but forgotten. As the very able Lebanese business/political elite ignored or rationalized the sociopolitical forces and dynamics that began to emerge in the Lebanon of the 1960s, the concern with greater accumulation of financial resources in and outside Lebanon took on new proportions. Lebanon's elites underestimated the dynamics of sociopolitical change and overestimated their ability to deal with adversity. It is during this period in Lebanon's modern history that the Lebanese ruling elites lost the war to protect a collectively vibrant and politically exciting Lebanon in favor of winning the short-term battle of economic interests. While the Lebanese elite class expanded and accumulated its wealth, the country was being taken over by outsiders and the political system undermined.

Toward the end of the 1960s, violence increased, the psychological quality of life became deformed, and the Lebanese who were obsessed with their financial success soon discovered that they would not be permitted to enjoy the fruits of their obsession. From 1967 to the present, the Lebanese have been on the run.

The fate of present-day Lebanon cannot be explained without a serious analysis of the decadence that beset the country in the post-1958 period. The intervention of regional and international groups and powers easily destabilized Lebanon because of the weak state and the unconcerned and materially preoccupied society.

The June 1967 war shattered all of the political and strategic calculations made by all the states in the Middle East, including Lebanon. In 1968–69, Lebanon found itself extremely vulnerable. Its territory had become a staging ground for the new phase of Palestinian–Israeli and inter-Arab conflicts. Thus, in 1969, a weak and insecure Lebanon had no choice but to accept the Cairo Accords, which gave the PLO the right to use southern Lebanon for its military operations against Israel. While other Arab League states have been reluctant to permit the PLO to use their terrritory to stage war against Israel, the entire Arab League, with the utmost disregard for Lebanon's freedom and integrity, encouraged President Helou's Government to sign these Accords and turn southern Lebanon into "Fatahland."

The defeat of the PLO in Jordan in 1970 added to Lebanon's misery, and paved the way for more destruction. As tens of thousands of Palestinian fighters and their families were driven into Lebanon and started to wage war against Israel from Lebanon itself, Israeli retaliation hurt the people of Lebanon as well. Many became refugees in their own country. Some turned to makeshift shelters in and around Beirut and the Beqa'a. Soon after 1971, physical and economic insecurity increased and spilled over into all other sectors of Lebanese life. Thus between 1968 and 1973, the victimization and destabilization of Lebanon began to take on ominous proportions and repositioned Lebanon on the course of protracted violence until this day.[16]

In the early 1970s the Lebanese Maronites and, by extension, the Christian community began to question the conditions that befell their country. Some political leaders saw that Lebanon had unwittingly become the arena for armed struggle and for international terror. The country had become a source of insecurity for its neighbors. By 1975, the cleavages and contradictions of the entire region found their way into Lebanon.

The PLO-Lebanese and Syrian-Lebanese wars of 1976-83 have been costly in human and material terms for all concerned. These wars divided the Lebanese population a dozen different ways and precipitated internal strife among the Lebanese religious and political communities. Lebanese instability brought about Israeli retaliation and occupation, and led to a very active and controversial involvement of the United States and some European states in Lebanon in 1982.[17] Emasculated by the National Pact of 1943, Lebanon invited external disrespect for its sovereignty and ultimately direct intervention in its own affairs. Having "internalized" the role assigned to it by the Arab League community, Lebanon paid little attention to its security needs and finally witnessed its own destruction as a national entity.

The events have had many sociological and political consequences. The past decade has sharpened the cleavages in the country but, paradoxically, these have reignited Lebanese nationalism and given new vigor to their particular political system and cultural pluralism. There is a new awakening on the part of Lebanese emigres, particularly in the United States. A renewed political seriousness has emerged which is historically significant. It is to these shifts that one must turn in order to understand present-day dynamics and potential trends in Lebanon. In another chapter in this book this question is addressed in more detail. In this chapter I will make some conjectures about the prospects of reconciliation and stability in present-day Lebanon.

## QUESTIONS AND CONJECTURES

Can Lebanon achieve domestic peace and reconstruction? Can Lebanon rebuild its institutions, economy, and intercommunal trust?

The answer is yes, if certain conditions are met. If the Syrian, PLO, and Israeli armed forces withdraw without extracting unreasonable prices and if regional and international support for the Lebanese regime increases openly and effectively, then the leaders of the Lebanese religious communities would be in a much better position to strike a compromise and effect reconciliation. Raw pressure on the Maronites to capitulate to Syrian demands and calling this reconciliation is both unjust and unworkable. Confidence-building measures have to be established and guarantees (both legal-conceptual and operational) have to be advanced so that the Christians of Lebanon will share power and not only give it up. Let me elaborate.

*Domestic Answers.* Lebanon makes sociopolitical sense to its nationalists only if it remains a pluralist society, confessional republic, and parliamentary democracy. It can only be an interesting country if it retains its unique role of being a haven for minorities, a primary link between the West and the Middle East, and a moderate and positive voice in regional and international affairs. This kind of Lebanon needs to conceptualize and clarify, at least in very broad terms, some of the more basic parameters of its political legitimacy and culture.

Lebanon's two clusters of religious communities need, first of all, to reassess their coexistence modalities, especially in light of the events of the past decade. Christians and Moslems in Lebanon have done well *only* at times when they allowed one another to satisfy their identity needs from within. The conflict between the two major groups has primarily centered over regional and international issues and identities. This was evident in the mid-1950s and the 1970s. Thus, present-day Lebanese reconciliation discussions must confront this issue head-on and come to grips with it.

Perhaps, in the case of Lebanon, the Moslem population would find it useful to reconfirm, assertively and convincingly, the historic compromise that Lebanon is the permanent and final homeland for them and the Christians. Furthermore, this homeland would remain unique, democratic, independent, and pro-Western. The Moslem community needs to demonstrate its recognition of the genuineness of the Christian fears and to cooperate in addressing this issue. Because the more the Christian groups in Lebanon feel secure, the more the Moslem groups will be and vice versa—it is a non-zero sum game.

The Christian communities need to work out ways to accommodate Moslem aspirations within the framework of a sovereign and independent Lebanon. The more the Moslem community perceives itself as part of the system the more it is likely to subscribe to Lebanese nationhood.

Christians and Moslems have to be able to live without the fear of extermination or absorption. Because the demographic shifts and the increased ideological rigidity in the Middle East translate into fear and anxieties among the Christian communities, the numerical size of a community must not be used as a basis for power sharing in any present or future political arrangement in Lebanon. It should be recognized that there are two communities which have to coexist with one another and to formulate power relationships without stirring fears in light of the present circumstances. Lebanon's religious communities will find practical ways to share the country's resources and political system, once they reassert the basic political principle of religious coexistence contained in the 1943 National Pact and rededicate themselves to protecting it.

*International Answers.* The international support for a just, independent, and democratic Lebanon makes a lot of sense. But this means that regional and international actors have to refrain from engaging in blatant intervention in Lebanese domestic affairs. It also means that capable and trusted international powers in the West have to continue to shoulder the responsibility of shepherding an orderly transition in Lebanon. Ten years of destruction and violence have left their own marks and dynamics, thus compounding the problems of rebuilding and reconciliation.

External intervention in Lebanese affairs, however, is not easily eliminated from a setting which has grown used to it. Some Lebanese groups might find it difficult to refrain from recruiting external allies to support them in altering the domestic balance, but it is essential that this self-entrapment mechanism be broken. Lebanon will have very limited success in calming intercommunal relations as long as its neighbors continue to take sides in its intercommunal competition and conflicts or insist on coopting various communities whenever their needs require it. As long as Lebanon is occupied and as long as its neighbors fight their wars on Lebanese territory, Lebanon cannot easily reclaim its sovereignty and independence. Lebanon can only succeed in achieving national integration and buttressing internal cross-cutting loyalties in a secure environment if external intervention aimed at destabilizing it is eliminated. If the above necessary conditions are not met, then it should be elementary for anyone to conclude that Lebanon will not be able to arrive at a durable and genuine reconciliation.

Whatever the Lebanese intercommunal elites do to effect a termination of hostilities and commence the process of social change, they must not do anything in the context of summit-type bargaining sessions alone. Once the decision to move towards rebuilding and reconciliation is made, then creative approaches to intercommunal dialogue at all levels need instituting. Continuous evaluation of the structure and process of reconciliation is required. The awesome task of rebuilding Lebanon is multifaceted—it involves psychological, institutional, political, economic, and physical reconstruction and development. The dozens of obvious difficulties stem from the fact that so many steps have to be taken simultaneously. But, is there a realistic alternative?

## NOTES

1. I am thankful for the contributions of several friends and colleagues who have contributed to the contents of this chapter. I am indebted for the generous assistance and constructive comments of Kate Shnayerson. Professor John Burton, Drs. Paul Jureidini and Ronald McLaurin, and Mr. Chung-in Moon all provided me with very valuable ideas.

2. Qaddafi, for example, has recently recommended that all Christians in the Middle East become Moslems in order that they may continue to exist happily in the region and save themselves from extermination.

3. Stephen P. Cohen and Edward E. Azar, "The Transition from War to Peace Between Israel and Egypt," *Journal of Conflict Resolution* Vol. 25, No. 1 (March 1981): 87–114.

4. Charles Malik, "Lebanon and the World," in Edward E. Azar, et al, *Lebanon and the World in the 1980s.* (College Park, MD: Center for International Development, 1983), 1–26.

5. For an excellent discussion of Lebanon under the Ottomans, please read the rich work of Zein Zein. A short but very good article to also read is Iliya Harik, "The Iqta' System in Lebanon: A Comparative View," *Middle East Journal* 19, 4 (1965): 405–421.

6. See Ceasar Farah, *The Problem of the Ottoman Administration in the Middle East.* (Ann Arbor: University Microfilm International). Ph.D. dissertation written at Princeton University, 1978.

7. John P. Spagnolo, *France and Ottoman Lebanon: 1861–1914.* (London: Ithaca Press, 1977). Cited in Footnote 27 to Chapter 1 of the volume, from L. de St. Armand, *Notes sur Les Affairs du Liban: Politiques Français, 1840¢1848.* AE/MD/T/122, item no. 29.

8. The transfer of sovereignty was neither voluntary nor very peaceful. The German occupation of France during WWII and continued British pressure ultimately left the French little choice but to transfer sovereignty of the country to its own people in 1943. For two years however, France continued to retain mandatory advantages and preferential status despite opposition from the Lebanese nationalists and Western powers. The French were forced to relinquish their mandatory administration in May, 1945 after conflict broke out and Britain and the United States demanded French departure from Lebanon.

9. J. C. Hurewitz, "Lebanese Democracy in its International Setting," *Middle East Journal* 17, 5 (1963): 498 says: ". . . Without British firmness in handling the Free French, the Lebanese Government and Chamber in November 1943 would not have succeeded so soon in unilaterally expunging from the constitution those articles that reserved to the mandatory transcendent powers. Free French clumsiness in attempting first to use the offer of elections and then to hold on to residual mandatory controls as bargaining levers for wringing preferential treaties out of the Lebanese served to unite the Confessions behind the program for keeping greater Lebanon intact and weakened the resolve of Sunnis to fuse Lebanon with Syria immediately and unconditionally."

10. In his book, *Conflict and Violence in Lebanon: Confrontation in the Middle East.* (Cambridge: Harvard University Press, 1975). Walid Khalidi cites the figures as 612,590 Christians vs. 423,364 Muslims, counting a certain percentage of emigrants on both sides. Footnote number 16, page 161.

11. See Ralph Crow, "Religious Sectarianism in the Lebanese Political System" *Journal of Politics*, 24, 2 (1962) 489–520. Richard H. Dekmejian, "Consociational Democracy in Crisis: The Case of Lebanon," *Comparative Politics* X, 2 (1978), 251–65.

12. However, it is important to note that in the electoral laws of 1952 and 1957, the districts were redrawn and the number single sect, single seat districts increased. Competitiveness for seats in this context may have boosted the chances of extremists within each group, since candidates from these districts had little incentives to appeal to diverse constituencies. See Michael Hudson, "The Electoral Process and Political Development in Lebanon," *Middle East Journal* 20, 2 (1966) 173–86.

13. For a good discussion on related issues see Ralph E. Crow, "Parliaments in the Lebanese Political System," in E. Kornberg and L. D. Musolf (eds.), *Legislatures in Developmental Perspective.* (Durham: Duke University Press, 1970), 273–302.

14. For a good discussion of the background of some of the issues we bring up here see P. Edward Haley and Lewis W. Snider, (eds.), *Lebanon in Crisis: Participants and Issues.* (Syracuse: Syracuse University Press, 1979.)

15. Edward E. Azar, "Lebanon and the West," in Azar, et al, *Lebanon and the World in the 1980s*, 77–87.

16. See Robert Pranger, "Perspectives on Lebanon's Political Future," in Azar et al, *Lebanon and the World in the 1980s*, 51–60.

17. R. D. McLaurin, "Lebanon and the United States," in Azar et al, *Lebanon and the World in the 1980s*, 87–112 and *Paul Jureidini*, in Ibid., 113–24.

# 3

# Lebanon and Its Political Change Events: The Pathology of Spasm Politics and the Challenge of Reconciliation

## *Robert J. Pranger*

To narrate events in Lebanon that have brought political change over the past decade would challenge the talents of a Mann or a Tolstoy, for if any country has experienced the depths of political pathology in recent times, it is Lebanon. Most important are the episodes of everyday existence as they have accumulated for nearly ten years in Beirut and elsewhere. Many Lebanese know fellow citizens like the permanently deranged man, old before his time, his wife holding him gently in the apartment elevator, a man who lost his mind one night when a rocket exploded in his bedroom as he slept. I am told that such cases have accumulated in the files of Beirut hospitals to the point where one can speak not only of a medical pathology, but of a political pathology as well.

## SPASM POLITICS

Thus Lebanon's experience with political change over the past decade has become a challenge for even the genius of existentialism: everyday life has assumed grotesque proportions, while major political personalities shrink in importance. What leads Lebanon after ten years of violence are not great political leaders but a myriad of events indeterminate in duration and outcome. Political change events in Lebanon seem to defy solution by the governments and officials ostensibly responsible for them, and yet those caught up in everyday life are equally powerless. All of the political actors are swept up in the cumulative force of events in Lebanon, spasmodically coming to the surface to show that they still survive. Lebanon changes constantly but has no direction. Events have taken over and have become the leaders of Lebanese political life, but they seem to have no logic of their own. Lebanon's politics has reached a surrealistic phase, a randomness like the spasm anticipated in the aftermath of nuclear war, a political pathology in the most authentic sense, where established political institutions and practices occasionally and spasmodically appear as important, but where everyone—officials and citizens alike—drown in the powerful flood waters of chaos.

A spasm politics, like that found in Lebanon, has little heart for its regeneration; plans yes, will no. Survivorship becomes a cardinal virtue for officials and ordinary citizens alike, yet few can define why survival has much importance. Under the terror of spasm politics, would it not be better to emigrate? To die? The Lebanese nation itself becomes problematic after those who constitute its membership begin to see all national problems as indifferently randomized events. What issue has the highest priority for Lebanon depends on which problem arbitrarily asserts itself in a given moment: a sniper's bullet; a powerful terrorist bomb; a battle between rival militias; an air attack; a government reconciliation effort; or an international peacekeeping mission. Perhaps all of these events and more may occur together, thereby creating bewildered confusion. Furthermore, in the past ten years Lebanon has experienced so much frightening violence that supposedly major political events must compete with a seemingly endless assault on defenseless persons by cruel, arbitrary, armed attackers with modern weapons. The environment for Lebanon's politics is one of incessant bloodletting and dying in which the words of politicians are frequently silenced by the screams of the victims in Lebanon. Surely what one hears in Washington will sound quite different in Beirut.

Spasm politics in Lebanon has a special sound as well as a unique political style of randomness: in Beirut there is the honking noisiness of Cairo against which the rattle of small arms and thud of explosives can be heard. It is as if Beirut has added a new contrapuntal theme of disorder to the Middle East, a constant reminder to other great cities in the region that the ordinary sounds of everyday life can be submerged by violent overtones. In a hotel by a Beirut beach one might awaken to the explosion of dynamite used by some fisherman to dangerously land his catch or the sound might be the concussion from an artillery attack on some nearby neighborhood. Traffic noise comes from taxis and tanks. Political change events in Lebanon have special sounds as well as unusual appearances, sounds carried by the arbitrariness of everyday violence and survival, in part like those existing in any other city and in part like in no other city on earth.

Against a backdrop of the politically spasmodic in Lebanon, governmental leaders make frustrated efforts to establish a more predictable, orderly politics. Lebanon's confessional partition of offices continues to produce visible personalities, but this activity bears little relationship to the militias fighting one another. Some taxes are collected by public agents, but the largest and most lucrative business is publicly reserved for those whose taxes are paid to private authorities. Lebanon has a regular army, but it is regularly challenged by other Lebanese armies. The amenities of Lebanese national identity are maintained, but most of Lebanon is ruled by foreign troops who have, as their official mission, the maintenance of Lebanon's integrity against foreigners, even while unofficially they engage in a de facto partition as occupying powers. Indeed, it is with outside intervention that one enters the most surrealistic dimension of Lebanon's spasm politics.

## FOREIGN INTERVENTION

At least five foreign powers rule most of Lebanon: Israel, Syria, Iran, Libya, and the PLO. The Israelis, Palestinians, and Syrians make bold to arrogate large territories of Lebanon—including the private property therein—for themselves, and then engage in their own rewriting of Lebanon's history as well. Despite common French mandate roots, Syria has always refused to recognize Lebanon's national independence; no matter how many Syrian troops move into Lebanon in the name of Arab peacekeeping, Syria will not open an embassy in Beirut. Under Arab protection with a weak Lebanese government's acquiescence, Palestinians established their provisional national capital in Beirut while proceeding to expropriate Lebanese property, by force, as it suited their interests. Along Lebanon's southern coast the PLO developed its own policy of territorial expansionism as it worked to link its central headquarters in Beirut with Israel's northern border. Not to be outflanked by the Syrians and Palestinians, Israel has rewritten Lebanese history in blood as well as ink: for the Israelis, Lebanon is a cesspool of Arab intrigue against them, not so much a country as a great military base for armed assaults by others. Because Lebanon is weak, reason the Israelis, rent by factional struggles between "warlords," it has become the victim of this Arab intrigue and, in some ways, a nation in name only. Israeli policy does not recognize its 1982 military activity in Lebanon as "invasion" at all, but simply as a kind of foray or "action" against enemy targets already under Israel's retaliatory policy in the past. This Israeli perception of Lebanon was clear as early as its attack on Beirut's airport in 1968. The great 1982 Israeli debate over Lebanon shed few tears for the Lebanese people

themselves. Such outside intervention, careless of borders and national aspirations, has its equivalent in the pages of Machiavelli's *The
Prince*, a book that analyzes connections between internal and external instability in the spasm politics of Renaissance Italy. Like many
Lebanese, Machiavelli was both fascinated and outraged by what he
saw as an international conspiracy against his nation's integrity.

## THE NEW POLITICAL ENVIRONMENT
## AND ITS POLITICIANS

As in Machiavelli's *The Prince*, political art in today's Lebanon is
practiced most skillfully by those aware of the unpredictability of their
craft and the indeterminacy of their environment. A new breed of
political leader has arisen in Lebanon during the past decade, creating
a politics separate from, but connected to, an older, polite confessionalism. Bashir Gemayel, Walid Jumblatt, and their ilk, are all
specialists in spasm politics. To described these new leaders is to
translate Machiavelli's advice to the princes of new republics into
Lebanon's peculiar pluralistic idiom: they rule as the lion and the fox;
they desire love as well as fear but will settle for fear; and they are well-
versed in the importance of the end justifying the means where others
also operate without fixed standards of behavior. In fact, the first
primer for political pathology is *The Prince* and it is as relevant for
twentieth-century Beirut as for sixteenth-century Florence. None of
the new militia leaders—for in the violent atmosphere of today's
Lebanon power most often flows from the barrel of a gun—will write a
clinical treatise on political pathology, but an outsider can learn much
from the events they create and inspire. The career of Bashir Gemayel
is perhaps the most astonishing instance of this new Lebanese leader.

Bashir admitted from the start of his leadership of the Lebanese
Forces that Lebanon was in a pathological condition and that he was
unsure that he could cure it. His principal mission was Lebanon's
renaissance from Syrian occupation, but he knew that this objective
was indeterminate, if not impossible. What he was convinced of was
the necessity for Lebanon's Maronite community, conservative supporters of the 1943 National Pact, to engage the reality of spasm
politics in the mid-1970s on its own violent terms instead of trusting
the half-empty formalities of a disintegrating Lebanese political
system. Disintegration was evident to Bashir in the Syrian presence
and in the physical destruction all around him: ordinary Lebanese
citizens needed no more rhetoric about the danger they confronted,
because the danger was incessant every day. So was the heroism of

these citizens. Political reality for Lebanon occurred in spasmodic, frequently violent events which ceaselessly changed Lebanon in ways no one could predict. Under the reign of such political indeterminacy, the older political order was passing away, but with very little hint as to what would emerge in place of the interminable fighting. The past was discredited in some ways, but the present was not in any sense to be exalted: the present simply "was," an existential politics of the grotesque everyday. In this environment, the new leader could hardly be called a "warlord," an epithet applied to Bashir and his foes by journalists, but, on the contrary, was more like the surviving helmsman at the end of Ingmar Bergman's movie on spasm nuclear war, "Shame." The vulnerability of a leader who is also a survivor was apparent to all of Bashir's followers.

The twentieth century has become an age of resistance leaders like Bashir, of course, but Lebanon has developed the political art of this leadership into a special form, the militia leader. Even during ceasefires and efforts at national reconciliation, few in Lebanon doubt the long-term persistence of this leadership in Lebanese politics: even if it should be tamed from its more extreme warlike expressions, it will remain a reminder that Lebanon's politics has passed through an era of spasm politics that will dominate Lebanese consciousness in the future. Further, the possible reversion of leadership to violent modes of action can never be doubted; for this new generation of politician there is a realistic appreciation of the close relationship between politics and force. There is also a keen awareness that in the distant origins of public justice, there was a sublimation of private vengeance, and that the public life of some nations, such as Lebanon, is closer to justice's primitive beginnings than in countries such as the United States. Americans sometimes consider themselves a violent people, but their politics is actually among the most institutionalized (and ritualized) on earth. The Lebanese, on the other hand, often see themselves as a merchant people with little patience for intricate national security measures, yet their politics for the past ten years has been the most violent on earth, to the point where political disintegration has become an everyday experience.

## THE WAYS OF RECOVERY FROM POLITICAL PATHOLOGY

Should a country like Lebanon wish to recover from a prolonged period of pathological politics, it will start by taking this pathology as its point of departure. "Business as usual" will prove impossible, because after a lengthy illness there can never be a simple, automatic recovery. As has been seen, the pathological state of spasm politics consists of the tyranny of everyday change events made dominant by the survival experiences of ordinary citizens in a randomly violent environment, where normally visible leadership is only occasionally relevant to political reality and the aberrent or grotesque becomes dramatically normal. All efforts toward national reconciliation in Lebanon find themselves mired in this surrealistic reality where established politicians of the old republic must compete with the princes of the new. In some instances, as in Amin Gemayel, both the old and the new may coexist in the same person.

Spasm politics is not revolutionary politics: as a result, the old and new can exist together, but in a volatile mixture that may produce no new synthesis. Revolutionary politics is dialectical, spasm politics is existential. Efforts at reconstruction during a spasmodic stage, therefore, must be less ambitious than a synthesis or even a compromise. While the art of leadership in spasm politics has its own character—the new prince, the militia leader, and so on—the leadership of reconstruction after a prolonged period of political pathology should have its own style, that of reconciliation.

Just as violently randomized change events call for a leadership adapted to spasm politics, so the reentry into Lebanese politics of more orderly change brings with it a need for a leadership adapted to reconciliation politics. However, the abnormal has become the norm, and that which is more orderly is now considered abnormal, even unrealistic, in the newer politics. Now a more organized form of politics will seem essential as the agent for change, not for stabilizing a pathological situation but for transcending it. The fallacy of a policy of stabilization is that, in spasm politics, stability brings only a temporary relief and no real answer to the indeterminacy one finds. Ironically, what much of the world takes for granted as "normal" politics, a process of settled expectations between leaders and led, for Lebanon is an "abnormal" politics that requires reorientation of the patient away from thinking of his disease as a permanent condition. The politics of reconciliation in Lebanon begins by trying to change fatalistic perceptions that favor a kind of status quo for surrealistic behavior. Yet, for citizens used to pathological politics, including a younger generation that may know little else, reconciliation will prove at least as demanding a political task as survival in a time of extreme political indeterminacy.

Moving away from spasm politics toward a reconstruction of more orderly political activity may prove impossible in Lebanon's case, short of some dramatic change events which signal a new beginning for Lebanon. It is possible that the only set of change events that would significantly affect Lebanese spasm politics enough to offer hope for national reconciliation would be an end to foreign occupation by Syrian and Israeli forces. This was clearly the Lebanese government's policy following Israel's June 1982 invasion and also became the American position. Any deviation from the objective of removing all foreign troops from Lebanon could well mean a continuation of spasm politics and its pathology in some form. This does not suggest that political pathology in Lebanon has only foreign causes, but international intrigue tends to focus attention in Lebanon away from what is specifically Lebanese in the current fragmented political situation: all sides are free to blame outsiders and the task of national reconciliation becomes absorbed in matters of foreign intervention. Is ending foreign occupation in Lebanon a feasible policy, at least in the near term? Short of this, can Lebanon's spasm politics somehow be better controlled, with the possibility that a more gradual process of reconstruction might begin? Both options merit consideration here.

What kind of political change events might bring an end to the presence of Syrian and Israeli forces in Lebanon? To ask this question in this way raises an interesting further question: Does policy alone produce this change? For example, the Arab states worked on various policies to bring about Israel's withdrawal from the Sinai, but Sadat finally went to war in order to create the appropriate conditions for Israel's withdrawal. October 6, 1973 was a date of momentous importance, but it was an event deliberately created. Similarly, Sadat's decision to go to Jerusalem, followed by his actual appearance in that city, could be classified as a specially contrived change event. Regarding Lebanon itself, the Israeli invasion of June 1982 was an artificially devised event of great importance for the subject of an appropriate policy for inducing foreign forces to leave Lebanon. If Syrian and Israeli troops are presently in Lebanon because certain catastrophic events—accidental and contrived—have brought them there, can they be removed without comparable events taking place? The answer is probably no. But what kind of events might lead to the withdrawal of these forces? This question requires that Lebanese leadership think in terms of political change events to achieve their policies and not simply in terms of the policies themselves. Does Lebanon have enough international leverage to create significant events that will precipitate the withdrawal of foreign forces?

Lebanon is too much at the mercy of outside powers in determining which events work for Lebanon's good and which do not. This means that Lebanese foreign policy remains too dependent on outsiders and has not shown enough initiative of its own. For example, with regard to Syria, the Lebanese government negotiates directly with Syria or indirectly through the United States and Saudi Arabia to influence Syrian decisions on the occupation of Lebanon. This manner of approaching the problem of Syrian troop presence appears deficient for Lebanese objectives. Perhaps a more dramatic armed confrontation between Lebanese and Syrian armies would make more sense, much as Bashir Gemayel employed his Lebanese Forces directly against the Syrians and PLO. Another dramatic event which might hasten Syrian withdrawal—though as big a gamble, at least, as armed confrontation—would be a direct Lebanese overture to the Soviet Union, or American cooperation with the USSR to support reconciliation. Lebanon has signed an agreement on Israeli troop withdrawal, even though Israel preferred a full peace treaty; suppose Lebanon were now to sign a peace treaty with Israel, much like the treaty between Egypt and Israel, with a full timetable with withdrawal of Israel's troops included in the treaty. These are but three examples of employing the technique of using dramatic change events to achieve objectives that seem stymied by more timid policies.

Turning to the more modest option of better control of Lebanon's spasm politics, short of the withdrawal of foreign forces, are there change events which might be of some assistance? Again, the point made about change events in the case of troop withdrawal is also pertinent here: a bolder policy that precipitates more dramatic initiatives and events could make sense. For example, should a radical revision of the 1943 National Pact be proposed, with the President of Lebanon himself resigning to allow for a national popular presidential election after a national plebiscite on a new fundamental law? What would happen if the President of Lebanon received emergency powers from the Chamber of Deputies allowing him to deviate from the National Pact in appointing the Prime Minister and other key officials? Is it not already the case that Lebanon has resorted to special authority for the President of the Republic during its crisis after the Israeli invasion?

What seems evident in an analysis of political change events in Lebanon over the past decade, is that events have often taken politics out of the control of established institutions and created alongside these institutions a spasm politics with a pathological tendency toward fragmentation. For example, it is clearly Syria's aim to treat the Lebanese central government, led by President Gemayel, as but one competing faction in Lebanon along with the Druze, Shi'a Moslems, and others. Where indeterminate events hold such sway, the only escape from such an intolerably surrealistic politics is to create events that will move Lebanese politics toward a more orderly process. Whether one is talking about the pathology of foreign occupation or internal violence, it is necessary to speak not only of "policy options," in the sense of proposals and planning, but also of policy action. An analysis of political change events inevitably leads one to the importance of the action dimension in politics and especially to the centrality of significant political acts or "great deeds," initiatives that create new beginnings. In other words, through an analysis of political change events, in Lebanon and elsewhere, one ultimately finds creative political action. What Lebanon needs after a decade of trauma and spasm politics, if it wishes to escape its pathological and surrealistic condition, is creativity in its politics. It must accept the consequences of such action, however, and prepare itself for political boldness. Does the contemporary Lebanese spirit have the will for this daring?

## THE DEGRADATION OF NATIONAL WILL AND THE STATE

The most tragic outgrowth of spasm politics is death of the will of citizens to maintain the integrity of their nation. When such will disappears, a state dies. Under the domination of outsiders, Lebanon has moved closer and closer to its own demise. Recalling again the Bergman film "Shame," those late images of the lifeboats with their mute survivors are ones of exhaustion. Is Lebanon on the verge of national exhaustion, where political leaders play their roles against a background of uncontrolled violence and fragmentation? Is the central government and its army, in truth, but one of several major Lebanese factions? Is Lebanon on the edge of partition into separate states or autonomous regions determined by internal and external forces? Will Lebanon's identity henceforth be determined not by confessional pluralism in a single state, but by sectarian armies defining citizenship in their realms according to the whims of Lebanon's enemies? The great danger of any pathological condition is its tendency toward deterioration and death rather than rejuvenation. Unless the current state of Lebanese politics is seen as spasmodic and pathological, neither the full danger of change events in Lebanon can be appreciated nor the small possibility for national salvation understood.

## THE THREATS BEYOND LEBANON'S BORDERS

The full danger of change events in Lebanon threatens the Lebanese and other countries in the Middle East and beyond. Terrors confronting ordinary citizens in Lebanon under deteriorating political conditions have already been noted here, but peril confronts others as well. Directly intervening in Lebanon's affairs are the Syrians and Israelis, but behind them are the Soviets and the Americans. From Beirut a fuse stretches to the Persian Gulf and Europe. So far, no combination of change events in Lebanon has lit this fuse, but it is apparent that some future combination of factors could ignite armed confrontation again between Syria and Israel and possibly the Soviet Union and the United States. Soviet advisors man special missile installations in Syria, while American Marines and their West European counterparts patrol Beirut. Off Lebanon sit Soviet and American naval combatants, while reinforcements on both sides are only a short distance away.

The attack on U.S. Marines in Beirut by a suicide mission on October 23, 1983 represented one of those dramatic change events common in Lebanon's spasm politics. As on so many occasions over the past decade, indeterminate politics has taken leadership away from established authorities, this time as Lebanon's central government was busily arranging a "reconciliation" conference in Switzerland (the latter location also necessitated by Lebanon's spasm politics, since the central government does not command enough authority to determine the location of this meeting in Beirut itself). Under circumstances of this kind of spasmodic violence, all notions of "national reconciliation" are mocked by another reality—that of division, fragmentation, and deterioration. Without any question, the type of violent event staged on October 23 demonstrates the pathological state of Lebanese politics: this political sickness should not be denied for the sake of official public relations in Washington or Beirut. Lebanon's central government has apparently become one faction in a bewildering mixture of warring tribes capable of destroying Lebanon but creating nothing else. This confusion is aided and abetted by outside powers, of course, with the U.S. Marines increasingly put in the position of being a form of external intervention on the side of one or another faction (in this case, on the side of the Lebanese "government"). It has surely been the policy of Syria and its Lebanese allies to foster this perception about American policy in Lebanon.

What is to be done about Lebanon's spasm politics and the possible dangers this politics has for both Lebanese and international security? One must begin in great honesty: with the attack on the U.S. Marines on October 23, the central government of Amin Gemayel was on the verge of being totally discredited as a focal point for national reconstruction. The policies pursued by the president came to enjoy almost no support, and no thread of a plan was visible. Candor would also recognize that the Gemayel government was becoming, in matter of political fact, a faction competing with others: it was losing control of the symbols and practical instruments of national unity. Whatever can be done positively for Lebanon will have to come from international sources without partisanship for one or another of the Lebanese factions. Realities in Lebanon seemed to be moving toward an internationally sponsored, de facto partition, with both the United States and the Soviet Union indirect parties to this partition behind the Lebanese central government, Israel, and Syria.

## WHITHER THE LEBANON OF TOMORROW?

The prescription of partition as a cure for Lebanon's political pathology may be a bitter pill to swallow for those, such as myself, who have supported the ideal of national unity in spite of Lebanon's spasm politics. Yet it is at least clear from the October 23 disaster—though it was probably clear before this—that Lebanon's pathology has reached such a dangerous stage for the Lebanese and the wider international community that the warring parties might, indeed, be partitioned into separate jurisdictions, if not into independent states then into a federation of semiautonomous confessional republics. American policy has tended, because of its long-standing allegiance to the territorial integrity of Lebanon, to miss the important point that many Lebanese seem no longer committed to their own national unity or seemingly helpless in the face of what Prime Minister Wazzan has called "evil" forces. The government of Amin Gemayel appears too weak to command enough consensus among Lebanon's warring factions to insure that the central government will become stronger rather than weaker: the prospect ahead looks very grim regarding Lebanese unity.

By agreeing to a reconciliation conference in Geneva for late October 1983, the various Lebanese factions—among whom must surely be counted the central government itself—appeared to be giving the idea of a united Lebanon one more try. American policy has been aimed at strengthening the Lebanese army as a focus for national unity and a stronger central government, but it has been apparent that this policy is deficient in two respects: 1) there are militias competing with the central government's army that are as strong as or stronger than the army, and 2) there is lack of political will among key Lebanese groups for efforts at unity. The Geneva conference approach to national reconciliation is symptomatic of Lebanon's spasm politics, however, and not a solution to it: being unable to agree on a site in Lebanon acceptable to all the warring groups, the Lebanese have resorted to a domestic reconciliation meeting in a city traditionally set aside for international conciliation. The symbolism of Geneva for Lebanon, as foreign center for settlement of Lebanon's internal political problems, should not be neglected: it reinforces the argument made here that any positive answer for Lebanon's pathological state will come under international sponsorship. Yet, Switzerland provides another symbolism for the Lebanese, in addition to that of international peace, and that is the Swiss solution to confessional strife, cantonization.

Is the selection of Geneva as a site for national reconciliation talks only an accident, or is there a powerful attraction to the Lebanese of the Swiss example for creating unity out of deep religious differences? The canton system of federalism in Switzerland has long attracted students of federalism who have confronted severe conflicts among confessional and language communities which have threatened the national unity of various countries. Some have recommended the cantonization model for Lebanon and perhaps this path is a way of stabilizing—even institutionalizing—the present chaos of Lebanon's spasm politics, assuming that political determination exists to find a national solution.

## CONCLUSION

It is time that the pathological nature of Lebanon's spasm politics be taken seriously as a progressively deteriorating national disease for which the cure may require change events more drastic than those so far employed. Yet, one again faces the problematic nature of the Lebanese national will to survive and to reconstruct Lebanon: the victims in the lifeboats may be too exhausted for anything other than drifting on the interminable political sea, indifferent to further tragedy and final destruction. Here, indeed, in the realm of spasm politics and spasm war, the world ends not with a bang but a whimper. Is Lebanon, in this sense, representative of how the twentieth century, the most violent in mankind's history, will end, as Eliot has prophesized? Is Lebanon, home to so many world cultures and religions, a microcosm of our common, fatal legacy in this most spasmodic of centuries? Are we seeing, in the interminable terror of Beirut and its environs, a glimpse of a future "post-attack" phase of worldwide nuclear war? Is Lebanon the fuse to this more general holocaust? Are we witnessing in the tragedy of Lebanon not only the deterioration of a Lebanese will to survive and to reconstruct, but an international failure of will to change course before final global destruction?

In the end, Lebanon is not only a pathological case for the Lebanese who must live there, but for the international community which must suffer its consequences far beyond Beirut's environs. The teams of pathologists needed to create a new politics in Lebanon must be cosmopolitan in representation and intention rather than narrowly involved with special national interests, because Lebanon is not only another stain on the twentieth century's conscience but also, perhaps, the most ominously destructive episode in this century. Political change events in Lebanon might well become something of an uncontrollable chain reaction, moving forward through indeterminate spasms and sweeping past Beirut's beaches to Dhaharan, Nice, Brighton, Yalta, Malibu, and Sydney. In the final analysis, then, Lebanon's political change events become a challenge for the threats they pose to Lebanese existence and what they portend for the existence of us all.

# 4

# Lebanon's Economy:
# The Costs of Protracted Violence

## *Joyce R. Starr*

The battles that have engulfed Lebanon since 1975 constitute, in large part, a struggle over power and resources—primarily political, but also economic. While the political determinants of this strife are now of central interest to leading governments and press alike, relatively little attention has been paid to the economic dimensions and consequences of the protracted conflict. Indeed, despite the remarkable resilience of the Lebanese in confronting the ravages of war over the past decade, Lebanon could emerge from the conflicts of 1983–84 with its economic base all but irreparable.

After World War II, Lebanon became a commercial and banking center for the entire Middle East, and by the 1970s Beirut was the nexus for trade between the region and the West, with a taste for the good life that rivaled Paris or London. But, as early as the 1950s, inequities in the domestic distribution of economic benefits and rewards were already posing major and ominous questions for the future. The strain of rapid growth and an exodus of manpower also taxed Lebanon's ability to meet burgeoning infrastructural demands. The creative adaptability of the Lebanese in withstanding the destruction of the 1975–82 period suggested that a "post-war" recovery could hold exciting promise for planners and entrepreneurs. But such indicators of Lebanon's inherent strength, while attractive and reassuring, could hardly balance the economic dislocations and disintegration caused by the years of warfare, previous decades of uneven development, and the lack of a national economic policy.

The Israeli invasion of June 1982 and its aftermath meant, for many Lebanese, that they could turn their thoughts to the economic restoration and reintegration of their state. By late summer and fall of 1982, economic analysts were again predicting that, given appropriate external assistance and a return to political stability, the Lebanese economy would rebound and possibly surpass previous levels. When Amin Gemayel, older brother of the slain president-elect Bashir Gemayel, assumed office as president of Lebanon on September 23, 1982, the parliamentary majority supporting his candidacy with only three abstentions was interpreted as a statement of historic consequence: the cycle of tragic violence had come to an end, thus enabling Lebanon to concentrate its energies on physical and political reconstruction.

Yet, by November 1983, the gap separating Lebanon's potential economic recovery from its further decline had widened to a dangerous and perhaps irreversible expanse. After nine months of relative calm, the violence of 1983 virtually exploded, on an otherwise unexceptional Monday, with the April bombing of the American embassy in Beirut—later to be exceeded in magnitude by the October and November suicide attacks on a U.S. Marine Corps compound, the French military contingent, and the Israeli military compound in Tyre. The shelling of Beirut during the summer months by Syrian-backed forces, intensified combat in the Shuf between Christians and Druze, and the warfare that ensued as the Israelis withdrew their troops from the mountain area on September 3, left more than two thousand people dead or wounded, and as many as fifty thousand Lebanese without basic shelter. Pitched battles in Tripoli between PLO factions also took its toll in hundreds of lives and extensive damage to an urban center that had remained largely unharmed during the previous eight years. By December, more than two hundred thousand of the six hundred thousand inhabitants of Tripoli had fled the area.

In projecting the conditions of post-1983 Lebanon, it is therefore mandatory to address the question: what impact might further and sustained conflict have on Lebanon's weakened economy, and how are the critical economic sectors likely to be affected? The following is a brief overview.

## DAMAGE ASSESSMENT AND ANTICIPATED ASSISTANCE

Studies undertaken at the close of 1982 by the World Bank, U.S. Government, International Monetary Fund, and Government of Lebanon generally agreed in estimating the extent of physical damage incurred between 1975–82 at approximately twelve billion dollars, including $1.5–$1.9 billion in destruction resulting from the Israeli invasion of Lebanon and its consequences during the summer of 1982. Physical destruction to the public sector alone, including losses generated by the fighting in Tripoli, the Shuf, and Beirut have skyrocketed to as much as 16 billion dollars, by Lebanese estimates. Furthermore, an important distinction must be made between physical destruction and the cumulative costs of unattended maintenance or repairs, and also stagnant development. Reconstruction estimates for Lebanon as of spring 1983, based on all three factors, were more realistically in the realm of fifteen to twenty billion dollars. These figures, of course, did not anticipate the hostilities that would erupt shortly after the May signing of the Israeli–Lebanese accord.

At the Tunis Summit Conference of 1979, the Arab oil states pledged two billion dollars over a five-year period for Lebanon's reconstruction. However, by December 1981 Lebanon had received a total of only $372 million in reconstruction aid, or slightly less than half of the $800 million pledged for this period. The United Arab Emirates alone fulfilled its commitments for 1980–81, while Saudi Arabia and Iraq delivered but half of their promised assistance. Libya withheld all of its promised funds.

Following the June 1982 Israeli invasion of Lebanon, the contributions of Western and Arab countries, the United Nations, the International Committee of the Red Cross, and other private voluntary organizations reached almost $165 million, the majority of it for immediate relief purposes. In the spring of 1983 the United States committed an additional $251 million in assistance, $150 million in direct AID grants, $100 million in military loans, and a one million dollar grant for military training. However, two weeks after the February 22 withdrawal from Lebanon of the last of the U.S. Marine contingent, the Reagan administration notified the government in Beirut that it was "borrowing back temporarily" almost one-third of the economic assistance package pledged by Congress for 1984: $40 million was rechanneled to programs in Grenada, including the completion of the airport facility. U.S. assistance providing in the best circumstances only a fraction of its needs had a high symbolic value and an importance much beyond the monetary figure.

Pledges from the European countries included fifty million dollars from the EEC, twenty million dollars from the European Investment Bank, nineteen million dollars from Italy, and a mixed credit protocol signed with France at a level of forty million dollars. Unofficial Arab assistance during this period was approximately sixty million dollars, principally from Saudi Arabia and channeled through the Hariri Foundation. (Rafiq Hariri is a prominent Lebanese Shi'a Moslem with strong economic ties in Saudi Arabia.) In February–March 1983, the World Bank identified and evaluated a $223 million short-term multisector project for the Greater Beirut area, but was in the midst of negotiations with prospective donor countries when heavy shelling from behind Druze and Syrian lines wrought new destruction on the commercial centers of the city. This project is presently suspended, with little prospect for its reactivation, given international unwillingness to risk future involvement.

Even under what appeared to be relatively positive conditions during the latter part of 1982 through mid-1983, pledges from the West and the Arab world covered only a fraction of Lebanon's larger needs. The government of Lebanon was optimistic through mid-1983 as the country slid into the netherworld of anarchy and intermittent ceasefires, that foreign aid would cover 75 percent of Lebanon reconstruction bill. It also held hopes that private initiatives, including investments by Lebanese at home and abroad, would play a critical role in the reconstruction process—serving as a further catalyst for urgently required foreign participation. But continuing uncertainty over the withdrawal of foreign troops and heightening fear produced overriding public caution. Between September 1982 and mid-1984 private investment in Lebanon was effectively frozen. Lacking a climate conducive to either foreign or internal investment, the central government's capacity to implement even emergency reconstruction measures is severely handicapped, with assessments for long-term development increasingly pessimistic.

## GOVERNMENT FINANCE AND DEBT

In spite of eight years of strife, Lebanon in the spring of 1983 could claim a minimal foreign debt of approximately two hundred million dollars, a strong currency (with the Lebanese pound appreciating by thirty-five percent in the last half of 1982), and a negligible balance of payments deficit. Inflation had been temporarily reversed, prices were falling moderately and sufficient foreign exchange was available to ensure that inflation could be kept within tolerable limits for 1983.

Lebanon's foreign reserves are substantial by any measure: approximately three billion dollars, and 9.2 million ounces of gold valued at four hundred dollars per ounce, or $3.7 billion. The government, however, has been extremely reluctant to draw on these reserves, fearing that such action would jeopardize Lebanon's international credit standing and might even lead to eventual bankruptcy. By contrast, while the Government of Lebanon faces extreme financial difficulty, the private bank deposits of Lebanese citizens are close to five billion dollars, with Lebanese abroad holding more than twice that amount in foreign banks.

Remittances from Lebanese working in the Persian Gulf and in Africa have averaged approximately two hundred million dollars per month since the mid-1970s, the principal vehicle by which the balance of trade deficit was offset during this period. Indeed, Lebanese remittances appear to be the highest in the Arab world. But as Arab oil-producing countries found it necessary to cut back economic development programs, remittances were also affected. By spring 1983 they had already dropped by almost twenty-five percent (to about one hundred and fifty million dollars per month), with further declines anticipated. A future Lebanon that faces a significant reduction in remittances without a parallel growth in internal economic activity would not only further erode the government's limited ability to function, but could also result in deepening poverty.

In the months of 1982 after the Israeli invasion, the government of Lebanon borrowed $1.6 million from Lebanese banks, but expended approximately $2.2 billion in early reconstruction planning and implementation, as well as government operations. The Lebanese public debt doubled in 1982 and by early 1983 stood at $3.7 billion, with only a small portion of that in foreign loans. One-sixth of the government budget is now applied toward interest on the debt.

The heart of the government's fiscal difficulties lies with its ability—or inability—to levy, collect, and tabulate taxes. In its effort to expand sources of revenue, the Gemayel government had initiated more effective tax collection procedures and was making some progress both on individual tax payments and port duties. Poor statistical records and inadequate or nonexistant data bases are additional handicaps, along with a shortage of professional and reliable civil servants—significant numbers regularly fail to report to their offices during periods of instability.

Further, illegal or extralegal economic activity is an important element in the Lebanese system, removing from the taxing authority of the central government substantial sources of revenue. Smuggling through official and illicit Lebanese ports has been costing the government as much as fifty million dollars per month, according to conservative estimates. In addition, with Lebanese paramilitary and political groups levying heavy taxes on the population they represent, many Lebanese citizens are understandably reluctant to pay further taxes to the central government. As the fighting resumed in Summer and Fall 1983, the paramilitary groups have increased their taxation at the expense of official government revenues. (Secret subsidies for various political groups and militias and the profits of Lebanese firms operating abroad also offset the balance of payments deficit.)

Illegal economic activity has proved extremely profitable to Lebanon's many factions, involving as many as one hundred thousand jobs and an annual value of more than three billion dollars. The hashish trade, for example, partially controlled by the Syrian Army in the Beqa'a Valley, is reported to be Lebanon's most lucrative agricultural export at a value of five hundred million dollars in a "normal" year. Illegal imports of consumer goods through nonlegal (i.e., noncustoms) ports also account for a significant portion of the Lebanese economy.

Combining the scope of Lebanon's "black economy" with the fact that forty percent of the country's GNP originates in the Persian Gulf, it is clear that the government's maneuverability would be limited in the best of circumstances. Early steps taken by the Gemayel administration to restore public confidence and reduce the public debt had barely begun when the country was divided again into warring factions.

## LABOR FORCE PROJECTIONS

Prior to 1975, Lebanon's population had reached just over three million. Death, disability, and emigration have left a work force shortage in all sectors. Between 1975 and 1982, for example, almost thirty percent of the construction workers had permanently emigrated from the country, as well as half of the industrial workers. By the fall of 1982 key workers for major reconstruction projects were difficult to locate, including carpenters, equipment operators, electricians, welders, etc. Accurate statistics are not available on the number of craftsmen remaining in the country, but throughout the latter part of the 1970s and early 1980s Lebanese contractors had come to rely heavily on Palestinian and Syrian labor for both skilled and unskilled labor. More than two hundred and fifty thousand Lebanese are presently employed in the oil-producing states of Africa and the Persian Gulf, a number which includes almost half of Lebanon's skilled work force.

Previously able to claim one of the highest literacy rates in the world, surpassing all other Arab countries, Lebanon today suffers from an alarming primary and secondary school dropout rate estimated at ninety thousand per year (of a total enrollment nearing five hundred and eighty thousand students), a high proportion of unqualified teachers in both the primary and lower secondary school systems, and extensive physical damage to schools throughout the country.

## INDUSTRY AND AGRICULTURE

Industrial activity in Lebanon increased in 1980-81, in large part due to accelerated construction in the Christian-controlled area of East Beirut. This surge, financed largely by remittances and the profits of Lebanese overseas firms, also had a stimulating effect on related industries—for example, cement and iron production, and the manufacture of paint and glass. Real estate activity exceeded pre-civil war levels and in 1981 climbed by thirty percent (principally within the Greater Beirut area.) Interestingly, by 1981 Palestinians and Syrians had replaced the Saudis and Kuwaitis as Lebanon's principal foreign property owners. (The issue of foreign property ownership was sufficiently worrisome to the Gemayel administration that new and quite stringent regulations were implemented in the early part of 1983).

Exports also increased by about thirty percent in 1981, reaching a level close to $1.3 billion in goods shipped, primarily to Iraq, Saudi Arabia, Jordan, and Syria. Lebanon's industrial sales to Arab countries constituted almost ninety-seven percent of total industrial exports. Lebanon has also been a major fruit exporter to neighboring Arab countries, with agricultural shipments in recent years accounting for almost eighteen percent of total exports. Syria has traditionally received nearly half of Lebanon's total fruit crop. The Syrian Army closure of the Beirut–Damascus highway resulted in the virtual interdiction of overland transit trade from Beirut to Arab markets. In spite of the significant black market trade between the Beqa'a and Damascus, principally in agricultural products, the Beqa'a is effectively isolated; produce from the area cannot be marketed in Beirut. The Saudi boycott of Lebanese goods after the Israeli invasion in 1982 also had its intended impact on overall exports, contributing to a worsening trade deficit.

With most of the irrigated agricultural areas of Lebanon located in the Syrian-controlled Beqa'a Valley, the continued presence of Syrian troops further threatens one of the most important sectors of Lebanon's economy. Agricultural production in southern Lebanon was adversely affected in 1982-83 by competition from Israeli producers, although Israel insists it is now restricting Israeli competition in Lebanese domestic markets. Nevertheless, even with the absence of fighting in the south, growing uncertainty has meant reduced agricultural output.

Industrial reconstruction in 1983 would have been hampered under peaceful conditions by the need for large infusions of working capital, the demands for substantial technological change and the exigencies of administrative reform. The Council for Development and

Reconstruction, the coordinating body for integrated reconstruction in Lebanon, was established in 1977. During the seemingly hopeful period of late 1982 and early 1983, the CDR assumed a major role in establishing reconstruction priorities and developing links between international lending institutions and firms, and donor countries. However, few reconstruction projects were actually undertaken before the Summer of 1983, when by necessity such plans were superceded by diplomatic and political events.

## HOUSING, WATER, AND ELECTRICITY

It is generally agreed that Lebanon's most acute need is for housing. According to recent studies, the country was short by 135,000 units in early 1983, a figure which was substantially increased by later hostilities in Beirut, the Shuf Mountains, and Tripoli. The Gemayel government had plans for sixty thousand units to be built during 1983–84, and a total of four hundred thousand new units by the year 2000.

Lebanon's water supplies and distribution systems were inadequate as early as the 1950s. Direct hits to the distribution system over the last eight years necessitate the creation of an entirely new network. The country's sewer systems are also overloaded, poorly maintained, and do not meet basic sanitation requirements. A complete reconstruction, development, and maintenance program that could upgrade water and sewerage systems through 1990 was calculated by the World Bank in early 1983 at a cost of roughly $1.5 billion.

The Electricite du Liban network, covering eighty-five percent of the nation's electricity needs, has suffered losses exceeding twenty million dollars. Illegal tapping of electricity lines by individual citizens and paramilitary groups has further complicated efforts to address this problem. Electricity imports come principally from Syria through the Beqa'a Valley, an additional area of vulnerability in Lebanon's relations with its neighbor. Outages and electricity rationing have become commonplace in the Greater Beirut area, and more recently in Tripoli.

## THE PORT OF BEIRUT, AIRPORT, AND CITY CENTER

The port of Beirut was a central component of Lebanese prosperity before 1974. It was closed for five months in 1978, forty-four days in 1979 and periodically in 1980–82. Reconstruction is a top priority, for only when transit trade can once again flow normally through its harbor will Lebanese recovery be assured. Total damage to the Port since 1975 exceeds seventy-one million dollars. The infrastructure, however, remains surprisingly intact, which is not the case for the superstructure, i.e., sheds, warehouses, cargo handling equipment, workshops, telephones, and powerlines.

The Beirut Central City is one of the most heavily damaged areas of Lebanon. Although a reconstruction master plan was formulated in 1978, only one major tender had been offered as of March 1983.

Public sector programs for the city center will require at least seventy-five million dollars annually for the next six years if existing plans for roads, bridges, tunnels, and related facilities are to be implemented.

The importance of Beirut International Airport to the commercial success of Lebanese business and the long-term health of the economy cannot be overemphsized. Damage to the airport or delays in repair have immediate and grave consequences, not only for ordinary business operations but for the tourism which until the late 1970s made up a significant portion of Lebanon's gross domestic product. Reconstruction and expansion of the Beirut airport was halted during the fighting in the summer of 1982, reopening in October after a four-month closure; during September–October 1983, the airport was again closed for more than five weeks. Total damage now amounts to at least twelve million dollars.

## SUMMARY

By the close of 1983, while there was as yet no unusual flight of money from Lebanon's banks, the long lines of Lebanese standing daily before Western consulates seeking permanent emigration suggests a further crucial weakening of the nation's skilled work force. The Lebanese pound remained strong throughout the winter of 1983, with Beirut shops generally well-stocked, yet for the first time the feeling was pervasive that "Lebanon is dying." If the caviar was still readily available, the critical element of hope seemed in short supply. The continuing isolation of different parts of the country—in effect, de facto partition—further compounds the stagnation which threatens to become a permanent rather than temporary feature of the economy. Ironically, the very resources that are at least partly at issue in the present crisis are rapidly being squandered by the principal players. Whether the Lebanese talent for coping with adversity can sustain the population through continuing conflict and despair is now questionable.

The key indicators of healthy economic growth suggest a grim scenario, with the likely prospect of Lebanon emerging as a newly impoverished nation.

# 5
## Lebanon and Its Army: Past, Present, and Future

### R. D. McLaurin

## INTRODUCTION

The armed forces of Lebanon have played an important historical role in the political and social evolution of the country.[1] It is often said of military forces that they represent microcosms of societies in general, though this is rarely—if ever—true upon close examination. Still, it is true that most military organizations reflect the stresses, strengths, and fissures present in the larger society, albeit in different proportions. Certainly the history and development of the Lebanese Army do reflect many dynamics of Lebanese society.

In view of the prominent role of the armed forces in Lebanese history, it is important to consider the nature of Lebanese society on which the military draws, and in which it is rooted. Lebanon in its present form is a relatively new country. The borders were formed by the French after a mandate over modern Syria and Lebanon (plus the area around Alexandretta or Hatay) was conferred upon France by the allied powers of World War I.[2] This is not to say that Lebanon had no discrete history prior to the mandate, but before that time, Lebanon, within its current boundaries, did not exist. Instead, the area was divided in different ways at various times. Mount Lebanon, the Christian heartland that formed the core of the new polity and gave it its name, had been separately administered for some time.[3] Since the creation of modern Lebanon through the marriage of Mount Lebanon with the surrounding territory, the issues of role and identity have been central to the country's political history.

This chapter on Lebanon's army does not permit us adequate space to address and analyze the identity issue, a question that in any case is discussed elsewhere in this volume.[4] However, Lebanon's legitimacy as an independent country is very much at the heart of the identity issue; it has also played a major role in the evolution of the Lebanese army, as we will point out below. The strong and enduring Sunni resistance to the emergence of an independent Lebanon— independent initially of Syria and later of other attempts at Arab unity—led the Sunni community both inside and outside the country to adopt an ambivalent attitude toward Lebanon. On the one hand, Sunnis sought to maximize the power and status of their community within Lebanon, especially after independence. On the other hand, many would not accept the idea of Lebanon as a separate independent polity, and refused to participate in institutions that symbolized that independence. No single institution represented a separate Lebanon more than its armed forces, and consequently the Sunnis boycotted the army during the mandate period and, to a lesser extent, after independence.[5]

Other minorities readily accepted the Lebanese State concept. Christian sects recognized Maronite predominance, but felt their values would be better protected in a non-Muslim state. The Druzes, and to a lesser extent the Shi'as, believed they would retain more autonomy and power as minorities in a country of minorities than as small minorities in a Sunni-majority state.

These divergent views and values persisted to some extent until 1982. Sunni conceptions of Lebanon and its role have always significantly diverged from those of other Lebanese communities. At the same time, the shifting demographic balance has increased the Shi'as to the position of a plurality in Lebanon today, while their political power remains far less than that of either the Sunnis or the Maronites, and their economic power is even less.

Lebanon achieved independence during World War II, due in part to united Lebanese reaction against several French acts (notably the attempt to overrule the election of Bishara al-Khoury in 1943 and to replace him with the French candidate, Emile Edde). However, this unity against the French was not synonymous with true Lebanese nationalism. Broad disagreements over basic issues of Lebanon's identity prevailed at the time of independence. While the Sunni community opposed French rule, it resisted the idea that Lebanon would remain independent from the Arab world. The National Pact of 1943, which remains a fundamental element of Lebanese political culture to this day, was formulated largely on the basis of the ideas of Lebanon's first Prime Minister after independence, Riyad al-Sulh. The Pact established a confessional structure for the political system to reassure all communities, particularly the three largest, that their 1943 positions could not be seriously altered later. However, obligations concerning

Lebanon's external relationships were addressed only symbolically. Despite the assertion of Lebanese independence vis-a-vis the Arab world, the Sunni community resisted the idea Lebanon would remain independent. Even the al-Sulh family had spoken of a "temporary" Lebanese independence. In the anti-French passion of the moment, this major consideration was set aside by all sides.[6] In short, the issue of identity has directly affected the Lebanese Army.

Numerous shocks have jolted the country in the period since independence: waves of Palestinian immigrants in 1948, 1967, and 1970; direct intervention and occupation of Syria in 1976 and by Israel in 1978 and 1982; the cycle of Palestinian raid and Israeli retaliation; and enormous social and demographic changes that have transformed the country extremely rapidly. These and other shocks have created circumstances that laid the groundwork for a second beginning in 1982: a new Lebanese Republic. There is every indication that, like many Lebanese institutions, the future of the Lebanese Army will differ significantly from its past, reflecting the lessons learned (some tragic) over the past four decades.

As the new Lebanese government begins to rebuild, it seems appropriate to focus on the past, present, and future of the Lebanese Army. The Army's reconstruction is a vital priority; it will serve as the anchor of the new republic. Reconstruction cannot commence until we determine exactly what has survived the years of turmoil and what has to be rebuilt.

## A HISTORY OF THE LEBANESE ARMY: THE ROOTS

Indigenous armed forces have existed in the area now called Lebanon for centuries. However, these forces can only indirectly be considered the forerunners of the Lebanese Army, because no organic historical links exist between them and the forces placed under Lebanese control after independence. Hence we shall not recount the centuries of warfare and martial competition in the Levant.[7]

The French Mandate in 1919 altered the status of military forces considerably. Upon establishing effective control, the French set up a military administration. The armed forces deployed in Lebanon and Syria were drawn both from France and from its colonies. They were designated *Troupes du Levant*. Within a few years, indigenous forces were created as auxiliaries, but the officers in the auxiliary units were overwhelmingly French. When a military school was opened in Syria for cadets of both countries (1924), slightly more than one-quarter of the total military forces in Lebanon and Syria (nineteen thousand) were indigenous auxiliaries, virtually all of them enlisted personnel.[8]

Eventually local forces (renamed the *Troupes Spéciales du Levant*) came to assume the predominant position numerically. Indigenous officers remained few until World War II, but increasing numbers of Lebanese attended the Syrian military school between the first and second world wars. One Lebanese, Fu'ad Shihab, enrolled in the *Ecole supérieure de Guerre* in Paris. (Shihab was the only Lebanese to attend St. Cyr prior to World War II.) By 1945, almost all the officers were local. Early in World War II, Lebanese troops fought with the Vichy administration against Free French and British forces, but after Vichy's Middle East forces surrendered in 1941, many Lebanese volunteers enlisted with the Free French.[9]

The Lebanese Independence movement, abetted by British pressure on the French, was galvanized by several incidents of high-handed behavior on the part of the French before and during World War II. Even after they transferred sovereignty to Lebanon in 1943, the French retained control of the *Troupes Spéciales du Levant*. It was not until two years after independence, on August 1, 1945, that the newly sovereign Lebanese Republic was given command of the local units. Colonel Fu'ad Shihab was the commander.[10]

Although the *Troupes Spéciales* were clearly a French creation and therefore inaugurated a new period of military history for Lebanon, their primary mission remained the same as that of other local forces since the mid-1800s: internal security. The *Troupes Spéciales* retained this as their mission, and it subsequently remained the principal concern of the Lebanese Army after 1945.

## THE LEBANESE ARMY, 1945-1958

When the Lebanese Army was created by the transfer of indigenous troops from French control, it was a small force of about three thousand men. The commander of the Lebanese Army from its inception until 1958 was Fu'ad Shihab, a Maronite. The provision that the army commander be a Maronite has become a major element of the confessional system. The officer corps of the Lebanese Army was also disproportionately Christian, as it was inherited from the French *Troupes Spéciales.*

For years, Arab nationalists have accused France of recruiting principally from minorities to staff local forces, both on the precept of divide and conquer, and because the minorities had a greater interest in retaining French suzerainty. While these charges are more or less

accurate, it is important to remember that many other factors contributed to the prominent role of non-Sunni officers in both Lebanon
and Syria:[11]

- Military service was disdained by the Sunnis who avoided it as much as
  possible. By contrast, poorer groups, particularly the Shi'as in Lebanon,
  saw military service as a means of achieving upward mobility.
- The fact that the Lebanese Army ultimately guaranteed the preservation
  of the Lebanese system gave Christians in general—and Maronites in particular—a strong incentive to join.
- Sunni resistance to the French mandate in Lebanon and Syria and to a
  Lebanon separate from the Sunni-majority Arab world was manifested in
  a boycott of French institutions, particularly the *Troupes Spéciales*.

All of these factors contributed to a serious imbalance in the
Lebanese Army. The officer corps was disproportionately Christian,
and while the rank and file included all major groups, Sunnis were not
equitably represented. Nor did recruitment patterns shift markedly
after the army became Lebanese. Such a change would have required
widespread Sunni acceptance of an independent Lebanon. Instead, a
grudging acceptance of the state, and a conditional acceptance at that,
emerged over time.

In the years after 1945, Fu'ad Shihab showed his wisdom as an army commander by stressing the importance of education, rigorous
standards, and professional behavior. The result of his efforts was a
Lebanese Army composed of an unusually well educated and professional officer corps by Middle East standards. He encouraged his officers to acquire all the education they could. He maintained high standards and insisted that promotion be based on performance. He
resisted the regional trend toward politicization and stressed professionalism instead.[12]

Recruitment procedures for the officer corps reflected and still
reflect the nature of Lebanese politics. Criteria included Lebanese
citizenship, a baccalaureate, the absence of a criminal record, successful performance on a battery of tests, and adherence to the confessional quotas. The quotas were broken down both by major and minor
religion, but favored the Maronites, the Sunnis, and the Shi'as. Between 1945 and 1958, new officers were overwhelmingly Christian,
largely because Sunnis did not participate and Shi'as had difficulty
passing the tests. (Most Shi'as served as enlisted personnel.) However,
informal factors also played a role in selection. These factors included
regional, religious, and familial considerations, specifically: regional
contacts and status; relationship to senior religious leaders; family
status; and contact with and relationship to G-2 (Army Intelligence)

Section, the Army commander, and the president.[13] Moreover, once cadets became officers, the tendency was to maintain the linkages that had served well. General Shihab diligently tried to discourage linkages between officers and their patrons in order to promote a neutral army. To some extent he succeeded, but officer recruitment regulations remain in place, and patron-client relationships remain strong.

During the formative years of the Lebanese Army, General Shihab's imprint was extremely important. The decision to eschew an active military role in the Arab-Israeli conflict both safeguarded Lebanon's territorial integrity and saved enormous sums that would otherwise have been diverted to the military. However, the decision also posed dangers to the clarity and legitimacy of the army's mission. The police and gendarmerie, the internal security forces, and the sûreté générale all had diverse internal security responsibilities. The Army was to assist the police and gendarmerie in preventing the spread of disorder. Similarly, the Lebanese Air Force was to provide air support to the ground forces for these duties. In reality, however, the role of the army was unclear and often superfluous. Moreover, to the the the extent that the armed forces focused on defending the constitution rather than the borders of Lebanon, they were often perceived by the Sunni population as a Christian army. Shihab exerted every effort to defuse this resentment by insisting on neutrality in sectarian matters. Thus the Lebanese Army, apart from its ephemeral "action" in the Palestine War, served as a police force of last resort, protected state officials, and umpired elections. As the guardian of the Lebanese system, it was expected to remain neutral with respect to all the country's parties and sects.

The first test of this neutrality arose in 1952. A general strike was declared against the first president, Bishara al-Khoury, in protest against the extent of corruption in his government. General Shihab refused to intervene and Khoury resigned, appointing Shihab Prime Minister until new elections could be held. Shihab refused to become a presidential candidate himself. The preservation of the army's neutrality in 1952 thus substantially increased its legitimacy.

A greater challenge was posed in 1958. During the fifteen years since independence, the Lebanese Army had policed internal security successfully and uncontroversially. By 1958, new and different problems had arisen. The unrest of 1958 was not of the same scope as that of 1952. While in 1952 the problems stemmed mainly from one individual's universally recognized toleration of corruption, the crisis of 1958 threatened the system itself.

The 1957 parliamentary elections were held at the height of pan-Arabism's passionate appeal to the surrounding Arab world. Elected in

1952 following Khoury's resignation, Camille Chamoun captured an overwhelming majority of supporters in the Chamber of Deputies. Chamoun had risen strongly against the pan-Arab and pro-Nasserist enthusiasm sweeping the region; he had even advocated adherence to the Eisenhower Doctrine. His electoral victory reconfirmed the degree of public support for Chamoun's position and it consequently undermined the power of the opposition view. Following the declaration of the United Arab Republic and the Iraqi Revolution in 1958, a distinct cleavage began to emerge in Lebanon's political life. Its danger was that the pan-Arabist, pro-Nasser movement tended to attract Muslims, while Chamoun's strong pro-Western and anti-Nasser stand was much more appealing to Christians. As positions hardened, many Lebanese felt each "side" had gone too far, perhaps violating the National Pact in spirit,[14] and many began to back away from the extreme postures. As the split developed, however, violence began to break out. When the president looked to his army commander to restore law and order, General Shihab once again demurred.[15] In part, he felt that, as in 1952, the conflict had become one surrounding the personality and presidency of one man, Camille Chamoun, and that the Lebanese Army should not protect a particular administration. There is also evidence that he feared the disintegration of the army.

The Lebanese Army in 1958 was a Christian officered army in which Muslims predominated in the ranks. Units were not significantly mixed in religion, however. Judging from army performance it might easily be concluded that Shihab's concern about army disintegration was exaggerated, because the army acquitted itself well when used, and confessional incidents were minor. LAF intervention prevented severance of army lines of communication, interdicted certain rebel sorties, and reasserted government control in specific sectors. Would the army have split in 1958 if it had been asked by Shihab to restore law and order throughout Lebanon? This is a question no one can answer with certainty. On the one hand, Shihab's intelligence service was excellent and he can be presumed to have had good information about potential problems within the armed forces. On the other hand, some have suggested that he may have coveted the presidency in 1958 and refrained from using the army for political reasons.

President Chamoun requested American intervention and U.S. Marines, followed by American forces, arrived in Lebanon soon thereafter. At first appalled by the inaction[16] of the indigenous armed forces in the face of serious violence,[17] the American soldiers eventually understood some of the reasons behind Shihab's position. The Americans were also surprised at the quality of Lebanese Army personnel and their potential.[18]

The crisis ended when Fu'ad Shihab was elected to succeed President Chamoun in 1958. Chamoun insisted upon completing his constitutional term, thus setting a precedent for future Lebanese leaders. The departure of Shihab from the position of Army commander would have seriously affected the army if only because Shihab had been its sole commander since independence. His elevation to the presidency reinforced the legitimacy and credibility of the institution as a neutral force in Lebanese politics, but it ushered in a new era in which, ironically, the army was to become much more intimately related to the presidency.

## THE SPREADING CRISIS, 1958-1969

Fu'ad Shihab entered the office of the presidency with widespread Muslim support and with a divided Christian community, whose members were bitter over his refusal to commit the Lebanese Army fully. The period from 1958-1969 was uneventful on the surface. Indeed, even the administration of Charles Helou, Shihab's hand-picked successor, retained that appearance until 1969. The army was not often called upon to act, and overt social violence was limited. Meanwhile, the Arab world experienced over twenty-five military coup attempts (about half of which were successful), two wars with Israel,[19] at least two other wars, and several internal conflicts. Lebanon appeared to be a stable island in a sea of turmoil.

The reality was distinctly different from the appearance. After Shihab became president in 1958, the Lebanese army took an active role in politics throughout the Shihab and Helou administrations, so much so that some say the army "took the form of a political party" or "constituted a military government" in civilian garb.[20] Distrusting politicians in the corrupt Lebanese environment, Shihab appointed senior military officers to key positions in both the government and the security forces. This, however, was only the military's public face. The army also became the primary security force, rather than the force of last resort, and it imposed an informal but effective censorship.[21] In addition, the deuxième bureau, the army's G-2 or intelligence section, became a principal actor. The deuxième bureau established a far-reaching network of agents, especially among Nasserite Sunnis.[22] The network was intended partially to supplant the traditional Sunni leaders, and partially to control parliamentary elections as well as the administrative machinery. While Shihab could manage the system with his own base of support, his successor (who had no independent power base) was largely managed by the system.[23] The Nahj political faction that Shihab forged came under substantial army G-2 influence and was subsequently used to control Helou.

Lebanon acquired a more distinctly Arab external face during Shihab's rule. Several leading Christians accused the military establishment of allying itself with Nasser and the radical left.[24] At the end of 1961, junior officers from the Syrian Social Nationalist Party attempted to stage a coup. Amateur and disorganized, the coup aborted.[25]

Surely the most important development during this period for Lebanon's future, however, was the second influx of Palestinians following the rout of the Arab forces in June 1967 and the substantial weakening of the Arab governments that resulted from the decimation of their armies. As a result of Arab impotence, the Palestinian movement, and particularly the Palestine Liberation Organization (PLO), took its fate into its own hands and gradually became a significant regional actor. The Palestinians had never had a free hand in Lebanon, and the power of the *deuxième bureau* under Shihab constituted an effective constraint on the inclination of some Palestinian groups to raid Israel, because G-2 maintained careful surveillance of the camps (although it did allow some training activities).

By themselves, the Palestinians in Lebanon could not have reduced the control the military exercised. However, the long-term implications of the 1958 crisis were already beginning to have ramifications for Lebanese unity. Increasingly, Christians, particularly Maronites, questioned Sunni intentions. They sensed a threat to Lebanon's structure and independence in each pro-Nasserist or anti-Israeli position. By the same token, the Sunnis increasingly perceived the government's behavior as an effort to effect a Christian state of Lebanon. Gradually they began to identify with the Palestinians as Sunnis, as Arab nationalists, and as protectors.

Meanwhile, the pervasive influence of the Lebanese Army, which sought to preserve the security of Lebanon but increasingly supported the *regime* of Shihab as well (ironic indeed in view of Shihab's reluctance to become involved in regime support while he was army commander) did not take sides in the growing religious divisions in the country. Nevertheless, the army was understandably seen as defending a Christian order not because it was more or less confessional but because the confessional divisions in Lebanese society were increasingly acute.

As the Lebanese Sunni community and its leaders and the Arab world as a whole were becoming more closely allied with the Palestinians, the omnipresence of the Lebanese Army was eroding its public support. Its procurement policies (specifically, the acquisition of equipment suitable principally for internal security operations) showed clearly that the army had no intention of conducting military operations against any foreign power. It seemed to many observers that the Lebanese Army, despite the government's rhetoric to the contrary, was perpetuating a Christian state that was both anti-Arab and anti-Muslim. This perception stemmed from the general assessment that the army seemed to be the real government of Lebanon. Furthermore, the officer corps was still predominantly Christian and the Christian community appeared to dominate the state. The army's efforts to prevent Palestinian border operations strengthened this idea. The effort to control the Palestinians continued, even after increased restraints were imposed on the army after 1965.[26]

Although the army was losing both legitimacy and the physical ability to exert control at reasonable cost by 1968, it might have succeeded in maintaining some control of the situation had it received support from some quarter. Christian communities insisted that the army was not doing enough and that vacillation would encourage Israeli responses and potentially far more serious consequences. The Muslim communities saw the army as anti-Muslim, anti-Arab, and anti-Palestinian. Israeli leaders did not consider the army willing or able to prevent attacks on Israel from within the Lebanese borders.

On December 31, 1968, Israeli commandos raided the Beirut airport and destroyed 13 aircraft. No single event had catalyzed the developing crisis as did the Israeli raid. The Lebanese Army was vehemently attacked for not protecting Lebanon. Muslim criticism of the army was based of its lack of readiness to combat Israel. The army was becoming a lightning rod of sectarian divisions in society, as Muslims who saw Israel as the Arab world's—and hence Lebanon's—principal enemy demanded Lebanese Army dedication to confronting Israel, while Christians believed that such a confrontation would inevitably lead to both a military confrontation with Israel in which Lebanon would be devastated and a militarization of Lebanese society in which Palestinians would become an uncontrollable force. Although government and army leaders endeavored to remain neutral in this increasingly dangerous debate, there is no question that they identified much more with the dominant Christian view. Meanwhile, Palestinian activity increased rapidly and was more and more openly supported by Syria.[27] The army, aware of the consequences of these developments, attempted to reestablish its control. As a result, violent clashes erupted in the south (near the Israeli border) and east (near the Syrian border) of the country. The ensuing crisis prompted the resignation of the Prime Minister and no other Sunni would assume the position. Finally, in November 1969 the army commander, General Emile

Bustani, signed the Cairo Accords. Under the terms of this agreement,[28] the Palestinians could establish and maintain armed units in their camps as well as fixed bases in the south. The Lebanese Army was to assist Palestinian groups to and from the Israeli border and guarantee their lines of supply. Palestinian leaders would meet regularly with Lebanese Army officials to coordinate activities. Palestinian interference in Lebanese affairs was proscribed.

The Cairo Accords were justifiably seen as the ratification of a new Lebanese role in the Arab–Israeli conflict. Because the shift they represented was wholly antipathetic to the view of most elements of the Christian community, they also symbolized the dramatic increase in Palestinian power within Lebanon. Thus, although many were dissatisfied with the Cairo Accords, they were signed because:

- First, they were the only available option to end the crisis;
- Second, it was hoped that the Palestinians would show greater deference to domestic Lebanese politics;
- Third, the respite from conflict they initiated was expected (by all parties) to provide an opportunity to prepare for further conflict seen by most Lebanese as inevitable.

The foundation was laid for a major conflict in Lebanon.


## THE LEBANESE ARMY AND THE CONFLICT IN LEBANON

The clashes of 1969 and the Cairo Accord sealed Lebanon's fate. As Palestinian raids continued, Israeli retaliation increased. Moreover, the Cairo Accord legitimized the construction of a Palestinian army in Lebanon. Given the limited manpower and weapons inventory of the Lebanese Army, the implications of this buildup were clear. They were so clear that the Christian militias soon began importing substantial arms for what they saw as the inevitable confrontation. Predictably, the non-Christian militias—sectarian, ideological, and regional—pursued a similar course. Armed militias had existed in Lebanon since the 1930s, but the level of armament was insignificant and primitive by contrast with the situation after 1969.

In 1970, Charles Helou was succeeded by Suleiman Frangieh. While Helou had symbolized the perpetuation of Shihabist policies, Frangieh stood for major change. Elected in August 1970, he was not yet inaugurated when the fighting began in Jordan that ultimately ousted the PLO from that country. He therefore faced a major new Palestinian emphasis on the salience of its role in Lebanon. Moreover, the level of Palestinian arms, and of Palestinian arming of friendly forces, vastly surpassed anything seen before in Lebanon. However, Frangieh gained support as a candidate because he was prepared to insist much more strongly than Helou had that the Palestinians respect Lebanese sovereignty.

As an anti-Shihabist,[29] Frangieh stood for significant change in the armed forces. He advocated and moved to effect a weapons acquisition program unprecedented in Lebanese history, making it clear Lebanon would no longer accept inappropriate, obsolete, or used materiel. This program was part of an overall expansion of the armed forces. On the other hand, he promised to "return the soldiers to their barracks" and to end the "duality of power," meaning that he intended to restrict the armed forces to a military role and to eliminate the army's (*deuxième bureau's*) farreaching political activities. Frangieh also pledged to bring a more equitable share of power to the Muslim community in all areas, including the armed forces.

The weapons acquisitions planned for the Lebanese armed forces were to be the first major purchases since the late 1950s. Leftists had insisted that acquisitions be "diversified," by which they meant that Lebanon procure at least some of the material from the Soviet Union. Some purchases were in fact arranged from Moscow, but they involved no training, because both the army command and political leadership were concerned about Soviet penetration of the armed forces.[30]

Frangieh planned to increase the size of the Lebanese armed forces significantly. He envisioned a five to six brigade force of thirty-five thousand to forty thousand men, about twice the size of the existing army. This plan was never implemented because the Chamber of Deputies never authorized adequate budgetary outlays for the expansion.[31] Even if money had been available, however, recruitment problems were already in evidence.

Because of the difficulty in securing Sunni officers, the Lebanese Army continued to have a disproportionately Christian officer corps. After 1970, Frangieh strictly enforced the proportional recruitment which had the effect of significantly limiting growth. Slightly over half of the officers were Christians. The rank and file was predominantly Muslim (slightly over 50 percent), most of the Muslims being Shi'as. Critical posts and operational commands tended to go to Christian officers, but the reasons had less to do with discriminatory planning than with seniority patterns, the reluctance of some Sunni officers to assume command responsibilities, and educational differences. Frangieh made a pronounced effort to push Sunni representation in commands and other key positions.[32]

Lebanese Army recruitment also suffered from the influx of capital to the Arab world in the early 1970s. The army was increasingly unable to pay salaries commensurate with those available in the private sector, limiting the overall growth of the institution. This was particularly true vis-a-vis the Christians, whose area east of Beirut was experiencing phenomenal growth, and the Sunnis whose skilled manpower and brainpower easily found more lucrative careers. The Shi'as continued to consider the Lebanese Army an effective vehicle for social and economic mobility. Christians (and Sunnis to a lesser extent) increasingly came from areas outside the city. A conscription bill was drafted to resolve this recruitment problem, but the magnitude of the change in the sectarian composition of the army frightened the deputies and sidelined the legislation.[33]

Ending the Shihab era of "military politics" entailed dismissing many officers of the Shihab and Helou eras,[34] which Frangieh proceeded to do. A new officer corps emerged. As indicated above, Lebanese Army officers are generally associated with a patron. Although Shihab had attempted with some success to reduce this phenomenon, the patron–officer relationship persisted and indeed resurfaced in Helou's later years. Chamounists and officers associated with other leaders filled the posts vacated by the dismissed Shihabist officers. The role of the *deuxième bureau* receded noticeably.

Between 1970 and 1973, the massive influx of Palestinians recently expelled from Jordan predictably led to increased raids on Israel. Predictably too, Israel retaliated against southern Lebanon, whence the raids originated. The Israeli retaliation brought massive devastation and constant threat to the south, whose Shi'a residents moved in alarming numbers northward to the southern suburbs of Beirut. Coincidentally, large numbers of Lebanese Shi'a began returning from Africa in the early 1970s as well. Unable to return to their "native villages" (the villages of their family origins), they too took up temporary residence near Beirut. Pressure on the Lebanese Army also increased: Christians awaited a crackdown on the guerillas; Muslims condemned the army's unwillingness to defend Lebanon's interests against Israel. Ironically, the de-Shihabization of the army crippled its one strong branch, intelligence, so that it was no longer as aware of dangerous developments before they exploded. The Palestinian presence had grown to such a degree that effective control of the guerillas was probably not much more feasible than defense against Israel.

On April 10, 1973, Israeli commandos raided Beirut and Sidon. As in 1968, the Israeli raids aggravated already simmering conflicts. After the Sunnis verbally attacked the army and its commander, a personal friend of the president, the Lebanese Army surrounded refugee camps in the suburbs of southern Beirut. Heavy fighting erupted on May 3, and continued for two weeks, during the course of which Saiqa[35] units entered Lebanon from Syria and attacked Lebanese security forces. The clashes led to a new agreement on the Palestinian role in Lebanon (the Melkart agreement), basically a restatement of the 1969 Cairo agreement. New militias formed, old ones redoubled their preparations, and contacts began between some militias and concerned officers in the Lebanese Army.[36]

After the clashes of 1969, many recognized that Lebanon was pointed in a direction that guaranteed further violence—a "showdown," as it were, between Lebanese nationalists and Palestinian fighters and their supporters. The influx of PLO combatants from Jordan, further clashes in 1971, the growing involvement of Syria, and the increasing militance of the PLO concerning its "rights" in Lebanon made such a confrontation inevitable. Numerous writers have tried to portray the polarization of Lebanon during this period as an economic or social phenomenon resulting from inequities in income distribution, from corruption, and from the feudal power structure in the country.[37] No one can question the problems caused by these aspects of Lebanese social dynamics, and certainly some were motivated by concern over these issues.[38] Yet, the question that truly polarized Lebanese society was that of the Palestinians, and this question relates very directly to the issue of Lebanese identity and nationalism addressed elsewhere in this volume.

Lebanese nationalists, particularly elements of the Christian community that tended to see Lebanese nationalism as distinct from Arab nationalism, were the most concerned about the implications of the Palestinian problem in Lebanon and about the catastrophe that the events of 1973 suggested was imminent. These Lebanese nationalists were found in number in the rapidly growing militias and in the army. Muslim Lebanese nationalists were also abundant in the army and in the Beirut merchant community. When the events of 1975 showed the army to be immobilized by political shackles, individual army officers began to meet and to coordinate plans with militias for the inevitable crisis. Muslim army officers who were equally concerned about the course of developments were aware of the growing closeness with the militias. While many seemed to have been uneasy about the phenomenon, they tended toward ambivalence because of their greater concern about the larger problem.

The Lebanese civil war, as it is often called, erupted in full force in 1975. The initial incidents in Sidon involved army officers by chance, but resulted in the imposition of a blockade by the army. Already the political command structure had become confused, and the (Sunni) prime minister's contradictory orders were paid little heed by an army command that seemed to be responding directly to the (Maronite) president.

> Until the early years of the [Frangieh] regime, the Lebanese Army, with its Maronite command, had managed to retain a general popular respect by maintaining the position of arbiter on all matters which [sic] were subject to confessional dispute. When the Shihabist core of the Army was liquidated after 1970 . . . the situation began to change. By 1973, the Maronite Army command was beginning to be viewed among the Muslim Lebanese as a political ally and instrument of the Maronite Presidency. This Muslim suspicion of the Army command was certainly encouraged by the Palestinian commandos, who had their own quarrel with the Lebanese military, and also by the Lebanese radicals, whose more underhand[ed] activities were all too often frustrated by Army intelligence.[39]

We shall not detail the Sidon incidents in 1975 that precipitated renewed violence except to note that during the conflict in February, and from April to June 1975, the PLO tried to remain outside the battles that often pitted Muslim and leftist groups against the army or against Christian and Nationalist units. However, PLO constituent elements such as the PFLP and DPFLP did not follow the lead of the parent organization, and even some Fatah members participated. In the wake of the spring and summer incidents, a shrill cry arose from the Sunni community for a reorganization of the Lebanese Army.

As fighting escalated and spread in 1975, especially when it began again in September, calls arose for a decisive action by the army. Throughout 1975, the army was only called in to protect certain facilities and buildings and to give effect to cease-fires. While both Christians and Muslims anticipated that the army might shift the balance of power in the Christians' favor, the changes Frangieh had instituted were reassuring to the Muslims. However, when the Tripoli Muslim community, after violent exchanges with local militias around Zgharta, requested the intervention of the army, they did so with the proviso that the army commander, who was a symbol of Christian domination of the army, be removed. He was subsequently placed on leave and a new commander was named to replace him. This step seriously affected the morale of the Lebanese Army which resented "politicization" of the command and generally felt that the previous commander had carried out orders. The army was deployed to separate the engaged forces in the north, but its role remained tightly constrained by national politics.

Even after the replacement of Iskander Ghanim by Hanna Sa'id, the Lebanese Army was not fully committed. Sa'id's strategy was apparently to await a "decisive moment" to bring stability, and of course he did not receive policy direction, much less orders, from a paralyzed government. Demoralization of the army was the result. The country's destruction proceeded, but the army still did not receive orders from headquarters. The September fighting wreaked massive destruction upon the heart of old Beirut. In September, December, and in the large-scale conflict that erupted in January 1976, army units were always deployed in small numbers to stop the fighting in some specific area. No overall attempt to restore law and order was undertaken.

In a real sense, all of the problems of the Lebanese Army came to the fore in 1975–76. First, the ambivalence of the Lebanese Army as an internal security force was at issue. There were, in fact, various government internal security forces, and the army had never relished this role. By 1975, however, the *legitimacy* of the army as an internal security force was—as we have noted—no longer clear. Second, the political chain of command, which under the constitution linked the army to the presidency, had been clouded over time such that no one any longer had undisputed rights to "call in the army." Because the issue was internal, the army command required clear authority from political powers who were divided. Third, the divisions of society which are characteristically reflected in the armed forces had begun to be felt within the Lebanese Army where some Sunni and Shi'a elements, largely unorganized and generally enlisted personnel, sought fundamental change in Lebanon's structure and essentially identified with Arab nationalist ideas.

It is not possible to say how much this deterioration affected the army's ability to act before February 1976. It is likely that at any time before that the army could have been used to stop the violence. There are few indications of irreparable schisms before February, and, in fact, it was the unwillingness to use the army and the demoralization that resulted that was the single most disruptive factor in army cohesiveness.

The inability of the Lebanese Army high command to commit the army to the country's defense paralyzed the entire body of the army. In the face of this paralysis, individual commanders followed several different approaches.

- Some commanders committed their forces independently of headquarters, acting in the name but without the imprimature of the Lebanese Army.
- Ahmad al-Khatib, an army lieutenant with a long record of earlier engagements against Palestinian forces (but who had been passed over for promotions), established what he called the "Lebanese Arab Army" (LAA). A number of Muslims and some Sunni units rallied to the LAA over the next few months, as it took the side of the Palestinians in the fighting.

- Some commanders, units, or individuals stayed in their installations, awaiting orders. Technically, they remained under the complete control of, and responsive to, the army commander.
- Many individuals went home. This was particularly true of army personnel of one faith assigned to installations situated in areas populated predominantly by other sects. Indeed, some commanders encouraged their personnel to return home in these conditions.

What is noteworthy about the Lebanese Army during the conflict is that it did not commit itself to one side or the other. Paralyzed by a lack of orders from headquarters, the army disintegrated—i.e., ceased to behave as a single entity. The attention garnered by the LAA and by other commanders who purported to act in the name of the army as a whole misled many into believing that the army had ceased to exist. In fact, the majority of the body of the Lebanese Army remained loyal to headquarters, whether by remaining in the barracks, going home but being prepared to rejoin units once they were deployed, or taking local action in the absence of GHQ direction. The threat to the army posed by its disintegration was overcome, and by late 1976 the army was, for the most part, again an integral, though still unused, unit, weakened by its reduced size and by the loss of its heavy weapons (to the militias and to disrepair), but prepared to fight if ordered to do so.

In a sense, subsequent incidents such as the activities of Major Sa'ad Haddad in southern Lebanon constituted political threats to Lebanon and its future, but they did not and do not constitute serious threats to the legitimacy of the army. The problems of 1975 and early 1976 undermined the integrity and therefore imperilled the existence of the Lebanese Army. However, the loyalty of the majority of its officers and enlisted personnel allowed the Lebanese Army to overcome these threats. Haddad and others never presented themselves as legitimate alternatives to the army, and if they had, they would have gained no support. There was never a question of overthrowing or replacing the army with some other force.

One of the interesting aspects of the crisis of 1975–76 and the turmoil that gripped Lebanon for the succeeding six years is that notwithstanding the appeals of Ahmad al-Khatib, the senior Sunni officer corps remained loyal to the state, to the government, and to the army. The Lebanese Arab Army and other armed factions attracted very few Sunni officers and virtually all were in the lowest officer ranks. That many Christian officers continued to stay with the army is not surprising, since it was widely seen as a key symbol of independent Lebanon. Similarly, Shi'a and Druze elements had realized even during the Mandate era that their situation would be better if Lebanon remained a separate state than if it was absorbed into Syria with its Sunni majority. But the loyalty of Sunni officers is an extremely important indicator that the concept of a Lebanese Army was, and remains, viable. Similarly, it provides evidence that the institution is much less fragile than many believe.

An example of residual loyalty was the attempted "coup" of General 'Aziz al-Ahdab, a well-known brigadier and ardent nationalist from an established Sunni family in Tripoli. One of the principal objectives of his initiative was to persuade Ahmad al-Khatib to bring his recently created LAA back into the Lebanese Army. Supported by the LAA and many leading Christians in his goals, Ahdab sought a united army and the end of domestic violence. Most of his objectives were shared by senior army personnel, regardless of sectarian background. However, the patent illegality of the approach dissuaded many who identified with those objectives from supporting the method.

Over the course of the conflict years, the Lebanese Army was called upon to bring limited force to bear against almost every participant at one time or another. By 1981 and 1982, virtually every community in Lebanon had come to recognize the symbolic presence of the Lebanese Army. More importantly, they had also requested its *real* presence—its force—to be used against one or another of the groups that threatened them. Once again, a number of factors frequently prevented the army from responding to these appeals—but the factors were *not* internal to the army.

At times, however, circumstances did allow the deployment and employment of the army. The Lebanese Army performed competently and effectively against the Syrian Army, the PLA, and other forces. For example, the Lebanese Army repelled attacks against the army's military academy at Fayadiyeh by the PSP militia and the Lebanese Arab Army in March–May 1976. Later, in 1978, the Syrian Army also attacked Fayadiyeh and was soundly beaten back with heavy casualties.[40] Under extraordinarily adverse conditions in which the army found itself over the last few years, this record is certainly a powerful indication that the Lebanese Army "can do" what is legally asked of it.

By 1982, the army, though slowly rebuilding, had no armor and therefore less ground-based heavy firepower than *any* of the major militias, the PLA, other Palestinian combatants, Saiqa, or, certainly, the Israeli or Syrian armies. The army commander, acceptable to Syria, was committed to a do-nothing course in terms of the expansion of army capabilities, as those foreign advisors and observers who tried to improve the army quickly discovered.[41]

In 1982, the IDF intervened massively in Lebanon. Although there were incidents between the Lebanese Army and the IDF near the army's

Tripoli garrison, the army was not involved in any major combat operations during the Israeli move north. Once again, the Lebanese government did not order the army into battle, but certainly it could have contributed little in any case.

As the Israeli forces moved north toward Beirut, it quickly became clear that the military operations underway would fundamentally change the course of Lebanese politics and therefore of the Lebanese Army. Army officers immediately understood that there would once again be a Lebanese central government and that this government would depend heavily upon its army. Morale within the army and across religion soared.

The denouement of the 1982 fighting did not, however, restore government authority to large areas of Lebanon. Instead, Israel occupied Lebanon south of Beirut, and the Shuf, the Syrians remained in the Beqa'a and in the north and northeast, and the Lebanese Forces controlled Beirut and Mt. Lebanon. Although the army was eventually given authority over West Beirut and then East Beirut, the vast majority of Lebanese territory remains occupied as this is written.

In September 1982, as a new Lebanese president was preparing to take office, he was assassinated, whereupon the Israeli army moved into West Beirut. Some Israeli officers had tried to persuade the Lebanese Army to assume responsibility for the Palestinian refugee camps south of the city, but the Lebanese government, believing such action would be seen as complicity in the unilateral Israeli move (which violated the agreements reached with U.S. envoy Philip Habib), refused. A grisly massacre of the residents ensued.

One result of the massacre in Sabra and Shatila (and Burj al-Barajneh) refugee camps was the reintroduction of multinational forces (initially, Italian, French, and United States) into Lebanon. (Such a force had earlier policed the evacuation of PLO fighters from Beirut, but had been withdrawn just prior to the assassination of the president-elect.) This development in turn facilitated a concentrated American effort to assist the building of a new Lebanese Army.

## THE FUTURE OF THE LEBANESE ARMY

In this section we shall consider the future of the Lebanese Army. In order to discuss the army's future it is necessary to review quickly the developments to date and particularly those since 1975.

The prevailing view is that the Lebanese Army divided into its sectarian components and took sides due to Lebanese internal conflict, thus escalating its intensification. In fact, however, this view is erroneous in several respects. First, the army, as we have seen, did *not* split in the early stages of the fighting between April and June 1975 or in the renewed fighting in the autumn. Only in 1976, as the fighting ceased to be a Lebanese affair, did the army disintegrate. Second, while it is true that the army became fragmented, it did not take sides per se. Rather, the army, lacking an appropriate mission and in the absence of orders to act, refrained from involvement in the fighting for the most part. Third, most of the army personnel either remained in their barracks or returned to their homes. They did *not* join one side or the other. Significantly, when the army was given an order, it carried out the order.

The official attempts to reconstruct the Lebanese Army, efforts supported strongly by the United States, fell short of the mark before 1982. The reason for this failure may well be that the effort itself was based on incorrect assumptions. The army was paralyzed by the effects of long-developing and recent societal and administrative problems.

The Lebanese Army, as we have seen, has always been equipped only for internal security purposes. Although its stated mission gives particular attention to the territorial defense of the republic from external attack, in fact the Lebanese Army has never been staffed or equipped to deter or defend Lebanese territory against its two possible attackers, Israel and Syria. In reality, the mission of the armed forces has been and remains unclear. One problem, then, is ambiguity of mission. Anyone familiar with other armed forces recognizes that an army without a clear mission is hamstrung. Organizations, like people, require a sense of purpose to thrive.

A second principal problem was the increasing politicization of the Lebanese Army. Although most observers have painted this portrait with sectarian colors, in fact religious differences were often more the form than the substance of the problem. Ambitions of some senior army personnel and politicians' fears and perceptions about those personnel were more at fault, even though some of the fears were probably well founded. The dismissal of two successive army commanders during the conflict is an example of this disarray *above* rather than within the armed forces.

The politicization of the Lebanese Army began or significantly accelerated as early as 1958 when the *deuxième bureau* evolved into a major actor in the country and came to be perceived as the 'power behind the throne' in national politics. Indeed, the activity of Lebanon's G-2 continues to this day to be the single most powerful and feared element in government.

Finally, the fact that the army's internal role has always been a consensual one hobbled the army to a large extent both in the south and, consequently, in its internal security functions after 1975. Again, if the army mirrors society, we can see how the society's government was built on the basis of consensus but that gradually, as social groups became increasingly unable to trust each other, the *society* split, and the army became paralyzed as a result of that division and the lack of a coherent hierarchy of command. The army itself, however, neither split nor took sides with any group.

The overlooked and misportrayed fact is that the Lebanese Army is one of the few Lebanese institutions that did *not* cease to function after 1975. Let us briefly consider this fact. The disintegration of the army was initiated by a few individual officers and enlisted men who attached themselves to various militias or established largely autonomous commands. But the army *itself* did not opt for one side or the other. Most of the army "sat out" the fighting, both literally and figuratively, either in military facilities or at home.

The distinction drawn here is not insignificant. Because the Lebanese Army survived the disintegration of 1976 it did not have to be *wholly* rebuilt. Instead, the Lebanese Army was paralyzed, for a variety of reasons, during the fighting and even before 1975—but it retains a good foundation, a good complement of fine officers, a history of professionalism, and substantial pride in itself, despite recent history.[42]

After the cataclysmic events of 1982, the United States, the president of Lebanon, and several regional governments as well favored the emergence of a strong central government in Lebanon, one that would symbolize a belief in Lebanon's unique historical and cultural role in the region, one able to represent and protect the interests of each and every Lebanese community. Clearly such a government would require a strong army. Although the bulk of the PLO's fighting forces had withdrawn from Lebanon, the amount of weapons in the country remained staggeringly high. Individual Lebanese and Palestinians, a plethora of militias, and the army of Major Haddad, were all armed. Israel and Syria occupied most of the country. If the central government were to implement its policies and terminate the state of anarchy that had prevailed, it would necessarily have to field and command an army stronger than any other group in the country following Israeli and Syrian withdrawal.

We do not suggest that Lebanon needed to develop an army like those of its neighbors—a military force with offensive potential. Lebanon cannot and will not participate in any renewed Arab–Israeli combat. Realistically, Lebanon cannot, should not, and does not seek to compete with Israel or Syria in armed forces size, offensive capability, or equipment inventories. The Lebanese Army will and should retain major internal security functions. However, the ability to overcome internal threats and to *deter* (rather than defeat) external aggressors certainly required a new "look" for the armed forces.

• First, a clear chain of command from the executive branch was required. The respective roles of the president and prime minister were far from clear.

• In addition, the armed forces' missions required much clearer and realistic delineation.

• Moreover, the armed forces needed to be reequipped for several reasons. For one thing, arms acquisitions had been heavily influenced by political rather than logistical considerations, with the result that effective training, supply, and maintenance were undermined. A second and more evident reason for reequipment was the large-scale loss of materiel over the previous seven and a half years. Finally, equipment should reflect the clearer and more realistic delineation of mission. Undoubtedly, such a mission would require an air-mobile army, upgraded air and naval components, with the ability to deploy rapidly anywhere inside Lebanon.

• The Lebanese needed to decide whether their army was to continue being a consensual force. If the Lebanese feared that a resort to armed force might potentially impose undue government control or provide an instrument for government overthrow, they might prefer to retain a consensual perspective. In any case, the consensual or compellent nature of the mission had to be decided.

The Amin Gemayel government was faced with several major problems in connection with the development of the armed forces. First, as a result of the foreign occupations, most of the manpower base required for recruitment—particularly in view of the intention to substantially increase army size and the determination to maintain a confessional balance—was denied. Second, the army was initially without facilities for training or even for housing its personnel. (Most army installations were either destroyed or in occupied areas.) Third, there were no concrete plans for the development of the army, and political and economic considerations and the occupations very significantly complicated the process of developing such plans. Beyond these developmental problems, the country as a whole was in a near-anarchy situation, having experienced continuation of the prolonged Palestinian and Syrian occupation, the culmination of over seven years of widespread violence and bloodshed in a major new Israeli invasion and occupation, the appearance and withdrawal of a multinational force, rapidly changing levels of territorial control by a variety of militias, the assassination of the president-elect, a highly emotional massacre of refugees, the reintroduction of a new multinational force, and a new presidential election—all within the space of a few months. Moreover, Bashir Gemayel had approached the presidency on a foundation of strong support by the Christian community, acceptance by the Shi'as and Druzes, who saw in him the only Lebanese president likely to be able to persuade Israel to withdraw from Shi'a and Druze lands, and fear by the Sunnis who believed Bashir might relegate their community to third in government *behind* the Shi'as if they did not cooperate. The Lebanese Forces, a Lebanese militia led by Bashir and fiercely loyal to him, was the single strongest Lebanese militia or paramilitary body in the country, with more armor and artillery than the army itself. By contrast, Amin Gemayel did not command the unconditional support of the Lebanese Forces or the Christian community. Though he was less feared by the Sunnis, the latter were almost powerless at the time he assumed the presidency, and their embrace weakened Amin's support among the Christians. The other communities had less confidence in Amin's ability to control Lebanon and to secure foreign troop withdrawals.

At the same time, the new president enjoyed some favorable developments as well. The Israeli invasion had resulted in the neutralization of 'Amal, the Shi'a militia, as a *military* force and the dissolution of the Murabitoun and some allied, smaller militias. Similarly, the PSP or Druze militia seemed to be neutralized as a result of Israeli occupation of the Shuf. Bashir's statements about the future of the Lebanese Army[43] had excited its officer corps, and although readiness (lack of training and equipment) was poor, morale had soared.[44] Moreover, as a result of the increasingly disastrous turn of events, a rebirth of Lebanese consciousness was evident. Whether Maronite, other Christian, Shi'a, Sunni, or Druze, the Lebanese sought with near unanimity the return of *Lebanon* and the speedy withdrawal of Israeli, Syrian, and Palestinian combatants.[45] Finally, and of considerable importance, the United States government had indicated both a significant commitment to Lebanese unification and reconstruction and a willingness to embark on a long-term program of reequipping and retraining the Lebanese Army.[46]

Amin Gemayel wisely carried through some of the ideas of his assassinated younger brother. The civilian chain of command above the armed forces was clarified, and the president's role once again emphasized. This development might have been hotly contested under different circumstances, but the Sunni prime minister was not anxious to be associated with army actions and the defense minister in Gemayel's first cabinet had no experience in military affairs. Moreover, the Lebanese–Syrian–Palestinian committee that had taken a major role in military matters clearly no longer was appropriate under the new circumstances. Gemayel named a new army commander, Ibrahim Tannous, and a new G-2, Simon Qassis, both of whom quickly impressed observers with their activism, competence, and brightness. The new president made it clear to the army that the internal security role was to be a temporary mission until withdrawal of foreign forces was secured and Lebanese government authority restored to all 10,452 square kilometers of Lebanese territory.[47] He and his new army commander continued to speak about the growth of the army to sixty thousand.

The Lebanese have tried, then, to come to terms with several of the core issues concerning their army, then. They resolved the chain-of-command problems. They determined that the army's principal mission should become defense of the national territory and security against hostile, non-Lebanese threats.[48] They concluded that, in view of this mission, the armed forces should be increased to at least sixty thousand, and include certain military units that are essentially border guards.[49] Some Lebanese officers even began to look at materiel procurement and Tables of Organization and Equipment appropriate to the evolving mission.

As the process of addressing and overcoming these hurdles took place, the army was also in the process of operational reconstruction. This process included intensive training by United States forces sent to Lebanon; expansion of areas under the security responsibility of the Lebanese Army with concomitant burdens on personnel, materiel, command-control, and logistics support; development of five-year plans; recruitment of personnel on the basis of confessional quotas and procurement of materiel from several sources (primarily France and the United States).

The training program had not been extensively planned. Nevertheless, both American trainers[50] in the Lebanese Army Modernization Program (LAMP) and Lebanese participants were pleased with the progress made by the Lebanese, whose morale and sense of national identity appeared high.[51] While press reports in the United States and the findings of some observers[52] were critical, most analysts on the scene believed that the Lebanese Army was capable of maintaining internal security and felt that within five to eight years it would be able to carry out its deterrent mission as well if foreign forces were to withdraw.[53] Senior Israeli officials who earlier pointed to the army's shortcomings as the reasons for a number of Israeli security requirements suggested by the summer of 1983 that the army, with United States help, could "impose the state's authority on all its territory."[54]

Although the case of unrest in the southern suburbs of Beirut and in the city in September was not purely "internal," it is a reasonable case to judge the ability of the LAF to safeguard internal security, because the personnel and weapons involved on the part of the miscreants *were* internal, even if encouraged by foreign elements. In this operation the LAF performed quite well except for a comedy of errors at the initial stages in regrouping and deploying forces. The unity of an army that was composed of sixty percent Shi'a enlisted personnel in the face of disturbances in a Shi'a area should not go without notice. Defections, which had been feared, did not arise as a problem, and the LAF acted with surprising unity.[55]

The expansion of the army's areas of responsibility occurred on a major scale three times, as the Lebanese Army officially took over, first, West Beirut, then the eastern sector, and, later, parts of the Shuf. The first two actions are quite distinct from the third. In both the east and west of the city there were few problems, and even critics of the army were surprised at the smooth and effective growth of army responsibilities. Negative incidents were minor. The problems in supporting the territorial expansion were minimized by the still relatively small area involved, but United States and foreign observers both felt that the Lebanese Army could control a substantially larger area—if the army did not have to confront foreign military forces.[56]

The Shuf operation was, however, very close to a combat environment against foreign forces. For some time, the Israeli government had indicated it intended to redeploy its forces, withdrawing most of those in the Shuf to more southerly positions. Attempts to coordinate this withdrawal with LAF movement into the positions to be evacuated were thwarted by political disagreements between Beirut and Jerusalem. Thus, no coordination was effected. Worse, unilateral Lebanese attempts to replace IDF units with their LAF counterparts resulted in a bloody ambush of the latter. The Lebanese Army prepared to move into the Shuf in the aftermath of the IDF withdrawal, recognizing that casualties would probably significant.[57]

At the same time, discussions were underway in Paris between Walid Jumblatt and the Lebanese government with participation by an envoy of the United States president. Although the discussions were political in nature, they took place against the backdrop of the imminent IDF withdrawal and the probable outbreak of hostilities in the Shuf if a suitable political arrangement were not reached. In fact, an agreement was reached, but Syria rejected it.[58] Immediately, violence erupted in Beirut and its southern suburbs, forcing the diversion of the two LAF brigades scheduled to move into the Shuf. Consequently, no LAF troops were available for deployment to the Shuf as the IDF withdrew. Moreover, Syria had been for some time building up the strength of Druze groups responsive to Damascus, in some cases with tacit IDF agreement. When the Lebanese Army was able to identify units to deploy to the Shuf, they now had to face a substantial military force already present, and one supported by Syria in terms of equipment, ammunition, LOC, and intelligence. Moreover, these forces included Palestinians and Syrian Druze.[59]

The battle in the Shuf was probably the closest thing to real combat the Lebanese Army had ever experienced. However, the intensity of the fighting led many Druze to see the conflict as a threat to the Druze community, and many Druzes therefore fought the army for the survival of their people. Under these circumstances, new and much greater pressures for desertion arose for the Druze *in* the army, and in fact several hundred did leave for their homes, although probably as many in order to protect their families as for any political reason.

The fighting around Suq el-Gharb was particularly intense, and served with several other battles to point up the weaknesses as well as the strengths of the army. Its cohesion remained far in excess of what anyone could have expected in the face of successive confrontations with groups whose coreligionists comprised well over half the army. The courage and morale of LAF forces were exemplary. However, the experience deficits of field grade officers, the very straitened stocks of ammunition, and the logistical shortcomings of the army were painted in stark relief.[60]

## THE LAF FROM THE SHUF OPERATION TO THE U.S. WITHDRAWAL

The army's development plans were still necessarily incomplete, since the pace of foreign withdrawals, and therefore of the availability of personnel and training areas, remained unsettled. Nevertheless, Lebanese Army development plans envisaged a slow, but steady growth toward a sixty thousand-man standing army. This army was expected to shift in mission toward national defense, especially toward the latter part of the development cycle.

By the fall of 1983, the Lebanese Army Forces had made surprising progress toward their goals. The army grew from about twenty thousand to about thirty-three thousand during the nine months from January to September 1983. Conscripts and volunteers contributed just about equal parts of this growth which was confessionally balanced and saw very large numbers of volunteers from the occupied areas. Stocks of major equipment increased substantially, so that by late summer the army was far and away the largest Lebanese armed force in the country. Training appeared quite successful, and junior officers and enlisted personnel impressed the trainers.[61]

Several major hurdles remained in front of the army, however, and by the end of the Shuf operation some ominous signs also emerged. The first and most important hurdle was the foreign occupation of most of Lebanon. Perpetuation of this occupation—which could not be ruled out—would adversely affect the high motivation and morale of the new army over time. Moreover, systematic recruitment would remain virtually impossible in areas denied to central government authority, which would seriously affect the quantity and quality of recruits available from each sect. The planning for the army had been based on the assumption of a unified Lebanon. If this assumption were to prove unrealistic, the entire structure and future of the army would require rethinking.

A second problem was that of the operational experience of the field grade officers. There was nothing wrong with the quality of the personnel, but their careers were interrupted for a crucial decade, and there was no simple way to overcome this interruption in the short term.

Similarly, the logistical shortcomings of the army, which were also clear in the Shuf battles, had to await a long-term solution. They reflected personnel areas, training deficiencies, and shortfalls in experience. Substantial time would be required in this area as well. At the same time, it should be noted that logistical problems are typical of developing countries' armed forces, and therefore it might have been assumed that threat forces might also have to cope with similar difficulties.

Even assuming eventual foreign withdrawal, Lebanon's Army would still have to deal with the issue of the militias. Most writers saw this as the principal problem the army faced. In fact, however, the militias' challenge could have been relatively easily met if foreign forces had withdrawn. In all of Lebanon, only two militias maintained any significant cohesion or firepower—the late Sa'ad Haddad's group in the south and the Lebanese Forces. The others were disorganized, lacked effective communications or logistical support for sustained fighting, and in any case lacked adequate heavy firepower.[62]

By contrast the Lebanese Army was, by September 1983, the dominant *Lebanese* military force in Lebanon, far outstripping either the Haddad militia or the Lebanese Forces.[63] The former, however, was backed by the IDF, and the latter retained the support of the Christian community. The relationship of the Lebanese Army to the Haddad militia would clearly be determined by the Israeli–Lebanese relationship. As a force, the militia was of little importance. As a surrogate for Israel, it was unlikely to be pushed by the Lebanese Army for some time. Had the Lebanese–Israeli withdrawal accord or some other agreement symbolizing Israeli–Lebanese cooperation entered into force, the absorption of the southern militia into, and dilution of the militia by, the Lebanese armed forces would not have presented a problem.

The Lebanese Forces had also received materiel and other support from Israel. However, the Lebanese Forces' strength is the Christian community, not Israel. The army would avoid a confrontation with the Lebanese Forces if possible. Both Bashir and Amin Gemayel referred to the possible absorption of the Lebanese Forces into the army. Absorbing the militia as a sort of territorial auxiliary for the Mount Lebanon area might have been an expedient. At the same time, a unified Lebanon under a strong central government might have allowed the Lebanese Forces to "fade away." The major problem the army would have faced under these conditions would be less a confrontation with the Lebanese Forces than a competition for manpower. In the past, qualified Lebanese Christians had been more attracted by the army than by the militias. (This was true until the army was paralyzed in 1976.) Despite the major structural and psychological changes that had wracked the country, a national Lebanese Army still had infinitely greater attraction, recruiting power, and resources in 1983 than any militia.

A much more significant question went to the heart of the Lebanese state. The Lebanese tragedy built a strong nationwide yearning for a return to a Lebanese Lebanon. However, it also polarized religious communities and led to a crisis of trust of unprecedented proportions in Lebanon's brief history. It would have been surprising if this development had not affected the army. United States military personnel and other observers attest to the strong national identity of Lebanese Army personnel, and certainly the sense of unity and nationalism is stronger in the army than in any other Lebanese institution. A Lebanese Army oriented to external defense would stay together. However, between here and there the army necessarily would have to face challenges in internal security that would test the institution's unity, and though the major "sectarian" problem for the Lebanese state may prove to be around Tripoli, the army's first major challenge was certainly to be in the Shuf.

Beyond immediate problems which, with the help of the multinational force, might have been resolved if foreign forces had withdrawn, the army still had to insulate its personnel from the command patron-client relationships that characterized the LAF to date. Although this was a sociological and a political problem, the answer to it was certainly

to be found in *planning*, planning the personnel, recruitment, assign-
ment, and rotation policies; the basing structure and training facilities;
and even the procurement patterns of the army. It is apparent that the
army's new leadership had begun to think in these terms.[64]

Another problem, perhaps more easily overcome, and certainly
less difficult than the others, was the disjunction between United
States and Lebanese concepts and planning. Since the United States
was seen by most Lebanese as the key partner in the future development of the army, these differences had more than passing importance. The United States continued to insist that the Lebanese Army
should grow to a size of only about forty to forty-five thousand men.[65]
Washington assumed this army would have a *de facto* mission of internal security. Little attention was given Lebanese planning figures, apparent Lebanese intentions to reorient the army to national defense
following the liberation of all national territory, or the consistently expressed Lebanese determination to add ancillary paramilitary structures (as territorial or border guards) and enlarge the Internal Security
Forces to assume responsibility for the internal mission. American
planners never understood the psychological and political importance
to the viability of a unified army of making this transition and
therefore provided no assistance in this regard.

Another problem resulted in part from Lebanese inexperience, in
part from the difference between the United States and Lebanon over
the future mission of the army. The Lebanese believed they had to
demonstrate to the Americans the practicability of rapid growth of the
army to the sixty thousand-man figure. The best means of making the
point that the army is, in fact, a national institution, seemed to them to
be to encourage its growth as quickly as possible, which, particularly
in view of the continuing occupation, would favorably impress the
Americans (as well as the Lebanese populace) with regard to the
potential of the army. In principle, the logic was sound. In practice, it
should have raised alarms to American trainers and managers as well
as to the more sophisticated Lebanese about the quality of the recruits
and the thoroughness of the training, because the growth rate of the
army far exceeded American or Lebanese planning figures. Many of
the new recruits had just fought with militias, and the loyalties of
others were suspect.

## AN END TO LEBANON'S NATIONALIST ARMY?

Sectarian appeals to Druze within the army to abandon the institution did have some effect before and to a lesser extent during the battle

of the Shuf in September 1983. Nevertheless, the number of persons affected was small, and the unity of the army as a whole impressed all observers. This unity was an accurate reflection of the flagging but still extant national unity of the time. It was clear by the end of the year that if national unity were allowed to further erode, if Lebanon ceased to exist as a national idea, communal appeals to army personnel would grow in impact. Whether national unity eroded was not, however, a factor subject to the control of the army. Rather, it depended upon the foresight of the Lebanese government at the political level, and probably upon the emergence of an identifiable, independent foreign policy for Lebanon.

Thus the impact on the army of national political trends was critical. Because the army (and hence the government) did not enter and establish itself throughout the Shuf, pressures on Druze personnel to leave the army increased, and by the end of the year most had removed themselves to Hammana barracks, nominally still part of the army but effectively beyond its control. Could the army survive without the Druze? Of course. The Druze constitute only about six percent of Lebanon's population, and their numbers in the LAF were representative of that proportion as well. The critical components of the army were the Shi'a (who formed the bulk of the enlisted personnel) and the Christians (slightly over half the officer corps and perhaps thirty to thirty-five percent of the ranks). These two groups had always been the most consistent advocates of a sovereign Lebanon and the most nationalistic groups in the country. Moreover, sectarian strains were greater between Druze and Shi'a than between Christian and Shi'a (notwithstanding the events of February 1984).

At the highest levels of government the first priority should have been attached to ensuring a greater degree of Shi'a participation, and principally to demonstrating through policies and appointments that the government both recognized the crucial role of the Shi'a community in the restoration of Lebanon and welcomed their responsible attitudes in this regard. Unfortunately, the government, beset with crises, did not pursue this approach.

The largely Shi'a southern suburbs of Beirut were heavily armed. While 'Amal was united prior to the 1982 war, this area was relatively completely dominated by moderate secular ('Amal) and religious (the Higher Islamic Council) groups. Although more strident voices existed, they carried relatively little influence.

Over the year and a half following the end of the 1982 conflict, substantial quantities of military materiel entered the southern suburbs, and a growing militancy arose as well. By late 1983, the moderate voices of 'Amal's Nabih Berri and the Council's Sheikh

Mohammed Mehdi Shamseddin still represented the views of the bulk of the suburbs' residents, but were no longer decisive. *Agents provocateurs*, militants, revolutionaries, and other extremists provoked numerous confrontations and carried out attacks on Western interests.

When violence erupted at the end of the first week in February 1984, the LAF responded to a Shi'a attack in East Beirut by counterattacking in the southern suburbs. This time the LAF itself did split. The Sixth Brigade in West Beirut, which continued to declare itself loyal to the government, refused to accept orders from the army command and returned to its barracks. Commanders of the Fourth Brigade "defected" to the opposition, intentionally using communications to betray and destroy the brigade.

What had happened? How could unity and nationalism that had endured the seven years between 1975 and 1982 dissipate between 1982 and 1984? There are several answers.

1. The problems of internal disarray, intercommunal distrust, and an ineffective government were cumulative rather than serial and were for that reason alone far more grave in 1984 than in 1982, 1980, or 1975.
2. The government by 1984 appeared to have no policy, no direction, no momentum, and virtually no chance of success.
3. The sine qua non for the restoration of Lebanon and for the reconstruction of the army was the early withdrawal of foreign occupying forces. By 1984 it was clear to everyone that neither Israeli nor Syrian occupying forces were planning to withdraw.
4. The army grew too quickly, incorporating large numbers of personnel who were not merely unseasoned in combat—which is after all true of the bulk of most armies—but were also of questionable loyalties and reliability.
5. To a great extent a function of the fact that foreign forces did not withdraw, the Lebanese Army—though its leadership sought to become a force for national defense—became first and foremost an internal security force, a role for which it was politically unsuited except as a force of last resort on an occasional basis.

## AFTER THE FALL

When the events of early February 1984 occurred, the appearance to the outside world was that of the collapse of the LAF. The Lebanese, especially in the Muslim community, did not see it that way. The Sixth Brigade, for example, still existed. Indeed, when the U.S. Marine contingent withdrew from the Beirut airport, the Sixth Brigade took over its positions. The Sixth Brigade also assumed security functions in West Beirut, but in conjunction with 'Amal. 'Amal continued to speak supportively of the army, and except for a brief period returned Shi'as who wanted to leave the LAF. This Shi'a support for the Lebanese Armed Forces reflects a continuing Lebanese nationalism so characteristic of the community. (Whether this moderate view will continue to represent the majority of the Shi'as is less clear. In the southern suburbs, as even more clearly in the south, militants whose views cannot easily be accommodated in Lebanon are ever more powerful.)

Unfortunately, the events of 1984 must be seen as constituting a turning point for the LAF. Prior to 1984, the bulk of the LAF remained loyal to the national government and the senior command. It was the government that failed the army and not the reverse. Although Shi'as recognize their actions of 1984 trod a thin line between betrayal and national loyalty, the community leadership seems to believe that these actions were responsible and within the parameters of loyalty to the state. Whether Shi'a leaders are correct or incorrect in this assessment, it is unlikely that the Christian community will ever again place credence in the army as a national institution, and Christian–Shi'a cooperation was always the essential element to measure the army's potential.

This is not to say that Lebanon cannot again have a national army, or even a nationalist army. The LAF, long the symbol of Lebanese sovereignty, may still reacquire that symbolic importance. Nor is this to say that the failure of the army in 1984 was a function of army mistakes. Certainly, the army erred—in growing too quickly, for example. Ultimately, however, the blame for what happened to the army must lie with the Lebanese government for failing to appreciate the implications of its own policies on the army, the one institution it could not afford to "lose."

For many years, the army was the single Lebanese institution that remained national on a multiconfessional basis. In the dark years after 1969 the army stood alone as the institution that united Lebanese across the barriers of religion and against foreign domination. It was precisely because of this character that the Syrians attempted to subvert and destroy the nationalism—and anti-Syrian nationalism—of the army. And the measure of the vitality of the national spirit within the army is that the Syrians failed.

It is unlikely in the foreseeable future that the Lebanese Army can recapture the confidence of the communities of Lebanon to return to its traditional role. Thus, the army's future may either be as a decentralized institution with several territorial components, each acting with substantial independence within a specified area; or as a small, back-up internal security force. The possibility of constructing an army oriented toward national defense is reduced by the distrust of the institution that will remain among the Christian and Druze communities and the lack of confidence in unity that will characterize all elements of the institution.

Over the long term, Lebanese security and stability will certainly be determined by a number of variables and not solely by a strengthened army. The Lebanese Armed Forces are not and should not be the only glue that holds the country together. As a result of the 1984 crisis, neither can the LAF be the principal symbol of Lebanese national unity.

## NOTES

1. It is particularly remarkable, in view of the Lebanese Army's important role in society over the history of the republic, that only one book has ever been written on the army itself—none in English, one in French, none in Arabic. Indeed, nor has any article or book chapter systematically studied the Lebanese Army. (The chapters devoted to Lebanon in J. C. Hurewitz, *The Middle East: The Military Dimension* [New York: Praeger, 1969], and Eliezer Be'eri, *Army Officers in Arab Politics and Society* [New York: Praeger, 1969], do not deal in any systematic way with the armed forces, but instead focus on the society at large.) The best source material on the Lebanese Army is found in books on other subjects that incidentally treat the armed forces.

2. The mandate was conferred upon France on the basis of the secret agreements reached between the World War I allied powers, and not on the basis of historical claims. Indeed, the British made promises to Sherif Hussein of Mecca that conflicted with the Sykes-Picot agreement, the basis of the French mandate in fact.

3. See Adel Ismail, *Le Liban: Histoire d'un peuple* (Beirut: Dar al-Makhluf, 1968); Philip K. Hitti, *A Short History of Lebanon* (London: Macmillan, 1965); and K. S. Salibi, *The Modern History of Lebanon* (New York: Praeger, 1965).

4. See in particular the discussion on this point in "The Search of National Identity," Chapter 3 in Labib Zuwiyya Yamak, *The Syrian Social Nationalist Party: An Ideological Analysis* (Cambridge, MA: Harvard University, Center for Middle Eastern Studies, Monograph Series, 1966).

5. Walid Khalidi, *Conflict and Violence in Lebanon: Confrontation in the Middle East* (Cambridge, MA: Harvard University, Center for International Affairs, 1979), 67.

6. See Salibi, *Modern History*, 197.

7. "Lebanese" military units of both segregated and mixed religions served effectively, but also broke down periodically along confessional lines.

8. Hurewitz, *The Middle East*, 55.

9. Hurewitz, *The Middle East*, Harvey H. Smith et al., *Area Handbook for Lebanon* (Washington, D.C.: Foreign Area Studies, the American University, 1969), 298.

10. Salibi, *Modern History*, 190–91.

11. See Be'eri, *Army Officers*, 336–38; William Hazen and Peter Gubser, *Selected Minority Groups of the Middle East: The Alawis, Berbers, Druze and Kurds* (Kensington, MD: American Institutes for Research, 1973) 81–2, 97–8; John Keegan, *World Armies* (New York: Facts on File, 1979), 442.

12. Mohammed Mughisuddin et al., *Aspects of Weapons Acquisitions in Iran, Lebanon, Saudi Arabia, Kuwait and the Union of Arab Emirates* (Kensington, MD: American Institutes for Research, 1973), 99, 106–7.

13. In its informal recruitment/promotion patterns, the Lebanese Army has been an accurate reflection of Lebanese society in its feudal aspects. The confessional quotas have favored Maronite and Sunni officers in particular. Appointments are based on a quota of 33 percent Maronite; 22 percent Sunni; 20 percent Shi'a; 7 percent each Greek Orthodox, Greek Catholic, and Druze; 3 percent other Christians; 1 percent other Muslim. However, the within-Christian division was less rigidly applied in the 1970s as fewer Christians were attracted to the army.

Paramount leaders (patrons) in Lebanon have a geographical base. Consequently, clients depend upon paramount leaders of their sect who also dominate their region. Thus, Christian non-Maronites have been faced with an absence of *any* coreligionist paramount leaders, and have depended upon Camille Chamoun, Majid Arslan, and to some extent the Jumblatts.

See Paul A. Jureidini, "The Politics of the Lebanese Army," Abbott Associates SR 49 (September 1979).

14. Part of the National Pact was the statement by Riyad al-Sulh that "Lebanon is a homeland with an Arab face seeking the best from Western culture." The operational meaning of this phrase was that Lebanon should associate itself neither with a pan-Arab movement that would submerge or threaten its independent identity nor with Western protection or status.

15. The army did act, but did not act to protect the regime, to suppress the opposition, or even to end the violence. Shihab's goal was to *contain* or limit the violence only.

16. But see note 15.

17. Lynn D. Smith, "Lebanon—Professionalism at Its Best," *Military Review*, XXXIX, 3 (June 1959), 37.

18. Smith, "Lebanon—Professionalism at Its Best," 38.

19. The June War of 1967 and the War of Attrition, 1969–1970.

20. Riad N. El-Rayyes and Dunia Nahas, *Politics in Uniform: A Study of the Military in the Arab World and Israel* (Beirut: An Nahar, 1972), 53, 56.

21. El-Rayyes and Nahas, *Politics*, 60.

22. These leaders were neighborhood strongmen (*Qabadais*). Among them was Ibrahim Quleilat whose Independent Nasserite movement became a major problem for the government in 1975–76 and thereafter. See Kamal S. Salibi, *Crossroads to Civil War: Lebanon 1958–1976* (Delmar, NY: Caravan, 1976), 11; Aziz el-Azmeh, "The Progressive Forces," *Essays on the Crisis in Lebanon*, ed. by Roger Owen (London: Ithaca Press, 1976), 63.

23. Khalidi, *Conflict and Violence*, 40.

24. Notably Chamoun's National Liberal Party. See Marius Deeb, *The Lebanese Civil War* (New York: Praeger 1980), 27.

25. See Yamak, *The Syrian Party*, 73–5.

26. Salibi, *Crossroads*, pp. 21, 26–28ff.

27. For a detailed study of this period, the problems with Syrian-supported Saiqa elements, and army activities designed to prevent commando raids, see Paul A. Jureidini and William E. Hazen, *Six Clashes: An Analysis of the Relationship Between the Palestinian Guerrilla Movement and the Governments of Jordan and Lebanon* (Kensington, MD: American Institutes for Research, 1971), 215ff.

28. The Cairo Accords were not made public, but their substance was quickly known.

29. When Fu'ad Shihab decided not to become a candidate, the *Nahj* decided upon Elias Sarkis as its candidate. Although *Nahj* supporters retained a majority in the legislature, the *Nahj* was a coalition rather than a party. As such, important elements did not support Sarkis' candidacy. It was the defection of certain *Nahj* deputies to Frangieh that brought about his election.

30. El-Rayyes and Nahas, *Politics*, 57; Mughisuddin et al., *Weapons Acquisition*, 73-4. The dispute over arms sources paralyzed the acquisitions process. Soviet ammunition proved to be problematical, U.S. production queues were too long, and so forth. Paul A. Jureidini and William E. Hazen, "Lebanon's Dissolution: Futures and Consequences," draft typescript, 1976, 37.

31. Jureidini and Hazen, "Lebanon's Dissolution," 37.

32. Salibi, *Crossroads*, 53; Khalidi, *Conflict and Violence*, 67-8.

33. Salibi, *Crossroads*, 53; Jureidini and Hazen, "Lebanon's Dissolution," 38.

34. Deeb, *The Lebanese Civil War*, 27.

35. Saiqa is controlled by Syria.

36. See Paul A. Jureidini, R. D. McLaurin, and James M. Price, *Military Operations in Selected Lebanese Built-up Areas, 1975-1978*, (Aberdeen, MD: U.S. Army Human Engineering Laboratory, Aberdeen Proving Ground, 1979).

37. See, e.g., Halim Barakat, "The Social Context," in P. Edward Haley and Lewis W. Snider, eds., *Lebanon in Crisis* (Syracuse: Syracuse University Press, 1979), 3-21.

38. A more balanced view is found in Fuad I. Khuri, "The Social Dynamics of the 1975-1977 War in Lebanon," *Armed Forces and Society*, VII, 3 (Spring 1981), 383-408; and Khalidi, *Conflict, passim*.

39. Salibi, *Crossroads*, pp. 95-6.

40. Both "Fayadieh I" and "Fayadieh II" are among the battles analyzed in Jureidini et al., *Military Operations*.

41. There are some indications that the army commander believed he could become a candidate for the presidency if he did not "rock the boat."

42. This assessment contrasts sharply with James Wootten, "Expanding U.S. Involvement in Lebanon," mimeo, Congressional Research Service, The Library of Congress, and the extraordinarily misinformed treatment by Daniel Pipes, "Lebanon, The Real Problem," *Foreign Policy* 51 (Summer 1983), esp. 148.

43. See Bashir Gemayel, "Rebuilding Lebanon: What We Must Do Now—and Why It Matters," *The Washington Post*, August 23, 1982, A15; Loren Jenkins, "Gemayel Seeks Aid to Expand Army," *The Washington Post*, September 8, 1982, A1.

44. Based on interviews with a number of Lebanese Army officers in late September 1982.

45. "One of the most important, if not the single most important, developments of the past few years has been a growing unanimity in Lebanon, across confessional groups, against any alien presence." Augustus Richard Norton, "Israel and South Lebanon," *American-Arab Affairs*, 4 (1983), 25.

46. See the remarks of Deputy Secretary of State Kenneth Dam in a speech in Chicago, Illinois, December 2, 1982. A follow-up Pentagon briefing discussed U.S. perceptions and objectives in greater detail. See also Wootten, "Expanding U.S. Involvement."

47. See Lucien George interview with Amin Gemayel, *Le Monde*, October 19, 1982, 1, 3,

48. Note that the Lebanese Army does not anticipate competing with Israel or Syria in armed forces size. The philosophy is one of *deterrence* in which the army seeks to create a force trained and equipped to make any attack too costly for an aggressor. The army need not defeat a potential attacker to deter it, but must be able to inflict unacceptable damage. Lebanese Army officers believe this is a feasible objective.

49. See note 47 above; interview with General Ibrahim Tannous, *as-Siyasah*, June 26, 1983.

50. An important part of the combat training is being conducted by U.S. Army Special Forces personnel.

51. See Jonathan C. Randal, "U.S. Training Officer Takes Issue with Critics of Lebanese Army," *The Washington Post*, March 26, 1983, A18; David Ignatius, "In

Bombing's Wake, Marines in Lebanon Press Their Mission," *The Wall Street Journal,* April 28, 1983, 1, 22.

52. E.g., Wootten, "Expanding U.S. Involvement."

53. David Ignatius, "How to Rebuild Lebanon," *Foreign Affairs,* LXI, 5 (Summer 1983), 1152; Randal, "U.S. Training Officer."

54. Charbyl Khouri interview with David Kimche, June 17, 1983, presented on Radio Free Lebanon, June 18, 1983.

55. See Paul A. Jureidini and R. D. McLaurin, "Army and State in Lebanon," *Middle East Insight,* III, 2 (Aug.–Oct. 1983).

56. Sources in note 53 and 54 above; interviews with U.S. and Lebanese armed forces personnel.

57. Interview by Joyce Starr of Col. Arthur T. Fintel, U.S. Army Liaison and Advisor to the Lebanese Army, August 1983.

58. Abdallah Bouhabib, "It Is Not a Civil War," *The Washington Post,* September 8, 1983, C8.

59. David Ignatius, "Syrian-Backed Palestinians Have Joined with the Druse Militia, Lebanon Charges," *Wall Street Journal,* September 8, 1983, 23.

60. See David Ignatius, "Lebanon Army Victory, With U.S. Help, Marked Turning Point for Both Nations," *Wall Street Journal,* October 7, 1983, 37.

61. See note 57.

62. Some writers (e.g., Pipes, "Lebanon") continue to refer to "the Phalange, Amal, Mourabitoun, Druze, and the other militias" (p. 140) as if the events of 1982 had not occurred.

63. We are not arguing here that either lacks firepower. Both have Israeli-provided armor and artillery, for example. Neither is a full-fledged combat organization, although the Lebanese Forces are close to that. On the weaknesses of Haddad's militia, see "Beirut Reports on Salim's Press Conference," Foreign Broadcast Information Service, *Daily Report: Middle East and Africa,* February 17, 1983, G2–G4.

64. See, however, the cogent warning advanced by Norton, "Israel and South Lebanon," 29–31. The intent of the Lebanese negotiators of the Lebanese–Israeli withdrawal accord was that the militia would be integrated. As Ignatius correctly observes, this kind of integration would be conducive to army growth and effectiveness, as long as the army command maintains its current emphasis on individual effectiveness in performance. ("How to Rebuild," 1151–2.)

65. See note 64.

# PART III

# SOCIAL CHANGE AND DEFENSE IN TWO LEBANESE COMMUNITIES

# 6

# The Lebanese Forces: Wartime Origins and Political Significance*

## Lewis W. Snider

## INTRODUCTION

### Who are the Lebanese Forces?

As a political group the Lebanese Forces have no close parallel in the West and therefore do not conform very closely to Western political experience. The Lebanese Forces are a political movement whose avowed aim is to liberate Lebanon from Syrian, Palestinian, and Israeli occupation, and restore control of Lebanon's political destiny to the Lebanese. Their creation and expansion as a political movement was basically in response to the vacuum created by the collapse of the central government, and particularly in response to the total absence of internal security and other essential government services. In fact many activities undertaken by the Lebanese Forces began as efforts to persuade or pressure various government bureaucracies to perform the services which by law they are charged to provide.

The name "Lebanese Forces" implies a nationalist political movement with a truly national following drawn from all confessional

*This chapter is a condensed version of a larger paper entitled "The Lebanese Crisis, The Lebanese Forces and American Foreign Policy", presented at a meeting of the California Seminar on International Security and Foreign Policy, November 8, 1983. This Chapter has benefited from critiques and suggestions from Richard Dekmejian, R. D. McLaurin, and Kate Shnayerson. Most of the information presented is based on research and interviews conducted in Lebanon in October 1982. Funding for the research and travel arrangements were provided by the Center for International Development at the University of Maryland - College Park.

117

groups. In fact, the Lebanese Forces are overwhelmingly Maronite in their composition. Thus their vision of what kind of Lebanon should emerge from the fighting of the last decade is a reflection of Maronite thinking. The Lebanese Forces are not a political party even though they are usually confused with the Kata'eb Social Democratic party (the Phalangists) in the news media. The Lebanese Forces began as a coalition of Maronite political and paramilitary groups, and is largely the creation of the late Bashir Gemayel to provide him with a power base that was independent of the Kata'eb. The parties that formed its original nucleus retain their independent identities and capacity for independent political action. However, that will not inhibit the Lebanese Forces from fielding their own candidates for public office—including that of the presidency—if the Lebanese Forces leadership decides this is the only way the interests of their principal constituencies—the Christian communities—can be protected. As long as Bashir Gemayel was alive this did not pose a problem since he was the Lebanese Forces' candidate for president. The eventual emergence of the Lebanese Forces as a serious political force to be reckoned with will remain regardless of whether their militia is disbanded or integrated into the Lebanese Army. As for the future of the militia itself, its commander, Fadi Frem, has stated that the militia must remain intact until all foreigners—meaning in particular Syrian and Palestinian forces—have left Lebanon.[1]

The enduring political strength of the Lebanese Forces does not ultimately rest with their militia, but with their organizational structure, the effectiveness of their social programs and their ability to mobilize the population they control for political action. The purposes for any such mobilization will be determined largely by the Lebanese Forces' vision of how an independent Lebanon should be reconstituted and how political power should be distributed among the sects.

In the short term the political role that the Lebanese Forces choose to play will depend upon how they respond to mounting pressures for a renegotiation of the terms of the National Pact of 1943 in a way that reflects the demographic reality of a Muslim majority. If the Lebanese Forces' vision of post-war Lebanon equates national reconciliation with the restoration of Maronite political hegemony over the country, more intercommunal fighting is inevitable. Under such circumstances, the closer the Lebanese Forces cooperate with the Lebanese government, the more the government will appear to be the instrument of one community's interests. The effect will become a self-fulfilling prophecy. The other sects will continue to resist the expansion of the government's authority and control over their populations, thereby creating the conditions favoring an alliance between

the government and the Lebanese Forces. If such a vicious circle oc-
curs, national reconciliation will be extremely difficult to achieve.
Similarly, since the Lebanese Forces represent the bulk of Christian
communities, the Lebanese government will find itself severely constrained in negotiating any new social covenant if its terms are opposed by the Lebanese Forces.

On the other hand, if the Lebanese Forces' vision of the rebuilding
of Lebanon includes acceptance of the redistribution of political power
and political representation that recognizes a Muslim majority, the
Lebanese Forces could play a decisive and constructive role in com-
mitting the Christian communities to that new social compact.

Most of the overlap of interests between the Lebanese Forces and
the government is in their stated common objective of securing the
evacuation of all foreign forces from Lebanon. The precedents for this
sort of collaboration exist in the very circumstances that led to the
creation of many of the activities of the Lebanese Forces in the first
place. Further, Bashir Gemayel had established the precedent of
covert cooperation with the regime of Elias Sarkis in an effort to
strengthen Sarkis' hand against the Syrians.[2] A positive symbiotic
relationship was thus established between the legitimate formal
authority of the relatively powerless Lebanese government and the *de
facto* military and political power of the Lebanese Forces.

However, in the event that the government begins to revert to the
conduct of politics as it was done before 1975, the Lebanese
Forces—with or without their militia—could provide the nucleus for a
social revolution. In this regard it is not just the objectives or accomplishments of the programs that are important to understanding
the staying power of the Lebanese Forces but their attitudes and
values concerning how Lebanon ought to be governed that count, too.
Chief among these is their conviction that the old style of politics pursued by the Christian and Muslim establishment in the past is both corrupt and bankrupt. There can be no returning to the old way of doing
business. Another is the premise that government employees are paid
by the citizenry and should therefore serve the citizenry. If the government officialdom cannot or will not do the job, the citizens must do it
themselves until such time as the bureaucracy is able and willing to
reassert its responsibility or until the citizens are able to sack the
nonresponsive personnel and replace them with more effective people.
This notion is relatively new in Lebanon, where the attitude of government leaders and public employees is a remnant of the legacy of
Ottoman rule—i.e., that government rule exists for the benefit of those
who hold power. If these values continue to be held by a majority of
the Lebanese Forces, some common ground exists between them and

the Shi'a populist movement, 'Amal. Any potential for cooperation, however, is likely to remain unexploited as long as sectarian tensions generated by dissatisfaction with continued Maronite domination of the government apparatus are unresolved.

Thus, if normalcy can be reestablished throughout the country, long-term support for and opposition to the Lebanese Forces may be less likely to manifest itself along sectarian lines than in the form of a struggle between those reform-minded Lebanese who are committed to meritocracy and effective performance in the operation of government versus those groups—Christian, Muslim, and Druze alike—who feel they have more to gain by a return to the old "neo-Ottoman" style of politics and government. Granted, the initial political battle lines appear at first to have a strong sectarian coloration for at least two reasons. One is an initial Muslim—especially Sunni Muslim—fear and distrust of what was essentially a Christian political movement and military force. As long as national reconciliation remains more of a slogan than anything else, this suspicion is not likely to subside. In fact, it has been reinforced by the ties the Lebanese Forces have with Israel, and by the Lebanese Forces massacres of Palestinians at Sabra and Shatila. The other reason is that political loyalties and claims to leadership in the Muslim communities have been more strongly based on ascriptive status—a cornerstone of the old style of politics—more than in the Christian communities.

## HISTORICAL CONTEXT

### Paralysis of the Government

The Lebanese Forces emerged in response to the increasing inability of the Lebanese government to carry out the tasks imposed upon it by its own mutually antagonistic elites, by various segments of the population and by pressures from the external environment. The history of that paralysis has been treated in detail elsewhere.[3] The basic factors that contributed to the government's inability to function effectively were:

*Lebanon's internal disunity stemming from a lack of consensus of Lebanon's political destiny.* At issue were such fundamental questions as whether Lebanon's existence as an independent and sovereign state was a permanent fact to be defended at all costs by the government and the armed forces. In this regard the conflict can be viewed as a clash between two fundamentally different political cultures. One can be labeled a conservative or "Lebanese nationalist" (with emphasis on the "Lebanese"). One's political identity is centered on Lebanon and satisfied within the Lebanese nation. Lebanon's independence and sovereignty are self-evident and permanent, not a transitory situation pending the country's absorption into some broader political order. For the Lebanon-centered nationalists, the ultimate purpose of government is to ensure the independence and sovereignty of Lebanon and the security of its population from internal and external threats. Particular stress is placed on Lebanon's uniqueness and its pluralist politics. While most of the adherents of the Lebanon-centered position are Christians, they include a large number of Druzes and Shi'as and a growing number of Sunni Muslims (particularly Sunni merchants).

The other political culture can be characterized as an Arab-centered culture with a strong pan-Arab orientation. Lebanese who gravitate toward this political culture would be quick to argue that they are more truly nationalist in a secular sense than their Lebanon-centered opponents. To them, Lebanon is an integral part of the Arab and Islamic worlds. Therefore one's political identity cannot be satisfied except by identifying with leaders, political movements or causes in the Arab world beyond Lebanon's borders. There is no perceived contradiction between loyalty to Lebanon and commitments to pan-Arab causes. First and foremost among these causes has been a commitment to the cause of the Palestinians, sometimes to the detriment of Lebanese territorial integrity or national security. Most of the political groups representing this culture either have branches operating in other Arab countries or are themselves branches of political parties operating in other parts of the Arab world. Thus this culture comprises many "non-Lebanese" political organizations and expressions. Their commitment to the permanence of Lebanon was equivocal in the eyes of the Lebanon-centered conservatives, often leaving the impression that they view Lebanon's existence as an independent entity at best as transitory and at worst, illegitimate. Those Arab-centered Lebanese who have believed that Lebanon should remain independent also believed that Lebanon's security could only be improved by full participation in inter-Arab politics and by closer alignment with the Arab states. While most supporters of the Arab-centered positions were Muslims they included a substantial number of followers from the Christian communities, particularly the Greek Orthodox.

The Arab-centered orientation of this political culture is underscored by the fact that the leadership in the executive committee of its most tangible expression, the National Movement, included a large number of non-Lebanese. In fact, the Palestinians largely controlled and coordinated most of the activities of the National Movement, a fact that even Kamal Jumblatt, the National Movement's leader, finally conceded.[4]

*A political system which was becoming increasingly unresponsive to the political demands from a growing number of "have-nots."* Most of these have-nots were concentrated in the Sunni, Shi'a, and Greek Orthodox communities whose grievances concerning discrimination in education, social services, and regional economic development were given only verbal acknowledgment by their own members of the ruling elite. The strength of the system had become confined to perpetuating the traditional governing elites and preventing the infusion of new blood at the top.

*The erosion of the political power of the traditional Sunni leaders.* The political power of the traditional Sunni leaders was based largely on ascriptive status and not on traditional tribal or clan loyalties or on geographically concentrated rural constituencies enjoyed by the Druze, Shi'a, or Maronite leaders. This erosion was caused partly by these politicians' inability to satisfy the growing demands of their followers for job opportunities and political reforms and partly because of the strong reformist appeal of the National Movement and the Palestinian Resistance Movement. This was combined with a high level of personal estrangement among the leading members of the Lebanese oligarchy in general even before the fighting in 1975. To forestall a further erosion of their political position the Sunni oligarchs concentrated on Christian–Muslim sectarian cleavages, blaming the ills of the political system on the Maronite 'monopoly' of power.[5] Consequently the traditional Sunni leadership was not in a position to cooperate with the Christians lest this cooperation lead to further defections of followers to the National Movement.[6] Given the pivotal role of an effective working rapport between the Maronite president and the Sunni prime minister, this estrangement among the members of the Lebanese ruling elite was a crippling blow to the continued functioning of the government. This problem was not confined to the Sunni communities. The traditional Shi'a leadership found itself confronted with a similar erosion of power to the charismatic Imam Moussa Sadr, the founder and leader of the Shi'a populist movement, *Harakat 'Amal.*

*Lebanon's inability to remain aloof from the Arab–Israeli conflict.* Although Lebanon was technically at war with Israel, it had managed to remain aloof from the Arab–Israeli conflict until the 1970s when the Palestinians began to use Lebanese territory as their main springboard for attacks on Israel. Syria, in turn, felt an increasing urgency to control Lebanese politics, partly for the purposes of retaining Lebanon as a buffer in any future war with Israel. Control of Lebanese politics required Syrian support of the Palestinian guerrillas in Lebanon and their pan-Arab allies.[7] One effect of this was fairly continuous Syrian pressure against any Lebanese attempts to suppress Palestinian guerrilla activity against Israel from Lebanese territory. Israel, in turn, felt compelled to intervene more directly in the conflict in Lebanon as the only way to compel Lebanese control over Palestinian activities within the country. This intervention involved escalating the severity and intensity of Israeli retaliatory strikes against targets in Lebanese territory until the government found the political courage to suppress Palestinian guerrilla activities from its territory.

The cumulative effect was total government immobility in foreign and domestic affairs that was intended to preserve Lebanon's fragile democracy without satisfying any of the principal antagonists, inside or outside the country. Unable to satisfy the demands of the Lebanese who wanted the repudiation of the Cairo Agreement and the expulsion of the Palestinians or the insistence of the National Movement and the traditional Muslim oligarchs on defense of the Palestinians and an alliance with pan-Arab and progressive forces against Israel, the government could only watch its position and authority crumble to total inaction by 1975.

The most obvious indication of government paralysis was the growth of private militias and paramilitary groups, particularly in the Lebanon-centered, mostly Maronite camp, matched by the growing dependence of the Arab-centered Lebanese and the National Movement on Palestinian military forces.

## Composition of Opposing Forces

Because Lebanese have fought on both sides and because the fighting has been confined to Lebanese territory, the conflict is usually viewed as a sectarian civil war. However, when the focus shifts to the national composition of the principal forces fighting on each side, it is seen that the war has been fought mainly between the predominantly Maronite militias (later absorbed into the integrated formations of the Lebanese Forces), on one side, against a coalition of Sunni and Shi'a Muslims, and some Christians plus the Palestinians and Syrians on the other, with the irregular forces of the National Movement (NM) playing a definitely subordinate role as an appendage of the Palestinian forces.[8] This is evidenced by the diversity of forces of which the NM is composed.

The NM was organized in 1969 by Kamal Jumblatt, a Druze feudal chieftain, who was its principal leader until his assassination in 1977. This group was a coalition of mostly Lebanese Muslim forces which supported the Palestinian Resistance Movement in Lebanon and branded as "isolationist" those Lebanese who were opposed to the expansion of Palestinian power and extraterritorial privileges on Lebanese territory. Its principal Lebanese military muscle consisted mainly of forces loyal to Jumblatt and the Mourabitoun, the military arm of the Independent Nasserite Movement (INM) lead by Ibrahim Qulailat and which was supplied and equipped by the Palestinians. Jumblatt's Druze militia, an extension of his Popular Socialist Party, seldom fought outside the Druze's ancestoral homeland, the Shuf. In addition, the NM fielded what might be called the Palestinian mixed forces led by Salah Khalaf (alias Abu Ayyad), the number two man in *al-Fatah*. It was Khalaf who declared that the road to Palestine ran through Jounieh, the predominantly Christian city north of Beirut.[9] To the Maronites and others in the Lebanon-centered camp, this was a clear indication of the extent to which the Palestinians had lost sight of their original objective. Militarily, however, the NM depended mainly upon military support from the Palestinian guerrilla forces in Lebanon.

As for its Lebanese constituency the National Movement's program for political reform appealed mainly to the Sunni, Shi'a, and some Christian communities but very little to the Druzes or Maronites. Many non-Maronite Christians, such as the Armenians, studiously avoided involvement in the conflict as did a very large portion of the Sunni community. Thus the NM's supporters and opponents cannot be said to correspond very directly to the Muslim and Christian communities respectively.

Similarly the confessional affiliations and the nationalities of many of the leaders in the NM belie the notion that war in Lebanon was largely a sectarian war reminiscent of the strife in Northern Ireland. Indeed the tendency to oversimplify the conflict in Lebanon by describing the adversaries in terms of confessional identities has undoubtedly contributed to the myth that the conflict has been mainly a sectarian war, in which the combatants were almost exclusively Lebanese. Prior to the Israeli invasion of Lebanon in June 1982 and the subsequent expulsion of the Palestinian forces from Beirut, the National Movement's Executive Committee consisted of three main factions, only one of which can be said to have been indigenously Lebanese. The main elements of the Lebanese wing were:

> Kamal Jumblatt's Progressive Socialist Party (PSP), whose major source of support has been the traditional Druze allegiance to the feudal Jumblatt family, but was also supported by some Christians. It is now lead by Kamal's son, Walid;

The pro-Libyan Independent Nasserite Movement, led by Ibrahim Qulailat, which derived most of its support from the lower middle class Sunni neighborhoods of Beirut;

A pro-Iraqi wing of the Ba'ath party whose supporters were a mixture of Sunnis, Shi'as and Greek Orthodox and;

Kamal Shatila's Union of Forces of the Working People (UFWP) which derived most of its support from lower class Shi'as in Beirut.

The second wing of the NM might be termed a mixed Lebanese–Palestinian wing. It consisted of a variety of Lebanese political groups who were closely aligned with various Palestinian guerrilla organizations. It was comprised of:

The Lebanese Communist Party (LCP), led by George Hawi, a Christian, and attracting followers from confessionally mixed districts but whose strongest support came mainly from individuals in the Greek Orthodox community;

The Syrian Social Nationalist Party (SSNP), the membership of which was a mixture of Greek Orthodox, Maronites, Druzes, Shi'as and Sunnis, with one wing led by In'am Ra'd, a Christian (aligned with al-Fatah), and another wing led by Abdullah Sa'ada (also a Christian) and aligned with the Popular Front for the Liberation of Palestinian (PFLP);

The Organization of Communist Action (OCA), led by Muhsin Ibrahim, a Muslim, a group appealing to workers and students in the urban areas and attracting mainly Catholics, Maronites, Sunnis and Shi'as; and

The Socialist Action Party, led by Hussein Hamdane, a Muslim, and closely aligned with the PFLP.

The purely Palestinian wing consisted of two major sub-groups;

That of Yasser Arafat, a Muslim, and leader of al-Fatah and the Palestine Liberation Organization; and Nayef Hawatmeh, a Christian, a Marxist, and leader of the Popular Democratic Front for the Liberation of Palestine (PDFLP); and

The Rejectionist Front represented by George Habash, a Christian, and commander-in-chief of the Popular Front for the Liberation of Palestine (PFLP), and Antoine (Ahmed) Jabril, a Christian, Marxist, and leader of the PFLP-General Command.

Thus the Palestinians largely controlled and coordinated most of the activities of the National Movement, a fact finally acknowledged by Jumblatt himself.

## The Political Context of the Fighting

The fundamental causes of political conflict in Lebanon have not arranged themselves very neatly around Christian-Muslim or rightist-leftist axes at all.[10] As pointed out earlier, one of the principal political divisions was not so much between left and right as between an Arab-centered versus a Lebanon-centered political culture. The Arab-centered vs. Lebanon-centered horizontal axis is not synonymous with the left-right continuum. This can be easily seen in Figure 6.1 by the fact that both wings of the SSNP are very much right-wing parties as far as the political philosophy is concerned. Therefore on a left-right continuum the SSNP would be located about three standard deviations to the right in the same quadrant as the NLP, the Kata'eb and the

**FIGURE 6.1   Location of major Lebanese political groups by political identity and confessional composition (ca. 1976–1981)**

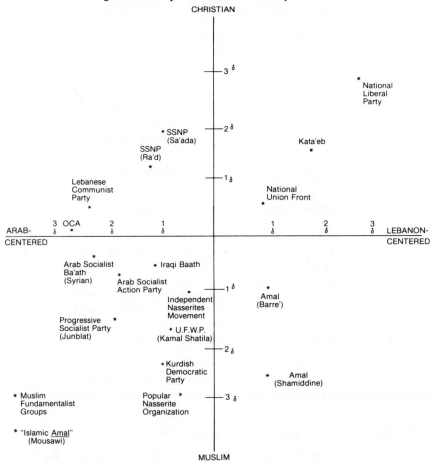

National Bloc. Similarly 'Amal would be located in the lower left quadrant instead of the lower right while the Muslim fundamentalist groups, of which the "Islamic 'Amal" is one, would be moved from the extreme left to the extreme right.

Most supporters of the Arab-centered position have been Muslims, but, as suggested earlier, they have included individuals of all ethnic and religious backgrounds who, since 1967, have been committed to the cause of the Palestinian resistance at the expense of Lebanon's security, independence and political sovereignty. The most tangible expression of the Arab nationalist political culture has been the National Movement described earlier. Its Arab-centered orientation is underscored by the fact that the leadership in its executive committee includes a large number of non-Lebanese. The most articulate expression of Lebanon-centered nationalism has been the Lebanese Forces.

## HISTORICAL ANTECEDENTS OF THE LEBANESE FORCES

The first observable manifestation of what was to become the Lebanese Forces was the necessity of the various Christian militias fighting in the Beirut area to operate as one coordinated force under a joint military command in the campaign to wrest control of the Tel al-Za'atar area from the Palestinians in June 1976. Prior to the Tel al-Za'atar operation, the militias had been fighting largely a defensive war just to prevent Palestinian and the National Movement forces from completely encircling East Beirut through the belt of fortified Palestinian positions surrounding the city. The belt began at Quarantina, at the north port of Beirut, and extended through al-Naba' to Tel al-Za'atar in the eastern suburbs, through Jisr al-Basha to Burj al-Burajnih and Sabra south of Beirut (see Figure 6.2). Strategically, Tel al-Za'atar was the most important of these as it occupied the high ground which dominated all of East Beirut and the port area. The Palestinians' control of the Qarantina district enabled them to cut the roads linking predominately Christian East Beirut to Jounieh and the north. Control of Tel Za'atar enabled the Palestinians to cut the roads linking East Beirut with the mountains. The only gaps in this fortified belt were portions of two predominately Christian neighborhoods in East Beirut, Ain al-Rummaneh and Sin al-Fil. These neighborhoods also dominated the few remaining roads linking Beirut to the hinterland that could not easily be cut by Palestinian forces. Principal among these were routes leading out of the city to the Beirut-Damascus highway. Had the Palestinians or their National Movement allies succeeded in occupying these neighborhoods, East Beirut would

## FIGURE 6.2   Map of Beirut, showing areas under Palestinian control (ca. December 1975)

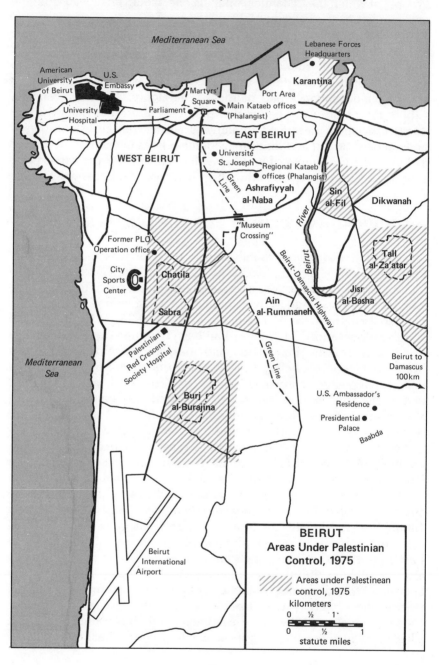

Mediterranean Sea

Lebanese Forces
Headquarters

American
University
of Beirut

U.S.
Embassy

Martyrs'
Square

Karantina

Port Area

University
Hospital

Parliament

Main Kataeb offices
(Phalangist)

EAST BEIRUT

WEST BEIRUT

Université
St. Joseph

Regional Kataeb
offices (Phalangist)

Ashrafiyyah
al-Naba

Sin
al-Fil

Dikwanah

Green Line

"Museum
Crossing"

Beirut River

Former PLO
Operation office

Tall
al-Za'atar

City
Sports
Center

Chatila

Beirut-Damascus Highway

Jisr
al-Basha

Sabra

Ain
al-Rummaneh

Green Line

Palestinian
Red Crescent
Society Hospital

Beirut to
Damascus
100 km

Mediterranean
Sea

Burj
al-Burajina

U.S. Ambassador's
Residence

Presidential
Palace

Baabda

### BEIRUT
### Areas Under Palestinian
### Control, 1975

Areas under Palestinean
control, 1975

Beirut
International
Airport

kilometers

0    ½    1

0    ½    1

statute miles

128

have been totally isolated from the rest of the country. Hence securing these neighborhoods (as well as parts of Ashrafiyyeh near the National Museum) had the highest priority for the Christian militias. As long as they were concerned mainly with defense, these militias could operate independently of one another without requiring very close coordination of operations beyond dividing the responsibility for the defense of various sectors. However, once the front stabilized to the point where the Christian forces could turn their attention to breaking the potential stranglehold of the Palestinians on East Beirut, coordination of these forces was absolutely essential. These militias had no experience to speak of in offensive operations requiring the close coordination of several forces. Prior offensive operations such as those against Dubayyah, Qarantina, or Maslakh either did not involve the participation of as many different militias or did not require very much coordination.

Tel al-Za'atar was the most logical target for two reasons. First, as was mentioned earlier, it was the strongest of the Palestinian fortified camps and dominated the predominately Christian sectors of Beirut and its links with the rest of Lebanon. Second, due to the paralysis of the political system the Christian militias could not count on the Lebanese Army to clear the area, as the army had begun to disintegrate by March 1976.

While the actual planning of the Tel al-Za'atar operation was done by career officers in the Lebanese Army working with representatives of the Tanzim[11] and the National Liberal Party (NLP), it soon became apparent to the planners that the size of the operation required the participation of all the nationalist militias operating in the area. The operation was carried out by six different military groups: 1) the Tanzim; 2) the Kata'eb militia; 3) the NLP militia (which provided about ninety percent of the logistical support for the operation); 4) the Guardians of the Cedars; 5) the Lebanese Youth Movement (a local militia defending the Dekouane quarter); and 6) infantry and artillery units of the Lebanese Army (mainly the Akkar Brigade). It was coordinated by a military command council composed of Bashir Gemayel (Kata'eb); Fouad Rouquis (Kata'eb); Dany Chamoun (NLP); Nabil Karim (NLP); Fawzi Mahfouz (Tanzim); and Etienne Sakr (Guardians of the Cedars).

## Significance of Tel al-Za'atar

The critical element sustaining the momentum toward increasingly unified operations was the awareness on the part of all the participants that they had to hang together or they would hang separately. Ideologically, these groups were quite homogeneous in that they all

perceived that they were fighting for the same basic purpose—to defend their homes and eventually to rid Lebanon of Palestinian occupation. The imperatives of a common defense took on a dynamic all their
own, independent of any political differences that existed between party leaders. Indeed, the Tel al-Za'atar campaign was planned by the
militia commanders and elements of the Lebanese Army independent
of the party leaders. The latter, who had constituted themselves as the
Lebanese Front (described below), simply approved the operation
after it was launched. This has implications for Lebanon's political
future. The relative independence of the military commanders from
the traditional or "historical" political leaders not only served to
minimize political differences, but thrust up a new generation of potential political leaders whose leadership qualities have been tested by a
decade of war and who have developed their own followings and their
own ideas about how Lebanon should be governed.

In an operational sense the Tel al-Za'atar campaign demonstrated
both the benefits and necessity of further coordination. While the
operation had been planned by career officers, most of the units that
took part in the battle were composed of irregulars. The number of
casualties they sustained and the equipment losses were extremely
heavy due to their inexperience and periodic breakdowns in coordination.[12] The experience at Tel al-Za'atar underscored the need for improved and standardized training of the Christian militias, and the continuing need for joint operations under a unified command. The formation of a joint command led to the pooling of resources and some stan-
dardization of procedures. Common radio frequencies, for example,
were established for all the militias. Another initiative was the pooling
of funds for purchasing of weapons and supplies. This was particularly
important as some of these militias were in competition with one
another for funds. The source of weapons was the black market.[13]
Some militias discovered that they were paying highly inflated prices
for the same weapons that another militia had acquired far more
cheaply from another source. By pooling their funds and sharing
sources of supply they were able to purchase their weapons less ex-
pensively than when each made its own purchases independently of
the others. Likewise, the unification of artillery efforts meant that
scarce ammunition could be husbanded and used more effectively
than if three or four different artillery groups were directly firing on the
same target. In short, there were very compelling incentives to unify
their operations on a long-term basis.

A permanent, unified command structure was formally established
August 30, 1976, with the creation of the Joint Command Council of the
Lebanese Forces with Bashir Gemayel as its first elected commander.

The evolution of its military formations is shown in Figure 6.3. In 1979 the Joint Command Council began creating integrated military formations that were separate and distinct from the party militias which all along continued to represent the military structures of their respective political parties. The integrated units were responsible only to the Joint Command Council. This was a critical step in reducing the political parties' capacity for independent action outside the framework of the Lebanese Forces.

**FIGURE 6.3   Evolution of Lebanese Forces, 1976–1980**

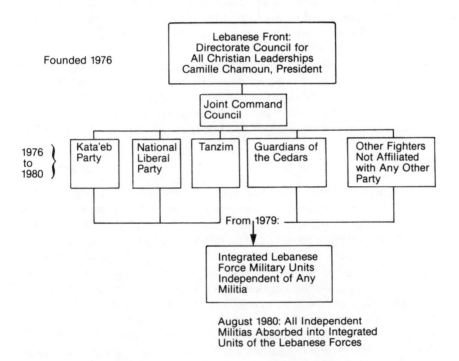

This integration, however, was not achieved without considerable friction. The Christian militias in northern Lebanon in particular, resisted the expanding presence of the Lebanese Forces. The growing friction between the Lebanese Forces and the Marada brigade led by Tony Frangieh, the son of former President Suleiman Frangieh, ultimately led to the former's death in June 1978.

The bloodiest clash occurred July 7, 1980, when Lebanese Forces units simultaneously attacked the barracks, offices, and other strongpoints belonging to Camille Chamoun's Tiger militia, killing as many as five hundred of their fellow Christians, most of whom were innocent bystanders according to the Chamounists.[14] Even though Chamounist sources later reduced the number killed to one hundred and fifty, the long-range repercussions went far beyond the shock of the magnitude of intracommunal bloodshed. The destruction of the Tigers and the absorption of their remnants into the Lebanese Forces meant that for the first time the Maronites were represented by a single organization. Those who were opposed to this consolidation could either seek the protection of the Syrians as had Suleiman Frangieh and remain in political isolation; or they could acquiesce to what was taking place by rationalizing that the "July seventh corrective movement" had eliminated a source of weakness within Christian ranks by ending the internecine fighting, and introduced a level of internal security unprecedented since 1975.

With the elimination of the Tiger militia, the autonomous existence of the original militias came to an end. This meant that the political groups comprising the Lebanese Forces no longer had any independent military structures of their own. They were completely absorbed into integrated units of the Lebanese Forces in August 1980.

## The Militia

The military arm of the Lebanese Forces remains a militia in the sense that it is basically a citizen army as distinct from a professional army. Many of its personnel hold civilian jobs or attend colleges at the same time as they are serving. The militia does not use the traditional system of military ranks. Authority derives from the responsibilities assigned to the commanders and other individuals.[15] However, as Figure 6.1 suggests, the organizational structure of the militia closely resembles that of a regular army (See Figure 6.3). Therein lies one of the militia's two most important sources of strength. Unlike the Morabitoun or the Popular Socialist Party forces, the Lebanese Forces' militia is now organized and trained to fight regular armies in nonurban terrain. This is worth noting, partly because most of the militia's combat experience was in city fighting, and partly because it says something about the type of war they expect to fight in the future.[16]

Currently the militia is organized along traditional military lines of brigade, battalion, company, platoon, and squadron. The formations are no longer limited to infantry but include armor (mostly Israeli-provided Super Shermans, AMX-13s, and Panhard armored cars), and artillery companies, as well as a special alpine brigade for fighting in the mountains, a corps of engineers, and a small navy. By 1983 it was estimated to have ten thousand to twelve thousand combat troops and the ability to mobilize at least another fifteen thousand reservists.

Doctrine specifies the kind of war an army must be prepared to fight and prescribes how that war shall be waged. Therefore, it implies who the enemy is likely to be. While the specifics of the militia's doctrine are difficult to obtain (partly because their doctrine was still in the process of being formally committed to paper as of early 1983), the broad outlines are reasonably clear.

The mission of the Lebanese Forces' militia is to rid Lebanon of all foreign forces. This implies being prepared to wage war not only against irregular forces, the Palestinian guerrillas, and their Lebanese allies like the Mourabitoun, but against regular armies such as Syria or possibly Israel. This means being able to wage war in rural as well as urban terrain. Since the Lebanese Forces militia can be expected to be inferior to a regular army in terms of manpower and firepower, its forces must be structured accordingly. Thus they must take advantage of Lebanon's mountainous terrain. Terrain in turn provides insights into force structuring and weapons procurement. Mortars, for example, are likely to provide more effective artillery support than howitzers and they are more mobile and easier to shield from air attack. Anti-tank weapons—especially Milan and TOW—enable Lebanese Forces to challenge tank formations more effectively in mountainous terrain with heavy vegetation than a fleet of M-60s or AMX-30s (although Panhard AML-90s might prove quite serviceable under these conditions). The terrain itself may serve as one effective form of air defense. Radar placed along mountain peaks can provide almost as much early warning of intruding enemy aircraft as an airborne platform such as the Grumman E-2C Hawkeye. Obviously terrain does not provide the answer to every problem, but the militia is trying to adapt tactics and weapons to its best advantage.

While the majority of the militia's personnel are volunteers, a system of conscription has been established as of July 1982. This system is based on a preconscription training program established two years earlier in the secondary schools. The preconscript program consists of a two-year program of training on weekends and in the summer (21 days) for all students (male and female) at the junior and senior grades in high school. After graduation, the conscripts undergo three months of basic training, and two months of specialized training, followed by ten months of actual military service. The number of people passing through this conscript program is not known for certain, but it could run as high as two thousand to twenty-five hundred a year considering that both men and women are conscripted.[17]

More important than sheer numbers, however (the militia more than trebled in size from four thousand to twelve thousand troops and reservists in 1981), is its social composition. That is its second main source of strength. Its ranks include lawyers, business people, engineers, college faculty members, and students as well as young people from both working and middle class strata. While the majority of its personnel are predominately Maronite, their ranks include Greek Catholics, Greek Orthodox, American Catholics, Assyrians, and other Christians. An estimated five to seven percent of the personnel are Muslims. It is definitely not a collection of urban *gabadai* commanding street gangs of lower-class inner-city youth with nowhere else to go as appears to be the case with, say, the Mourabitoun.[18] The quality of the personnel cannot help but have a positive impact on the combat effectiveness of the militia.

## The Lebanese Front

Parallel to the development of a unified military force was the creation of the Lebanese Front, which is a directory council for all the Christian leaderships in Lebanon and in that capacity it defines the broad lines of the general policy that are implemented and enforced by the Lebanese Forces. The first attempt at forming a front was the creation of the Front for Freedom and Man in Lebanon in early 1976.[19] It was composed of a mixture of "historic" party leaders and heads of militias. The Front was initially a response to the fighting that erupted in Beirut in April 1975, when various Maronite political leaders, recognizing the gravity of the threat to their community, began to grope for a formula for unified political action, as government services deteriorated to the point of collapse. In addition to Camille Chamoun, Pierre Gemayel, Suleiman Frangieh, Charles Malek, and Father Sharbal Qassis, head of the Maronite Order of Monks, this front included Fouad Shamali, head of the Tanzim militia, Sa'id 'Aql, head of the Guardians of the Cedars, and Marun al-Khouri, head of the Lebanese Youth Movement.

The composition of the Front has remained fairly stable with the exception of the withdrawal of Suleiman Frangieh. Frangieh had stopped attending the meetings of the Front in May 1978 reportedly because of his opposition to turning to Israel for military and political support against the Front's erstwhile ally, Syria. He became estranged from the Front altogether after the killing of his son Tony by Lebanese Forces gunmen at the Franjieh summer residence in Ehden on June 13, 1978.[20]

Currently the Front is composed of:

- Camille Chamoun, President of the front, former president of Lebanon and leader of the NLP;
- Pierre Gemayel, president of the Kata'eb Social Democratic Party;
- Edouard Honein, secretary of the front, member of Parliament, and formerly a member of the National Bloc Party;
- Abbott Boulos Na'aman, head of the Permanent Congress of the Lebanese Monastic Orders;
- Dr. Charles Malek, former Minister of Foreign Affairs and former president of the United Nations General Assembly;
- Dr. Fouad Ephrem Boustany, former president of the Lebanese University, historian and writer.

What might be regarded as the "national charter" of the current Lebanese Front is a set of guidelines for political action drawn up during a retreat held at the monastery of *Sayyaditna Bi'r* (Our Lady of the Well), in January 1977 and attended by all the leaders of the Christian communities. The document was signed by the major "historic leaders" of Lebanon at the time: Camille Chamoun, Pierre Gemayel, Suleiman Frangieh, and Father Sharbal Qassis. The document can be considered a formal expression of the political will of the Maronite Christian communities in Lebanon.[21] The principal elements of the charter are:

- Lebanon's sovereignty and political independence cannot be qualified in any way;
- Lebanon will not be absorbed into some greater political entity or transformed in any way that will cause its distinctive characteristics (i.e., its republican, democratic, parliamentary, pluralist, and free and open society) to disappear;
- It is necessary to reconsider the structural formula (The National Pact) of 1943 which is a basic determinant of Lebanese politics, with the aim of "modifying it in such a way as to prevent any friction or clash between the members of the same Lebanese family." Such a reconsideration might take the form of an alteration of the National Pact formula to accommodate some sort of decentralization or federation within a comprehensive framework of a single unified Lebanon. The aim of any such alteration is to insure that no disaster like the many disasters which have plagued Lebanon since 1840 will recur in the future;
- The Christian communities do not want more for themselves than they want for other communities, but they do not accept less for themselves than other communities want for themselves;
- Absolute rejection of the settlement of foreigners, "particularly of Palestinians" on any part of Lebanese territory including the abrogation of all sales or transfers of real estate which have occurred enabling Palestinians—directly or indirectly—to own property in Lebanon; and
- No partition.[22]

While these declarations can only be considered the legitimate expressions of the Maronite Christian communities, they are expressed in a tone which gives them more of a national character than one which is Maronite or even Christian in any particularistic sense. This is quite apparent in the declared willingness of the Maronite leadership to consider some alteration of the National Pact formula for determining the future politics of Lebanon.

The point about partition is particularly significant since circumstances favoring partition have actually increased since 1980. For example:

- Geographically the Christian communities are concentrated in areas that are territorially contiguous and therefore relatively easy to defend.
- These areas are unoccupied by foreign forces.
- Governmental infrastructure has already been established to the point that if necessary, a new "state within a state" (in a far stricter sense than the Palestinians were accused of building) could spring up with its capital at Jounieh.

The Maronites and other like-minded Christians have had ample opportunity to ponder the costs and benefits of partition and have found it singularly unattractive.[23] This position on partition and a willingness to renegotiate the terms of the National Pact not only imply a willingness to negotiate much-needed, overdue reforms with other confessional and political groups; they also imply that continued occupation of Lebanon by Israeli forces is as odious as is the continued presence of the Syrians and the Palestinians. Thus the Front's position is not merely a lofty-sounding defense of a status quo in support of a privileged position for the Christian communities in Lebanon's politics. What is not clear is what, in the Front's view, constitutes an acceptable range of negotiating partners. A source of concern is the apparent absence of a leadership in the Muslim communities that will be able to commit those communities to any agreement that is eventually negotiated.

From the time of the declaration of *Sayyiditna Bi'r* the Front for Freedom and Man in Lebanon simply became the Lebanese Front. It was also in 1977 that the composition of the Front was modified to comprise only civilian political leaders and intellectuals. The heads of the militias had already organized themselves in their own Joint Command Council in August 1976. Militia leaders attended meetings of the Front when military matters were discussed. This structure reinforces the division between the "historical" Maronite leadership, which dominates the Front and a generation of much younger leaders on the

Joint Command Council. It is the Joint Command Council, not the Lebanese Front, which is the real executive organ of the Lebanese Forces, *and* the Lebanese Front. This division of labor makes sense as long as active defense of the Christian communities is the principal and immediate concern. However, as negotiations over the restructuring of Lebanese political life proceed apace, differences between the historical leadership and the younger leaders over what sort of concessions should be made to the other communities may emerge.

Historically, then, what emerged as the Lebanese Forces initially represented the Maronite Christian community. However, the language, the policy orientation and some of the activities of the Front suggest a view of Lebanon's problems, politics and approaches to post-war recovery that speak to a much broader constituency than just to the Christians. It is to a description and evaluation of the Lebanese Forces as a potential national political movement that we now turn.

## CURRENT STRUCTURE AND ACTIVITIES OF THE LEBANESE FORCES

Figure 6.4 presents an overview of the organizational structure and breadth of activities of the Lebanese Forces. This structure was formally constituted August 26, 1980, after the approval of all parties. Even a cursory glance at the chart of Figure 6.4 strongly suggests that the Lebanese Forces cannot be considered a mere collection of militias operating under the direction of a group of politicians. The military constitutes only one wing of the Lebanese Forces. In addition, the military wing has been restructured along the lines of a regular army with a formal chain of command and a clear-cut division of responsibilities. The civilian activities are what make the Lebanese Forces a political movement, not just a military organization.

It would be a mistake to assume that the Lebanese Forces are merely an extension of any of the original political parties or militias from which it has evolved. While the Kata'eb party appears to be a dominant component of the Lebanese Forces, the appearance is stronger than the substance. The Lebanese Forces were created as an organization independent of the Kata'eb. Many of the personnel in positions of responsibility and authority have weak or no formal ties to the Kata'eb. Further, a large proportion of the Lebanese Forces militia are drawn from the urban areas, particularly from the working class suburbs of Beirut. The traditional source of manpower for the old Kata'eb militia was from the villages in the mountains. The Lebanese Forces include another large group sometimes referred to as *Ansar al-Kata'eb*

**FIGURE 6.4 Organizational structure of the Lebanese Forces as of November 1980**

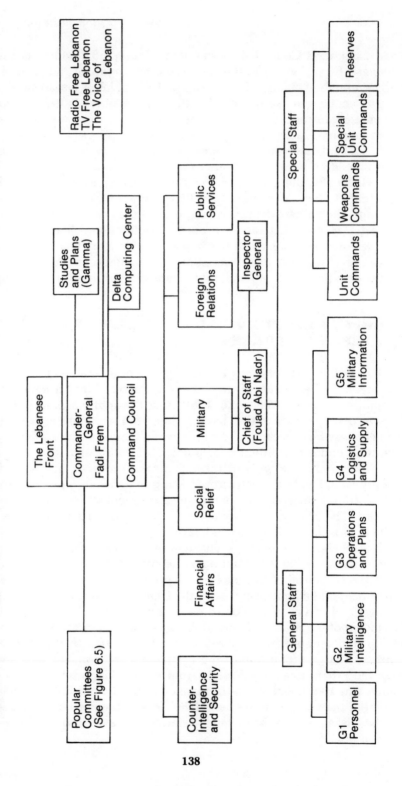

(Associates of the Kata'eb). These are mainly Christians who were either displaced by the fighting or who originally gravitated toward the Kata'eb at a time when it was one of the few paramilitary organizations able to provide many anxious Lebanese with the weapons and training to defend themselves. The commitment of these people to the Lebanese Forces may be taken for granted, but their commitment to the Kata'eb cannot. Thus the Lebanese Forces cannot be considered a reliable instrument of Amin Gemayel.

## The Command Council

As Figure 6.4 suggests, the key executive organ is the Command Council of the Lebanese Forces. The chief executive of this body is the Commander General. Bashir Gemayel occupied this position until September 13, 1982. He was succeeded by Fadi Frem who was elected to the position the day before Bashir's assassination. The Command Council is composed of eight representatives of the four principal militias that made up previous joint commands: the Kata'eb, the Tanzim, the NLP, and the Guardians of the Cedars. The Command Council also includes as nonvoting members the heads of the offices of Foreign Relations, Finance, Public Services, and the Chief of Staff of their armed forces. The Command Council is also the executive organ for the Lebanese Front. It has centralized control of all the activities of the Lebanese Forces.

## ACTIVITIES OF THE LEBANESE FORCES AND CENTRAL GOVERNMENT AUTHORITY

The official position of the Lebanese Forces is that none of its activities has been aimed against the Lebanese government, nor are they intended to compete with the government's administrative apparatus. That position is open to question, since the tax collection and conscription activities of the Lebanese Forces by definition assume an alternative legitimacy structure to that of the central government. Another awkward contradiction is the Forces' habit of ignoring or overriding the authority of the Lebanese Army when it suits their purposes.[24] Nevertheless, many of the public services performed by the civilian offices of the Lebanese Forces began as efforts to prod various branches of the government to perform the functions and responsibilities with which they were formally charged. The stated policy of the Lebanese Forces is to use its resources and its organization to support the government in whatever areas the government chooses to reassert itself. Further, the civilian components of the Lebanese Forces have been very careful to operate within the framework of written Lebanese Law. For example, in the absence of effective government, the Lebanese Front today considers its representation of the communities controlled by the Lebanese Forces to be legal in the sense that the Front is a legitimate expression of their collective will.

The expression of legitimacy extends only to the Lebanese Forces' caretaker role pending the restoration of government authority. The organization chart in Figure 6.4 represents in effect the activities and responsibilities assumed by the Lebanese Forces in response to the void created by the collapse of government services and the need to mobilize the civilian population in times of crisis. As shown in the chart in Figure 6.4, the Commander General and the Command Council maintain direct contact with the population down to the village/neighborhood level through the Popular Committee (discussed in detail below). The Command Council is further able to remain in constant contact with the population and to mobilize it in times of crisis through its operation of two radio stations (Radio Free Lebanon and the Voice of Lebanon) and a television station (TV Free Lebanon) which has not yet begun telecasting. For example, on July 1, 1978, when Syrian artillery suddenly began shelling Ashrafiyyeh, Lebanese Forces radios broadcast the telephone numbers of an emergency hotline where people could call if they needed assistance. Similarly these radios broadcast the names of people arrested for profiteering (e.g., selling gasoline diluted with diesel fuel and selling items above the price-control ceilings set by the Lebanese Forces). This helped maintain public order and served as a deterrent to other would-be profiteers.

The Command Council is also supported by the Delta and Gamma groups. The Delta Group is the Lebanese Forces' computing center. Established in 1981, its initial purpose is to provide for automation and systematic management of the Lebanese Forces' enterprises and the storage and retrieval of data. Gamma is a planning group composed of technicians and experts who are engaged in studying Lebanon's fragile physical and social infrastructure and in preparing plans for its reconstruction and future development. The studies and planning include the economy as a whole, agriculture, industry, finance, electricity, water, sewage, roads, telecommunications, and education.

The work of the Gamma Group is one observable manifestation of the Lebanese Forces' gradual evolution from a Christian political movement to a potential national political movement.

## Civilian Services and Social Relief Functions

Most activities performed by the Lebanese Forces that have important long-term political and social implications fall under the areas of public services, social relief, financial affairs and foreign relations. It has already been mentioned that most of the Lebanese Forces' civilian activities originated from the need to provide essential services and public order to the populations under its control in the wake of the collapse of all government services. Moreover, experience showed that their combat units fought harder and more effectively if they were defending heavily populated areas instead of empty neighborhoods which had been evacuated.

## Public Services

Just as the unification of the Lebanese national militias and the political groups was an evolutionary process born of necessity, so too was the Office of Public Services. Initially many neighborhoods responded individually to various emergencies and then gradually began to pool their resources and to unify their efforts. Among the more important activities that continued to be carried on are:

- A transportation organization to move people, most of whom do not have automobiles (the government has not operated any trains or buses since 1975).
- The creation of more public beaches in Lebanon. Previously most of the beaches in Lebanon were private and charged entry fees that were prohibitively expensive for lower income Lebanese.
- Traffic managment and security involving the marking of dangerous intersections and the creation of public parking lots inside the city.[25]
- Price control, which is probably the most difficult public service project. Every morning the prices of 200 items deemed essential for daily living are published in the newspapers and broadcast over the Lebanese Forces' radio. The population is also urged to turn in the names of merchants selling these items at prices above the ceilings. The names of those arrested and punished are also broadcast.
- Consumer protection such as checking to make sure that service station dealers are not mixing cheaper diesel fuel with the gasoline they were selling or altering the calibration on their pumps to register a higher volume of gasoline pumped than was actually sold.[26]
- Preservation of public assets by taking a complete inventory of all vehicles, movable property, and materials belonging to the ministries and municipalities in areas under Lebanese Forces' control.
- The documentation of major public service problems in Lebanon in such areas as water, electricity, telephones, roads, and traffic control.

These services are available to all members of the population—Christian and Muslim alike—living in areas controlled by the Lebanese Forces. All of these activities have been undertaken by volunteers and the only paid personnel are a secretary and two drivers. The attendants who operate the parking lots are disabled fighters who are also paid a salary supported by the revenues taken in by charging one Lebanese pound (about 25 cents) per car per day.

## Public Order and Security

The most essential public service in any organized society is the maintenance of public order and the personal security of the population. This was the public service that was the first victim of the fighting which broke out in 1975 and the lack of it led to the entry of Syrian Forces into Lebanon in 1976 (as part of a deal brokered by the United States between Israel and Syria) and eventually the Syrian occupation of most of the country in 1978.

Table 6.1 presents a comparative tabulation of crimes committed across various categories of criminality between the areas controlled by the Lebanese Forces and the rest of Lebanon in 1981. The data are from the files of the Lebanese Internal Security Forces who, even if they were powerless to intervene in acts of criminality or to arrest the perpetrators, at least kept records of the incidence of crime. The Internal Security Forces were about the only government organization that maintained very much coherence and continued to function (if not very effectively) throughout the country regardless of which forces were occupying particular regions or districts.

In evaluating the data presented in the table attention should be paid to the differentials in population densities between the sectors controlled by the Lebanese Forces and the rest of Lebanon. The population density in Lebanese Forces' controlled territories is 1,244 per square kilometer whereas the average density of the rest of Lebanon is 285 per square kilometer. Thus the potential for incidence of criminality is higher in territories controlled by the Lebanese Forces than in the rest of the country. However, even a cursory glance at the figures in the table indicates that the opposite happened in 1981. In every category of crime the incidence is higher—usually dramatically higher—in the territories not under Lebanese Forces' control.

Particularly interesting is the near absence of incidents in the category of "armed clashes" for Lebanese Forces' territory. Assuming no systematic distortions in the data, this is rather remarkable when it is remembered that the population is very heavily armed and that gunfights between citizens over such incidents as contested parking places

**TABLE 6.1 Comparative Table of Criminality in Lebanon From January 1st To December 31st 1981**

| Type of Crime Event | January O.F. | January L.F. | February O.F. | February L.F. | March O.F. | March L.F. | April O.F. | April L.F. | May O.F. | May L.F. | June O.F. | June L.F. | July O.F. | July L.F. | August O.F. | August L.F. | September O.F. | September L.F. | October O.F. | October L.F. | November O.F. | November L.F. | December O.F. | December L.F. | Total O.F. | Total L.F. |
|---|---|---|---|---|---|---|---|---|---|---|---|---|---|---|---|---|---|---|---|---|---|---|---|---|---|---|
| Murders | 18 | 3 | 26 | 5 | 41 | 3 | 24 | 1 | 50 | 2 | 33 | 4 | 40 | 1 | 46 | 3 | 31 | 2 | 46 | 3 | 29 | 3 | 33 | 5 | 417 | 35 |
| Attempted Murders | 9 | 2 | 22 | 1 | 24 | 2 | 21 | 1 | 29 | — | 18 | — | 28 | 1 | 44 | 4 | 31 | 1 | 45 | 3 | 16 | — | 36 | 1 | 323 | 15 |
| Theft | 20 | — | 43 | 2 | 44 | 4 | 19 | — | 26 | — | 23 | 4 | 39 | 3 | 56 | 6 | 38 | 3 | 36 | 3 | 42 | 5 | 44 | 4 | 430 | 34 |
| Armed Robbery | 10 | — | 18 | — | 14 | 1 | 22 | 2 | 43 | — | 32 | — | 40 | 2 | 26 | 1 | 45 | — | 30 | — | 36 | — | 40 | 1 | 356 | 8 |
| Kidnappings | 3 | — | — | — | 1 | — | 1 | — | 1 | — | 2 | — | 7 | — | 1 | — | 4 | 1 | 6 | 1 | 3 | 3 | 4 | — | 33 | 6 |
| Fraud and Swindles | 2 | — | 3 | 1 | — | — | 1 | — | — | — | — | — | 1 | — | 2 | — | 4 | — | 2 | — | 3 | 1 | 4 | — | 22 | 2 |
| Drug Smuggling and Dealing | 8 | 1 | 9 | — | 12 | — | 4 | — | 1 | — | 4 | — | 5 | — | 3 | 1 | 10 | — | 13 | — | 11 | 1 | 9 | — | 89 | 3 |
| Terrorism and Explosives | 41 | 1 | 46 | 10 | 60 | 6 | 56 | 3 | 2 | 1 | 32 | 5 | 26 | 5 | 41 | 1 | 48 | 3 | 88 | 3 | 44 | 8 | 61 | 5 | 568 | 51 |
| Aggression Against Embassies | 1 | — | 2 | — | 4 | — | 5 | — | 4 | — | 4 | — | 3 | — | 1 | — | 2 | — | — | — | — | — | 2 | — | 28 | — |
| Aggression Against Police and Army | 3 | — | 1 | — | 5 | — | — | — | 3 | — | 4 | — | 5 | — | 10 | 2 | 13 | 3 | 16 | 3 | 11 | 1 | 9 | 1 | 80 | 10 |
| Aggression Against UNIFIL | 3 | — | — | — | — | — | — | — | — | — | 4 | — | — | — | 2 | — | — | — | 4 | — | 2 | — | 2 | — | 17 | — |
| Aggression Against ADF | — | — | — | — | — | — | — | — | 1 | — | 1 | — | — | — | 2 | — | 1 | — | — | — | 3 | — | 1 | — | 9 | — |
| Armed Clashes | 10 | — | 4 | — | 14 | — | 16 | — | 24 | — | 19 | — | 21 | — | 27 | — | 20 | 1 | 24 | — | 10 | 1 | 17 | — | 206 | 2 |
| Total Crimes By Month | 128 | 7 | 174 | 20 | 219 | 16 | 169 | 7 | 207 | 3 | 176 | 13 | 215 | 13 | 261 | 19 | 247 | 13 | 310 | 16 | 210 | 23 | 262 | 16 | 2578 | 166 |
| Dead | 59 | 4 | 45 | 9 | 95 | 4 | 37 | 3 | 57 | 2 | 45 | 4 | 64 | 2 | 78 | 2 | 47 | 2 | 54 | 3 | 41 | 6 | 100 | 6 | 722 | 47 |
| Wounded | 50 | 5 | 54 | 8 | 60 | 5 | 40 | 1 | 47 | — | 63 | 2 | 137 | 7 | 113 | 4 | 46 | 2 | 108 | 6 | 59 | 10 | 201 | 4 | 978 | 54 |
| Automobile Thefts | 8 | — | 11 | — | 9 | — | 10 | 1 | 24 | — | 26 | — | 24 | — | 19 | — | 22 | — | 18 | — | 20 | — | 20 | — | 211 | 2 |
| Money Thefts in Million of $L Lebanese | 2605 | — | 1624 | — | 1468 | 160 | 1923 | 1 | 2239 | — | 1338 | 45 | 4080 | 202 | 3532 | 362 | 9589 | 30 | 1668 | — | 1448 | 62 | 4089 | 340 | 35.503 | 1,202 |

* O.F. = Other Forces
L.F. = Lebanese Forces
Source: Rep. of Leb. Internal Security Forces

Population Estimate in millions
1.00 in 804 km² areas controlled by Lebanese Forces
2.75 in 9648 km² areas controlled by Other Forces

Population Density:
1.244/sq km areas controlled by Lebanese Forces
286/sq km areas controlled by Other Forces

143

and failure to yield the right of way used to break out rather frequently. Equally interesting are the lopsided totals for dead and wounded in the Lebanese Forces sector as compared with the rest of the country.

## Social Relief

Most of the programs under the heading of Social Relief are those which concentrate on aiding citizens who have been victimized by the war. The most prominent of these is HELP Lebanon (Humanitarian Endowment for the Lebanese People). With a voluntary staff of over 350 people, many of them trained psychologists and psychiatrists, the program concentrates on rehabilitating children and adolescents who have been traumatized by the war. Founded in 1978 at the behest of Bashir Gemayel, HELP Lebanon has concentrated its efforts on five principal programs.

- Summer camps for children who have emotional disturbances caused by the war. Each year some three thousand children are taken to these camps in order to introduce them to a semblance of normal life.
- J.A.D. (Jeunesse Anti-Drug) which is aimed at reversing the effects of drug abuse among Lebanese youth that developed during the war (prior to the war drug abuse was not a serious problem among the Lebanese population). Its two principal activities are: a) finding as many drug dealers as possible and having them arrested; and b) finding as many addicts as possible and entering them in a detoxification program followed by counseling by two psychiatrists for a period of one year or more.
- CAMP or *Centre Aide Medio-Psychologique* which treats all children in the areas traumatized by the war. Here children are given a battery of psychological tests so that emotional or psychological problems can be treated as early as possible.
- A career guidance and counseling program for Lebanese youth at the junior and senior years in high school to channel them into occupations that are in high demand in Lebanon and away from those (such as law) which are overcrowded.
- ROOTS, which establishes and strengthens contacts with the children of Lebanese emigrants abroad. It includes sponsoring trips to Lebanon for children from the emigrant communities who are brought there in groups of twenty at a time for a period of one month. During this period they are shown the country and introduced to their cultural heritage.

All of these programs and services are available to the populations living in the areas controlled by the Lebanese Forces without any distinction made regarding confessional membership.

## Foreign Affairs

Mobilizing the expatriate Lebanese communities is also one of the responsibilities of the Lebanese Forces' Foreign Affairs office. Apart from mobilizing Lebanese communities abroad, the principal mission of the Foreign Affairs office is to make the Lebanese Forces' positions known to governments and to the public. This work does not necessarily imply that the Lebanese Forces have a foreign policy which is separate and distinct from the Lebanese government. Since 1976 and the Syrian occupation of Lebanon, the Lebanese government has not articulated, let alone pursued, a coherent foreign policy as such. President Sarkis, for example, did not attend the Arab summit conference in Amman in November 1981 because of Syrian pressure. For similar reasons, the government could not very well develop a strictly *Lebanese* response to the Camp David accords. Nor has it taken a stand on the Reagan peace initiative of September 1982.

The Foreign Affairs office was originally created with the aim of activating the Lebanese embassies in key capitals which had become dormant. The need to explain the positions of the Lebanese Forces and the communities they represent directly to various foreign powers became particularly important as the United States government became persuaded of the need for Syrian intervention in Lebanon in order to separate the combatants and to restore order. The need for such direct representation grew under the Carter administration whose position toward Lebanon was one of benign neglect. Currently the Foreign Affairs branch operates offices in Washington, Paris, Geneva, and Bonn.

## Finance

All these programs require financing. Since the Lebanese Forces operate as a governing body in the areas under their control, but without the formal authority of the government, the levying and collection of taxes is a delicate business.

While the Lebanese Forces do levy a graduated surcharge on households, most of the revenues come from indirect taxes. Apart from lacking formal authority to collect taxes, the Lebanese Forces seemed to have realized as far back as 1976 that there were limits to how much revenue could come from direct taxes. One reason was that the war had caused so much unemployment. Therefore, it was impolitic and unfair to try to generate much revenue in this way. A persistent effort to levy direct taxes only risked undermining the popular support the movement enjoyed.

Tax revenues are collected through a rather elaborate system that includes a one pound (roughly twenty-five cents) surcharge on cinema tickets and a two percent surcharge on restaurant meals and gasoline. Until 1982 sizable proportions of revenues came from duties levied on goods entering and leaving the ports of Jounieh and the northern port area of Beirut. Lebanese Forces officials claimed their ports handled three to five times as much tonnage as the official port in Beirut. One reason is that a cargo at Jounieh could be unloaded and in the receiver's hands in one day while it took an average of three days to turn around a cargo at the official port in Beirut. The Lebanese Forces turned their port in Beirut over to the government in 1982.

Additional revenues came from businesses. The transportation company operated by the Public Services office, for instance, is supported by a business called "Busstop". This is a company that was created to build sheltered waiting areas for the riders served by the Lebanese Forces' transportation system. These covered waiting areas sell advertising space on the walls to generate the revenues needed to support the transit operations.

The proportion of total revenues received from foreign assistance is unknown. Israel had been providing military aid including training since 1976, but the amount of Israeli financial support has not been made public.

More important than the actual amount of revenues raised through taxation is the fact that an effective system of taxation exists. The Lebanese Forces have arrogated for themselves the prerogatives of the state as long as they enforce their special tax levies and continue to control any port revenues. Inevitably these activities, which are the sole prerogatives of the government, must lead to a clash of interest between the Lebanese Forces and the central government—even a government run by a Phalangist president. The reason is not hard to understand. Taxation in its many forms is one government activity that links the population with political elites. Very few government activities affect the lives of most individuals in society so directly as taxation. Fewer still are avoided so persistently or levied so vigorously, and for good reason. Without a steady flow of revenue there is no government control, and no organized society. The levying and collecting of taxes are two activities that are clear indicators of the government's ability to penetrate the population and extract resources from it in pursuit of government objectives. Since taxation is one instrument for maintaining control over the population, the Lebanese Forces are not likely to relinquish these activities gracefully. Yet as long as they continue to siphon off state revenues, the Lebanese Forces will constitute a potential threat to the government that is far more serious than the size and organization of their militia alone would suggest.

## The Popular Committees

Apart from the tax levies, the key element that keeps the Lebanese Forces in close contact with the population and *vice versa* is the system of popular committees. These committees began as an effort by the Kata'eb to enlist the cooperation and participation of nonparty members in mobilizing community resources to support the militias and to fill the void left by the government in providing basic social services. As of 1982 there were 122 popular committees operating in territory controlled by the Lebanese Forces.

Figure 6.5 summarizes the organization structure of the popular committees. The organization of the popular committees is parallel to the administrative organization of the country itself. That is, the office of the General Coordinator functions at the equivalent to the Muhafazat (governorate) level. It might be considered as a central committee since the division of its responsibilities is parallel to those at the county and village level. It is in direct contact with the popular committees organized at the caza (qadhā or district) level. The Lebanese control those parts of seven cazas that are not occupied by Syrian forces or Druze militias. These are the six cazas in the Mount Lebanon governorate—Jubayl, Kesrouane, Metn, Ba'abda, 'Aley and the Shuf—plus the caza of Beirut which is a governorate by itself. Each popular committee at the caza level supervises the popular committees organized at the village or neighborhood level within that caza. Every popular committee has the same organizational structure at every level. Its executive organ consists of a president, or chairman, a vice-president, a secretary, a treasurer and a head of subcommittees of which there are 11:

1. *Health,* which is concerned with the operation of hospitals, pharmacies, and dispensaries. Activities include providing surgeons blood plasma, establishing vaccination programs, administering blood tests, providing drugs for pharmacies, and handling all medical emergencies as well as testing water, foodstuffs, and responding to epidemics such as typhoid.
2. *Education,* which involves supervising schools and in some cases opening schools, providing teachers and providing educational facilities for needy people.
3. *Finance,* which handles the funding of the committee which comes from a budget provided by the Lebanese Forces.
4. *Environment,* which is concerned with cleaning streets, beaches, preventing the cutting of trees, and reforestation.
5. *Civil Defense,* which is responsible for maintaining shelters, supplies of blood plasma, providing first aid facilities, and directing the population on where to go and what to do during an emergency.

# FIGURE 6.5 Organizational structure of the popular committees

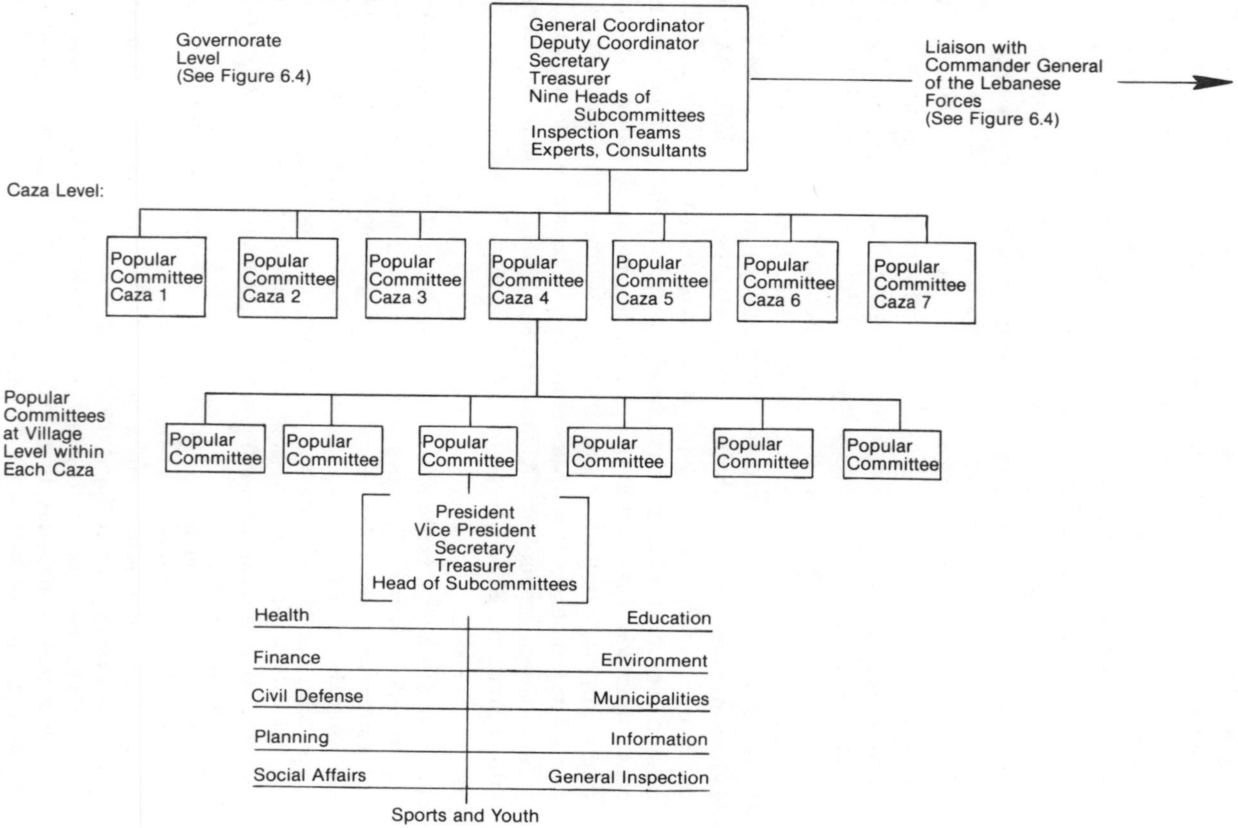

Governorate
Level
(See Figure 6.4)

Liaison with
Commander General
of the Lebanese
Forces
(See Figure 6.4)

General Coordinator
Deputy Coordinator
Secretary
Treasurer
Nine Heads of
Subcommittees
Inspection Teams
Experts, Consultants

Caza Level:

| Popular Committee Caza 1 | Popular Committee Caza 2 | Popular Committee Caza 3 | Popular Committee Caza 4 | Popular Committee Caza 5 | Popular Committee Caza 6 | Popular Committee Caza 7 |

Popular
Committees
at Village
Level within
Each Caza

| Popular Committee | Popular Committee | Popular Committee | Popular Committee | Popular Committee | Popular Committee | Popular Committee |

President
Vice President
Secretary
Treasurer
Head of Subcommittees

Health

Finance

Civil Defense

Planning

Social Affairs

Education

Environment

Municipalities

Information

General Inspection

Sports and Youth

6. *Municipalities,* which is concerned with garbage collection, repair of water mains, preventing the theft of electricity and water, and maintaining the telephone system.
7. *Planning,* which is necessarily the "brains" of all the other subcommittees.
8. *Information,* which is responsible for preparation and dissemination of information that is broadcast over the Voice of Lebanon and Radio Free Lebanon as well as published in two newspapers, *al-Amal,* and *Le Reveil.*
9. *Social Affairs,* which is responsible for price controls, prevention of profiteering, and refugee resettlement.
10. *General Inspection,* which monitors the performance of the other subcommittees and intervenes in situations requiring action by the police.
11. *Sports and Youth,* which is basically responsible for organizing recreational activities.

These popular committees are the units that implement many of the plans and decisions taken by the various offices described in the organization chart discussed earlier in this section (Figure 6.4).

While the initiative for the creation of the original popular committees originated at the local level, the establishment of most of the subsequent popular committees has been a combination of local initiative with direction from above. The first step in establishing a new popular committee in a village or neighborhood is generally taken by the local chapter of the Kata'eb which tries to stimulate public interest in the idea. If sufficient local interest is apparent, a meeting is arranged between the General Coordinator and the local population to see if they accept the idea of establishing a popular committee. No village popular committee is formed unless sixty-five to seventy-five percent of the population votes to accept one. The personnel, however, are appointed by the caza popular committees in consultation with the local population. Presumably most of the appointees are from the village that the popular committee represents.

The procedure for establishing the popular committees has some interesting implications for the future. First, the involvement of the citizens in a more direct form of self-government than was the case in the past undoubtedly will change their expectations about what government is supposed to do for them. Second, the procedure for establishing popular committees may have the effect of establishing an alternative political structure which may involve bypassing the old loyalties and patronage system that dominated Lebanese politics in the past. Third, the opportunities for personnel to use their positions on the popular committees for personal gain or to engage in corruption are minimized by the use of inspection teams at every level. The personnel on these teams are rotated frequently so that they in turn have few opportunities to abuse their authority. This increases the prospects that the population will become accustomed to having public affairs conducted effectively and relatively free of corruption. Therefore they will not be willing to accept a return to what they perceive as a corrupt and less effective handling of public affairs that existed before 1976.

So far the popular committees have been most successful and most effective in villages or neighborhoods that are almost exclusively Maronite. Those popular committees that had been established in confessionally mixed localities have reportedly been less successful in their operation or have met with considerably less acceptance by the non-Maronite populations. There is no reliable information on the degree of acceptance of the popular committee system by the other Christian sects. Nor is there any reliable way of ascertaining if the other Christian sects view the popular committee system as an instrument for extending Maronite dominance, or a means for mobilizing the Christian population for defense of their communities, or, for that matter, as a secular populist instrument for securing much-needed political reforms. The reservations by the Muslim populations might be due in part to the fact that the popular committees were initially a Christian creation for predominantly Christian neighborhoods. Therefore the whole popular committee system may be perceived by the Muslims as an instrument for extending or consolidating Christian—especially Maronite—control over Muslim communities. These fears could be reinforced if the establishment of popular committees does in fact bypass the traditional structure of patronage or political loyalties which, in the Muslim communities in particular, are based primarily on ascriptive status (mainly family prominence) and relatively little on personal achievement. Further, the tradition of political action originating at the local level is much weaker in Muslim communities than in the Christian sectors. Therefore, the whole concept of the popular committee could be largely outside the realm of Lebanese Muslim traditions and experience.

However, if the popular committees in confessionally mixed areas eventually demonstrate their commitment to serving all members of the community equally, many of the initial reservations or opposition by the Muslims or Druzes may ultimately diminish. What is important is that the popular committees are credited for a series of accomplishments that should be highly visible at the grass-roots level. The popular committees are credited with having:

- established the municipal parking lots mentioned earlier;
- provided the necessary maintenance for the water, electrical, and telephone systems;

- provided vocational programs for Lebanese youth;
- contributed to the alleviation of housing shortages; and
- established clinics and equipped them with specialists and provided free medical treatment and medication to the needy.

One factor responsible for the success of the popular committees is that the area in which they operate is controlled by one military force, not several. Therefore political authority is consistent, predictable, and supportive.

The popular committee system is not intended to compete with or displace the authority or the function of governmental agencies. Rather they evolved to fill the void left by an absence of government authority. The system was formally dissolved in 1977 when it appeared that the government was about to reassert its authority and resume its responsibilities. When this did not materialize, the popular committees were revived.

## THE FUTURE

### The Role of the Lebanese Forces in Post-War Lebanon

The Lebanese Forces began as an extension of the Christian party militias, but have developed a political and military identity of their own which is separate and distinct from any of the original component groups that contributed to its creation. Therefore the Lebanese Forces can be expected to have political interests, political objectives, and policy preferences that are not identical with the Kata'eb, the National Liberal Party, or any other of the "historical" political groupings or leaders. Thus it is useful to give some consideration to how the Lebanese Forces can be expected to relate to the government, the army and the other major confessional and political groups.

### The Lebanese Forces and the Central Government

Recall that the organizational structures and activities of the Lebanese Forces evolved in response to the absence of effective government authority. The Lebanese Forces did not intend to establish themselves as an alternative legitimacy structure to the government. The question, then, is whether the Lebanese Forces will relinquish the quasigovernmental prerogatives and responsibilities they assumed during the fighting and if so, under what circumstances?

Although Amin Gemayel is a long-standing member of the Kata'eb party and even though the Kata'eb constitutes a major component of the Lebanese Forces, the latters' support of the Gemayel government is qualified and tinged with suspicion. The Lebanese Forces have yet to be persuaded that Gemayel can achieve the withdrawal of all foreign forces from Lebanese soil. Hence they are not about to consider disbanding until after that task has been accomplished to their satisfaction. The Lebanese Forces support the strengthening of the central government and the extension of its authority throughout Lebanon, but are not certain that Gemayel is equal to the task. Should the Lebanese Forces withdraw their support of Gemayel the central government could become little more than a facade.

However, on occasions when the government has asserted its authority the Lebanese Forces have cooperated fully. One example, already cited, was the dissolution of the Popular Committees in 1977 in anticipation of the reassertion of government authority. Another is the support the Lebanese Forces lent former President Sarkis against Syrian pressures. A more important precedent occurred in late 1982 when the Lebanese Forces allowed the government to take over the port they controlled in northern Beirut. They also turned over their port at Jounieh to the Lebanese Army. This was a significant concession since the ports were a critically important source of revenue for the Lebanese Forces. In fact whenever the government has sought to expand its presence and authority into East Beirut, the Lebanese Forces have always yielded to the government. This is tangible evidence of the formal legitimacy accorded the government by the Lebanese Forces.

The only time the Lebanese Forces are likely to challenge the government is when it fails to discharge its responsibilities as interpreted by the Lebanese Forces' leadership. As long as the principal issue is the withdrawal of foreign forces from Lebanon, there are few sources of friction between the Lebanese Forces and the Lebanese government. However, some foreign forces (e.g., Syrian, Palestinian, Iranian, Libyan) are more foreign than others (Israeli). Presumably the Lebanese Forces are more concerned about securing Israeli evacuation of Lebanese soil than in retaining Israel as their chief supplier of arms, ammunition, and other military equipment. It is not certain how the Lebanese Forces are prepared to deal with this inherent conflict of interest.

Implicitly, however, the Lebanese Forces' interpretation of government responsibilities includes protecting the interests of the Christian communities in any renegotiation of the terms of the National Pact or other social covenant. This is an area where the interests of the Lebanese Forces and those of the government do not converge very neatly. For example, Fadi Frem declared in late September 1983 that the Lebanese Forces would not necessarily be bound by the recommendations of the National Dialogue Committee, the multisectarian reconciliation council created to bring peace to war-torn Lebanon. "The Lebanese Forces will adhere to the cease-fire but remain on the alert . . ., rejecting any result which may be inconsistent with the higher interests of the Christian people in Lebanon."[27] Such a statement suggests that the Lebanese Forces do not believe their interests are adequately represented by such members of the Lebanese Front as Pierre Gemayel or Camille Chamoun, and that the Lebanese Forces are prepared to challenge government acceptance of any recommendations by the National Dialogue Committee which the Lebanese Forces find objectionable. Fadi Frem's declaration underscores two points made earlier. First, it remains to be seen how long the Lebanese Front, composed of the "historical" Maronite leaders, will be able to speak for the younger leadership on the Joint Command Council and commit the Lebanese Forces to the terms of a bargain worked out in the National Dialogue Committee.[28] Second, the Lebanese Forces are not synonymous with Pierre Gemayel's Kata'eb.

Assuming the government can accomplish the withdrawal of all foreign forces from the country, it will actively extend its authority over all of Lebanon. In that event, the government must be able to impose its writ on the country without the help of the Lebanese Forces. At that point the Lebanese Forces will be confronted with the choice of relinquishing their quasigovernmental activities such as tax collection and conscription and so disbanding many of their operations, or challenging the government.

## The Lebanese Forces and the Army

What has been said about the Lebanese Forces' relations with the government applies to their relations with the army. They allowed the army to take up positions in East Beirut and to patrol that section of the city. There are close ties between senior personnel in the army and senior personnel in the Lebanese Forces. This facilitates a positive but limited symbiosis between the army and the Lebanese Forces as long as Lebanon remains under occupation. If evacuation of foreign troops does not occur then Lebanon will become partitioned *de facto* between Syria and Israel with a predominately Christian ministate in between. In that event the Lebanese Army could easily disintegrate with some elements of it merging with Lebanese Forces military units.

However, assuming evacuation takes place, the positive symbiosis between the two military forces can be expected to erode rapidly. Unless all militias including Lebanese Forces' formations are either disbanded or absorbed into the army, the two forces will find themselves competing for recruits since both will need to attract people from the same manpower pool. The Lebanese Army is not likely to tolerate this sort of competition. The army is the closest institution to being a wellspring for *Lebanese* nationalism that can be found in multisectarian Lebanon. It was humiliated both by the Palestinians and by their Lebanese allies—even at times by units of the Lebanese Forces—and will not tolerate the existence of any competing military force, including the Lebanese Forces. However, since the Lebanese Forces see themselves as being a defender of Lebanese nationalism pending the restoration of central government authority, friction over the dissolution of the Lebanese Forces' military wing may be minimized or avoided if the nationalism of the Lebanese Forces overlaps sufficiently with the nationalist outlook of the army. Ultimately the Lebanese Forces' relations with the Army may be a crucial test of the extent to which the Lebanese Forces have the potential to become a truly national political movement.

## The Lebanese Forces and Other Political Groups

While the Muslim and Druze communities and other political groups still view the Lebanese Forces more as a Christian political movement than a national political movement, the Lebanese Forces' persistent demand that all foreign forces depart Lebanon and the Lebanese Front's declared willingness to negotiate modifications of the National Pact offer positive potential for a dialogue with other groups. Since 1980 a growing consensus has developed in Lebanon, cutting across confessional lines, against any foreign presence. The Shi'a, now the largest confessional group in the country and once the allies of the Palestinians, fought pitched battles against the Palestinians and their Lebanese allies with increasing regularity between 1980 and 1982. A continued Israeli presence in southern Lebanon undoubtedly will spark similar opposition. The Shi'a movement, *Harakat 'Amal*, has consistently called for the deployment of the Lebanese Army throughout Lebanon. Like the Lebanese Forces, 'Amal is committed to the reestablishment of the central government's authority. All the territories in which the Shi'a are a majority are occupied by Syria (the Beqa'a) or Israel (the south). In the absence of a strong central government, the prospects for the evacuation of these areas by foreign forces, including the Palestinians, are nil. At some point the Lebanese Forces and 'Amal could conceivably find it to their mutual advantage to form a coalition. In 1861 the Maronite and the Druze formed a coalition that helped stabilize Mount Lebanon in the wake of bitter sectarian fighting.

In 1943 a Maronite–Sunni coalition was instrumental in establishing the modern Lebanese state. A Maronite–Shi'a coalition could be equally instrumental in stabilizing post-war Lebanon. Despite the initial positive reactions of the Shi'a in Lebanon to the Iranian revolution, events in Iran are now viewed much more equivocally by Lebanese Shi'as. While the Iranian example is still important, the brutality, extremism and fanaticism of the Khomeini regime has diminished the Shi'as' sectarian ardor. In any event, there is no evidence the Shi'as of Lebanon ever wished to establish an Islamic Republic in Lebanon. If anything, the agony of the past few years has reinforced and intensified the nationalistic sentiments of the majority of the Shi'as. A small splinter group of 'Amal, led by Hussein Musawi, operates in the Beqa'a Valley and calls itself the "Islamic 'Amal." However, this type of Iranian-inspired political Islam, reinforced by the presence of several hundred Iranian Pasdaran, does not reflect the mainstream of Shi'a political thinking. Thus the possibility of growing Shi'a commitment to "political Islam" becoming a barrier to a future Maronite–Shi'a alliance is very remote.[29] Further, a Maronite–Shi'a coalition would reflect one of the most important changes that has taken place in Lebanese society, and Maronite recognition and acceptance of that change—the fact that the Shi'a community has become the largest community in Lebanon.

Unless a new social compact is negotiated that reflects the Shi'a plurality, no lasting political stability is likely to be achieved. The National Pact of 1943 was negotiated at a time when the Sunnis were the largest Muslim sect in Lebanon. The Prime Minister's office, therefore, has always been reserved for a Sunni. The Shi'as can legitimately lay claim at least to the premiership on the basis of their demographic strength, if a renegotiated National Pact continues to reserve the top offices for the largest communities.

One obstacle to establishing closer rapport with other confessional and political groups is the close ties between the Lebanese Forces and Israel. Israel has contributed generously to the financing, training, and equipping of Lebanese Forces military units. The Lebanese Forces will have to distance themselves from Israel and if possible be able to take some of the credit for Israel's withdrawal from the country if they are to convince other groups that they are not just attempting to restore the Maronite-dominated political status quo. At present, this seems to be a nearly impossible task since the most visible distance that has developed between the Lebanese Forces and Israel has come from the Israeli side. In July 1983, Israel ordered the closure of three Lebanese Forces bases in southern Lebanon. The bases were located in villages east and southeast of Sidon, an area where the Lebanese Forces were attempting to expand their influence. Similarly, during Israel's invasion of Lebanon, the Israelis allowed—some reports say encouraged—the Lebanese Forces to enter the Shuf and establish control of Christian villages under the protection of the Israeli occupation forces. The Shuf is the ancestral Druze homeland, but the Christians, mainly the Maronites, have traditionally constituted a plurality in parts of that region. Druze forces had established their control over these areas during the fighting in 1975 and 1976, thereby establishing themselves as the uncontested power in the Shuf.

While the Lebanese Forces expected the Israelis to support the extension of their control against the Druze, the Israelis did not oblige. When Israeli forces withdrew from the Shuf, they not only did not allow the Lebanese Forces or the Lebanese Army to occupy their positions, but reportedly turned over some of them to Druze forces. To the extent that Israel viewed the Lebanese Forces as an ally, the alliance was against the Palestinians, not necessarily against other Lebanese groups—even those once allied with the Palestinians—once the Palestinians themselves were pushed into the Beqa'a. Hence another community with whom the Lebanese Forces must mend their political fences is the Druze. This, too, is nearly an impossible task until after a new political covenant is negotiated. In the meantime all the major confessional groups can be expected to maneuver—politically and militarily—in order to obtain the strongest bargaining position possible in anticipation of the negotiations for national reconciliation. The avowed aim of the Lebanese Forces is to secure the interests of the Christian communities. Thus any aspirations that they may retain to becoming a national political movement are not likely to be fulfilled in the forseeable future. Assuming they still want to, another factor that will affect the extent to which the Lebanese Forces are ever accepted as a national political movement is the apparent leadership vacuum that has developed in the non-Christian communities. Apart from 'Amal, the absence of effective leadership on the Muslim side may stem partly from the fact that many Muslim leaders were coopted by the Syrians and the Palestinians or simply lost effective leadership authority altogether (i.e., Rashid Karami and Sa'ib Salaam). Since the National Movement has been so heavily penetrated by the Syrians and Palestinians, a new generation of Lebanese Muslim leaders, able to commit their communities to a new National Pact, has yet to emerge.[30]

Conversely, the Lebanese Forces have produced a whole new generation of young leaders—most notably the late Bashir Gemayel—who not only have proven their qualities for a decade, but who have a clear idea of what direction Lebanon's political destiny ought to take. More important, these people are relatively very young. The average age of the militia commanders is 28. The Chief of Staff, Fouad Abi Nadier, is 30. The Commander General, Fadi Frem, is 31. Bashir Gemayel was 34 when he was killed. The youth of these people, seasoned by eight years or more of combat and administrative experience, helps to account for much of the Lebanese Forces' success. The leadership and the rank and file have the energy, enthusiasm, and motivation to work very long hours to produce the results they seek.

The apparent leadership vacuum in the other communities can work either to the advantage or the disadvantage of the Lebanese Forces, and ultimately to that of Lebanon. It can be to their advantage if, over time, the Lebanese Forces, by their policies, programs, and performance, can demonstrate to the Muslim communities that they are concerned with the interests and needs of all Lebanese. Those who remain unconvinced may see no alternative but to press more urgently for the strengthening of the central government's authority throughout all of Lebanon in the hope that this will blunt the influence of the Lebanese Forces. The strengthening of the government's authority, however, is one of the principal objectives of the Lebanese Forces, so ultimately this works in their favor, and hopefully for all of Lebanon.

Ultimately, however, the political role of the Lebanese Forces will turn on whether the overwhelming majority of Lebanese can arrive at a shared view of Lebanon's political destiny to which they can direct their primary political allegiance.

## NOTES

1. See Robert J. McCartney, "Lebanese Christian Seeks Troop Pullout," *The Washington Post* (October 25, 1982), A1.

2. A prominent example of this concerns the cooperation between Gemayel and Sarkis in August 1981 with the creation of the Follow-up Committee. This was a committee created by an agreement between Syria, Saudi Arabia, and Lebanon to arrange for Syria's withdrawal from Lebanon. Composed of the Saudi and Kuwaiti ambassadors to Lebanon plus representatives of the Secretary General of the Arab League and Syria, the first item on the Committee's agenda was a demand by Syrian Foreign Minister Abdel Halim Khaddam that the Lebanese Forces issue a public declaration severing any ties with Israel and demanding Arab League control of Lebanese ports. Had Bashir made such a statement it would have confirmed past ties with Israel and so would have undermined the Lebanese Forces within Lebanon and with most of the Arab countries, especially Saudi Arabia. Therefore Bashir and Sarkis agreed in advance that Bashir would agree to make such a statement in response to a request from Sarkis, as long as it remained secret until Sarkis would ask Bashir to make it public. This would enable Sarkis to move to the second item on the Committee's agenda, the timetable for the withdrawal of Syrian forces from Lebanon. When the committee met, Sarkis promised

to guarantee that Bashir would issue the statement so the committee could move on to the second item on the agenda. Sarkis secured Bashir's agreement to this in a telephone call with the Follow-up Committee members present. With Bashir's agreement thus secured Sarkis could insist that the Committee move to the question of Syria's withdrawal from Lebanon. The Syrian Foreign Minister balked, insisting he had to return to Damascus to advise his government. This demonstrated to the other members of the Committee that Syria was opposed to withdrawal of its forces from Lebanon, but that the Lebanese Forces were not opposed to severing their ties with Israel if this action would help strengthen Lebanon's independence. This maneuver also helped to establish positive relations between the Lebanese Forces and Saudi Arabia.

3. Thorough treatment of the subject can be found in Marius Deeb, *The Lebanese Civil War* (New York: Praeger, 1979); P. Edward Haley and Lewis W. Snider (eds), *Lebanon in Crisis: Participants and Issues* (Syracuse, NY: Syracuse University Press, 1979); and Walid Khalidi, *Conflict and Violence in Lebanon: Confrontation in the Middle East* (Cambridge, MA: Center for International Affairs, Harvard University, 1979).

4. Jumblatt mentioned this in his memoirs which are serialized in *al-Watan al-Arabi*, Vol. 66 (May 20–26, 1978), 39.

5. Walid Khalidi, *Conflict and Violence in Lebanon*, 73.

6. A complete description of the composition of the National Movement and its political program is provided in Marius Deeb, *The Lebanese Civil War*, Chapter 3.

7. The extent to which Syria succeeded in this endeavor was underscored by none other than Abd al-Halim Khaddam, the Syrian Foreign Minister, who admitted at a meeting of the Arab League, October 24, 1976, that "half the leaders of the National Movement were from the Syrian secret services and were paid money," including Kamal Jumblatt. See excerpts from the text of a meeting of the Arab League October 24, 1976 and republished in the original Arabic in *Lebanon News* (December 23–30, 1981), 7.

8. See, for example, the chronology of the fighting which specifies the contending forces, the sectors/districts where they fought, the dates of the battles and other pertinent information in Paul A. Jureidini, R. D. McLaurin and James M. Price, *Military Operations in Selected Lebanese Built-Up Areas, 1975–1978*, Aberdeen, MD: U.S. Army Human Engineering Laboratory, Aberdeen Proving Ground, Technical Memorandum 11-79 (June 1979), Appendix B. The beginning date of the chronology is April 13, 1975 (the clash in Ain al-Rummaneh between Palestinian and Kata'eb forces) and ends October 8, 1978. Of the events listed in the chronology which clearly identify the opposing forces, only thirty percent of the engagements appear to have been fought by combatants that were indigenously Lebanese nationals.

9. Norman Howard, "Tragedy in Lebanon," *Current History*, Vol. 72, No. 423 (January 1977), 3.

10. The location of the political groups in Figure 6.1 is an approximation and is not intended to represent precise measurement beyond an ordinal level. The values on the axes represent standard deviation units. The zero point on the vertical Christian-Muslim axis represents insignificant sectarian orientation in policies and confessionally mixed membership. The same zero point on the horizontal axis represents a "centrist" position on a left-right or Arab nationalist vs. Lebanese nationalist continuum. The actual location of each political group was made according to the following rules:

> The group's political behavior, particularly the groups with which it is aligned and against which it is fighting, plus statements concerning political preferences;
>
> The ideological orientation and confessional membership of the paper leaders, and;
>
> The confessional make-up of the membership as a whole.

For example, if the leadership and the rank and file are predominantly from the same confession, the group was placed three standard deviations from the origin on the Christian-Muslim vertical axis. If the party leader was a Christian while most of the party's supporters were Muslim, the deciding factor was the leader's confessional membership and the group's political alignments. Such groups were usually located two "standard deviations" above the zero point. If the leadership was Christian and the rank and file confessionally mixed, the group was placed within one sigma above the origin. If the leadership was Muslim and the rank and file confessionally mixed, the party was placed within one sigma below the origin on the vertical axis. In assigning the political groups locations on the horizontal axis, the procedure followed was to begin with the most extreme group and assign it to the third standard deviation to the left or the right. The other groups' positions were determined by their position relative to these extremists.

11. The Tanzim, which in Arabic means "the organization," was founded in 1969 after the first major clashes between the Lebanese Army and the Palestinian guerrillas. It originated as a splinter group from the Kata'eb after its founders failed to persuade the Kata'eb leadership to support large-scale military training of Lebanese citizens in response to the expansion of Palestinian power in Lebanon and to Arab League pressure on the Lebanese government to neutralize Lebanese law in its application to the Palestinians. Therefore the founding members decided to build a paramilitary organization to defend Lebanon and support the Lebanese army. The Tanzim's principal goal—to develop a sense of self-defense for Lebanon—is reflected in its logo which is a map of Lebanon—*all* of Lebanon.

Since the Lebanese Army was against independent military preparations by private organizations, the Tanzim began secret military training programs in camps in the mountains. The rudimentary beginnings of this effort are suggested by the fact that wooden dummy rifles were used in the early stages of the program.

The military training program which began in April 1969 was open to all Lebanese civilians who pledged to keep the source of their training a secret and to be ready to defend Lebanon in times of crisis as the army could not do it alone. The Tanzim made its first "public appearance" in May 1973 during the prolonged clashes between the Lebanese army and the Palestinian guerrillas. The army indirectly called on the Tanzim for help when it announced over the radio for the Lebanese population to stop any 'foreigners' from entering army-controlled areas. The 'foreigners' in question were Palestinian guerrillas. From 1969 to 1975 the Tanzim claims to have trained fourteen thousand Lebanese. It did not become a truly separate and distinct organization until 1975.

With this background in mind, it is easy to see how Tanzim, Kata'eb, and NLP militia leaders could develop a close working relationship.

12. Lebanese Forces representatives estimate that on the first day of the Tel al-Za'atar operation the nationalist militias had about thirteen thousand fighters. By the end of the campaign they had sustained over five hundred dead and another five hundred seriously injured.

13. The black market included the Palestinian camps. In the initial rounds of fighting in 1975-76, many Lebanese who fought in the nationalist militias purchased Kalashnikovs and other weapons from the Palestinians who had far more weapons than they could use and who were interested in the additional income that could be gained from selling weapons that the Palestinian resistance forces would never miss.

14. See the account of Jonathan C. Randal, *Going all the Way: Christian Warlords, Israeli Adventurers and the War in Lebanon* (New York: Viking Press, 1983), 135-38.

15. Although the ranking system is ambiguous, responsibility is not. As of December, 1981, any person whose duties involve the acquisition or distribution of

materials and supplies or is involved in the collection or disbursement of funds, must complete a declaration of assets and personal wealth. This is placed in an envelope which is sealed and deposited in the Commander General's office. These declarations are used in the event that an individual is accused of malfeasance or corruption.

16. Much of the information presented in the discussion of the militia is based on interviews with Fadi Frem, the Commander General of the Lebanese Forces, other commanders in the militia and on material presented in Jureidini, McLaurin, and Price, *Military Operations.*

17. This "guesstimate" was made based on the following fragments of evidence:

Between 1969 and 1975 the Tanzim claimed to have trained over fourteen thousand people which averages twenty-seven hundred per year. This was accomplished using very primitive facilities and a relative handful of instructors.

According to the UNESCO Statistical Yearbook the number of students in secondary schools in Lebanon is 902 per 100,000 population. The population living in Lebanese Forces-controlled territory is slightly over one million which suggests there are around 9,020 students in secondary schools in territory controlled by the Lebanese Forces. Assuming a four-year high school curriculum, then the pool of high school graduates each year averages 2255. However, most of the population under Lebanese Forces control resides in urban areas, which means that the number of students per 100,000 population is likely to be slightly higher.

HELP Lebanon reportedly handles about twenty-two hundred secondary students per year in their career counseling program.

18. The political role of the *gabadais,* especially their importance in maintaining the material power base of the traditional Sunni political leadership, is described by Khalidi, *Conflict and Violence in Lebanon,* 97–9.

19. Much of the information on the Lebanese Front was obtained during an interview with Dr. Charles Malik, October 16, 1982 in Lebanon.

20. Whether Tony was the intended target depends upon which version of the events one is willing to accept. The Lebanese Forces' version is that Tony and his family were not supposed to be in the house, that the objective of the raid was to arrest two men accused of murdering a Lebanese Forces leader in Zghorta. The two men were using the Frangieh residence as a refuge. *Washington Post* correspondent Jonathan Randal, however, claims that years later a member of the Ehden operation confided that Tony's death was the main objective. See Randal, *Going all the Way,* 119.

21. An updated edition of this document is the Lebanese Front, *The Lebanon we Want to Build,* Deir Aoukar, December 13, 1980. It may not represent the views of other Christian communities such as the Armenians or the Greek Orthodox.

22. *The Lebanon we Want to Build,* 5.

23. This point was reiterated to the author by Charles Malik in an interview at Dr. Malik's home in Lebanon, October 16, 1982, and again in April, 1983.

24. One incident, for example, occurred in October 1980 when Lebanese Forces troops brushed aside Lebanese Army units that were protecting remnants of Camille Chamoun's Tiger Militia in Ain al-Rummaneh.

25. Land for these parking lots was acquired by first making an inventory of all empty land inside Beirut, and then finding the owners and persuading them that the Lebanese Forces did not intend to seize their land, only to use it until the owners were ready to build on it. The Lebanese Forces promised to return the land within 48 hours upon demand. In addition, most of the land contained vast amounts of refuse which

were cleared. Therefore conversion of vacant land into parking facilities improved sanitation conditions as well.

26. Inspection involves taking twelve samples a month from service stations or fuel distributors. The samples are sent to a petroleum laboratory for analysis. Any dealer selling gasoline that is less than 92 octane is arrested and his business is closed for seven days. All arrests are broadcast on the radio. Regular inspection of fuel pumps is also made to ensure that consumers are not paying for more fuel than they actually receive.

27. William Tuohy, "Christian Falangists Remain Wild Card In Deck of Lebanon Power Politics," Los Angeles Times (September 28, 1983), 16.

28. Apart from members of the Lebanese Front, the Lebanese Forces do not have any of their own representatives (i.e., leaders on the Joint Command Council) on the National Dialogue Committee. The JCC and the militia are represented on the National Security Committee. The latter is composed of representatives of the principal militias involved in the fighting in August-September 1983: the Lebanese Forces, the Popular Socialist Party militia, led by Walid Jumblatt, and elements of the Shi'a militia, 'Amal, led by Nabih Berri, in addition to representatives from the Lebanese Army.

29. See Augustus Richard Norton, "Aspects of Terrorism in Lebanon: The Case of the Shi'as," Clandestine Tactics and Technology, Volume IX, No. 4 (1982), 5–6.

30. The fact that eventually the Palestinians largely controlled and coordinated most of the activities of the National Movement is even conceded by the late Kamal Jumblatt, the National Movement's leader, in his memoirs which are serialized in al-Watan al-'Arabi, cited in footnote 4. The apparent absence of leadership among the Muslim Lebanese, particularly the Sunnis, however, cannot be attributed solely to the cooptation by the Palestinians. Geography and demographics, too, have contributed to this vacuum. The Sunni communities generally are concentrated in the urban areas of Tripoli, Beirut, and Sidon. By contrast the Shi'a, Druze, and Christian communities are territorially contiguous. Consequently in times of strife, the lack of contiguity among the Muslim communities often restricted communication among these communities and their local leaders. This apparently continues to be the case as southern Lebanon is occupied by Israel and Major Sa'ad Haddad's Christian-Shi'a militia; the Tripoli area is occupied by Syrian and Palestinian forces.

# 7

# Harakat Amal*

## Augustus Richard Norton

The cascading violence in Lebanon has—over the span of nearly ten years—confounded all but the most recalcitrant optimists, while it has swelled the pessimists' ranks. As the situation has gone from bad to worse and from worse to seemingly worst, spectators and participants alike have learned to be skeptical about even the dimmest rays of hope. Thus, only a fool would venture any specific hopeful prediction as to the future of Lebanon, or even the possibility that Lebanon has a future. However, there is one prediction that is safe to make, and that is the following: whatever the future will hold for this ill-fated country, it is indisputable that the Lebanese Republic's plurality, the Shi'a, will play a decisive role in shaping it—for better or worse.

Long on the periphery of Lebanon's political system, and on the bottom of the country's economic system, the Shi'as only began to find their political voice in the late 1960s. Notwithstanding the political activities of individual Shi'a *zu'ama* (political bosses) who controlled respective segments of the community, the Shi'as as a group have been marked by quiescence and even irrelevance for politics in Lebanon.[1] This chapter treats, in three parts, the mobilization of the Shi'a community by the movement that has come to be known as Harakat Amal.†

---

*I would like to thank Brian Jenkins and the splendid staff of the RAND Corporation for the extraordinary research assistance that was made available during my September 1982 stay at that unique institution. Naturally, only the author is responsible for any errors or shortcomings in the present chapter. This chapter should not be construed to represent the position of RAND, or any organization, branch, or agency of the U.S. Government.

This chapter is dedicated to the memory of Musa Baddah.

†Harakat Amal means, literally, The Movement of Hope; however, 'Amal is also an acronym for *Afwai al-Muqawimah al-Lubnaniyah*—the Lebanese Resistance Detachments, a meaning that is now seldom mentioned by movement officials.

Part I discusses the socio-economic status of the community and describes the processes of social change that have affected the Shi'as. Part II takes the reader from the late 1960s through the civil war years of 1975-76 and the key events of 1978 and 1979, and concludes on the eve of Israel's June 1982 invasion. Part III analyzes the reaction to the invasion, and the adaptive responses of the Amal leadership to the dramatically changed political context of post-invasion Lebanon.

## BACKGROUND

While population estimates for Lebanon are always risky—the last official census was conducted over fifty years ago—many observers agree that the Shi'as presently comprise the largest single confessional group, representing approximately thirty percent of the population which is to say from nine hundred thousand to one million members.[2] Thus, the Shi'a population now surpasses both the Maronite and Sunni sects that have dominated the republic since the attainment of self-rule in 1943. Lebanon's confessional political system institutionalizes a Maronite presidency, a Sunni premiership, and a Shi'a speakership in the chamber of deputies, all by virtue of the respective population shares established by the 1932 census. Should the Shi'as successfully demand that the political system reflect the logic of changed demographics, it is clear that a substantial reallocation of political power in Lebanon would result. However, for the most part, the Shi'as have been occupied by far less grand objectives, in particular, the amelioration of their economic plight and the rampant insecurity that they have suffered, especially in *al-junub* (the south).

Lebanon's Shi'as have long been considered the most disadvantaged confessional group in the country. By most, if not all, of the conventional measures of socio-economic status, the Shi'as fare poorly in comparison to their non-Shi'a cohorts. For example, using 1971 data, Joseph Chamie noted: the average Shi'a family's income was 4,532 Lebanese pounds (£L; 3£L = $1, in 1971), in comparison with the national average of 6,247£L; the Shi'as comprised the highest percentage of families earning less than 1,500£L; they were the most poorly educated (fifty percent with no schooling vs. thirty percent state-wide); and, the Shi'a was the *least* likely, in comparison with other recognized sects, to list his occupation as professional/technical, business/managerial, clerical, or crafts/operatives, and the *most* likely to list it as farming, peddlery, or labor.[3] In his 1968 study, Michael Hudson found that in the two regions where the Shi'as predominate, *al-Beqa'a* and *al-junub*, the percentage of students in the population (about thirteen percent) lagged by as much as five percentage points behind Lebanon's other three regions.[4] Riad B. Tabbarah, analyzing educational differentials, found that in 1971 only 6.6 percent of the Shi'as had at least a secondary education, compared to at least fifteen percent and seventeen percent for the Sunnis and the Christians, respectively.[5] Citing official Lebanese government statistics for 1974, Hasan Sharif found that while the south had about twenty percent of the national population, it received less than 0.7 percent of the state budget.[6] Sharif's description of the underdevelopment of the south illustrates the conditions under which many Shi'as have had to live.

> The South has the fewest paved roads per person or per acre. Running water is still missing in all villages and towns although water pipes were extended to many areas in the early sixties. Electricity networks were erected at about the same time, but they are inoperative most of the time. Sewage facilities are available only in large towns and cities. Outside the larger centers telephone service is completely absent except for a single manual cabin which is usually out of order. Doctors visit the villages once a week and sometimes only once a month. Clinics are maintained only in large villages and do not function regularly. Hospitals and pharmacies are found only in the larger population centers. [The] Elementary school is usually run in an old unhealthy house provided by the village. Intermediate schools were introduced to the large towns in the mid-sixties.[7]

Based on this writer's field work in Lebanon from 1980 to 1982, Sharif's description is still essentially correct. While there have been some minor improvements, the conditions depicted are for the most part at least as bad as noted, and in many respects have only been exacerbated by nine years of conflict and social disruption.

## THE SOCIAL MOBILIZATION OF THE SHI'AS

Even before the onset of civil war in 1975, Lebanon was experiencing profound and rapid social change. The importance of this social change is anticipated in Karl W. Deutsch's important 1961 article, where Deutsch elaborates the concept, "social mobilization."[8]

Social mobilization, in effect, has two dimensions: first, it is an indicator of the modernization process (while Deutsch cautions, it is not identical with the "process of modernization as a whole").[9] Second, it speaks to the consequences of modernization. As an indicator, the concept subsumes a wide range of variables that when measured over time signal the extent of the changes that are taking place in a given country. Thus, Deutsch counsels that we pay attention to the following clusters of change: exposure to aspects of modern life (e.g., the media, consumer goods, and technology); changes in residence, in particular rural to urban migration; occupational changes, for example shifts away from agrarian employment; literacy rates; and, changes in income.

The consequences of social mobilization were described by Deutsch as follows:

> In whatever country it occurs, social mobilization brings with it an expansion of the politically relevant strata of the population.[10]

> Social mobilization also brings about a change in the quality of politics by changing the range of human needs that impinge upon the political process. As people are uprooted from their physical and intellectual isolation in their immediate localities, from their old habits and traditions, and often from their old patterns of occupation and places of residence, they experience drastic changes in their needs.[11]

Taking Deutsch's concept as his inspiration, Michael Hudson examined social mobilization phenomena in Lebanon and offered persuasive, if sometimes circumstantial, evidence that the country was—in the late 1960s—undergoing rapid, but uneven, social mobilization.[12]

While reliable data are scarce, especially by confession, the limited available data point to profound socioeconomic change in Lebanon over the past several decades. Of particular importance are changes in employment and residence patterns, changes which are central to Deutsch's concept of social mobilization, and which can reasonably be inferred to have disproportionately affected the Shi'as.

From 1960 to 1980 the percentage of the total labor force employed in agriculture declined from thirty-eight percent to eleven percent, with most of those displaced moving to the services sector which increased from thirty-nine percent to sixty-two percent of the labor force over the same period.[13] The reasons for this occupational shift are complex, but in addition to the dislocations incidental to warfare, they include: stagnant prices for cash crops (viz., tobacco and sugar beets); an increase in capital-intensive citrus-crop cultivation; a relatively high rate of growth in the labor force (three percent per annum in the 1970–1980 period); an uncertain and dangerous security environment (especially in al-junub and al-Beqa'a, areas accounting for well over fifty percent of the Shi'a population—the remainder are found in Beirut and its suburbs); and a decisive lack of budgetary support from the government, and bank credits from the private sector (respective rates were 2.3 percent of the state budget in 1973, and 2.3 percent of total bank credits in 1974). Not surprisingly, the result has been a growing impoverishment of the small freeholder, who typically owns three hectares or less and accounts for about three-quarters of the rural population. (One 1973 estimate shows an annual per head of household income of 500£L for agriculture, as compared to 1,100£L in industry and 8,060£L for the services sector.) By the late 1960s—well before the onset of serious conflict—fifty-six percent of those engaged in agriculture in south Lebanon took second jobs, usually as laborers.[14]

The decline of the agrarian sector has been an important impetus for internal migration, usually to Beirut and its environs, as well as for external migration, for the Shi'as typically to West Africa. Even before the events of 1975, about forty percent of the population of south Lebanon, and about twenty-five percent of the population of al-Beqa'a had emigrated.[15] Coupled with other important if less dramatic changes, such as a doubling of per capita energy consumption in the period 1960–1979, Lebanon was experiencing profound changes of the sort anticipated by the social mobilization construct.

While under some circumstances the end result of the social mobilization process is the emergence of a shared nationality, Deutsch recognized,[16] a propos of Lebanon, that in some political settings the social mobilization of a population would not lead to assimilation, but to differentiation.

> ... the same process may tend to strain or destroy the unity of states whose population is already divided into several groups with different languages or cultures or basic ways of life.[17]

The data, sparse as they may be, certainly hint that ever larger numbers of Shi'as would be available to political action (i.e., for recruitment); however, the forms of their political activity as well as the context were clearly not predetermined. That the Shi'as should act qua Shi'a-Lebanese and not as Lebanese was not unexpected as the preceding quotation from Deutsch emphasizes. But, that the rural setting was seemingly as important as the urban as a locus for political mobilization, is, at least at first glance, something of a surprise. Finally, that the successful political mobilization of the Shi'as should have fallen to Harakat Amal is a result of several developments that are addressed below.

The most obvious explanation for the relative solidarity of the Shi'as is the commonplace that it is nearly impossible to escape from one's confessional identity in Lebanon. From the identity card specifying religion to the allocation of political privilege and reward along particularist lines, the Lebanese citizen is constantly reminded that he is a hyphenated Lebanese (e.g., Shi'a-Lebanese, Druze-Lebanese, etc.). Not that fervent religiosity is necessarily widespread of course, but religious identity defines one's primary social organization through which political security is maintained.[18] The Shi'as' confessional consciousness was even further enhanced by the widespread—and not unjustified—belief that they had suffered the costs of the continuing conflict in Lebanon far more grievously than any other group in the country.

As for the several hundred thousands of Shi'as who settled, both permanently and temporarily, in and around Beirut, it is now well acknowledged that urban residence does not necessarily erase sectarian identities and often has quite the opposite effect.[19] As Hudson remarked, "the crucible of Beirut does not appear to be molding less particularistic Lebanese citizens. . . . Urbanization appears to fortify, rather than diminish Lebanese parochialism. . . . "[20] Furthermore, even if the urban dweller seeks to cut his village ties, electoral law makes it difficult, even impossible to do so. (The complicated and lengthy legal process involved in an attempt to shift voting rights from one constituency to another effectively forecloses the possibility for most Lebanese.) As Fuad I. Khuri notes, while only seventeen percent of Lebanon's population remained rural after the migrations of the 1950s, 1960s, and 1970s, these important demographic shifts remained unrecognized in the electoral law.

> A citizen, irrespective of where he was living or for how long, was required to return to his home-town to exercise the right to vote. Shifting voting rights from one constituency to another is a complicated procedure that requires a court decision. Had the electoral law been amended to give seventeen percent of the parliamentary seats to the rural areas and eighty-three percent to the urban areas, the political structure of Lebanon would have been turned upside down. As it was however, the electoral law helped to bind the voter to his village. . . .[21]

Thus, the village followed the villager into the city in both the social and the political realms; and yet, as argued below, the city is both figuratively and literally close to the village.[22]

As we shall see, the villages of southern Lebanon have been at least as important as Beirut's urban quarters and the surrounding poverty belt as a spawning ground for the political mobilization of the Shi'as. This may be mildly surprising, even taking into account the extraordinary security situation in the south, since some of the fundamental tenets of political development theory claim an important relationship between urbanization and manifestations of increased political activity (viz., participation). Before reconciling this apparent divergence between the actual and the theoretical, it is pertinent to briefly review some representative authoritative statements on the subject of urbanization and political participation.

Daniel Lerner, in *The Passing of Traditional Society*, treats urbanization as the first phase of modernization and he claims:

> It is the transfer of population from scattered hinterlands to urban centers that stimulates the needs and provides the conditions for "take off" toward widespread participation.[23]

Karl Deutsch equates, in large part, the very process of change that transforms a society from traditional to modern ways of life with urbanization. Thus, as noted above, to measure social mobilization such variables as "changes in residence," "changes from agricultural occupation," and, specifically, "urbanization" are proposed. As a society experiences greater social mobilization (hence, urbanization), we are taught to expect an expansion of "the politically relevant strata of the population,"[24] which in turn leads to "increased political participation."[25] Finally, Samuel Huntington makes the point most directly.

> Urbanization, increases in literacy, education, and media exposure all give enhanced aspirations and expectations which, if unsatisfied, galvanize individuals and groups into politics.[26]

Obviously, the object here is not to trivialize the work of other scholars, but to make an important point with respect to Lebanon. The special meaning of urban residence for political participation has been lost in Lebanon, not because of faulty theorizing, but because for Lebanon the urban-rural distinction has lost much of its meaning.[27] In a country of 4,015 square miles, a country in which traveling by road to major urban centers from even the most remote villages is possible in three hours and usually much less, a country in which external migration (and return) is a tradition, and in which brutal pulses of violence have propelled cycles of internal migration, the vast preponderance of the population is psychically nonrural.

The pristine village is not just uncommon in Lebanon, it is a rarity. For reasons that are well expounded by Fuad Khuri, the isolated village, safe in its customs and traditions and unaffected by the dynamics of modernity, is a vestige of dusty ethnographies.

Generally speaking, no community (village, suburb, or city) in Lebanon today has physical boundaries corresponding to its sociocultual limits, although this is a matter of degree. What emerges is a phenomenon in which social groups transcend territorial boundaries, a phenomenon more characteristic of suburban than city or village traditions.[28]

Khuri's work, published in 1975, is even more relevant in light of the changes that have taken place since its publication.

Thus, in considering the political emergence of the Shi'as, which is described in the remainder of this chapter, it should hardly be surprising either that an important locus of political mobilization has been in the village or that the patterns of recruitment have followed confessional lines rather than alternative, nonparticularistic ones.

## FROM THE 1960s TO THE 1980s

Notwithstanding their relative impoverishment, the Shi'as were not, as we have seen, divorced from the processes of social change underway in Lebanon. Nonetheless, politicization is one thing and political action is another. The question in the late 1960s seemed not to be whether the Shi'as would find their political voice, but who, or what organization(s) would provide it. As Hudson noted in his prescient 1968 book, *The Precarious Republic:*

> One of the more interesting political developments in the postwar period has been . . . the gradual modernization of Shi'a leadership, a trend accompanied, of course, by demands for a greater share of power.[29]

### Musa al-Sadr

Of those contending for the leadership of the Shi'a community, the most important was no doubt a charismatic religious leader, Musa al-Sadr.[30]

Al-Sadr was born in Qum, Iran, in 1928, the son of Ayatallah Sadr al-Din Sadr. He was educated in Tehran, and received his religious training in a Qum *madrasa* (religious school), one of the many such institutions referred to as *Maktib-i-Islam* (or school of Islam). He first visited Lebanon, his ancestral home, in 1957. In 1959, after receiving an invitation from the Shi'a community in the southern port city of Tyre, he relocated in Lebanon.[31] By a special presidential decree, President

Shihab (1958–1964) granted him Lebanese nationality, a rare act that was an early confirmation of his growing influence in Lebanon.[32]

By the end of the 1960s, al-Sadr had established himself as the leading Shi'a cleric in the country, a status that was confirmed when he was named, in 1969, to be chairman of the newly formed Supreme Shi'a Council by the government. The Council, created by the Lebanese parliament, was a direct response by the government to the growing demands of the Shi'as, demands which were loudly and effectively voiced by al-Sadr (who had by this time taken the title "Imam"). The creation of the Council with Musa al-Sadr at its head was a significant political victory, and was one of the many rounds in the battle for supremacy between the Imam and Kamal al-Asad, the most powerful Shi'a *za'im* (political boss).

In 1970, one year after the formation of the Supreme Shi'a Council, al-Sadr organized a general strike "to dramatize to the government the plight of the population of southern Lebanon vis-a-vis the Israeli military threat."[33] Shortly thereafter, the government created the *Majlis al-Junub* (Council of the South), which was capitalized at thirty million £L and was chartered to support the development of the south. Unfortunately, the *Majlis al-Junub* quickly became more famous for being a center of corruption than for being the originator of beneficial projects.[34]

With the influx of thousands of fedayeen in 1970 and 1971, following the bloody conflict in Jordan, the already difficult social and economic problems of the Shi'as were compounded by a rapidly deteriorating security situation. As the pace of fedayeen attacks and Israeli counterattacks accelerated, life in the south became increasingly perilous. With the Lebanese government unable to protect its citizens, al-Sadr made armed struggle one of the motifs of his campaign to mobilize the Shi'as. Following the October War of 1973, he declared that there was "no alternative for us except revolution and weapons."[35] He asserted that "arms are a symbol of manhood,"[36] and at one rally, he angrily declared:

> From now onwards we're not *metwallis* [a somewhat derogatory term for Shi'as]; we are rejectionists; we are avengers; we are a people who revolt against any kind of oppression.[37]

Citing the government's failure to provide either security or economic well-being for its Shi'a citizens, Musa al-Sadr became increasingly vehement, and finally, in 1974, he founded the *Harakat Mahrumeen* (the Movement of the Deprived). With his new movement, he vowed to struggle relentlessly until the social grievances of the

Shi'as (and other deprived Lebanese) were satisfactorily addressed by the government. As Kamal Salibi reports:

> He even warned that he would soon have his followers attack and occupy the palaces and mansions of the rich and powerful if the grievances of the poor and oppressed were left unheeded.[38]

Just one year later, al-Sadr's efforts were overtaken by the onset of civil war in Lebanon. By July 1975, it became known that a militia adjunct to the *Harakat Mahrumeen* had been founded.[39] The militia, *Afwaj al—Muqawimah al-Lubnaniyah* (the Lebanese Resistance Detachments), better known by the acronym Amal (which also means "hope"), was initially trained by Fatah, and it played a minor role in the fighting of 1975 and 1976. Musa al-Sadr's movement, including the Amal militia, was affiliated with the reform-oriented Lebanese National Movement (LNM) and their fedayeen allies during the first year of the war, but when the Syrians intervened in June 1976 to prevent the defeat of the Maronite-dominated Lebanese Front, al-Sadr split with his erstwhile allies and staunchly supported the Syrians. The movement's estrangement from the LNM has continued ever since, as has its close association with Syria.[40] Subsequently, the name *Mahrumeen* fell into disuse, and the movement that al-Sadr founded came to be known as Harakat Amal (or simply, Amal, *not*, as is sometimes thought, al-Amal).

## The Decline and Reemergence of Amal

The growing influence of Imam Musa (as he is called by his followers) prior to the civil war was certainly a bellwether for the increased politicization of the Shi'as; however, in point of fact, Musa al-Sadr only led a minority faction of the politically affiliated Shi'as. Indeed, it was the multiconfessional reform-oriented or revolutionary parties and militias that attracted the majority of the politicized Shi'as. Musa al-Sadr had significantly reduced the power of the traditional Shi'a elites, the *zu'ama,* but it was the civil war itself that made these personalities increasingly irrelevant in the political system.

Many young Shi'a men joined such groups as the (pro-Syrian) Ba'ath organization, the Syrian Social Nationalist Party, the (Iraqi-supported) Arab Liberation Front (ALF),* or one of several Com-

---

*Strictly speaking, the ALF (*Jabhat Arabiyya*) is a constituent group in the PLO. Its Lebanese counterpart, within the LNM, is the Iraqi faction of the Ba'ath Party. However, there have been Lebanese in both segments, and, as a result, most Lebanese do not distinguish between the two in common usage.

munist organizations.[41] Such groups represented a wide range of grievances and programs, and their only common denominators were opposition to the Kata'eb-dominated Lebanese Front, and their support for the Palestinian Resistance Movement (PRM). While the discernment of the motives of individual recruits is patently difficult, there were clearly those who were motivated by ideological and revolutionary objectives, but many simply found membership the requisite for a fairly attractive salary. (It is probably impossible to find a Shi'a village or urban quarter where stories about unemployed *shabab*—young bloods—departing one day to join a militia and returning a few weeks later sporting a Kalashnikov rifle or a pistol and a wad of Lebanese lira are not told.)[42]

Thus, while al-Sadr's partisans sometimes played consequential roles in the 1975–1976 fighting, they were only one group among several that counted a significant Shi'a membership. In fact, the most valuable political currency from 1975 forward was armed strength, and Musa al-Sadr's not inconsiderable charisma (his devotees typically described him as a giant among men) was no substitute for his inability to field a more substantial force than the fifteen hundred or so fighters in Amal. Overshadowed by the military might of his many competitors for political influence, and somewhat discredited for his alleged complicity in the August 1976 fall of the Palestinian-held Shi'a quarter of Beirut, known as Nabaa, to the Kata'eb,[43] al-Sadr retreated to the south with a coterie of dedicated followers. While he remained active giving speeches and buttressing his following in the south, his national influence waned significantly between 1976 and 1978. There are reports that he played an important role during this period arousing opposition to the Shah among Iran's Shi'as, but the specific nature of his activities is still somewhat obscure.[44]

Three events transpired in the ten-month period from March 1978 to January 1979 that accelerated the political mobilization of the Shi'a community and contributed to the growing consolidation of the Shi'as' political influence in a revitalized Harakat Amal. In March 1978, the Israelis launched their first major invasion of Lebanon, the Litani Operation: in August 1978, the Imam Musa al-Sadr disappeared during a still enigmatic visit to Libya; and, in January 1979, the Ayatollah Khomeini's Islamic Revolution toppled the Shah. It was the occurrence of these three events that, on the one hand, focused the resentment of the previously empathetic Shi'a community on the Palestinians, and, on the other, provided an important myth and an exemplar which facilitated the recruitment of Shi'as by Harakat Amal.

## The Litani Operation

Israel's 1978 invasion, which claimed some one thousand—mostly Shi'a—lives and resulted in the destruction of a number of homes throughout *al-junub*, not only demonstrated the heavy human price that the Israelis would exact from the residents of the area as a result of the extant armed Palestinian presence, but also signaled the conclusive end of one Israeli security policy—a policy of retribution—and the beginning of another—a policy of relentless disruption. After the Litani Operation the IDF moved far beyond all but the slimmest pretense of retaliation in its military operations in south Lebanon. Instead, the IDF sought to keep the PRM (and its supporters and sympathizers) constantly on the defensive with an active campaign of air attacks, raids, kidnappings, and house bombings. Until the cease-fire of July 1981 the disruption campaign was remarkably successful. Palestinian-initiated actions in or from south Lebanon were rare as the fedayeen found themselves almost constantly reacting to Israeli military initiatives. The IDF's guiding principle was confirmed by then-Chief of Staff, General Rafael Eytan, when he noted:

> We will continue to take action where we want, when we want and how we want. Our own self-interest is supreme and will guide us in our actions not to allow terrorists [i.e. *fedayeen*] to return to the border fence.[45]

A significant consequence of the IDF's offensive was that the residents of the south were constantly reminded that a continuing Palestinian presence in the region would preclude any surcease to the Israeli campaign. Villagers, particularly those living in areas adjacent to the border strip controlled by Israel through their agent, Sa'ad Haddad, lived in fear of nighttime raids carried out against those who sympathized with the Palestinians or who were suspected of being members of Lebanese groups hostile to Israel or Haddad. (Such raids sometimes cut a wide and bloody swath as villagers found that by denouncing their adversaries they could enjoy the nectar of revenge and settle old feuds: more than a few political innocents suffered the unwitting IDF's heavy hand.) In a typical raid, carried out in December 1980, Israelis and Haddad's militiamen attacked five villages, killing three in cold blood, wounding ten, and damaging or destroying 14 houses.[46] Such raids had several important effects. First, persons affiliated with the LNM tended to stay away from their villages, and hence from additional recruits. Thus, the field was increasingly open to Amal which was viewed with favor by the IDF. Second, heretofore apolitical villagers learned that the best protection against unwanted early morning visitors was affiliation with a movement (viz., Amal) that would prevent "undesirables" from entering their villages. In a number of towns and villages, local residents even established their own local security forces, which would patrol during the hours of darkness. Over time, these ad hoc militia groups tended to affiliate with Amal. Third, the net result of the campaign was a clear and widening gulf between the PRM and the villagers of the south. Simultaneously, similar developments were underway in the Shi'a quarters of Beirut.

By 1980 and 1981, many of even the simplest peasants adopted anti-Palestinian slogans. Rather than casting blame on the Israelis—as had been the case in the past—the cause of the villagers' plight was often said to be the Palestinians. This alienation represented an important and easily understood success for the Israeli security apparatus. However, it should be noted that it was the intensity of the Shi'a villagers' feelings that was remarkable rather than their originality. In fact, the roots of the villagers' disenchantment may be traced to the early 1970s when the Shi'as rallied in support of the Lebanese Army after clashes between the army and the *fedayeen*.[47]

As the conflict in Lebanon progressed, the Shi'as were increasingly isolated as a community. In the early stages of the civil war, the Shi'as provided the cannon fodder for most of the groups aligned with the PRM. Indeed, as a dispossessed people they were often and aptly described as the natural allies of the Palestinian people. However, they increasingly became the communal victims of the Palestinian–Israeli war for Palestine–Israel. In a mean dialectical process, the Shi'as found themselves targeted by the Israelis for their geographic proximity to the *fedayeen*, and as they attempted to put distance between themselves and the *fedayeen* they were viewed with increasing contempt and suspicion by the *fedayeen*. Israel's campaign would not have been nearly as successful had it not been enhanced by the often arrogant, insensitive, and capricious behavior of the *fedayeen*.[48] By the late 1970s, it was common when visiting Shi'a villagers, to hear all kinds of vignettes in which Palestinians were the villains and Lebanese the victims. The IDF's intensive campaign, beginning in 1978, served to bring the latent contradictions and tensions to the surface,[49] and the resultant alienation of the Shi'as from the Palestinians served as a fertile context for the growth of an organization, Amal, that promised to fill a most basic need, security.

### The Disappearance of Musa al-Sadr

Accompanied by two associates, Sheikh Muhammed Shahadeh Ya'qub and Shafi 'Abbas Badr al-Din, Musa al-Sadr arrived in Libya on August 25, 1978, for a visit of unspecified length and purpose. One of Imam Musa's close associates has indicated that the visit was in response to an invitation from the Libyan leader, Mu'ammar al-Qaddafi, which al-Sadr accepted so that he could "advocate the return of peace to Lebanon and to work for peace."[50] Prior to his arrival in Libya, al-Sadr had visited Saudia Arabia, Kuwait, and Algeria, ostensibly for the same purposes.

According to a sympathetic account, the Iman Musa decided to leave Libya on August 31, 1978, the eve of the Libyan national holiday commemorating the September 1, 1970 Revolution. During the visit, al-Sadr was met by the Chief of the Libyan Foreign Relations Office, al-Sayed Ahmed al-Shahatey and presumably, al-Qaddafi. The Libyans claim that Musa al-Sadr and his companions left Libya on an Alitalia flight bound for Rome, but his followers deny this and claim that he never left Libya.[51] One senior associate, who claims he urged al-Sadr not to go to Libya, states that the Libyans sent three persons intended to pass for the traveling party, along with the party's luggage on the flight to Rome.[52] At any event, Musa al-Sadr has not been heard from since, although occasional reports of dubious origins indicate that he is still alive.[53] Most impartial observers believe him to be dead, as do a good number of his followers—when speaking privately.

Several explanations have been offered for the disappearance, but only one has been supported by more than conjecture or rumor, and that version, which involves the Syrians, is anything but a conclusive account. It is germane to at least touch upon the proffered explanations, since they each tell us a bit about al-Sadr's opponents, if not about the fate of Iman Musa himself. According to one version, al-Qaddafi had earlier provided three million £L (about one million dollars) to al-Sadr, and he could not satisfactorily account for the money, which allegedly ended up in a Swiss bank account. As a result of this malfeasance, the Libyan leader had al-Sadr murdered or incarcerated. There are several reasons to doubt this report. First, Libyan monies have been distributed to a number of Palestinian and Lebanese organizations (e.g., the *Ittihad al-Ishtiraki al-Arabi*—the Arab Socialist Union) without any semblance of close or even cursory accounting. Second, al-Sadr's closest companions claim that he was deeply in debt (two million dollars) when he disappeared, largely as a result of loans he had personally signed to support the large Technical Institute in Burj al-Shamali (near Tyre). An examination of his personal accounts revealed very modest sums of money. Third, al-Sadr's life style was simple, if not ascetic, and there is no reason to believe that he would have hoarded money that might have been used to support his movement. Indeed, interviews with individuals who knew him, including some of his adversaries, have not produced even one accusation of corruption on his part. Finally, al-Sadr's followers claim that they have told al-Qaddafi that if he can substantiate any financial misconduct on al-Sadr's part they would gladly agree to his imprisonment or even execution.[54]

Another version of the story has the Shah of Iran employing his intelligence service, SAVAK, to eliminate the Imam who apparently played at least a minor role in exciting anti-Pahlavi sentiment in Iran. There has traditionally been a very close relationship between Lebanese and Iranian Shi'a religious leaders, particularly since many Lebanese *sheikhs* were trained in the *madaris*—religious schools—of Iran. (Musa al-Sadr of course studied in Qum.) Furthermore, al-Sadr was not only an Iranian by birth, but he was linked by marriage to the Ayatollahs Khomeini and Taba'taba'i. (His sister is married to Khomeini's son, and his daughter is the wife of Sadiq Taba'taba'i, the son of the elder Taba'taba'i.) Thus, there is a certain plausibility to this variant of the story. In fact, when the United Nations Interim Force in Lebanon (UNIFIL) was formed in the spring of 1978, Iran provided a battalion—reportedly well manned by SAVAK agents—to the force. The Iranian unit was, according to a correspondent's report, busy "identifying and isolating followers of the anti-Shah leader, Imam Musa al-Sadr."[55] Nonetheless, while the Shah had the motive and no doubt the means to eradicate al-Sadr, Imam Musa's followers as well as the current Iranian regime—both with every incentive to blame the Shah—persist in placing the blame on al-Qaddafi's shoulders. As an Iranian official noted in 1980, "we consider the Libyan Government directly responsible for the mystery that continues to hover over this matter."[56]

Yet another version of the disappearance saga is offered by Shahpur Bakhtiar, to whom the Shah handed power when he fled Iran in 1979. Bakhtiar claims that al-Sadr was sent to Lebanon by the Shah in furtherance of a scheme to create a Shi'a state consisting of Iran, Iraq, and Lebanon. They subsequently fell out over the failure of the Shah to disburse a promised five hundred thousand dollars. However, it is not the Shah that Bakhtiar claims was responsible for the disappearance, but Khomeini, for whom al-Sadr was purportedly a very strong and dangerous competitor.[57] Especially well-informed observers have noted that even after the triumph of the Islamic Revolution, there was real fear that the "Amalists would take over the revolution." Interestingly enough, the latter explanation is given credence by one of al-Sadr's close associates, who believes that the Imam was murdered as a result of a Syrian-Libyan-Khomeini plot. This individual adds that al-Sadr and Khomeini did not like one another, marital and religious ties notwithstanding. Apparently, it was the Syrians, and particularly Foreign Minister Abdul Halim Khaddam, who urged al-Sadr to accept the Libyan invitation; obviously, it takes a rather substantial inferential leap to arrive at a full-blown assassination plot, but the possiblity cannot be dismissed.[58]

While the mystery of Musa al-Sadr's fate remains, his disappearance has been of enormous symbolic importance to Harakat Amal. His persona has been elevated to that of a national martyr for many of Lebanon's Shi'as. By 1979, his face had been added to the panoply of posters that testify to the multitude of causes and movements in Lebanon. The movement's newspaper, Amal, uses a picture of Imam Musa on its masthead and regularly reprints his speeches and commentary (usually accompanied by additional photographs). From time to time, movement members will identify themselves as "Sadrieen." Most of the younger members of Harakat Amal wear a button or a pendant with al-Sadr's visage on it, and some even sport silk-screened t-shirts depicting him. In a country with precious few contemporary heroes, Imam Musa has achieved an especial degree of fame.

Had Imam Musa passed quietly from the scene, it is likely that Shi'a politics in Lebanon would have been far more fractious than they have been for the past four years. While his followers applaud his humanity, selflessness, and staunch commitment to Lebanon's "disinherited," and to Lebanon itself, Musa al-Sadr's detractors point to his tactical shifts of alliances, the witting or unwitting role he played to the benefit of "counterrevolutionary" institutions and interests (viz., the deuxième bureau—Army Intelligence), and his political ambitions. Hence, had he continued his efforts in Lebanon, it is unlikely that he would have been able to repair or surmount the fissures that divided him from the Shi'a zu'ama and their followers, and from many of the groups that were affiliated with the LNM. While his disappearance has not eliminated the fissures, it has made them somewhat irrelevant. Many Shi'as find in the vanished Imam a compelling symbol for the expression of their discontent with the cruel malady that they have had to suffer. Al-Sadr's disappearance has complemented and fed a political mood and has been propitious for the crystallization of the populist movement he left behind, Harakat Amal.

More than a few Amal leaders concede that a "disappeared" Imam is doubtlessly of greater value for the political mobilization of the masses than a "present" one. Not only did the Imam's mysterious disappearance make it much more difficult for adversaries to criticize the movement that reveres his memory and which symbolizes his work, but his "occultation" is plainly reminiscent of the Shi'a dogma of the hidden Imam, a fact which lends further authenticity to the only wholly Shi'a political organization in Lebanon. As one thoughtful movement member conceded, the disappearance of Musa al-Sadr is the single most important thing that has happened for Harakat Amal.

## The Islamic Revolution

There is no question that the victory of the Islamic Revolution in Iran was keenly affective among the Shi'as of Lebanon. The deposition of the Shah in January 1979 served as an important exemplar demonstrating what a pious, well-organized, and motivated *ummah* could accomplish in the face of oppression and injustice. Even more important, the new regime in Tehran promised to be an important source of material and political support.

One interesting example of the close relationship between Tehran and the Lebanese Shi'a community is the case of Doctor Mustafa Chamran. Chamran, an Iranian, was the director of the Burj Ash-Shamali Technical Institute—which was probably partially financed with Iranian monies—until 1979, when he departed Lebanon to become a member of the Supreme Defense Council in the new Islamic Government. While it is not illogical to presume that such a well-placed official would have been of immeasurable assistance in securing substantial assistance for Amal, the mysterious death of Chamran in 1981, reportedly while visiting the Iraqi front, casts some doubt on such presumptions. Many Lebanese affiliated with Amal believe that Chamran's death was the work of persons or parties affiliated with Khomeini's regime who saw the American-educated engineer as a threat to their control of the regime. Thus, it may well be that popular notions about extensive and consistent support flowing from Tehran to Amal are inaccurate. It is not possible to accurately gauge the extent or dimensions of the support provided by Iran to Amal, but it appears to be quite possible that the relationship is much more problematic than glib press reports indicate.

Even in the event that the Iranian Government provided no more than rhetorical support, the very fact that the Islamic Revolution succeeded has been an important source of pride and inspiration to Lebanese coreligionists. But, while the Islamic Revolution is an important exemplar, it is not widely seen as a model for Lebanon, but rather as a sample that is more important for its emotive significance than for its political form. Some minor Shi'a clerics in Lebanon have attempted to mimic their brethren's success by taking a militant role in secular affairs, but such cases have been the exception rather than the rule. for the Muslim mainstream in Lebanon, there has been no indication that

Shi'as or Sunnis would care to transplant the Islamic Revolution to Lebanon; indeed, many Lebanese Muslims are both contemptuous and fearful of what they sometimes describe as Khomeini-ism.

The steady growth of Harakat Amal since 1978 is no doubt interesting. However, the fundamental significance of this dynamic movement is not to be found in its structural characteristics, but rather in its sociopolitical meaning to which we now turn.

## Sociopolitical Dimensions

Harakat Amal has been, to a large extent at least, the beneficiary of a number of circumstances that it did little to foster. The movement was rescued from obscurity because it offered a hero, an exemplar, and the promise of security for Lebanese Shi'as, who had tired of paying *diya* (blood money) on behalf of Palestinians, Israelis, and non-Shi'a Lebanese. There was nothing deterministic about the emergence of Amal or an organization like Amal. Had Musa al-Sadr returned from Libya, or the Shah prevailed in Iran, or the fedayeen comported themselves less antagonistically in their dealings with their host Lebanese, the past few years would have been very different—in political terms—for the Shi'as. It is not difficult to conceive of circumstances in which the political mobilization of the Shi'as might have been a centrifugal rather than a centripetal process. The fact that the process has tended to be centripetal was in large part especially due to the security situation in south Lebanon where the Shi'as paid in spades for the misfortune of being caught in the Israeli–Palestinian crossfire.

The credit that Amal's leadership deserves is for capitalizing on a fertile context—indeed, perhaps recognizing an historic opportunity—and having done so, filling a vacuum that under other conditions might have been filled by the *zu'ama*, the government, or the parties affiliated with the LNM.

The early 1982 comments of Nabih Berri, who has served since early 1980 as the Chairman of the Amal Command Council, as to the price paid by the Shi'as are notable in that they accurately represent the communal sense while they are also very restrained in comparison to the vehement opinions one would hear in the villages of the south. (Berri is a lawyer whose family home is in Tibneen, a major town close to the Israeli border.)

> The people of the south, including the Shi'as, have given the Palestinian cause more than all the Arabs combined have given it. They have given the cause their land, their children, their security, their orchards— everything but their honor and dignity.[59]

For the villager, for whom Berri's eloquent language was a strange diplomatist's tongue, it could all be put more simply: "We gave the Palestinians everything and they gave us back insults, corpses, and a lesson in corruption." Asked who or what was the source of their problems, Shi'a peasants as well as those higher up on the economic ladder would answer "the basis of our problem is the Palestinian presence." (Incredibly enough, I have even heard this muttered as the Israelis were attacking Lebanese territory.) Thus, peasant, worker, farmer, and teacher were ready to support a movement that would *protect* them and their families.

We tend to view events through familiar structural prisms, so much of the attention devoted to Harakat Amal has been in the sense that the Shi'as had simply organized themselves in a paramilitary organization that was challenging many of the other paramilitary groups that populated the Lebanese scene.[60] But such notions entirely miss the significance of Amal. As a combatant, the movement has more often than not been overshadowed by its adversaries; even its leaders have been quick to recognize its military weakness.

> If you go by arms, ammunition, and equipment, we are probably the weakest party in Lebanon: The smallest organization is probably better armed and better equipped than we are, but our strength lies in our ability to make the people, the masses, carry out our orders, and they do it because they know we are out to meet their demands.[61]

While the preceding assertion by Berri somewhat overstates Amal's military weakness, it does highlight what has been the movement's real strength—its capacity for transcending raw military power, and having done so, exerting not insubstantial political influence in Lebanon.

In the south, where Amal has drawn much of its strength, and nurtured its growth, the number of actual members (as opposed to sympathizers) has been extremely small. In one major Shi'a village only ninety persons even held membership out of an active male population of over fifteen hundred. In two other important villages only thirty to forty were officially members. Yet each of these villages was considered an Amal stronghold. The point is not that the significance of the movement has been exaggerated, but that we have to consider Amal in its wider meaning, viz., as a political statement to which Shi'as affiliated ideationally, if not officially.

In more than a few village in al-junub, residents identified themselves as Amalists, yet they often had no official connection with the organization. Of course for many villagers the best politics was no politics at all, a feeling that is well summed up in the folk proverb, *"Ra'ih al bagir ahsan min siyasat al-bashar"* (the intellect of a cow is better than the politics of the people). But politics, especially in violent variants, was impossible to escape. Thus, it was quite common to encounter a village replete with posters depicting Imam Musa and the Ayatollah Khomeini where the *mukhtar* and the village notables, as well as the peasants voiced the mottoes that so well exemplified Amal, and yet discover that Amal officials, who had every reason to claim a large membership in the village, could not claim one registered member in the village. When the villager said, "I am with Harakat Amal," he was merely confirming that Amal's populist message was striking a fundamental and authentic chord. While the Amal leadership might contemplate the restructuring of the Lebanese political system and the role of the Shi'a sect in such a restructured system, the villager's objectives were far less ambitious—in a word, he sought *security.* Hence, the appeal of a movement that called, without equivocation, for the reestablishment of the legitimate government and its institutions (and especially the army); for the support of the Palestinian struggle *in* Palestine, *not* Lebanon; and, for the disarming of militias, thugs, and marauders that have proliferated in all parts of the country.[62]

It was from the villages and towns that Amal drew its strength, and at the same time derived its weakness. Merchants, the small agrarian middle class, and overseas Shi'as were important financial supporters of the movement, but these people did not represent readily mobilizable coercive strength. In other words there was no functional equivalent to the armed militias of the LNM (or the Lebanese Front). For example, the wealthy Shi'a citrus growers of the southern coast (especially south of the Rashidiyye refugee camp), were keenly ardent contributors to the movement; yet beyond an occasional meeting (which in itself could be dangerous), their active participation in Amal affairs outside their respective villages was nearly nil. (Having attended several of these meetings, this author can attest to the very elementary level of organization enjoyed by the movement in 1980 and 1981.) Dependent as it was on a geographically diverse base of support, of which the basic unit was the village, Harakat Amal was only infrequently capable of concentrating coercive military or political power. Thus in al-junub, but less so in al-Beqa'a or in Beirut, Amal was defensive in orientation. This was certainly true at least through 1981.[63] In short, Amal was usually at a decided disadvantage when it had to confront its adversaries on the adversaries' terms.

Arguably it is not even accurate to speak of one Harakat Amal. In an important sense, for every village where pro-Amal sympathies predominated, there was a separate Harakat Amal. The result was an organization that accurately claimed wide support, but that often was unable to translate its affective force into effective control over its members and their activities. Indicative of this lack of control is the following candid comment made by an important movement leader:

> Remember that Amal is a movement. Thus, direct orders can often not be given. Instead leadership must be a combination of persuasion, moral example, and the like.[64]

While not lacking in funds or weapons, the movement's infrastructure in the south was very weak as late as 1982. Beset by constant clashes with its Lebanese and Palestinian adversaries, many of its most competent leaders spent the vast preponderance of their time quelling armed clashes and attempting to maintain at least the fiction of a brotherly relationship with the overtly less hostile segments of the *Quwat Mushtarikah* (i.e., the "Joint Forces" which brought together PLO and LNM fighters). Organization-building efforts were further stalled by the simple fact that many of the principal leaders continued to pursue a livelihood (usually out of necessity). Physical security was also a major preoccupation in that many leaders lived in villages that while internally secure were located adjacent to military positions manned by the *Quwat Mushtarikah*. In one extraordinary case, a key leader in the south lived less than two hundred meters from a military position that had apparently been sited for the express purpose of intimidating and observing him. The movement was much less vulnerable in the Beirut suburbs, especially in its Ghobierre stronghold, where larger concentrations of Shi'as and the self-contained nature of the community facilitated both the growth of the movement and the exclusion of "aliens." (One Ghobierre resident bragged that "fedayeen and leftists do not dare to enter.") Hence, in a violence-ridden environment like contemporary Lebanon, it was the degree of geographical integrity of respective Shi'a population clusters that largely determined the extent of Harakat Amal's "official" or public growth.

In the south (and al-Beqa'a), the result of the absence of a well-integrated organization was that the label "Amal," was sometimes free for the taking. For many Shi'a villagers the movement's name was merely a synonym for any collective self-defense activity carried out in the village. This, in itself, was a persuasive if ambiguous indicator of the degree to which Harakat Amal had come to be seen as the quintessential Shi'a organization. The Amal name was adopted, in at least a few cases, by local *shabab* (young bloods) who found that it provided them and their activities a certain legitimacy that they could not otherwise provide. Furthermore, more than a few Shi'as who had previously belonged to the ALF, or any of the several communist organizations, tested the wind and found that the time was propitious for a change of labels. This latter tendency was serious enough that in the spring of 1981 Harakat Amal termporarily suspended its recruitment activities, at least in the south, because of the well-founded suspicion that it had recruited quite a few members of questionable loyalty and background. (Lest the reader be misled, it is germane to note that while the parties of the "left" were being overshadowed by Amal in the early 1980s, successful recruiting campaigns were conducted by the Lebanese Communist Party right up to the 1982 invasion.)

The characteristics and developments described above are neither surprising nor dysfunctional for an emergent communally-based organization such as Amal. However, the movement's weak infrastructure had made it potentially vulnerable to cooptation by those who could manipulate the same symbols as Amal, viz., the Shi'a clergy. The leadership that replaced Imam Musa in Amal is basically secular in orientation and while contacts with Shi'a religious leaders are assiduously maintained, there is very little evidence of any participation in Amal per se by individual *sheikhs*. Doubtlessly, there are those within the movement who would like to see the integration of Amal with the Shi'a clergy, but this seems to be a minority tendency.[65] In early 1982 there was some evidence to indicate that the Imam Muhammed Mahdi Shams al-Din, Deputy Chairman of the Supreme Shi'a Council (Imam Musa is still officially the chairman), was challenging Nabih Berri for the leadership of the Shi'as—and doing so successfully. While this particular power play seems to have been short-circuited by the Israeli invasion, it was, as we shall see, reinitiated after the invasion.

On the local level, a few *sheikhs* who were sympathetic to Amal's objectives were reluctant to concede a leading role to its secular leaders. Taking the Iranian mullahs as their role models, several of these men took a direct part in organizing village chapters of Amal replete with militiamen and security activities. One colorful case involved the southern village of Siddiqine, where the local *sheikh* was incensed because his house had been bombed, reputedly by the ALF. Ignoring movement representatives in the village, he directed and apparently led the village militia. When Amal officials attempted to bring the maverick *sheikh* under control, he refused to concede their authority. It was only after Shams al-Din, at the behest of the Amal leadership, convinced the *sheikh* of Siddiqine to cooperate that he began to do so, and then only grudgingly. Contemptuous of the right of secular officials to represent his constituency or direct his efforts, the *sheikh* remarked: "I am Siddiqine and Siddiqine is me."

## The Movement's Agenda

With the plethora of militias and political groups in Lebanon, there has been a surfeit of political programs replete with prescriptions for curing the country's ills.[66] Before examining Amal's contribution to this crazy quilt of political platitudes and proposals, it is pertinent to briefly discuss the reasons it is difficult to definitively present the political program for Amal—or any other political grouping for that matter. Most obviously, among the early casualties of any war are the grand ideals for which men believe that they fight. The Lebanese conflict that began in 1975 was different only in that the idealism of the participants faded with astonishing rapidity. While each of the militias that fought could—to a greater or lesser extent—claim some semblance of a political rationale, the (il-)logic of the conflict quickly reduced the basis for individual campaigns and clashes to military pragmatism. Wars start with objectives writ large, but are fought for objectives writ small. Indeed, even the tactical rationale for specific clashes was suspect, given the large number of violent incidents sparked by affronts at checkpoints, killings, or kidnappings of friends and relatives, or merely the opportunity to loot and pillage.[67] War becomes its own justification, and men engaged in it have little time or inclination to reflect on their collective future. Thus, in an environment of near anomie, prescriptions for eradicating the conditions that engendered the conflict often must wait until the combatants exhaust themselves (or each other), or until decisive results (i.e. "victory" and "defeat") are achieved.

It is important to recognize that Harakat Amal was, before the 1982 invasion, acting on two complementary agendas: a first, implicit, and publicly unacknowledged by its officials, and a second, explicitly enunciated agenda. Before dealing with the latter, it is a propos to elaborate the movement's implicit or hidden agenda.

As we have seen, at the local level the primary motive for joining or supporting the movement was—plainly and simply—to find some relief from the rampant insecurity that gripped much of Lebanon. As the increasingly serious and frequent Amal-*Quwat Mushtarikah* clashes of 1981 and 1982 indicated, the primary threat to the Shi'a community's security was believed to emanate from the fedayeen and their supporters in the Lebanese National Movement.[68] In that the presence of the Palestinian fighters and their allies was seen as an invitation for Israeli attacks, villagers were not surprisingly opposed to the location of fedayeen positions in their midst. Furthermore, not only was there the ever-present fear of Israeli strikes, but all too often the propinquity of the fedayeen meant the expropriation of agricultural lands, and communal and privately owned buildings, not to mention exposure to constant coercion and physical intimidation. (These unsavory side effects were of course not restricted to locales occupied by the fedayeen, but were only one symptom of the devolution of coercive power to armed groups and paramilitary groups throughout Lebanon.)

The frequent Israeli raids, artillery bombardments, and air strikes dictated the dispersion of fedayeen positions; otherwise the Palestinians would have been even easier targets for Israeli guns. But the dispersion of Palestinian resistance forces fed the anxiety, resentment, and resolve of those who paid the heaviest price—the villagers. Accordingly, as Harakat Amal gained strength it would only further limit the freedom of action of the *fedayeen* and render the fedayeen ever more vulnerable to enemy attacks. Thus, Amal's implicit agenda that aimed at denying the *fedayeen* access to the Shi'a community could only weaken the *fedayeen*. It is hardly surprising that the consequences of the growth of Harakat Amal were recognized both by movement officials and leaders of the various organizational components of the *Quwat Mushtarikah*. Those groups that were most directly threatened by the resurgence of Amal pursued an aggressive campaign to stifle and even eliminate the movement. In particular, the *Jabhat Arabiyya*, which because of its close association with the Baghdad regime of Saddam Hussein was anathema to the pro-Iranian Amal, and the various communist factions that were prime competitors for Shi'a recruits, were among the most militant in their opposition to Amal.

While Fatah officials recognized the threat represented by a strong Amal, they also recognized the imperative of maintaining at least the appearance of good relations with the most important organization in the Shi'a community. Hence, Fatah strove to avoid any public involvement in open hostility to the movement. For their part, Amal officials were quick to express their distrust of Fatah, which they believed was instigating anti-Amal activities, but they also recognized the temporary utility of the largest PLO group as a *wasita* (mediator). In fact, Fatah was unquestionably the preeminent organization in the *Quwat Mushtarikah*, and the only group that was capable of even attempting to impose any discipline on Amal's adversaries. The significant if transitory importance of a relationship with Fatah was illustrated in late March 1980, when bloody street battles erupted in Beirut between Amal on the one side, and the *Jabhat Arabiyya* and the Popular Nasiserite Organization on the other. The fighting, which left twenty-seven dead, so alarmed Yasir Arafat (leader of Fatah and chairman of the PLO Executive Committee) that he interrupted his attendance at the Fourth Fatah Congress, then in progress in Damascus, and returned to Beirut to mediate the conflict.

By the Summer of 1980, two tendencies with respect to the armed Palestinian presence in Lebanon were discernible within Harakat Amal. The more moderate tendency, stemming from sympathy for the Palestinian cause and a recognition that the *fedayeen* presence was not likely to be soon terminated by a peaceful solution, held that Amal's enemies were those who were affiliated with despicable governments (viz., Iraq and Libya). Fatah for those espousing this point of view, was not only a useful *wasita*, but a worthy ally. The second tendency, which even in 1980 clearly represented the mainstream in the south, held the Palestinian fighters and *all* foreign interlopers responsible for the continuing troubles in Lebanon. According to the latter perspective, any relationship with Fatah (or any fedayeen organization for that matter) was merely tactical and transitory.

Despite the public posturing of Amal's officials and the staunchly pro-fedayeen line of the movement's weekly organ, *Amal*, the delicate partial entente between Amal and Fatah steadily deteriorated between 1980 and 1982. Clashes occurred with increasing regularity and all but the pretense of amity vanished. While Fatah attempted to maintain a modicum of control over the movement through local joint security committees (which in practice it dominated) and various forms of pressure and intimidation, the movement's geographic dispersion, diffuse leadership, and a rapidly growing amount of public support, made such attempts increasingly ineffective.

One corollary of the movement's hidden agenda that bears noting at this point is the consistent public support that it declared for the deployment of the Lebanese Army throughout Lebanon. While the LNM and the Lebanese Front represented alternative legitimacy structures, Amal firmly committed itself to the reestablishment of the central government's authority—an essentially conservative position that seemed to well serve the interests of a constituency that sought security *plus* a fair share of political rewards. Amal's stand on the deployment of the army did not endear it to its erstwhile allies who continued to see the army as a Maronite-dominated force that was opposed by definition to the reformist National Movement (and its Palestinian allies).[69] Thus, Amal's support of the army further emphasized its antithetical position to the *Quwat Mushtarikah*, and it also fed the suspicion that the movement (or at least segments of it) was no more than a stalking horse for the army's intelligence bureau, the *deuxième bureau.* (While Amal's support certainly warmed some hearts in the Lebanese Army, it is not clear that the Army directed or buttressed Amal to any significant extent.)

In addition to supporting the army, the movement sought to associate itself with any program or institution that symbolized legitimate governance in Lebanon. Furthermore, it seized every opportunity to compel the government to extend its authority. As previously noted, one consistent focus for Amal has been governmental indifference to the plight of those living in al-junub. A palpable symbol of that neglect has been the *Majlis al-Junub* (Council of the South). Originally chartered in 1970 to foster economic development, the council has languished corruption-ridden. Amal made the council a constant target for criticism and protest, and in September 1980, occupied the council's offices in Saida and prevented its employees from entering the building. Simultaneously, Nabih Berri announced a series of demands, including the more timely and adequate compensation of those who had been displaced or who had suffered property damage due to hostilities. The movement threatened to take over the operation of the *Majlis al-Junub* if its demands were not met.[70] It is hard to conceive that a more politically lucrative target could have been chosen. By attacking the council, Amal raised an issue of widespread concern, forced the feeble government of Prime Minister Salim al-Hoss to take—or at least purport to take—a keener interest in the welfare of its citizens, and astutely identified itself with a legitimate governmental function.

While it is beyond the scope of this chapter to fully explore Harakat Amal's relationship with Syria, it should be acknowledged that the relationship has been close indeed. Amal's weapons were acknowledged to be supplied "via" Syria,[71] and the Syrians seem to have played a role in training Amal militiamen, especially since 1980. Berri affirmed his movement's relationship with the Damascus government in February 1982, when, in an enunciation of Amal's goals, he included:

> The definition of special military, security, economic, and cultural relations between Lebanon and Syria, and the specification of Israel as Lebanon's arch-enemy.[72]

The Amal–Syria relationship served as yet another proof of the danger that Amal represented for the *Quwat Mushtarikah.* Certainly since the June 1976 Syrian intervention on the side of the Lebanese Front, relations between Syria and Fatah (and its allies) had been frosty to say the least.[73] It should be recalled that Imam Musa broke with the LNM in 1976 when he supported the Syrians against his former allies. It is not unreasonable to presume that Amal was, to a degree at least, a means by which Hafiz al-Assad could temper and even control the actions of those groups which he could not directly influence. Plainly the strongest fedayeen presence was south of the "red line" delimited by Israel, and thus in the area from which Syrian forces were excluded, and its influence limited.

By early 1982 relations between Amal and its adversaries further deteriorated as widespread skirmishes broke out in a number of southern villages. Then in April 1982 fighting erupted in Beirut and in sixteen villages in al-junub. According to an Amal account, elements belonging to or aligned with Fatah conducted a ten-hour bombardment of the Technical Institute in Burj al-Shamali during the April fighting.[74] These serious clashes represented an important watershed for several reasons: When the fighting was brought to a halt, Amal forces—for the first time—remained in control of formerly disputed villages.[75] While the movement was far from being a well-oiled military organization, it showed significant tactical skill, even to the extent of mounting diversionary attacks and feints. Most significantly, through the auspices of the Syrian-dominated Higher Coordination Committee (comprised of representatives from the PLO, Amal, the LNM, and Syria), it was agreed that the PLO "should henceforth not involve itself in Lebanese internal security matters" but should concentrate on "strategic security." No one really expected the PLO to fulfill the agreement, but its very promulgation served as an indictment.

In the months preceding the Israeli invasion, the contradictions separating the *Quwat Mushtarikah* from Amal had become highly salient. The deteriorating character of the relationship was well illustrated by the contrasting statements of Salah Khalaf (whose *nom de querre* is Abu Iyad and who is usually identified as the second-in-command in Fatah) and the leading Shi'a cleric, the Imam Muhammed Mahdi Shams al-Din. When Khalaf was asked in December 1981 about Fatah's relationship with Amal, he replied:

> In fact, there is no conflict between the [Palestinian] resistance and the Amal movement. Indeed relations are good.[76]

Commenting on the same subject, just two months later, Khalaf had clearly lost his patience with Amal:

> We address our brothers in the Amal movement, not the schemers in Amal, but the brother nationalists whom we know take the initiative in the Amal movement and participate in the joint command

and the joint forces in the South so that we can prevent all evil elements and schemers in various areas from scheming in southern Lebanon. We reaffirm that we are concerned about the Amal movement . . . so that they will be with us in the same trench, within one joint command.[77]

Following the April fighting, Shams al-Din offered his first public criticism of the fedayeen and the LNM. His strongly worded statement, which follows, was widely interpreted as an important hardening of the Shi'a (and the Amal) position.

The Supreme Shi'a Council urgently asks *those responsible in the Palestinian resistance and the Nationalist Movement* to stop the shelling of the villages immediately, to pull the gunmen out of them and to withdraw the weapons directed at them. The continuation of this situation portends grave consequences for the entire Arab situation. The people of the South are now facing Arab bullets, which are supposed to be directed at Israel, and are being displaced from their homes not by Israelis but by fellow Arabs. [italics added][78]

Even Nabih Berri, who had previously adopted a conciliatory public stance,[79] did not hesitate to contradict the PLO leadership's claims that Palestinians were not involved in the April clashes.[80]

## Amal's Public Agenda

Harakat Amal's publicly proclaimed agenda has combined a call for the restoration of unified Lebanon with demands for the gradual reformation of the polity. As alluded to above, the movement's immediate objectives have included the reimposition of state authority and sovereignty.[81] Consistent with these goals, the movement opposed any effort to proliferate alternative governmental structures. Nabih Berri even suggested that the heavy fighting in April 1982 was precipitated by the LNM's attempt to elect "local councils" in Ras Beirut. The election of such councils was seen by Amal as a "form of autonomy" that might be preliminary to the partition of Lebanon.[82]

While the immediate goals have been relatively modest, the longer term prescriptions promoted by the movement amount to changing the criterion—confessional identity—by which political rewards have traditionally been allocated in Lebanon. Berri has argued that confessionalism has precluded the development of a Lebanese nationality and has been the root cause of the country's troubles.

> This [confessional] hallucination that we have in our minds has made us behave like tribes instead of like people of one country. The 1943 National Pact that we created is a partitionist pact. It helped us to build a farm, not a country. . . . I say this Pact is the root of all our troubles.[83]
>
> Because here the economic and employment competition is built on a purely sectarian basis. Sectarianism is imposed on us. They are making us wear turbans and priests' robes and forcing us to think confessional.[84]

Consistent with Berri's remarks, until early 1982 Amal called for the abolition of confessionalism "from the top of the pyramid to its base,"[85] excepting the top three political positions only so long as necessary to demonstrate that deconfessionalism was working. However, by February 1982, the position had softened somewhat, although deconfessionalism was still proclaimed the ultimate goal.

> The abolition of sectarianism must at least start in the army and in education, in the hope that this will lead to the total abolition of political sectarianism in Lebanon eventually.[86]

At first glance the position publicized by Berri is not complementary to the collective interests of the Shi'a community that would stand to benefit from a reallocation of political positions and rewards proportionate to their share of the demographic pie. However, on closer examination, two factors justify the call for jettisoning—albeit slowly—confessionalism. Most important, it was the proliferation of parochial sectarian interests that, according to one principal's interpretation, made the civil war possible and thwarted the cessation of violence. Berri's deputy, Hasan Hashim, has asserted that the outside powers—especially the East and West military camps—were able to exploit sectarianism in furtherance of their aim of controlling the Palestinian Revolution. Hashim notes:

> Lebanon is a victim of the dirty political game laid out by the Eastern and Western Camps. All of the organizations active on the Lebanese stage (except Harakat Amal) were connected and affiliated toward one of the Arab countries or an outside foreign power, and all of these groups and organizations were deeply and thickly involved in Lebanon and in the developments which took place in it.[87]

Thus, to leave the Lebanese system unchanged is to maintain its vulnerability to meddling by outside powers. Obviously there is a very good dose of truth in this analysis, but here is another side to the position, and that is the position, voiced from time to time in the movement's weekly, that the Shi'as were the only sect lacking an outside sponsor. Lacking a political sugar daddy, the Shi'as suffered accordingly.[88]

Deconfessionalizing Lebanese politics is obviously a profoundly difficult matter and one that requires the support of precisely those who stand to lose the most if it is to be implemented. Less radical reforms that preserve confessional politics, but recognize Shi'a claims through the reallocation of political privileges, may well satisfy an assertive Shi'a community without exacerbating the existing insecurities in other confessions. As Fuad Khuri notes, the formula (i.e., the 1943 Covenant) might be preserved, but the equation by which political roles have been distributed would be changed to reflect new realities.[89] There is certainly evidence that Amal is aiming at an important revision of the political equation. Specifically, Nabih Berri and others in the movement have made statements which betoken a blurring of sectarian-based allocations between the Shi'as and the Sunnis. By minimizing or even denying differences between the two Muslim sects, the way may be opening for Shi'a claims to Muslim (i.e., Sunni) seats of power (viz., prime minister). For example, speaking in the wake of the Israeli invasion, Berri observed:

> There is one Muslim community in Lebanon, and there are no differences. Regrettably, however, we still have the mentality of 1943, and I dread to say the mentality of 1864. I say it is absolutely impossible to disregard any side in the Lebanese arena. The Muslim community in Lebanon constitutes half of the population of Lebanon and even more, and it has its rights. It has discharged many duties. I add that our Christian brothers cannot be dispensed with or replaced. As a cohesive national unity, we must rise with Lebanon from a Lebanese premise and not from a sectarian premise.[90]

Although the Amal position has expressly excluded federalist or confederalist solutions,[91] such as the Lebanese Front has proposed from time to time,[92] the movement has been careful not to exlcude the discussion of any political program. In short, it has striven to project a conciliatory pose that makes it a natural interlocutor for any party willing to discuss incremental reforms. Berri has stated that any changes that are undertaken should result from a dialogue between "all active forces in Lebanon without exception."[93] Given the movement's troubled relations with the PLO, its strong relationship with Syria, and its promotion of Lebanese nationalism, its presence in any Lebanese government might solve problems for the Maronite community and salve any misgivings about power-sharing arrangements with the Shi'as.

In discussing the movement that venerates Musa al-Sadr, it is appropriate to note that observers often found al-Sadr's intentions elusive. As one writer put it, "no one could specify where he stood politically."[94] One great admirer of Imam Musa, whose relationship began over twenty years ago, often remarked that "Imam Musa was a pragmatist, not an ideologue." Thus, we should probably not be surprised to find that Imam Musa's political heirs proved to be rather more interested in short-term gains than in long-term consistency.

## AFTER THE 1982 INVASION

By early 1982 relations between Amal and the Quwat Mushtarikah had passed the breaking point. After the serious clashes of January and April, it was a foregone conclusion that Shi'a interests could no longer be reconciled with the fedayeen presence. While the movement was still significantly outgunned by its opponents, tactical improvements and a militarily wiser leadership helped to make the movement an increasingly formidable threat. With its fighters scattered from village to village, Amal lacked the geographic concentration of its brethren in the Beirut suburbs, but it compensated for its weakness by launching hit-and-run attacks, diversionary actions, and careful defense of village strongpoints.

No doubt Amal's growing effectiveness played an important role in the Israeli decision-making that led to the June invasion. While Israeli planners grossly misinterpreted the longer term meaning of Amal's militance, they were certainly correct if they anticipated a paucity of indigenous support for the fedayeen. No Amal leader of stature could accept an overt relationship with the IDF or with its puppet, Sa'ad Haddad, yet there was no lack of understanding of the benefits of a tacit alliance. In fact, after hearing the definition of an "objective alliance," one key leader acknowledged that that was indeed a good description of the movement's relationship with the IDF and Haddad. Some reports have exaggerated the level of collaboration between the invading IDF and Amal, but it is clear that especially in the first weeks of the invasion, residents of the south provided assistance in such matters as pinpointing fedayeen arms caches or identifying leaders of adversarial groups.

It is no understatement to claim that many southern Shi'as welcomed the Israeli invasion. One leader even stated that had Israel not invaded a war between Amal and the fedayeen was inevitable. It should be stressed, however, that the mood in the south was not neatly replicated in the other two Amal strongholds—Beirut and the Beqa'a. It was only in the south that the Shi'as were constantly exposed to the deadly weight of Israeli military power and it was only in the south that the fortunes of geography forced the Shi'as to choose between supporting or resisting the Palestinian presence. It was the shortsightedness of the PLO, and in particular the preeminent Fatah, which helped to decide the choice. Notwithstanding an active Israeli program to alienate the people of the south from the guerrillas, the brash, arrogant, and often cruel behavior of the *fedayeen* rendered the choice really no choice at all. Outside of the south, Amal defined its adversaries more narrowly. Thus, south of Beirut, around Burj al-Burajinah for example, fighting involving Amal tended to be against forces perceived as viscerally anti-Shi'a (or anti-Iran), such as the Iraqi-sponsored *Jabhat Arabiyya*. The contrast in situations is well illustrated by the fact that while the Amal fighters in the south watched as the Israeli tank columns rolled by, those from al-Shiyyah, Ouzai, and Ghobierre mounted some of the most spirited and aggressive defensive actions against the invaders.

True, the invasion accomplished what Amal could not, namely the expulsion of the fedayeen from the south, but the glee of the Shi'as was short-lived as it became clear that for the cost of their suffering they may merely have witnessed the supplantment of one occupation force for another. With the invasion Harakat Amal found itself faced with a new panoply of problems, which if not satisfactorily resolved could well threaten the viability and even the survival of the movement.

Just as an earlier phase in the political mobilization of the Shi'as by Musa al-Sadr was interrupted by the cascading violence of 1975–76, so the events of the summer of 1982 seemed likely to short-circuit the renewed mobilization efforts that had commenced in 1978 and 1979. At first glance it even seemed that Amal's very raison d'être—communal security—had been obviated. While the Iranian exemplar and the disappearance of the imam were important mobilization symbols, the decisive factor was the increasingly serious and violence-fraught estrangement of the Shi'as from the Palestinian Resistance Movement. With the fedayeen excised, the critical question to be faced was whether a membership fed by the attraction of collective security could be maintained when the imperative of collective security was much weaker or at least less obvious. Put another way, could Amal redirect its efforts so as to retain its primary leadership role for a politicized Shi'a community, or would the organization prove to be an anachronism in the "New Lebanon"?

In effect the organization faced challenges at three distinct levels: from within the organization, from within the Shi'a sect, and from other—non-Shi'a—actors in Lebanon's political system.

## Internal Challenges

As we have noted, Amal was never a tightly integrated organization and the possibility of fissure has always been latent within the organization. Not unexpectedly, given the organization's inchoate quality, there were keen regional splits which roughly corresponded with relative proximity to the Israeli (and Syrian) border(s). In addition to disparities born of locale, the movement subsumes an admixture of political perspectives and ideological preferences. While the critical mass of active members and leaders agree that the appropriate focus of their demands is a reformed Lebanese political system, there are segments that reject this relatively modest objective.

In addition, Amal has always contained its share of agents and opportunists who were perfectly willing to return to patron-client relationships outside the organization. For these people, the movement's instrumental value was simply as a substitute for preferred patrons—whether they be this or that za'im or organization. (One of the more fascinating political spectator sports has been watching the zu'ama who had been made increasingly irrelevant by the continuing civil war, attempt to elbow their way back into power after the invasion. Kamal al-Asad, whose constituency is unapparent, is typical of the genre.) Moreover, more than a few secularly oriented Shi'as had merely found it astute, and even advantageous, to support or join the movement rather than overtly opposing it. Many of the latter category dropped away from the movement after June 1982, when this pragmatic rationale became much less compelling.

Further threats to the movement's viability were mounted by those who raised serious challenges regarding the political objectives of Amal, including questions as to its very authenticity as a Shi'a movement. One such challenge was mounted by a member of the 25-member Command Council, Hassein Musawi. In July 1982, Musawi charged the movement's leaders with blatant collaboration with the invading Israelis, and, apparently with Iranian support, attempted to reorient the movement to what he saw as its proper objectives: the replication of Iran's Islamic Revolution in Lebanon. Musawi was subsequently expelled from the movement during the summer of 1982. He is, as of late 1983, ensconced in Ba'albek, in the Syrian-controlled Beqa'a where he leads the Islamic Amal Movement in apparent cooperation with a contingent of *Pasdaran* (Revolutionary

Guards) dispatched by Iran to Lebanon. He has been implicated in a number of acts of political violence, including the kidnapping of the president of the American University, David Dodge, and the destruction of the U.S. Embassy in April 1983. While Musawi's following is limited, his activities, buttressed as they are by the Syrian occupation of the Beqa'a, serve to remove the sizable Shi'a population of the Beqa'a from the organizational grasp of the mainline Amal organization.[95]

## Shi'a Competitors

As alluded to above, the post-invasion period brought a reemergence of a number of the traditional leaders, who while lacking sizable constituencies still maintained important political ties outside of the Shi'a community. Of course, the most notable was Kamal al-Asad, but there were others as well with familiar names like Hamadeh, Khalil, and Ossiran. These *zu'ama*, often denoted "semi-feudal leaders" by articulate Lebanese, were increasingly anachronistic. Their control of segments of the Shi'a community was tenuous even before 1975, as demonstrated by the successes of Musa al-Sadr in the early 1970s. Indeed, the very processes of mobilization that helped to bring about a politicized Shi'a community, had, by definition, reduced the fragmentation of the community and concomitantly the ability of a *za'im* to control geographically isolated communities. This is not to say these sociopolitical changes have been recognized (or accepted) by the Shi'a *zu'ama* or their Lebanese and non-Lebanese allies. As we shall explain below, attempting to turn back the clock of Shi'a politicization can be an attractive—albeit naive—maneuver for devotees of a Maronite-controlled Lebanon, as well as for outside powers thwarted in their attempt to manipulate Harakat Amal. While external manipulation may keep the *zu'ama* off the endangered species list, it is very doubtful that they will ever recapture the influence and control that they once enjoyed.

Without question, the most serious challenge to Amal's primacy in the leadership of the Shi'as has come from one individual, Mufti Muhammed Mahdi Shams al-Din. Shams al-Din, while technically a principal in Amal (he is a member of the Command Council), is probably the most important Shi'a cleric in Lebanon. His only real competitor for that distinction is the Jafa'ri Mufti al-Mumtaz, Adb al-Amr Qabalan. Since the disappearance of Musa al-Sadr, who led the movement while simultaneously chairing the Higher Shi'a Council, the two positions have been split along secular-clerical lines. Hussein Husseini, a parliamentary deputy, and now Nabih Berri have led Amal, while Shams al-Din has chaired the Council (while retaining the title, Deputy Chairman).

The details of the struggle for supremacy between Shams al-Din and Berri are unavailable; nonetheless it is clear that a competition has been underway. In early 1982, for example, press reports indicated that there was a power struggle between Berri and Shams al-Din. The Israeli invasion seemed to push Berri closer to the Mufti, although there was some controversy between the two concerning the extent to which Amal fighters should confront the IDF. Berri, according to some informants, was pushing for a more aggressive role, especially in Ras Beirut, but he was successfully overruled by Shams al-Din. In the months following the invasion, the two men temporarily overcame, or at least accommodated their differences. Berri, arguably the weaker of the two in terms of legitimacy and elite constituencies, may have been somewhat buttressed through the active support of Sheikh Qabalan. The competition again became heated in early 1983, when it was announced that Shams al-Din had broken off all relations with the leadership of Harakat Amal.[96] Whatever the motives behind the announcement, it had the effect of placing the Mufti above the fray, validating his prospective claim for the principal leadership role of the Shi'as. Since the dramatic announcement, Shams al-Din has continued to deal with Nabih Berri and other movement leaders, so it is quite possible that the severing of ties may have merely been an object lesson for Amal. At this writing, it remains clear that the consolidation of leadership within Amal is an ongoing process, and the outcome is anything but predetermined.

## Extra-communal Actors

At this juncture it is appropriate to note what has undoubtedly been the most serious challenge to Amal's authority in the south. This refers to Israel's attempts to coopt and emasculate Amal. Buoyed by its reception in June 1982, Israel set about using the existing Amal organization in the south as an adjunct to, or even substitute for, Sa'ad Haddad's militia. In what can only be described as a supreme miscalculation, the IDF or Mossad mistook the alienation of the Shi'as from the Palestinians as positive evidence for the possibility of establishing close ties between Israel and the Shi'a community. In fact, most of the population had no desire to trade one foreign overlord for another. Such wishful thinking on the part of Israel is not altogether surprising, however. Notwithstanding some sycophantic reporting in the United States, the Israelis seem to have clearly understood that Haddad and his weak militia were, as one IDF adviser put it, "unacceptable" to the majority of the population.[97] As Clinton Bailey, an Israeli who served as an Arab affairs adviser in south

Lebanon, observed in December 1982, the Shi'a members of Haddad's militia were "looked upon as the dregs of Shi'a society."[98]

Initial efforts to coopt Amal intact promptly failed. While the southern leadership did not eschew a dialogue with Israeli personnel, they were both unwilling and unable to allow themselves to follow the Haddad prototype. Nonetheless, there were no outward displays of belligerence, and there were a number of cases of small-scale collaboration. The first phase was short-lived as the Israelis arrested thirteen of the movement's leaders and began a process of alienation that still continues.

The initial phase was followed by an Israeli campaign to recruit individual Amal members and Shi'as into a network of village militias that would form a regional grouping paralleling Amal. Simultaneously, the IDF apparently sponsored the return of the traditional leadership, which would further undercut Amal influence in the area.

Faced with an obdurate Amal leadership, the Israelis created an organization purportedly independent of Haddad's force. The organization, the *haras al-watani li-qura' al-Junub* (National Guard for the villages of the South), was intended to unite village militias created under Israeli pressure. While there have been some local successes, the attempt has basically been a failure. The principal cause of failure has been the inability of Israel's and Haddad's agents to recruit locally respected leaders. Even where the militias have been relatively active, as in Jwayya, Majdel Silm, and Sarafand, the groups remain transparent implantations. In Sarafand, for example, a local Amal leader was arrested and the village notables were told that the price of his release was the formation of a militia.[99] In a number of cases, the only leaders available have been those who are, for one reason or another, held in disrepute by the villagers. This is not to say that the militias will wither away, though, because they serve two complementary Israeli interests. First, they provide a justification and façade for Israeli involvement. Second, and this may well explain their morphology, while spawned of coercion, the militia may be converted into the partisan forces (*al-ansar*) which are ensconced in the Lebanese–Israeli agreement of May 1983. Thus, the existence of these militias will have been given a stamp of legitimacy. Along these lines it is important to note that the *haras al-watani* has been renamed *ansar jaysh lubnan al-hurr* (Partisans of the Army of Free Lebanon) or briefly *al-ansar*, thus corresponding in title to the government of Lebanon-created militia—a shrewd psychological gambit.[100] However, without Israeli shepherding, it remains doubtful that the militias, as constituted, will ever attain any significant role in the security of the south. They are, for many Shi'as, merely a symbol of continuing Israeli occupation.

Of less significance, but also indicative of Israeli intentions, has been the return of a few of the Shi'a *zu'ama* to the south under IDF sponsorship. For example, after an absence of seven years, Kazim al-Khalil, a political affiliate of Camille Chamoun's National Liberal Party, returned to Tyre. When Khalil first returned in July 1982, he attempted to reach a rapprochement with Amal, but as one Amal leader reported, the *sulha* (reconciliation) quickly evaporated after a few acts of violent intimidation authored by Khalil's son.[101] With IDF assistance, Khalil did establish a small (40-man) militia which was armed and uniformed by the Israelis. While few southerners believe that Khalil could retain his parliamentary seat in anything approaching a fair election, his presence in Tyre does serve to modestly undercut Amal and it is part of this whole cloth of the Israeli campaign to fragment a Shi'a community it cannot control as a single unit.

## AMAL SURVIVES

Admittedly, Amal has lost a number of marginal members and sympathizers since the Israeli invasion, but it has weathered what could have been a fatal organizational crisis extremely well. While its militia days have not been totally surmounted, the movement has increasingly moved to the center stage of the Lebanese political scene, while simultaneously consolidating its constituency. In the latter regard, Amal has identified key social welfare activities that meet pressing needs while giving the organization a high and favorable profile in the Shi'a community. Thus, in *al-junub* it has opened a series of Spartan yet adequate clinics which are accessible to all citizens for a modest fee (with free care available when justified). The clinics are well-planned and are clearly not a fly-by-night operation. The first important evidence of the movement's sustained vitality came in September 1982 when as many as two hundred and fifty thousand gathered in Tyre to commemorate the fourth anniversary of Musa al-Sadr's disappearance. A similar, but smaller demonstration was held in Nabatiyyah a few days later. Periodic strikes have also served as continuing evidence that the movement's fundamental influence has not waned.

While Israel's massive invasion was still in progress, Nabih Berri was serving as a member of the National Salvation Committee formed to begin what will continue to be a bumpy road of national reconciliation. While the movement could not openly support the election of Bashir al-Gemayel, it did privately pledge support, as did the two major Shi'a religious leaders. Given Amin al-Gemayel's less problematic resume, Amal was able to support Amin's election largely on the presumption that Amin would continue his brother's political program which included cutting the Shi'as in for a larger share of power. Unfortunately, President Amin al-Gemayel has seemed to be much more confortable dealing with the established *zu'ama* than with their challengers in Amal. Thus, the old rivalry with *zu'ama* like Kamal al-Asad has been resurrected with a vengeance.

In the fall of 1982 Amal had adopted a patient stance, expecting that *al-sabr miftah al-faraj*—patience would be the key to success. Many of the movement's principals merely expected modest incremental concessions from the government, as well as the extrication of foreign forces from Lebanon. Sadly, neither expectation has been met. Over time, the Shi'as have come to believe that they are serving as the whipping boys for a president who cares more for his weak Maronite constituency than for his larger constituency. Thus, it should hardly be surprising that the Shi'as came to lose patience. The result has been a series of clashes with the army as well as a purely tactical (and very cynical) alliance with the customarily distrusted Druze.

The prevailing attitude within the Amal leadership is well summarized by a joke that was printed in a column that appears in the movement's paper, *Amal*:

A man was on an airline flight, and after the airplace took off, this man entered the plane's cockpit drawing a pistol, and indicating that the plane was being hijacked. "For what reason?" the captain asked him, "and to what destination?" The hijacker insisted on going to Los Angeles, and the plane's stated destination was Los Angeles, anyway. When the plane arrived at the Los Angeles airport, the man routinely disembarked with the rest of the passengers. The newsmen on the scene asked him, "Why did you do this?" So he said, "This is the third time that I have taken off on a plane to go to Los Angeles to meet my family, and each previous time the plane was hijacked to another place, so I wanted to hijack it this time before some other hijackers took it to another place.[102]

The point of course is that the danger of the Lebanese ship of state's being hijacked is seen as a real one. Thus, so long as the danger persists Amal must be ready to guide it to its proper destination. The Lebanese Shi'as may not be able to ensure that the plane reaches Los Angeles, but they are capable of preventing it from reaching any other destination. If Lebanon has a future—and it may not—Shi'a interests as mediated by Harakat Amal will have to be accommodated; that much, at least, is clear.

## NOTES

1. One measure of the marginality of the Shi'as is the fact that most political studies written prior to the civil war almost totally ignored them. The following two books are notable exceptions: Michael C. Hudson, *The Precarious Republic: Political Modernization in Lebanon* (New York: Random House, 1968); and, David R. Smock and Audrey C. Smock, *The Politics of Pluralism: A Comparative Study of Lebanon and Ghana* (New York: Elsevier Scientific Publishing Co., 1975).

2. Useful population estimates may be found in the following two sources: Joseph Chamie, "The Lebanese Civil War: An Investigation into the Causes," *World Affairs* 139 (Winter 1976/1977): 171–88; and, Riad B. Tabbarah, "Background to the Lebanese Conflict," *International Journal of Comparative Sociology* vol. 20, nos. 1–2 (1980): 101–21.

3. Chamie, "Lebanese Civil War," 179.

4. Hudson, *Precarious Republic*, 79.

5. Tabbarah, "Background to the Lebanese Conflict," 118.

6. Hasan Sharif, "South Lebanon: Its History and Geopolitics," in *South Lebanon*, eds. Elaine Hagopian and Samih Farsoun (Detroit: Association of Arab-American University Graduates, August 1978), 10–11.

7. Hagopian and Farsoun, *South Lebanon*, 11.

8. Karl W. Deutsch, "Social Mobilization and Political Development," *American Political Science Review* vol. 55, no. 3 (September 1961): 493–514.

9. Deutsch, "Social Mobilization," 493.

10. Deutsch, "Social Mobilization," 497–498.

11. Deutsch, "Social Mobilization," 498.

12. See Hudson, *Precarious Republic*, esp. 53–86.

13. World Bank, *World Development Report* (New York: Oxford University Press, 1982), 147.

14. Salim Nasr, "Backdrop to Civil War: The Crisis of Lebanese Capitalism," *MERIP Reports*, no. 73 (December 1978), 3–13.

15. Nasr, "Backdrop to Civil War," 10.

16. For a useful critical discussion of Deutsch's position on assimilation versus dissimilation, see Walker Connor's important article; "Nation-Building or Nation-Destroying?" *World Politics* vol. 24, no. 3 (April 1972): 319–55, esp. 321–28.

17. Deutsch, "Social Mobilization," 501. See also Deutsch's *Politics and Government: How People Decide Their Fate*, 3d ed. (Boston: Houghton Mifflin Co., 1974), 544, where he notes:

> Social mobilization makes people more available for change. It does so by inducing them or teaching them to change their residence, their occupations, their communications, their associates, and their outlook and imagination. It gives rise to new needs, new aspirations, new demands and capabilities. *But all these patterns of behavior may disunite a population or unite it. They can make people more similar or more different. They may produce cooperation or strike, integration or succession.* [Italics added]

18. See Hudson, *Precarious Republic*, 21.

19. On the preservation of sectarian identity in Beirut, see Fuad I. Khuri, "The Social Dynamics of the 1975–1977 War in Lebanon," *Armed Forces and Society* vol. 7, no. 3 (Spring 1981): 383–408; and, Khuri, "A Comparative Study of Migration Patterns in Two Lebanese Villages," *Human Organization* 26, no. 4 (1967). See also Smock and Smock, *Politics of Pluralism*, 93.

20. Hudon, *Precarious Republic*, 61.

21. Khuri, "Social Dynamics of the War," 392.

22. For an instructive (and controversial) fictional treatment of a young Shi'a woman's attempt to "escape" from her village and her sect, see Tawfik Yusuf Awwad, *Death in Beirut*, trans. Leslie McLoughlin (London: Heinemann Educational Books, 1976).

23. Daniel Lerner, *The Passing of Traditional Society: Modernizing the Middle East* (New York: Free Press, 1958), 61.

24. Deutsch, "Social Mobilization," 497-8.

25. Deutsch, "Social Mobilization," 499.

26. Samuel P. Huntington, *Political Order in Changing Societies* (New Haven: Yale University Press, 1968), 47.

27. While the urban-rural distinction may have lost much of its meaning in the context of political development, there is no denying that the individual Lebanese finds the distinction very important, since the rural village is a place of relaxation, refuge, retreat, and retirement.

28. Fuad I. Khuri, *From Village to Suburb: Order and Change in Greater Beirut* (Chicago: University of Chicago Press, 1975), 8.

29. Hudson, *Precarious Republic*, 31-2.

30. Before the civil war began in 1975, the political loyalty of the Shi'a community was fragmented. In addition to al-Sadr, the principal contenders for power included Kamal al-Asad, the scion of a famous Shi'a *za'im*; the al-Khalil family of Tyre; and various political parties, including the several Ba'ath factions, Communists, the Syrian Social Nationalist Party, and a few Nasserist groups.

31. Biographical data have been extracted from al-Sadr! (Beirut: Dar al-Khalud, 1979), 11-17.

32. Raphael Calis, "The Shiite Pimpernel," *The Middle East*, November 1978, 52.

33. Smock and Smock, *Politics of Pluralism*, 141.

34. Sharif, "South Lebanon," 18.

Many Lebanese refer to the council as the *Majlis al-Juyub* (the Council of the Pockets) in recognition of the council's reputation for bribery and illegal diversions of funds. As will be noted below, the *Majlis al-Junub* became an important target for Amal activism in 1980.

35. "Rivalry to Lead the Shi'a in Lebanon," *The Arab World Weekly* (Beirut), February 16, 1974, 11.

36. Calis, "The Shiite Pimpernel," 11.

37. Calis, "The Shiite Pimpernel," 11.

38. Kamal S. Salibi, *Crossroads to Civil War: Lebanon 1958-1976* (Delmar, NY: Caravan Books, 1976), 78.

39. Salibi, *Crossroads to Civil War*, 119.

40. The precise dimensions of the relationship with Syria are difficult to discern. My impression is that conjecture to the effect that the relationship is based on religious affinities is incorrect. While Hafez al-Assad does belong to the 'Alawi sect that some consider to be an offshoot of the Shi'a, the relationship is pragmatically founded. Syria's proximity—as one Amal official said: "You can ignore history but not geography"—and utility as an ally explain the ties.

41. The authenticity of Shi'a Communism is—prudently—treated with skepticism by Kamal S. Salibi. See *Crossroads to Civil War*, 143. See also Iliya Harik, "Lebanon: Anatomy of Conflict," *American Universities Field Staff Reports*, no. 49 (1981), 3.

42. John Kifner estimates that twenty-five million dollars per month flowed into Lebanon to support the various militias. "Life Among the Ruins in Beirut," *New York Times Magazine*, December 6, 1981, 162.

Amal officials claim that their members are not paid, and, in fact, that they pay monthly dues (from 5–10 £L upward). While the truth of this claim may be questioned, I do know that many rank-and-file members take great pride in their lack of remuneration.

43. In his very useful book, John Bulloch argues that the August 6, 1976, fall of the Nabaa district of Beirut to the Kata'eb was facilitated by al-Sadr's defection (in league with his longtime adversary, Kamal al-Asad) to the Syrians who were at that time supporting the Maronite militia. See *Death of a Country: The Civil War in Lebanon* (London: Weidenfeld and Nicolson, 1977), 172–3.

44. Calis, "The Shiite Pimpernel," 54.

45. Quoted in the *Jerusalem Post,* March 25, 1981.

46. *Monday Morning* (Beirut), December 22–28, 1980, 13.

47. See Smock and Smock, *Politics of Pluralism,* 142; and Salibi, *Crossroads to Civil War,* 63–4.

48. For a noteworthy recounting see David K. Shipler, "Lebanese Tell of Anguish of Living Under the P.L.O." *New York Times,* July 25, 1982.

49. See Walid Khalidi, *Conflict and Violence in Lebanon: Confrontation in the Middle East* (Cambridge, MA: Harvard University, Center for International Affairs, 1979), 115–16.

50. Based on a private communication.

51. *al-Sadr!,* 61–2. The documentation produced in this book substantiates the claims of al-Sadr's followers.

52. Private interview.

53. A report of September 9, 1980, indicated that al-Sadr was being held in a Libyan military camp near the Algerian border. *New York Times,* September 10, 1980.

54. Private interview.

55. *Christian Science Monitor,* April 17, 1978.

56. *L'Orient-Le Jour,* September 16, 1980.

57. Shahpur Bakhtiar, "The Catastrophe," excerpts from his book, *Ma Fidelité, Al-Watan al-Arabi,* October 8–14, 1982, 54–6. See esp. p. 56.

58. Private interview.

59. Lydia George, interview with Nabih Berri, *Monday Morning,* February 1–7, 1982, 14–25, trans. by Foreign Broadcast Information Service, *Daily Report-Middle East and Africa,* February 10, 1982, G1–G6, quote at page G-4. Foreign Broadcast Information Service is hereafter referred to as "FBIS."

60. For example see John Yemma, "Lebanon's Shiite Muslims Flex Their Military Muscles," *Christian Science Monitor,* January 12, 1982; Thomas L. Friedman, "One Civil War Is Over, Others Fast Multiply," *New York Times,* May 23, 1982; "The Rise of Yet Another Enemy for the Palestinians," *The Economist,* May 1, 1972, 65; and Scheherazade Faramarzi, "Shiites Get Some Hope: New Force Arises in Lebanon," *Sunday Record* (Middletown, NY), February 28, 1982. Cf. Augustus Richard Norton, "Lebanon's Shiites," *New York Times,* April 16, 1982.

61. Nabih Berri interview, February 1–7, 1982, G2.

62. For descriptions of the situation in Lebanon circa 1981 and 1982, see Augustus Richard Norton, "Lebanon's Shifting Political Landscape," *The New Leader,* March 8, 1982, 8–9; Norton, "The Violent Work of Politics in Lebanon," *Wall Street Journal,* March 18, 1982; and William Haddad, "Divided Lebanon," *Current History,* January 1982, 30–35.

63. Lest the reader be left with the wrong impression, it should be noted that members of the movement were not reluctant to take offensive action when possible. Nor was the movement shy about taking action against its opponents. For example, on February 18, 1981, an attempt was made to kidnap a cleric, Sheikh Ahmad Shawkey al-Amin, of Majdal Silm who opposed Amal. In Beirut, Amal was thought to have initiated hostilities on a number of occasions.

64. Private interview.

65. *Le Matin* (Paris), May 28, 1982.

66. For the positions of various groups and factions prior to June 1982, see *Monday Morning* issues of December 22–28, 1980; December 29–January 4, 1981; January 12–18, 1981; January 19–25, 1981; and January 26–February 1, 1981.

67. For a personal account stressing this dimension of the civil war, especially in Beirut, see Lina Mikdadi Tabbara, *Survival in Beirut: A Diary of Civil War*, trans. Nadia Hijab (London: Onyx Press, 1979).

68. Note that it was only in early 1982 that the public statements of Amal officials began to match their private assessments.

69. Figures on the confessional profile of the Lebanese Armed Forces are closely held, and even authoritative estimates are hard to find. It seems that officer recruitment is being carried out along strict confessional lines, with a 50–50 split between Muslims and Christians and proportionate allocations within each major category for the respective 17 sects. Some estimates hold that there is a 60–40 split among the enlisted ranks in favor of the Muslims, and a 60–40 split in the officer corps favoring the Christians (reflecting Maronite overrepresentation in the grades of major and above). See Chapter 5 above.

For a rare detailed discussion by the Armed Forces Commander, see interview with Ibrahim Tannous, *Al-Watan al-Arabi*, June 17–23, 1983, 44–6. Tannous concedes that in 1983 there are three Muslim recruits for every two Christians.

70. *An-Nahar*, September 18, 1980.

71. Nabih Berri interview, February 1–7, 1982, 62.

72. Nabih Berri interview, February 1–7, 1982, 62.

73. See Abu Iyad (Salah Khalaf) with Eric Rouleau, *My Home, My Land: A Narrative of the Palestinian Struggle*, trans. Linda Butler Koseoglu (New York: Times Books, 1981, *passim*.

74. Private communication.

75. *The Economist*, May 1, 1982, 65.

76. *Al-Watan* (Kuwait), November 25, 1981.

77. From a speech by Salah Khalaf, broadcast by the Voice of Palestine, trans. by FBIS, February 4, 1982, p. G3.

78. Interview with Mufti Muhammed Mahdi Shams al-Din, *An-Nahar al-Arabi wa al-Dawli*, May 24–30, 1982, 13–15, trans. by FBIS, June 3, 1982, G2. (Emphasis added.)

79. A number of Amal officials, among them moderates, were critical of Berri's penchant for equivocation.

80. Interview with Nabih Berri, *Monday Morning*, May 10–16, 1982, 14–19, reprinted by FBIS, May 25, 1982, 63.

81. Interview with Nabih Berri, 64.

82. Interview with Nabih Berri, 64.

83. Berri's analysis is certainly shared by a number of longtime observers, including Michael Hudson: "The confessional system itself—as the embodiment of a consociational model—was the root of the problem." In "The Lebanese Crisis: The Limits of Consociational Democracy," *Journal of Palestine Studies* 5, nos. 3–4 (Spring/Summer 1976): 114.

84. Berri cited in Lydia Georgi, "The 'New Lebanon' File—Part 6: The Amal Movement: The Myth of Pluralism," *Monday Morning*, January 26–February 1, 1981.

85. Georgi, "The 'New Lebanon'," 23.

86. Georgi, "The 'New Lebanon'," 23.

87. Interview with Hasan Hashim, *Amal*, April 17, 1981, 8.

88. See, for example, an interesting commentary by a movement writer on an article that appeared in the *Kata'eb* organ, *al-'Amal,* on the subject of Harakat Amal. *Amal,* April 17, 1981, 6–7.

89. Khuri, "Social Dynamics of the War in Lebanon," 393–5.

90. From a program broadcast by the Beirut Domestic Service, July 19, 1982, trans. by FBIS, July 20, 1982, G2.

91. See Berri's comments in : *An-Nahar al-Arabi wa al-Dawli,* April 20–25, 1981, 10–11.

92. See footnotes 66 and 91.

93. Quoted in Georgi, "The 'New Lebanon' ," 26.

94. Calis, "The Shiite Pimpernel," 54.

95. See Augustus Richard Norton, "Aspects of Terrorism in Lebanon: The Case of the Shi'as." *Clandestine Tactics and Technology: Update Report,* 9, no. 4 (1983). Published by the International Association of Chiefs of Police.

96. Interview with Muhammed Mahdi Shams al-Din, *al-Mustaqbal,* March 5, 1983, 28–31.

97. Clinton Bailey, "A Change of Partners," *Jerusalem Post,* December 14, 1982.

98. Bailey, "A Change of Partners."

99. *Christian Science Monitor,* September 8, 1983.

100. Voice of Hope broadcast, May 13, 1983, trans. by the Joint Publications Research Service, *Near East/South Asia Report* (no. 2759), May 26, 1983, 133.

101. Private interview.

102. *Amal,* October 25, 1982.

# PART IV

# LEBANON AND
# THE WORLD

# 8
## Lebanon's Regional Policy

## *Paul A. Jureidini*

## INTRODUCTION

Given eight years of bitter conflict which ravaged Lebanon and almost destroyed the very fabric of its society, and recognizing that crises such as that of 1958 were precursors, the overriding goal of Lebanon's foreign policy, whether at the systemic or subsystemic level, should be the insulation of the country from the variety of factors that have twice plunged it into turmoil and that today give every appearance of once again aligning themselves to force it into another crisis of even greater proportions.

Twice in its brief history as an independent state have Lebanon's internal stresses and strains been exploited and manipulated by outside forces, and twice it became the arena in which outside forces attempted to settle their differences directly or through surrogates. Both times Lebanon was caught up in conflicts not of its own making, and both times Lebanon found itself dependent on others for its salvation and the preservation of its territorial integrity. In several important ways, Lebanon's foreign policy goals and objectives should derive from answers to two fundamental questions: What went wrong? and, What should be done to ensure not only survival but the enhancement of Lebanon's prospects as a state vital to the stability of the region? There is little doubt anywhere these are desirable goals.

## NEUTRALITY OR ALIGNMENT?

The question that arises next—one that will lead to debate and possible disagreement—is, which of two policies can best achieve the above goals?

1. a return to neutrality, or
2. the adoption of a flexible if not aggressive policy that incorporates concepts based on strategic relationships and alignments.

Before turning to a discussion of the appropriate policy, however, it may be helpful to consider an ingredient vital if either policy is to succeed—namely, the development of a Lebanese Army capable of enforcing the security commitments of the state while simultaneously deterring aggression. In other words, what is necessary, and as soon as possible, is the transformation of the Lebanese Army from an army equipped primarily for internal security missions to one capable of external deterrence (with internal security as a secondary mission).

The notion that "Lebanon's weakness is its strength" contributed in many ways to Lebanon's becoming the arena for regional conflicts, as has the absence of a clear army mission and chain of command. Thus, the army should not exhaust its financial credits on end-items that can only be used in internal security missions, nor should army training be limited exclusively to internal security missions. The restoration of internal security is of course vital at the moment, but the foundations of the future army role—a credible deterrent—should be established concurrently with present efforts aimed at enhancing its internal capabilities. Past experience demonstrates, and the demands on Lebanon's limited manpower (especially in the reconstruction period) require, that no attempt should be made to compete with either of Lebanon's neighbors. Israel has crossed the line that separates the purely defensive army from one designed to project itself beyond its borders, and Syria has also moved in that direction. Lebanon, by contrast, requires an army equipped with and trained on the most advanced weapon systems, the latest, "state-of-the-art" technology. An army so equipped and trained can remain numerically inferior to, and yet inflict unacceptable costs on, an aggressor. It is with this kind of deterrence that Lebanon can opt for either of the two policies.

Viable neutrality must be based on two fundamental ingredients: first, the state seeking neutrality must in fact be prepared to remain neutral; and, second, other systemic and subsystemic actors must perceive that neutrality to be in the best interests of all concerned, be prepared to respect it, and support that neutrality when it is threatened by one or another actor.

When Lebanon emerged in 1945 as an independent state and opted for neutrality, all prerequisites appeared to have been met. The Lebanese accepted neutrality as desirable, the members of the Arab League accepted Lebanese neutrality as important to the region, and undertook to respect and protect that neutrality ideologically. The members of the Arab League were relatively compatible, all of them maintaining a Western connection. And the Lebanese Army was adequate to its mission in a lightly armed region. Lebanon could remain neutral in inter-Arab conflicts. In 1948, with the creation of the state of Israel, a fundamental change occurred. A new regional actor was added, and Lebanon was not neutral in the first Arab–Israeli War. Lebanon thus could not seek, and did not get, Israel's support for its neutrality. Between 1948 and 1958 a number of fundamental changes occurred: *coups d'état* shook the Arab world, basic compatibility was replaced by incompatible relationships, the Soviet Union emerged as an important actor, an arms race began to shape up, and the second Arab–Israeli war was fought. Lebanon's attempt to adhere to a strict interpretation of the 1945 understanding of neutrality brought about the Lebanese crisis of 1958. An additional word, "positive," had now been added to neutrality, and positive neutrality implied distancing oneself from the West in general (and the United States specifically), improving relations with the USSR, and alignment with those nations that professed positive neutrality. Initially, and as a means of buying time, Lebanon began to reorient its policy. It distanced itself from the United States, somewhat improved its relationship with the USSR, and attempted to improve its ties with the radicals in the hope that these policies would not harm its relationship with its traditional conservative friends. Gradually and almost imperceptibly Lebanon slid into a kind of limbo. The Arab world's willingness to underwrite the Cairo Accord, and to force the Melkart Accord on the Lebanese government, alarmed many officials. Neutrality in inter-Arab affairs had in fact become a myth, and Lebanon's ability to remain outside of the Arab–Israeli conflict depended very much on Israel. In 1974 Lebanon stood alone.

It is interesting here to note that Lebanon's policy between 1959 and 1976 increased the general level of hostility aimed at Lebanon. It engendered the apathy or actual hostility of many of its former friends, without substantially improving cooperation with those it sought to placate. Thus, where none but cooperation existed before, relations with the United States, Jordan, and Saudia Arabia became more conflictive, while relations with the USSR, Egypt, Syria, and Iraq did not improve substantially or (as in the case of Israel) deteriorated seriously.

Can a policy of strict neutrality, in the present circumstances, secure the evacuation of foreign troops from the 10,452 square kilometers that make up Lebanon? And, more importantly, can it assure Lebanon success in achieving its goal? The answer is clearly no.

Most regional actors are willing to accept neutrality only if it implies some form of alignment, and until the Arab–Israel conflict is settled, one important actor is still not going to be allowed to participate in the process. Moreover, Lebanon lacks the means by which it can force others to respect its neutrality. Thus, if Lebanon decides that a policy of neutrality is, in fact, what is most likely to ensure success in achieving its goals, it will have to work for it. It will not be practical, and the interim policy that can lead to the adoption of a neutralist policy in the future is one that is active, if not aggressively so. It is Lebanon that has to convince its neighbors and other regional actors that it must be given the flexibility, if they are to avert alignment of one sort or the other.

## AFTER 1982: WHENCE THE DISASTER?

In spite of the evident need to pursue an active policy of alignment rather than neutrality, it is clear that Lebanon embraced, or was forced to espouse, neutrality. How did this transpire in the face of the disasters that clearly might attend—and in fact did attend—such a policy?

In the aftermath of the crisis of 1982, Lebanese leaders entertained several options. Israel sought the full cooperation of Lebanon, and in October or December, or even in early 1983, Israeli leaders might have been willing to coordinate policy with Lebanon for a limited short-term price, against the pledge of a peace treaty and full normalization within some reasonable period. A second option lay in Damascus which had had much better relations with Amin Gemayel in the past than with his late brother. The Syrian option was never considered for the simple reason that few believed Damascus was prepared to leave Lebanon, and fewer still to leave Lebanon without a prior Israeli withdrawal. The third alternative was the American option—to align Lebanon with the United States, and follow the American policy lead.

The American option had several assets to command it. First, unlike either Israel or Syria, the United States had no territorial ambitions, either for domination/control or for actual annexation, in Lebanon. Second, since opting for either Israel or Syria appeared to be a zero sum game, moving toward the United States was attractive simply as a means of avoiding such a cataclysmic decision. Third, the United States was a superpower and was believed to have important interests in the area. Lebanon could, therefore, exert some leverage as an American partner to attain the kinds of military and other assistance to which we have already adverted. Fourth, the United States was believed to have influence on Israel, which might be useful in securing Israeli withdrawal from Lebanese territory.

The Lebanese government did not see, perhaps did not have the time to see, and probably did not have the experience to see, that although three options presented themselves as exclusive themes of policy in fact *no* single one of the three could secure Lebanese objectives if wholly pursued. That is, some mix of *Lebanese* initiative and action was required to dilute the options if any one was to be attempted. In the event, the Lebanese aligned themselves fully with the United States and in the course of time became totally dependent upon the United States, subordinating critical and legitimate Lebanese needs to those of Washington. It may be that Lebanese and American interests were parallel; they were not, however, coincident.

One major difference between Lebanese and American interests was obfuscated by Lebanese misperception of United States behavior. Many Lebanese believed that the sudden American support was due to a new awareness of Lebanon's importance to United States regional and global interests and to a new consciousness about Lebanon itself. In fact, almost the opposite was the case. The principal American interest was to prevent a regional crisis, and the concern about a regional crisis was precisely the reason the United States had intervened in Lebanon. Indeed, the whole shift of American policy toward Bashir Gemayel in late 1981 and early 1982 was precisely a reflection of the determination to avoid or limit regional crises, *not* some newfound awareness of Bashir's leadership.

Many in Washington had come to the conclusion that sooner or later Israel would intervene in Lebanon. Despite the cease-fire negotiated by Philip Habib in 1981, American intelligence verified what American diplomacy had already discovered: too many parties were interested in provoking an Israeli intervention for the cease-fire to be indefinitely effective. As a result of the likelihood of an Israeli move, Bashir Gemayel appeared to have a very good chance to become the next president of Lebanon. It was not difficult to see that if Israel intervened (good chance), and if Bashir Gemayel was elected president (good chance if the first condition was filled), and if Bashir was given no option to Israel, a regional crisis would erupt anew based on an Israeli–Lebanese entente. The presence and availability of the United States as an alternative option would, if accepted by Bashir, reduce the risk of such a regional crisis. However, the means by which the regional crisis would be avoided was important—by internalizing the crisis.

Everyone recognized privately, and even many enemies of Israel avowed with surprising openness publicly, that without the Israeli intervention in 1982 Lebanon would have had no chance to recover its independence. What few seemed to grasp was that it was not the physical violence per se that had offered new hope for Lebanon, but rather the threat of a regional crisis in place of a Lebanese crisis.

In choosing the American option, the Lebanese government should have separated itself from the United States at certain points, notably where American approaches might lead to internal rather than regional crises. In other words, it was in Lebanon's interests—but not in the United States'—for the crisis of occupation to remain regional. And, in fact, a regional crisis would have allowed the United States more flexibility, too, since to the extent Beirut was not following Washington's suggestions, the United States could have disowned responsibility for the course of action.

A second difference between the United States and Lebanon was in the premium each placed upon the passage of time. Although it can be argued—and I would argue—that the United States could not afford a slow movement toward the resolution of the Lebanese crisis if it hoped to score progress in the overall Arab–Israeli domain, still it is quite clear that many American decision-makers preferred caution and deliberateness in discussions. Moreover, United States–Lebanese cooperation with respect to the tripartite discussions, like the cooperation when the United States served as a bilateral interlocutor with each party, demonstrated that Washington placed less value on speed in the talks than was warranted for Lebanon's interests. Why? Because late 1982 and early 1983 witnessed a renaissance of Lebanese identity and nationalism, a determination to restore the unique Lebanese experience and state to validity. However, the passage of time allowed both the emergence of internal problems that would impede such a restoration and the growth of new inter-Arab problems that would complicate withdrawal. In the late 1982, Syria was defeated, humiliated, and, fearing further Israeli strikes in Lebanon, may have been persuaded to withdraw at a reasonable price. One year later, Syria had emerged as the uncontested winner, using the complex Arab political scene to wily advantage.

It is true that the success of the American peace plan enunciated by President Reagan on September 1, 1982, would have solidified Lebanese internal stability. However, linking the withdrawal process in Lebanon to the peace process was a disaster. Lebanese leaders recognized that this linkage was a serious blow to Lebanon's interests. What is surprising is that they do not seem to have asked the logical, follow-up question: if the United States could do this to us to pursue its own regional objectives, what does this mean in terms of our immediate needs in Lebanon and what should be our response to this and similar differences of view? Apart from candid discussions of these differences, however, Lebanon continued to put all of its eggs in the American basket.

Both Lebanon and the United States agreed that the withdrawal process should be begun by negotiations on the Israeli front. There were several reasons for such a choice. First, one had to begin on one side or the other, and the two occupiers would not talk with each other. Moreover, Syria refused even to discuss the subject in any substantive way pending Israeli movement. The Syrian leadership insisted its brotherly forces were a legitimate presence in Lebanon, and would of course withdraw when Israeli forces left, but would not discuss any "conditions" for such a withdrawal. But there were other reasons to focus first on Israel. Israel was the stronger of the two occupiers, and could remain indefinitely. Too, progress seemed more likely on the Israeli front, and progress was required to keep both the Lebanese and the overall Arab–Israeli settlement processes alive. Moreover, while the Syrian presence in Lebanon could not be claimed to have major implications for Israeli security, many believed the Israeli presence did in fact threaten Syrian security. Thus, if negotiations reached a successful conclusion on the southern front, Syria would then have strong reasons to withdraw.

That the approach pursued by the Lebanese and American governments failed is now quite clear, and it is certainly timely to consider some of the reasons for the failure.

First, the impression that Syria would be interested in the overall process of Arab–Israeli settlement and mutual withdrawals from Lebanon, an impression only peripherally encouraged by Syria vis-a-vis the Americans, was incorrect. Syria was concerned neither with the former nor the latter. Syrian leaders never believed, and do not now believe that the American initiative would return the Golan Heights to Syrian control. Nor had they ever any intention of retiring from Lebanon. Syria's reasons for being in Lebanon were not Lebanese; rather they were internal Syrian and regional reasons. Lebanon had nothing to offer Syria that would come near compensating for the domestic Syrian or the regional pay-offs Syria derived from its occupation. It is barely conceivable that a United States–Syrian entente or an Israeli–Syrian entente might have been able to make withdrawal worthwhile for Syria, but such alternatives, which in any case were not profferred, could only have come at Lebanese expense.

Under the circumstances, the need for either Lebanon or the United States or both to undertake discussions with Syria to unearth more accurately what the Syrians would do in specific contingencies is clear.

The course and content of Israeli–Lebanese negotiations took place in an atmosphere in which Israeli leaders concluded more with every passing day that the Gemayel government would never sign a full peace and would never fully normalize relations. Consequently, the talks reflected this belief, and the provisions of the accord that emerged reflected it as well. The agreement provided a strong incentive to go to a treaty and normalization—the termination or modification of the security provisions in the south—along with the safeguards Israel wanted in the event matters went no further than the immediate agreement.

In the months subsequent to the conclusion of the accord, Israelis became more convinced than ever that Lebanon would never become a true partner. Indeed, the tone of the government in Beirut disturbed them to such an extent that a new policy evolved, one of limiting the effectiveness of the central government in favor of subnational groups, some of which (those close to the Israeli borders) could be influenced by Israel. Many events and developments—cooperation with the Druze and the lack of coordination between the redeploying Israeli forces and the Lebanese Army—in the Shuf in late summer 1983 reflected this policy.

By the autumn of 1983 two optional courses remained for the Lebanese government. It could "go with Israel," or "go with Syria." This is not to say that Beirut had turned its back on the United States. On the contrary, the two governments continued to cooperate very closely. However, events in September of 1983 recalled a warning the Lebanese had heard from Israel a year before. At that time they had been warned that, yes, the United States was a superpower, but its interest and presence in Lebanon could and would disappear just as quickly as it had surfaced. (By contrast, was the implication, Israel's interest in Lebanon is perpetual, sealed by the contiguity of the two states. Israelis did not add the obvious, of course—that for the very same reason they were far more dangerous, should policies diverge. Moreover, the same argument applied for Syria.)

The Lebanese could abrogate the agreement with Israel and move toward an alignment with Syria. Such a policy might spare the country a renewed offensive by Syrian-sponsored forces. More important, it might, by confronting Israel, provoke a regional crisis necessitating continued American action. The cost of the policy would, of course, be the loss of the south.

By contrast, the Lebanese could still move toward a full peace and normalization with Israel, aligning their country with their southern neighbor politically. Such an approach would probably have averted the Shuf crisis, but would result in the loss of Lebanese territory in the north and northeast to Syria.

The United States has favored neither approach. In the absence of a clear United States preference, the Lebanese government has been unable itself to arrive at a decision between them. The result is in many respects worse than either of the choices—loss of the south *and* the north *and* the northeast; the continuation of Israeli policies to undermine the effectiveness of the central government of Lebanon; and the continuation of Syrian policies to "capture" the government of Lebanon. Moreover, the indecision between the two options, or the pursuit of an activist policy to force the development of additional options internalizes the Lebanese problem, with all such an internalization entails—loss of Arab support for the restoration of a truly independent Lebanon, loss of such Arab agreement on the Lebanon problem as existed, and an open invitation for the United States to relegate the Lebanese issue to the back burner and to turn to other regional and global problems. All this is in addition to the disastrous domestic consequences inside Lebanon of internalization—loss of the consensus necessary to restore effective government and, in fact, encouragement to various factions to undertake anti-state activities.

## THE PROSPECTS

Following the September 26, 1983 cease-fire agreement the stage was set for something like a return to the 1976 period. That is, should the cease-fire accord be carried out in all its details, a national unity government would be created that, by including elements responsive to foreign powers, must necessarily hobble the Lebanese government and once again paralyze the security forces, notably the army. Spheres of influence are thereby solidified in Lebanon and the government of Lebanon is relegated to a secondary role in the country except perhaps in the small area around Beirut.

In fact, however, there are some pronounced differences between the situation in 1976 and that promulgated by the 1983 cease-fire accord, differences that further dim the prospects for Lebanon. Coincident with the disintegrative activities fostered by Israel and Syria in Lebanon in the spring and summer of 1983 was a major offensive by Syrian-sponsored elements in the Palestine Liberation Organization to wrest control of the PLO from Yasser Arafat and place it squarely in the hands of Syria. By the time of the Lebanese cease-fire, this process had reduced the area under the control of the Arafat-led PLO to the area around Tripoli, but evidence indicates that all Palestinian forces in Lebanon will be subjected to Syrian control eventually. Thus, the PLO as an independent actor—one principal element in 1976—will no longer exist in Lebanon.

A second difference concerns the other independent actors. The Lebanese resistance was relatively independent in the period after 1976. Supplied by Israel, the Lebanese Forces maintained an active role and autonomy from their supplier. It demonstrated strong, nationalist leadership. Even should outside support return to its previous levels—and there is no indication that it will do so at this time—the Lebanese Forces do not reflect the strong leadership that once characterized the organization. Other elements of the resistance in the Christian community have withered away almost completely. Nor do the Muslim resistance organizations, whether Shi'a or Sunni, demonstrate anything like their previous independence and activism. All are not merely supported by, but are to an unprecedented degree in Lebanon controlled by, foreign governments.

The importance of these differences between 1976 and 1983 are more significant than some observers have recognized, for the absence of independent actors means that there are few levers in the hands of Lebanese or others to disrupt or threaten the spheres of influence in Lebanon. This is a far more solid de facto partition than existed in 1976 or at any time thereafter.

Eventually—that is, over time—the Israelis and Syrians will not be able to control activities within their spheres of influence. For the present, these spheres should be much more stable than in the past. However, Israeli leaders have misread the nature of their Lebanese allies if they believe anything short of continued occupation will ensure their dependability. Similarly, the Syrians will probably be forced to provide a front to the Palestinians in Lebanon, and this front will become increasingly difficult to control over time. Moreover, the nature of the Syrian area in Lebanon is inherently resistant to control by virtue of its size and diversity, incorporating Maronites and other Christians, Sunnis, Shi'as, and Druzes, all with divergent interests. The result of the slow degradation in Israeli and Syrian control over their spheres is likely to also be different from the post-1976 experience. This time, the pressure will more likely be directed to each other's sphere. That is, the stage has been set for another confrontation in Lebanon, but this one will probably be between Israel and Syria.

Yet another difference between the new situation and that of 1976 is that Lebanon, having failed to secure either of its neighbors as an ally, will not enjoy even a single safe border. Israel and Syria will be able and ready to intervene in Lebanon whenever they feel it is in their interest to do so, the only restriction being that they will intervene in their own spheres and not in each other's.

Nor has the Lebanese regional status equation that somehow endured 1976—albeit in a crippled fashion—survived. No longer will anyone recognize or accept Lebanese claims of neutrality in the Arab–Israeli conflict. Nor should they, for when we say that the Lebanese government has become irrelevant, when we point to Syrian and Israeli control over virtually all of Lebanon, we are really saying there is no independent authority that can be neutral. The decision by Israel in late summer of 1983 to curtail its involvement in Lebanon north of the line of IDF troop deployments led to a full-scale Syrian move to take over the rest of Lebanon through the installation of a new, pro-Syrian regime in Beirut. Should the new Syrian policy succeed, with a Lebanese government much more responsive to Syrian wishes, there are enormous implications for Israel, of course, but also for Jordan, Iraq, Egypt, and Saudi Arabia. Under the circumstances, one could fully expect such a Syrian victory to lead to rather far-reaching changes in the political alignment structure of the Middle East.

Thus, Lebanon has already entered a stage of clear-cut spheres of influence. To some who have supported cantonization of Lebanon for internal political purposes in the past, the present situation may seem an appropriate one to broach such a solution once again. Cantonization is now—sadly—not a national political option but a recognition of international political reality. This is not to say it is the right or proper course; only to say it may be decided by non-Lebanese rather than Lebanese. Certainly, in view of the creation and consolidation of Israeli and Syrian spheres of influence in Lebanon, the immediate issue is to find a practicable way for the Lebanese to retain some kind of legitimate authority for all of Lebanon that may, some day, be able to reunite the country. Thus, the immediate concern is to find an approach to optimize the effectiveness of the national government and the Lebanese Armed Forces. Without an early move to provide a new legitimacy to these institutions, the future of Lebanon may be even bleaker than the present.

The transition from 1982 to 1983 can be seen as an inter-war period for Lebanon and for the Middle East, a period in which the results of the conflict of 1982 were manipulated by the parties to ready themselves for future conflict, political, economic, and military. In this perspective, a review and analysis of the policies of Israel, Syria, the United States, Saudi Arabia, and of course Lebanon itself with respect to the issues discussed here could prove enlightening. However, it is equally valid to view the 1982–83 period as war, that is, to reverse the dictum that "war is the continuation of politics by other means." In the protracted Arab–Israeli conflict, and in the view of at least one party, politics is surely the continuation of war by other means. Although Israel clearly "won" the military war of 1982, Syria just as clearly won the political war of 1982–83 subsequent to the military action. There is not a party in the Middle East unaware of this reality. As 1983 in turn becomes historical, and given the Syrian desire to play a regional extremist role (probably the only role left open for the Syrians), will Damascus be able to control the forces of extremism once unleashed? Or will momentum force Syria once again into a confrontation with Israel or the United States?

# 9
# United States–Lebanese Relations: A Pocketful of Paradoxes

## Edward E. Azar and Kate Shnayerson

After the summer of 1982, Lebanon became a household word in the United States. It emerged from a shadowy, unnoticed existence to become a primary focus of American attention—diplomatic, military, economic, and journalistic. Lebanon had more or less thrown herself to the mercy of the United States, hoping for a long-term commitment to the resolution of her severe problems. Many Lebanese, embittered by American nonchalance throughout their ten years of turmoil, felt that the United States owed them a debt of enormous proportions. Most Americans, on the other hand, had very little knowledge of the country prior to 1982; surely many had no idea that the United States and Lebanon had had a longstanding relationship for over a century. But the scope of involvement in the year 1982–83 was unprecedented: with the Marines stationed in Beirut as part of the Multinational Force and the American Green Berets helping to rebuild the Lebanese Army, it was clear that President Reagan had invested vast quantities of money, men, and personal prestige in Amin Gemayel and his government. The cost of the commitment was paid in lives, with the largest single American military loss of life since Vietnam suffered on October 23, 1983.

At the time of this writing, the future of American involvement in Lebanon remains uncertain; it would be futile to forecast its outcome. But a review of the past and the patterns it reveals might shed more light on the present status of United States–Lebanese relations. This chapter will attempt to provide, in some detail, exactly such a review. Its goal is to trace and to document the history of relations between the two countries and to provide food for thought to both Lebanese and Americans about the possibilities—and limitations upon—future relations.

The essence of the United States–Lebanese relationship cannot easily be captured or characterized. Peaks of intensive interaction and cooperation have been followed by lulls of inactivity and bilateral withdrawal. High expectations and mutual admiration have not precluded frequent frustration and miscommunication—indeed, they may have partially precipitated such disappointments. Inherent contradictions make the relationship an especially intriguing one to study: apparent similarities exist, but on closer inspection, differences abound; stated goals and policies have been accompanied by actions of precisely opposite intention; a small country of about three million people has drawn American Marines to its shores twice in the last quarter century; a protracted war raged in Lebanon for eight years while an America that proudly advocated world-wide rights did little. These and similar contradictions punctuate the Lebanese–American story at all periods of its history.

This chapter will concentrate on pinpointing and explaining some of these paradoxes. A partial explanation for such contradictions might be rooted in the diverse nature of the American–Lebanese connection, and an exploration of its various layers will provide a background context for the discussion. One of these layers, political culture, has been both a unifying force and a source of confusion. A brief look at each country's political culture will promote understanding of the assumptions it makes about the other, particularly as the two are assumed to be so similar in fundamental ways. In fact, many differences separate them, and this has often misled their leaders. Finally, in order to articulate key features, we will examine moments of crisis. A review of the four high points of United States–Lebanese relations over the last century will reveal pivotal underlying dynamics. Thus the bulk of the chapter will investigate interaction in 1941–1944, 1956–1958, 1975–1976, 1981–1983.

In general, we hope to demonstrate that United States policy on Lebanon has been rooted in domestic considerations, regional events, or global tensions *more* than in any genuine desire for Lebanon's well-being. Lebanese responses and initiatives emerged out of illusions about the importance of Lebanon in American politics, lack of understanding of the complexity of a superpower's problems, and domestic requirements. Thus we might posit that while Lebanon based its policy on a misguided image of the United States, the United States conceived policy in broad, regional terms in which Lebanon mattered little, if at all.

## CONTEXT

### The Superpower–Small State Dynamic

Any relationship between a nation of about three million people and a superpower will usually exhibit several characteristics that stem from the immutable inequality between the two. At the risk of stating the obvious, we would point out here that this basic fact has shaped the connection between Lebanon and the United States in a number of critical ways.

In general, the superpower–small state relationship contains an inherent asymmetry in dependency. Often the smaller nation cannot survive without superpower aid; if lucky, it may have a precious resource that the powerful nation needs that lends it some leverage. Excepting a virtual monopoly on that resource, however, the leverage will rarely be very strong, and the superpower usually determines events. The smaller country can only react and try to strengthen its position by forming regional alliances, cultivating personal networks, or advertising its unique strategic advantages. In Lebanon's case, only one special resource had graced the country, namely, a human talent in entrepreneurial leadership. Thus a relatively strong economy had forestalled economic dependence until 1975–76. Furthermore, Lebanon had longstanding societal, cultural, and educational ties with the United States that had a significant impact on their political interactions. An asymmetry in dependency indisputably existed, but a few fortuitous factors mitigated its severity.

The relationship did not remain stable over time. Some years brought intensive political interaction between the two; others, almost none at all. This inconsistency demonstrates two things. For the United States, Lebanon was not a top priority—it only became so at specific points in time. Had it been of high importance, the number of annual interactions between the two would have been steadier and far more frequent. Instead, as is clear from Figure 9.1, two types of situations triggered an increase in diplomatic interaction: regional turbulence (1967 and 1973) and internal Lebanese disturbance (1958 and 1976). The same applies to Lebanon's overtures to the United States. During President Shihab's term (1959–1964), for example, a very low level of interaction took place. Shihab (and to some extent his successor Helou) de-emphasized the American–Lebanese connection at the height of the Cold War and focused instead on France as a more "neutral" ally and protector.[1] In general, erratic levels of interaction typify relations between superpowers and small countries.

Furthermore, small, newly independent states tend to assume that superpowers have the ability to accomplish miracles. At times when neutrality did not preclude cooperation, Lebanese officials held such high expectations of the United States that they were repeatedly disappointed. The United States, the monolithic giant, could certainly push a button and send troops, or aid, or mediators, or whatever the moment called for. If the expected goods did not arrive, speculation immediately arose regarding a hidden motive, and conspiracy was presumed to be brewing. Unfortunately, over-expectancy can

# FIGURE 9.1 United States-Lebanese interactions 1948-1978

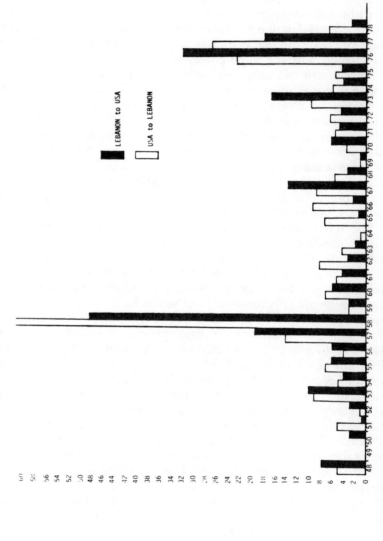

*Source:* Conflict and Peace Data Bank—COPDAB, University of Maryland.

222

sometimes grow to become first passivity, then psychological dependency. Newly independent, formerly colonized nations tend to assume that only superpowers have the expertise to resolve their political, societal, and economic dilemmas, so they either model their new state after their hero, accept this "expert" outside advice as the best available, or assume that in their dire hour of need the superpower knight will come on a white horse and rescue them from disaster. . .

A small nation often cannot accept that a superpower tends to be overloaded and must respond hourly to dozens of other small and large nations whose problems are equally, or perhaps more, urgent than its own. This is one source of overinflated expectations. Similarly, small countries may simplify the global power as a concept and reduce its entire foreign policy to one or two high officials to whom they have access. The degree of complexity in superpower affairs, foreign and domestic, is both difficult to grasp and more comfortable for small states to overlook. When a high, one-sided dependency exists, particularly in moments of crisis, the realization of one's own insignificance might be frightening indeed.

These dynamics often interacted with unique features in Lebanon's case to produce miscommunication and disappointment. One thing that cushioned their impact for a long time was the existence of other channnnels of Lebanese-American interaction that provided additional channels of communication. As these other dimensions of interaction lend important insights to understanding the relationship, we shall explore them now in some depth.

## A Multilateral Link

The United States-Lebanese relationship derives perhaps its greatest asset from its manifold nature. Diplomatic exchange constitutes only its most obvious aspect. Social, cultural, and economic ties had more depth. Perhaps they explain why Lebanon receives such great prominence when it does arise on the American foreign policy agenda.

Early relations between Lebanon and the United States had almost no political dimension at all. As with the rest of the Middle East in the age of American isolationism, missionary expeditions laid the most important foundations for future interaction. The first two missionaries to the Middle East were sent officially to Palestine to set up a mission in Jerusalem.[2]

Palestine, however, did not prove to be the most fertile ground. After four years of wandering—in Smyrna, Jerusalem, and

Malta—they chose Antoura, Lebanon, as the site for the first Protestant Missionary Conference in the Middle East. They subsequently established their first mission in Beirut in November of 1823. Despite the fact that "Beirut was so unimportant politically, that Saida (Sidon), twenty five miles to the south, gave name to the province,"[3] Beirut

> . . . was preferable to Jerusalem as the headquarters of a mission, in view of its climate, the character of the people, the proximity of Mount Lebanon as a summer retreat, its accessibility, its communication with Europe, and the ease with which books could be sent from it to Damascus, and the cities of the coast. The decision to occupy Beirut, then a town of less than 5,000 population, was divinely directed.[4]

The large resident Christian population in Syria and Lebanon must have been an important consideration, because by 1826 the missionaries had decided to concentrate their efforts solely on the local Christians and to rely on them to spread the word. Beirut must also have been an auspicious site for the establishment of new Protestant schools, the accomplishment of which had become the mission's second major goal.[5] A flock of schools followed: from one, in July of 1824 with seven pupils, to thirty-three in 1860, with 791 boys and 176 girls.[6]

Eventually, the success of these small schools prompted the American Board of Commissioners for Foreign Missionaries to intervene with a warning that primary emphasis should be placed on transmission of religious doctrine, and not on popular education. But the missionaries stubbornly insisted that a college was essential because the inhabitants had no access to education, and Protestantism could be spread through education. They saw this endeavor as a competition with other religions, in which Americans in particular had some unique advantages.

> It is for us to defeat their efforts, by taking possession of the field ourselves; and it is a well-known fact that American Christians can enter upon this work with prospects of success which no others enjoy. We are free from political entanglements to the East, and have already, by years of missionary labor, secured the confidence of the people, and in other important aspects prepared the way.[7]

And indeed, undaunted by the Druze–Christian upheavals in 1860 and the American Civil War,[8] the missionaries successfully raised enough money to open the Syrian Protestant College in Beirut on

December 3, 1866. In their vision of the college, its founders were adamant that Arabic be the language of instruction and that indigenous cultures, texts, and ideas should shape the education contained therein. Concern was expressed about the denationalizing effects of education, ". . . to be corrected by emphasizing the vernacular part of the educational course . . . ."[9] They also believed that the utilization of Arabic texts and teachers would make education more accessible to the local population and hence provide the most effective means of disseminating Christian ideals. However, despite their desire to preach and spread the ideas of Protestantism, the college's founders took pains to build an institution that would accept students of all denominations and refrain from active proselytization which might interfere with studies or repel potential students. That they successfully merged American ideals with missionary work in this most crucial and delicate respect is nowhere more apparent than in the statement of the college's president, Daniel Bliss, in 1871:

> This college is for all conditions and classes of men without regard to color, nationality, race, or religion. A man white, black, or yellow, Christian, Jew, Mohammedan, or heathen, may enter and enjoy all of the advantages of this institution for three, four, or eight years, and go out believing in one God, in many Gods, or in no God. But it will be impossible for anyone to continue with us long without knowing what we believe to the the truth and our reasons for that belief.[10]

The Syrian Protestant College grew into, and continues to be, a very influential regional institution. It brought a flood of Western ideas to the East, among them the notion of collective learning rather than individual scholarship, national pride, the importance of patriotism, and freedom for all.[11]

The enduring missionary commitment and contribution to Lebanon reaped long-term, tangible results. By 1940, seventy-one American schools existed in Lebanon, and the American University of Beirut student body had increased to two thousand, making the missionary and educational institutions "the largest private noneconomic investment of Americans in any part of the Middle East" excepting that of American Jews in Palestine.[12] By 1972, AUB had become the largest American university overseas, with a student body of four thousand.[13]

Cultural influence and population exchanges were not any means restricted to a one-way flow of traffic. Between 1880 and 1930, around two hundred thousand Lebanese emigrated to the U.S. in their quest for enhanced economic prospects.[14] At a time of severe hardship and famine, tantalizing rumors from America took on a mythic quality.[15] Many would return home at the end of their lives, taking with them some intangible set of American ways and values.

At first, Americans had more influence and played a bigger role in Lebanon than did their Lebanese counterparts in the United States. Lebanese-Americans initially had little input into politics or American foreign policy. The State Department's attitude of the early 1940's explains why:

> As a professional bureaucracy, the Department replied to any and all such (Lebanese-American) concern with formal courtesy. But that concern was not seriously considered a component of the national "interest." Nor were Levantine-Americans regarded as a significant pressure group, real or potential, for Americans to deal with. . . . In contrast, the interests and views of the "unhyphenated" American nationals long resident in the Levant—educators and supporters of the American University of Beirut, Presbyterian missionaries, the American expatriate "colonies" in the larger cities—were more important to the Department. These nationals represented wealth and prestige and were of the same social background as, and were ofter personally acquainted with, Departmental officers.[16]

Gradually, however, as time passed, the role of American expatriates in Lebanon decreased somewhat, while the role of Lebanese-Americans increased, particularly as they began to organize as an interest group and work within the American system in late 1970s. Particularly after 1978, Lebanese-Americans organized several groups and took it upon themselves to work persistently at mobilizing support in the U.S. and improving U.S.–Lebanese relations.

A strong economic connection later complemented educational, societal, and early missionary links. The combination of its financial strength and Western orientation made Lebanon an accessible and appealing country. As Lebanon grew to be the financial center of the Middle East, it attracted many American companies. The most "laissez-faire" state in the region, Lebanon became a nexus for American businessmen, and soon all regional offices of American companies were based in Beirut. Economic expansion in the 1950s and 1960s doubled the number of American companies between 1961 and 1965, and by 1964, five hundred U.S. companies were represented in Lebanon. The trade that began to develop between the two countries became a channel to closer relations between the two. The resultant strong trade bond is reflected in Table 9.1. The United

**TABLE 9.1 Lebanon's Imports From the United States, 1973-1980**

| Year | Imports for U.S. in millions of dollars | Relative rank of U.S. as a source of imports |
|------|------|------|
| 1973 | 146.8 | 1 |
| 1974 | 315.5 | 1 |
| 1975 | 405.3 | 1 |
| 1976 | 53.6 | 4 |
| 1977 | 136.0 | 4 |
| 1978 | 156.5 | 3 |
| 1979 | 250.5 | 4 |
| 1980 | 333.3 | 1 |

States had become the top supplier of imports until the Civil War. But the sharp decrease in 1976 volume did not prove permanent: U.S. imports rose again until they had regained their pre-war level. The United States did not, however, provide a market for Lebanese exports. Rather, services and banking accommodations constituted the major resource that the Lebanese sold to the U.S.[17] Relations between businessmen played an important role in the rebound of the trade volume after the war.

### Political Culture

Close ties between Lebanon and the United States over the past four decades have emerged out of, and reinforced, a perceived similarity: a sense of common political culture. By this term, we mean:

> The set of attitudes, beliefs, and sentiments which give order and meaning to a political process and which provide the underlying assumptions and values that govern behavior in the political system... A political culture is the product of both the collective history of a political system and the life histories of the members of that system...[18]

The early missionary presence in Lebanon introduced American political ideas during the country's formative, prenascent stage in the nineteenth and early twentieth centuries. Conversely, after the establishment of the only democracy in the Arab world in 1943, a perceived convergence in political culture predisposed Americans to view the country favorably and to expect certain behaviors from it. This vague partnership may be at the root of the strong mutual assumption of common interest. It thus merits a separate and thorough examination.

Lebanon and the United States share a number of basic political and social features, the first and most obvious being their democratic systems. The stark contrast between Lebanon and her neighbors served to enhance her democratic image. Although seldom remarked upon, Lebanon's institutionalized religious freedom distinguishes her from all other Middle East countries and creates congruence with the United States. Lebanon does not impose any one state religion on its citizens: pluralism, freedom, and institutionalized political protections more closely approximate an American model than a regional one.

Both political systems originated in revered founding documents: the American Constitution of 1787, and the National Pact of 1943.[19] Although never formally written, the latter certainly represents a national pillar of comparable salience to the former. Both agreements constitute, at heart, arrangements for a balance of power, and institutionalization of "checks and balances," a guarantee against an hypothetical "tyranny of the majority."[20] Both documents established a presidential system of leadership with limited terms—the Lebanese president serves one term of six years as opposed to the American four-year, optionally renewable, term.

Renowned freedom of the press in Lebanon also finds favor with Americans. Unlike much of the region, Lebanon's freedom of the press has been so open that it has sometimes been termed excessive. Virtually all political groups inside and many outside the country published at least one newspaper through which they communicated their ideas. In 1972, there were forty-nine newspapers, forty-eight weekly political journals, one hundred and thirty-three non-political weeklies, four monthly political magazines, and one hundred and forty non-political monthlies.[21]

On a more abstract plane, several aspects of the Lebanese social heritage have striking parallels in American history. Both combine essentially Christian origins with a melting-pot, multicommunal present. In the United States, the Anglican/Puritan society was gradually transformed by increasing waves of immigrants from all corners of the world; the original area of Mount Lebanon had a Christian majority until the creation in 1920 of Greater Lebanon, when a large population of Muslims was amalgamated into the state.[22] Despite this unique mix of traditions, however, Lebanon has always retained a Western outlook and character, as the continuing bilingualism demonstrates.

Briefly, because a detailed analysis cannot concern us here, let us review this apparent congruence in three areas. Although both countries are democracies, their functional performace rests on different principles. The United States operates on the principle of majority rule. As a country of minorities, no one of which is strong enough to dominate for any appreciable length of time, Lebanon functions by consensus decision. No group can ever be left largely unsatisfied, because it can generally mobilize the resources to sabotage the decision that was taken against its will. It may force the fall of the cabinet or pursue extra-legal methods. This system has been appropriately compared to the classical system of an international "balance of power" where there is no ultimate arbitrator of conflict and no monopoly of the instruments of force.[23] In Lebanon, there is no equivalent to the U.S. Supreme Court whose decisions are accepted as final and eminently legitimate. Politics is a constant bargaining process, with issues decided behind the scenes and the outcome of formal votes often predictable.[24] While the role of traditional local leaders has some limited parallel in contemporary American consciousness (e.g., Mayor Daley of Chicago), the phenomenon of traditional leadership in Lebanon (za'im) is far more complex. Leaders are the ultimate decision-makers, the nuclei of the multiple loci of power, whether or not they are formally in the government.[25] Americans often expect Lebanese to take drastic steps toward change in a given area, to decide and to implement. They are repeatedly baffled by Lebanon's unique and highly unfamiliar form of politics. As with the U.N. Security Council, politics by consensus ultimately produces stagnation. The result is a compromise acceptable to all and, ergo, a continuation of the status quo.

Religion in Lebanon plays a different role than it does in the United States, despite the absence of a formal state religion. In a sense, the lack of a state religion represents again a consensus compromise: the minimum acceptable to all. This in turn reflects the real state of affairs: religion is a differentiating force in Lebanon. Everything revolves around it: people describe others as "a Maronite" or "a Druze" first and foremost; political power is distributed according to religious denomination; bureaucratic positions must be proportionally distributed amongst the religions; education remains largely undenominational, and so on.[26]

It was precisely the overwhelming importance of religion in Lebanon that made the imposition of a state religion unthinkable. However, and this point is crucial, the importance of religion should be kept distinct from the attribution of religion as the sole cause of the war in Lebanon. Its roots have a myriad of sources that cannot, unfortunately, be explored here. Religion is one of many.

Finally, on a less crucial point, the Lebanese democracy is really a parliamentary system, not a presidential one. The popular American characterization of the Lebanese government illustrates the point: Americans use the phrase "the Gemayel government" while Lebanese refer instead to the "Wazzan government." Technically, as in all parliamentary systems, the prime minister is the head of the government. But again Lebanon refuses to fit neatly into a category: the president has more power than the prime minister, overall.

Thus, while political culture presents an image of congruence, ultimately it exhibits major differences. Hence America has been as confusing to Lebanese as Lebanon has been to Americans. In the remainder of this chapter, we will observe the impact of this background context upon actual interactions.

## 1941-1944: THE PARADOX OF INDEPENDENCE

The years between 1941 and 1944 gave birth to independent Lebanon with the formal end of the French mandate (July 1941), and inaugurated United States–Lebanese relations at the diplomatic level in September of 1944. The period between the two events frames the first set of paradoxes: at a time when nationalism was burgeoning into the dominant regional impetus, and the Lebanese urged American recognition of their independence, why did the United States, concurrently fighting a "war for democracy," extend only lukewarm support to the Lebanese struggle for self-determination? Specifically, why did the United States refuse to follow Britain's lead in 1941 and recognize Lebanon, and why did the United States campaign for the postponement of Lebanese elections in 1942? Why in 1943 was this policy reversed, when the United States pressured the French into holding elections? Finally, given all the cumulative recalcitrance of the previous three years, why was recognition finally and rather abruptly extended on September 19, 1944? The keys to these curious American responses lie outside of Lebanon: relations with the Allies, progress on the war fronts, personnel shifts in the embassy, and domestic American politics played the major roles in shaping American policy. Thus analysis of the era must be prefaced by some initial background on the war's progress and the overriding goals of the four most pertinent parties: the French, the British, the Americans, and the Lebanese.

Both de Gaulle's Free French and the Vichy administration that took office after the occupation of France had similar plans for Syria and Lebanon: the temporary setback of occupation would not be allowed to diminish French privilege or rights in the Middle East.

Indeed, the humiliation of domestic occupation made it doubly imperative not to lose the prestigious influence over France's overseas territories—the symbol of French grandeur and power. All local forms of national protest and independence (insofar as they threatened French dominance) would be suppressed. Thus despite a 1936 treaty promising Lebanese independence within three years, the Vichy French had suspended constitutional life and dissolved the cabinet at the outbreak of World War II. After they took over from Vichy in June 1941, the Free French pursued an identical policy. De Gaulle announced that the mandate would remain in effect until new treaties regarding the "rights and interests" of France could be drawn up.[27]

For the British, the Middle East represented a top priority. Secure access to Suez guaranteed passage to India. A major wartime priority would be the defense of the Middle East from the Axis: the British were adamant on this point, and thus they had wartime responsibility for the area's security.[28] The ultimate goal was a Hashemite union, led by Iraq or Egypt, that would secure in the long term Britain's Suez holdings and allow her some input into local politics.[29] Prerequisites for the achievement of both these aims included: 1) guarding against French obstructionism and interference in the overriding goals; 2) curtailing or eliminating French presence; 3) cultivating local support as the foundation for such a plan.

Hence the British and Free French forces invaded Syria and Lebanon together on June 6, 1941, to wrest them from Vichy and secure them from Axis invasion. Temporary collaboration proved very short-lived, and a bitter struggle soon emerged between the two over the independence of Lebanon.

In this context, the United States dilemma becomes partially clear. Naturally, the defeat of the Axis took precedence above all else.[30] As that required harmonious relations between the Allies, the United States took care not to alienate either Britain or France, and opted for the least objectionable course of action in the region. Of secondary importance, American rights as guaranteed by the Franco-American convention of 1924 had to be protected and preserved. These concerned the two main areas of pre-war United States interest in the region: schools and economic accessibility.[31] Cultivation and advocacy of American prestige *per se* were not particularly important at the outset of the war, but it was deemed prudent in any event to maintain some distance from Britain's unpopular policies. As it became clear that opportunities would soon open up with diminished French and British sway, as Middle Eastern groups began increasingly to approach the United States with great awe and admiration, and as the war shifted to an offensive rather than a defensive tack, considerations of American options in the area increased in importance. Plans for long-term policy were drawn up to replace the policy of "no policy" that had served in the early stages of the war.

Finally, the Lebanese stood united on their goals: independence had become a matter of pressing urgency. French obstreperousness only galvanized them into action. The Lebanese sent periodic appeals to the United States for support in their efforts to wean the reins of power away from the French. The American image at that time was particularly stellar—champion of democracy and independence, defender of small nations and the right to self-determination, sponsor of the plan for a new United Nations. American standing was particularly high in Lebanon.[32] Thus it seemed natural to many Lebanese to turn to the United States for support in their case, and many did: Foreign Minister Frangieh, Riad as-Solh, three thousand ordinary citizens (in a petition), successive presidents (Naccache and Khouri), the Maronite Patriarch,[33] the Greek Orthodox Archbishop, and many others. The Archbishop's appeal captures the essence of the predominant American image in Lebanon at that time:

> We have every reason to hope and believe that with the active participation of the United States of America in the war, the possibilities of the ultimate triumph of right over might, of good over evil, and the safeguarding and the sanctity of the liberties of the small nations, have been further upheld and consolidated, and that Lebanon, as one of the small nations whose future prospects depend so largely on Allied victory, will be given every chance and freedom to assert at the end of the war its self-determination. . . .[34]

These and similar impassioned petitions received supportive but insubstantial responses: noncommittal statements without any evident willingness to act.

The above outline of goals provides some clues to the paradox of independence, but closer examination reveals more. The first sign of American reluctance emerged after the British–Free French "liberation" of Syria and Lebanon from Axis influence, whereupon the Free French Commander, General Catroux, proclaimed:

> The Lebanese State shall enjoy, as from now, the rights and privileges appertaining to the statutes of an independent state. These rights and privileges shall be subject only to such restrictions as are dictated by the present war situation, the security of the country, and that of the Allied Armies.[35]

The British issued a supporting statement from Cairo. Hopes were raised very high in Lebanon; the French had proclaimed the end of the Mandate! Very shortly, however, the divergence between the two "liberators" surfaced and became pronounced. While the French made "independence" conditional upon so many restrictions thereof, the British promptly recognized Lebanon's independence without conditions and urged the United States to do the same. The British motive, as the secretary of state explained in a confidential communique to his Beirut representative, was that "our recognition would strengthen the position of Great Britain and her allies in Arab countries and would have a stabilizing effect on the Near East generally. . . ."[36] But his grasp of Britain's motives did not prompt the American secretary to follow their lead. Indeed, it led him in precisely the opposite direction. American recognition would have tipped the regional balance of power into Britain's hands, enraged France and necessitated the cessation of relations with Vichy, possibly implicated the U.S. in unwanted commitments, and linked America in Arab eyes with Britain's "imperialistic" goals, thus jeopardizing the abundant reserve of good will toward the United States that existed.[37] It also might have jeopardized American rights under the Franco-American convention of 1924. Hiding behind the excuse that the continuation of privileges would be imperiled in the event of recognition, Secretary of State Hull advised Consul General Engert that the United States would instead opt for a neutral, unoffensive, bland course of action.

> Response was made that . . . American treaty rights could not be given up by executive action alone, and that those rights might be jeopardized if Syrian [and Lebanese] independence were to be recognized unaccompanied by a new treaty. Moreover, we would doubtless require clarification of the continuing special rights and privileges claimed in Syria [and Lebanon] by France. . . .
> The Department feels that the objects which the British have in mind . . . can be attained through the issuance by this government of a sympathetic public statement which, however, would not repeat not constitute recognition, is contemplated soon after the independence of Lebanon is proclaimed.[38]

Both the Lebanese and the Syrians tried to transcend the stated American concern for rights in the event of recognition by offering special provisos, arrangements, interim agreements, and promises of long-term cooperation.[39] In one sense, this demonstrated ingenuity; in another, naivete. The Lebanese seemed to take the Americans at their word and failed to absorb the complexity of American global commitments and the gravity of the extenuating circumstances. The consul general reflected precisely this feeling in numerous communiques, like the following one regarding Riad as-Solh's appeal for support:

> From a purely constitutional or legalistic point of view there is doubtless much in what Mr. Solh has to say, but he seems to forget that while the war lasts the problem of protection, stability, and security are of paramount importance. Even the most ardent Lebanese or Syrian patriot must admit privately the futility of talking about constitutions and elections and national aspirations while the enemy may still be in a position to snuff out all thought of independence forever.[40]

Perhaps this comes as no surprise, for the Lebanese were just learning to guide their ship of state, and domestic turmoil engrossed their entire energies and attention. But insofar as it reflects a tendency toward national self-absorption combined with an inflated notion of American capability that would surface repeatedly over the next four decades, it has relevance as far more than a passing phenomenon.

The British, bent on achieving their goal of reducing French influence and enhancing their own prestige, would not give up so easily. In April 1942, their representative in Beirut began to place great pressure on the French to hold free elections in Lebanon.[41] The American consul general was baffled by British adamance and incorrectly assumed its source to be the British commander in the Levant, Spears. In fact, he later discovered that the policy originated in London with Churchill himself.[42] Once again, the U.S. discouraged the idea and tried to mediate in a rising atmosphere of crisis between the French and the British. Developments on the war front played a pivotal role in the regional policies of all the concerned parties (excepting Lebanon). Wartime policies provide the best explanation for motives, reactions, and strategies.

After the Japanese attacked Pearl Harbor on December 7, 1941, the United States joined the war. Churchill immediately prevailed upon the American president to consider a Middle Eastern operation—or, more accurately, the invasion of North Africa as the key to the defense of the Middle East.[43]

The idea grew into a tentative plan which subsequently was dropped due to an unexpected development in the third week of March 1942.[44] Immediately thereafter, elections became Britain's top priority in Lebanon. It seems probable that, an American–British military invasion having been barred, the British decided to "up the ante" and play another Levantine card: defense through popular support. They thus intended to decrease the credibility of Axis propaganda and to forestall, somehow, the onset of intolerable setbacks in the region. Unfortunately, the French perceived their advocacy as direct interference in local affairs, the governance of which had been explicitly restricted to French auspices. The resultant hue and cry, as Engert (and his successor Gwynn) noted with some alarm, probably gave the Axis propagandists unlimited evidence of strains in the Alliance, in addition to effecting and exacerbating a split between Lebanese into pro-French and pro-British camps.[45] Engert wrote to Secretary Hull:

> Until conditions are normal and elections can be held it would . . . be absurd to make a change which would only encourage Axis to believe that the Allies are hopelessly disunited and had been unable to gain confidence of native population despite their high sounding promises. We are probably on the eve of grave military events compared to which local politics are of but little interest.[46]

For the United States, elections in Lebanon were entirely unthinkable at that time. Relations with Vichy France could not be jeopardized. They provided access to indispensable sources of intelligence and held the key to possibly preventing French military resistance to a North African landing (eventually readopted on July 24, 1942, amd carried out in November as Operation TORCH) if a secret agreement with Vichy could be obtained.[47]

In short, planning for TORCH and thwarting Axis forces were the primary American considerations. There was simply no will, desire, nor time to consider local elections, or to worry about possible outcomes after elections in an area of such high strategic importance.[48] At the expense of the Lebanese, therefore, the Americans placated the French and tended toward censure of the British for their untimely disruption of the status quo.

Why then did the United States reverse itself and begin to put strong pressure on the French to hold elections and to relinquish privileged status in the summer and fall of 1943? The answer is simple and completely consistent with the foregoing explanation. The entire constellation of forces on the battlefield had changed. TORCH had been successful. Good relations with France therefore no longer ranked as a high priority: indeed, de Gaulle saw the British–American landing in North Africa as an omen of future French disaster and prepared for a strong resistance to French concessions in foreign holdings.[49] The top priority, defeat of the Axis, was on the road to achievement; now the State Department would turn its attention to the second priority: ". . . planning the unseating of British and French hegemony, with careful attention to questions of how, when, where, and to what degree."[50] Accordingly, American planners at the State Department had finally drawn up a coherent strategy for the Levant by the summer of 1943. The first paper on the subject argued that

> ... if Washington but behaved prudently, it would reap an abundant harvest in the Arab world. On the Levant specifically, private American missionary, educational, and philanthropic activity had established a necessary preconditions [sic] for success namely, "a reputation above reproach."[51]

Prudence indeed characterized American policy late in the summer of 1943. The American position was delicate. Reduction of French influence was slowly being achieved, but the United States did not want to submit to British designs on the area either. Public distance from both countries was necessary, but *excessive* pressure might have triggered an alliance of expedience between Britain and France to the detriment of the "Open Door" policy, an eventuality which Hull greatly feared.[52] Isolation of the French had to be achieved without alliance with, or alienation from, the British.

After their November 1943 debacle in Lebanon, French claims lost any shred of legitimacy they may have formerly held in Washington. The delicacy of the American position became acute. Distance from French aims was imperative, avoidance of identification with the British highly desirable, preservation of the facade of a harmonious Alliance preferable. The instructions transmitted by Acting Secretary of State Stettinius to Consul General Wadsworth, on the occasion of French abrogation of Lebanese parliamentary resolutions, reflect the delicacy of the American position:

> It is the opinion of this Government that the French Committee of National Liberation should take practical steps to implement the "independence" promised the Levant States. . . . it is expected that your British colleague will shortly be instructed to make similar representations. You are authorized to discuss this matter with him, but because of special interests which might be imputed to the British in this area, it would appear preferable that your action be independent of any which he may take.[53]

Thus during the summer, the United States had placed great pressure on the French to allow elections; after the November arrest of all the cabinet ministers in their beds, more drastic action was required. The situation had an aura of challenge; in the eyes of the Lebanese, it had become ". . . a test of the sincerity of the assurances of the United Nations in respect of the right of smaller states . . ." By *threatening* public condemnation of French actions (despite the potential benefits for Axis propagandists[54]) the United States could effect a French retreat without an open clash. Its minimalist strategy enabled the United States to remain on the "right" side in regional eyes, while avoiding full recognition as the British would have liked.

Clearly, we can conclude that American policy in Lebanon during World War II had little to do with the Lebanese themselves. If it had been more cognizant of Lebanese desires, recognition would have been extended on November 22, 1943, the day that the French released the imprisoned government members—the day that Lebanese now celebrate their independence. But global circumstance and maximum opportunism vis-a-vis the British and the French determined American policy. The decision, finally, to recognize the Lebanese Republic came almost a year later. The war in Europe had effectively been won, and "war exigencies" no longer provided a plausible excuse. Having fought the "war for democracy," the U.S. could no longer withhold recognition without appearing hypocritical. Russian recognition of Syria and Lebanon in July and August probably triggered a reevaluation of past recalcitrance. The advent of an election year[55]—in which equal rights for small nations in the proposed United Nations had become an issue[56]—no doubt helped. Formal recognition of the Lebanese Republic by the United States was extended on September 19, 1944.

## 1956-1958: THE PARADOX OF INTERVENTION

A short decade after the achievement of Lebanon's independence, the world and the region had already undergone many significant transformations. Having emerged after World War II as a superpower and as a major actor in the Middle East, the United States sought to preserve global and strategic superiority over the Soviet Union and to make it clear that the Middle East, an increasingly pivotal area, did not constitute an acceptable arena for challenges to that superiority. At the height of the Cold War, the first priority was unquestionably the battle against international communism on both the economic and political fronts, and the Middle East gradually emerged as the crucible for a rapid succession of plans aimed at that all-consuming goal. Soviet attainment of nuclear parity in 1955 and her entry into the Middle East via an arms deal with Nasser in the same year served to rivet American attention on the region and stiffen United States resolve to support the moderate pro-Western states.

For Secretary of State Dulles, the Suez War demonstrated the vulnerability of British and French—and ergo, potentially American—influence in the region. Despite a temporary convergence of views with Russia on the illegality of the tripartite invasion and the legitimacy of Egypt's claims, Dulles soon became alarmed by the increasing number of Soviet advisors in Egypt and decided that the spread of international communism—which he considered to be the sole motive behind all Soviet policies—necessitated immediate action. He perceived a power vacuum in the area, left by the departure of Britain and France, that the United States must fill before international communism took over. The power vacuum had unfortunately emerged in an area where newly independent states were basking in burgeoning nationalism and experimenting with ideas like "positive neutralism." Dulles was convinced that areas experiencing new and zealous nationalism were far more vulnerable to communist influence than others.[57] President Eisenhower's later explanation made it clear that the White House imputed widescale aims of a drastic nature to the Soviet Union:

> The leaders of the Soviet Union, like the Czars before them, had their eyes on the Middle East. . . . the Soviet objective was, in plain fact, power politics: to seize the oil, to weaken Western civilization.[58]

The signatories to the Baghdad Pact—Iraq, Iran, Turkey, and Pakistan—encouraged this outlook and urged formal action on Washington's part. Jordan and Lebanon were also apprehensive of regional developments, and advocated a strong United States position.[59]

In response, the American president proposed the enactment of the Eisenhower Doctrine on January 5, 1957. Designed to allow large-scale and effective American response to the perceived threat of international communism in the Middle East, the proposed measure would give the U.S. almost a free hand in the region. As Eisenhower outlined it,

> International Communism, of course, seeks to mask its purpose of domination by expressions of political, economic, and military aid. . . . The action which I propose would have the following features:
>
> It would . . . authorize the United States to cooperate with and assist any nation . . . in the Middle East in the development of economic strength dedicated to the maintenance of national independence.

> It would . . . include the employment of the armed forces of the United States to secure and protect the territorial integrity and political independence of such nations . . . against overt armed aggression from any nation controlled by International Communism . . . direct or indirect.[60]

The Doctrine became law on March 9, 1957, after extensive and heated debate. However, it provoked little positive reaction in the region to which it was directed. Of all the Arab states, only Lebanon embraced the Doctrine fully and publicly. She did so in a joint Lebanese–American communique on March 16, 1957, barely a week after the Doctrine's formal acceptance and enactment. Lebanon's quick and unique acceptance had its roots in numerous developments, both regional and domestic.

On the regional front, Lebanon found herself in the eye of a storm. Nasser's coup in 1952 and his subsequent meteoric rise to power had sharp repercussions all over the Middle East, but particularly in Lebanon. As the foremost proponent—indeed, the creator—of Pan-Arabism, Nasser's appeal and legitimacy often rivaled those of Arab governments. In some cases, "shadow governments" sprang up that could serve as guardians to ensure conformity with the Nasserist line.[61] In Lebanon, Nasser's popular appeal jeopardized the status of traditional Moslem leaders who hastened to present their credentials in Cairo, causing much consternation among the Christians.[62] Nasser's popularity and his vocal support for overthrowing traditional leaders alarmed many Arab governments. Some looked to the West for protection from the oncoming hurricane. Iraq joined the Baghdad Pact and attempted to form a rival, alternative nucleus of Pan-Arabism. The notion of dependence on Western assistance outraged Nasser. He vehemently opposed the Baghdad Pact and urged the expulsion of the British from the Middle East. On the other hand, he embraced the concept of "positive neutralism" and tried to steer a course between the United States and the USSR and to receive support from both. He accused President Chamoun of pretending neutrality while secretly favoring Iraq,[63] which so angered him that he began to sponsor Chamoun's opposition openly.[64] A fierce rivalry between the two camps resulted, and the regional polarization soon spawned a mirror image inside Lebanon.[65]

Chamouns' supporters, mostly but not exclusively Christian, feared the Pan-Arab alternative. They wanted Lebanon to remain independent and they wanted to retain their traditional position within the country. They believed that a real threat to Lebanon's short-term survival existed, and thus began openly to seek Western protection to counteract Nasser's magnetism. The domestic opposition, on the other hand, identified with and felt that Lebanon could not remain isolated from regional movements and trends and must not embrace the American plan so vehemently. Some may have believed that the union with Syria was desirable or inevitable; others wanted to con- tribute to Nasserism by showing support and reaffirming Lebanon's place as an "Arab" state.[66] Those who believed in merger with Syria were more likely to be Muslims, although not all Lebanese Muslims wished to see Lebanon disappear. Indeed, the Muslim leadership prob- ably dreaded such an eventuality, as they would have been the first to lose their traditionally-based power.[67] In short, the division inside Lebanon reflected regional polarization. Religion played a role insofar as it contributed to shaping beliefs and images, thereby predisposing both Muslims and Christians to be responsive to historical fears and desires. But the conflict, despite some of the language that surrounded it, primarily concerned Lebanon's future identity, not religious issues.

It was against this internal, regional, and international backdrop that Chamoun accepted the Eisenhower Doctrine on March 16, 1957, sparking a wide-scale debate inside Lebanon. His motives for doing so clearly included counterbalancing Nasser's influence and providing a backup support system in the event of an attempted takeover by Syria or Egypt. Chamoun and his supporters felt that outside interference in Lebanon (e.g., Nasser's support for the opposition, vehement radio campaigns, and even arms smuggling from Syria, the extent of which was never conclusively determined) merited international interven- tion—that, in a sense, Lebanon's neutrality could only be preserved by resorting to temporary protection. The opposition, on the other hand, considered the association with the United States as simply a replace- ment for the hated French—the penultimate abrogation of the Na- tional Pact of 1943, in which the Christians had specifically foregone French protection in favor of neutrality.[68] The international regional climate rendered neutrality in Arab disputes well-nigh impossible.

The tenuous balance between the regional and international poles tipped decisively and irrevocably with the birth of the United Arab Republic on Feburary 1, 1958. The merger was not considered solely a Syro-Egyptian marriage; rather, it would trigger a dynamic process that would end in comprehensive Arab unity.[69]

President Quwwatli of Syria extended invitations to Lebanon to join the union.[70] A surprise visit from Nasser to Damascus prompted thousands of Lebanese to travel to Syria to share in the excitement of the moment.

Tensions inside Lebanon escalated from that point onwards. Pas- sions rode high: for Chamoun's supporters, all their instincts told them to resist the wave of the moment, to find a branch to clutch at to halt this perilous hurtling journey down a mountain cliff; to do everything in their power to prevent any gains by the opposition, because the opposition was, in their eyes, funded and encouraged by Nasser himself, and its victory might mean the end of Lebanon as they had known it. The Lebanese opposition thought that American protection was unnecessary. They felt no threat from the UAR, nor from international communism, and they wanted very much to partake of the force that was sweeping the region. Thus when Chamoun's supporters won the 1957 elections, which were characterized by rampant corruption on both sides, the country exploded.[71] Shortly after Chamoun made it known that he intended to run for a second term, the war broke out on May 8, 1958.[72]

## American Involvement: Timing And Scope

Less than a week after the outbreak of hostilities, Chamoun sent an exploratory cable to the White House and received a lukewarm response: American troops would be sent only if American lives were endangered.[73] Another version has Chamoun writing out an (undated) request to Ambassador McClintock in Beirut, whereupon the latter convinces him to destroy it; and submitting thereafter a second verbal request via an emissary who is sent back to the president for a written copy, but never returns with it.[74] There is little doubt that Chamoun would have preferred substantive American assistance at the outset of the disturbances, but the United States held off. It took a few symbolic steps: doubling the strength of the Sixth Fleet, airlifting police equipment, promising to send tanks, and issuing statements of *readiness* to help. But United States officials made it clear to Chamoun that unless clear-cut evidence of massive infiltration and takeover by a country "dominated by international communism" could be proven, they would not interfere in the domestic affairs of Lebanon. Secretary Dulles made it clear how likely he thought that might be in a press conference on May 20:

> . . . we do not consider under the present state of affairs that there is likely to be an attack, an armed attack, from a country which we would consider under the control of international communism. . . . we are not anxious to have a situation which would be in any sense a pretext for introducing American forces into the area. We hope and believe that will not be called for.[75]

President Eisenhower confirmed the secretary's view on June 14 when he termed the Lebanese situation "serious—but not alarming."[76] The official policy called for awaiting the completion of the UN report to determine the extent of UAR intervention and therefore the applicability of the Eisenhower Doctrine.

On July 4, the UN issued its verdict: no evidence of an externally fomented plot. Despite the dispute surrounding this conclusion,[77] it would seem that the United States accepted it and decided to hold off on sending troops to await developments.

The development that triggered an immediate response erupted on July 14. Nuri as-Said, the prime minister of Iraq and an important American ally, was toppled in a bloody coup. Chamoun urgently requested American troops to land within 48 hours; he feared for his life.[78] Secretary Dulles informed the president that Chamoun was deeply embittered by the American failure to come to his aid earlier.[79]

On July 15, 1958, thirty-six hundred Marines landed on the beaches of Lebanon; the next day they marched into Beirut. By August 5, the total number of Marines had been brought up to 14,300, and the entire Sixth Fleet (with forty thousand men on board) backed them up at sea. They had all withdrawn by October, and suffered only minor casualties. By the time they left, the situation had calmed considerably, and Lebanon had elected a new president.

In his message to Congress on July 15, President Eisenhower explained that the troops were being sent "to protect American lives" (although an evacuation had commenced the previous day) and "to assist the Government of Lebanon in the preservation of Lebanon's territorial integrity and independence."[80] He elaborated on this point:

> Our government has acted in response to a request for help from a small and peaceful nation which has long had ties of closest friendship with the United States. Readiness to help a friend in need is an admirable characteristic of the American people, and I am, in this message, informing the Congress of the reasons why I believe the United States could not in honor idly stand by in this hour of Lebanon's grave peril.[81]

In actual fact, however, "readiness to help a friend in need" was clearly not the primary U.S. motive; if it had been, troops might have been sent in earlier amd Chamoun would not have been left with such resentment.

Herein lies the crux of the "paradox of intervention," although it has several faces. From President Chamoun's point of view, the United States had done too little, too late. His bitterness was compounded by the fact that once the Marines arrived, the United States set about orchestrating the election of President Fu'ad Shihab, the commander who had declined to commit his troops to either side in the fighting and who had, therefore, singlehandedly engineered a stalemate in the war, preventing Chamoun from winning. What Chamoun in fact expected from the United States remains unclear. Varying reports indicate that he wanted any or all of the following: guaranteed reelection; a means of placing his choice for successor in office and thereby ensuring the continuation of his policies and a role in future policy decisions; or some kind of international trust for Lebanon's sovereignty or even for the Christian population in times of peril.[82] Whatever the correct version (and it may in fact span all three), Chamoun's expectations were far higher than what the United States could deliver, and he remained bitter about the incident long afterwards.[83]

From the other Lebanese perspective, that of the opposition, the American troops were seen at first as foreign invaders to be resisted tooth and nail. However, their remarkable restraint on Lebanese territory won them respect and high marks from the opposition.[84] When the Americans facilitated the election of Fu'ad Shihab, the opposition choice for the presidency, the paradox on the Lebanese side was complete. The two camps had completely reversed their initial assessments of American motives. Chamoun resented their interference, while the opposition welcomed the weight of their presence.

From the American perspective, the paradox of intervention had numerous aspects as well. The first concerned motive: the massive landings of American Marines occurred in a country that was not, most agreed, truly threatened by international communism in the proper sense of the term. Indeed, the Administration itself had taken that position prior to July 14. Justification for the decision, as it was presented, was therefore called into question.

But the public presentation of United States motives did not touch on the central reasons why the Marines landed on the shores of Lebanon July 15. American policy was rooted in global and regional considerations once again. The initial reluctance to send in troops stemmed from the failure to engineer a coup in Syria in 1957,[85] a desire to give the UN a chance to mediate the dispute,[86] and a sense that although regional turmoil was indeed simmering, certain key anchor states were not actually threatened. The coup in Iraq and the turmoil in Jordan altered the assessment drastically.[87]

Various signals were intended for various parties. The American allies in the region—Iran, Pakistan, Turkey, Jordan, and Saudi Arabia— would not lose faith in American commitments. The Soviets would recognize the Middle East as an "untouchable" sphere of influence. Consequent Soviet inaction would demonstrate the shakiness of Soviet commitment to the Nasserist bloc. The rebels in Jordan would be stymied. Finally, and perhaps least importantly, the situation in Lebanon could be defused in some way that was acceptable to all parties involved. That Lebanon itself did not constitute the primary motive for the American action has been noted elsewhere: "There are very strong indications that, had the Iraqi revolt not taken place, the United States would not have dispatched its troops to Lebanon."[88] U.S. troops went to Lebanon to prevent a "domino" effect originating in Iraq and spreading to the rest of the Middle East.

The second aspect of the paradox from an American perspective concerned the landing's outcome. The entire episode, seen with hindsight, can be viewed both as a great success *and* as a failure. The success can be found in the mission's impact on Lebanon, the goal for which it was least intended. Order was restored in Lebanon; only one Marine died a combat-related death, and no Lebanese were injured in any way by the American troops.[89] The Marines had a well-defined mission in Lebanon: to separate the opposing forces while the politicians worked out a political solution. They achieved their mission, and, after a smooth transition of government, they left. They had succeeded in winning the admiration of many Lebanese.

With respect to the region, however, the mission was less successful, perhaps because it originated out of a murky policy. The Eisenhower Doctrine did not suit the Middle East. It failed to address the real roots of turbulence. Had some kind of Marshall Plan for newly independent Middle East states been designed, the course of United States relations in the area might have been completely different. Instead, the Administration labelled nationalism "Communism" and went on the offensive. Two final ironic details clinch the paradox. First, President Eisenhower did not in fact send the Marines to Beirut under the Eisenhower Doctrine; instead, he invoked Article 51 of the UN Charter and the 1950 "Unity for Peace" UN resolution.[90] Secondly, after the United States had worked so hard to install a new acceptable government in Lebanon, its president, Fu'ad Shihab, reversed the policy of his predecessor and withdrew Lebanon's commitment to the Eisenhower Doctrine. With the withdrawal of its only Arab supporter, the Eisenhower Doctrine died a quiet death.

## 1975-1976: THE PARADOX OF INDIFFERENCE

Seventeen years later, in 1975, some aspects of 1958 appeared to be repeating themselves as internal conflict erupted in Lebanon. This time the stakes had risen significantly, because regional and international constellations had changed dramatically. One marked difference lay in American apathy and hesitation to become involved despite the fact that a moderate, pro-Western friend was gradually being demolished before the world's closed eyes. We have chosen in this section to focus solely on the period between 1975 and 1976 although, as we will indicate, the apathy and the underestimation of the situation's gravity pertained for the most part to Carter's Administration as well.

Despite the immediate temptation to view 1975 as a direct sequel to 1958, the link did not actually apply except in that some of Lebanon's 1958 instabilities remained unaddressed until 1975, by which time they had become explosive beyond control. But most of the variables at the global, regional, and Lebanese levels had changed.

The Cold War of the 1950s had given way to the detente of the 1970s. Nixon's *weltanschauung* entailed a joint United States–Soviet global settlement of all outstanding issues, and the introduction of China into the game added more complexity to the challenge. It was expected that negotiations would be undertaken on all issues at once, thus augmenting the bargaining potential of all parties.[91]

In the Middle East, this policy translated into countering Soviet influence with a strong Israel in order to augment bargaining clout at the global negotiating table. Thus prior to 1973, the Middle East was construed in terms of the United States–USSR conflict rather than regional complexities, in part because regional complexities were presumed insoluble.[92] In Vietnam, it meant "peace with honor" or peace on American terms, without humiliation or capitulation to the North Vietnamese, a goal that sounded lofty but remained elusive—and ultimately unattainable—in practice. With respect to China, relations were established for the first time in 1972 in a move that approximated quintessential balance-of-power politics.

But these early grand designs began to disintegrate in the spring of 1973 under the dual onslaught of Watergate and Vietnam. The Watergate break-in of spring 1972 had become a full-fledged political scandal by summer 1973. As Congressional hearings commenced, it even appeared that Nixon's exit from power was possible. The situation had a tremendous impact on foreign policy, as Kissinger has described:

> With every passing date [sic] Watergate was circumscribing our freedom of action. We were losing the ability to make credible commitments, for we could no longer guarantee Congressional approval. At the same time, we had to be careful to avoid confrontations for fear of being unable to sustain them in a miasma of domestic suspicion.[93]

Growing alienation and desperation certainly contributed to frantic efforts to bring the Vietnam War to a decisive close. Hence the Paris Peace talks, the Christmas bombings of 1973, and the final withdrawal of American troops in January of 1974. But a fundamentally flawed policy in Vietnam would not expire quietly. Weakness at the core of the American system—so clear for all the world to see in the humiliating resignation of Richard Nixon—made "peace with honor" an absurdity. When South Vietnam finally collapsed in April of 1975, much of American will and self-esteem went with it. The fall of Cambodia and Laos in the same period called the previous decades of policy into question, and the nation retreated to nurse its wounds. At that time, only thirty-six percent of Americans polled agreed it was important for the United States to make and keep commitments to other nations, and only thirty-four percent were willing to send troops to West Berlin if the Russians were to invade.[94] The prevailing mood of disillusionment that settled over the country had a dampening and disquieting effect that had a sharp impact on the American public's ordering of priorities.[95]

Nixon's grand strategy of detente scored many highly significant and visible successes for the United States in its relations with the Soviet Union and China, but it did little for the Middle East. That area of the world remained locked in a stalemate, apparently by virtue of an explicit or implicit agreement between the superpowers not to jeopardize the progress of detente.[96] However, the October 1973 War and the Arab oil embargo jolted the White House into the realization that the Middle East could not be placed on hold for long. A new sense of foreboding emerged regarding the region's potential explosiveness. When conflicts did break out, it seemed that an irreversible, unintended process drew the superpowers into the conflict despite their best intentions. The region suddenly became the focus of Kissinger's diplomatic energy, but the Middle East he was attempting to mold consisted solely of Israel, Syria, Jordan, and Egypt.[97]

Indeed, Kissinger's frantic diplomatic shuttles had regional fallout effects that rapidly hit Lebanon as well. Their cumulative effect resulted in, *inter alia*, the following outcomes:[98]

1. Egypt and Israel pledged to abstain from violence with one another.
2. President Assad of Syria tried to bring together a regional coalition, the "Eastern Front,"[99] to counterbalance Egypt's deviation, but did not really succeed.
3. The United States developed an interest in good relations with Syria in the event of a "Golan II" agreement.

4. The Israelis stepped up their retaliation in Lebanon briskly, making a resolution of the terms of Palestinian presence inside that country almost impossible.
5. The Conservative Front became convinced that Lebanon's Palestinian dilemma could be resolved only by force.
6. The Palestinians, having been expelled from Jordan in 1970, forged an alliance with local Lebanese leftists in anticipation of the coming battle that—although they tried to remain on the sidelines—they could not afford to lose.
7. Various internal incidents sparked the Lebanese civil war in April of 1975.
8. Syria decided to carve out a leading role in Lebanon for herself in order to prove to the United States that she could not be overlooked in a settlement, prevent a potential leftist victory in Lebanon, and consolidate an additional flank for her proposed "Eastern Front."[100]

It should be self-evident that these events were highly interdependent but not necessarily causally related one to another in the order given. The Lebanese habit of seeking foreign sponsors has been rivaled only by the region's enthusiasm for intervening in Lebanon. This phenomenon has always meant a very high degree of linkage between regional events and developments inside Lebanon. 1975 provides a clear illustration. Once again, the Arab–Israeli conflict was showing signs of moving toward a settlement. No one intended to be left out, but most were also unwilling to bargain on American terms. They intended to set their own, and Lebanon was a good place to begin.

Regional waves had a severe impact on Lebanon. The war broke out in April 1975 and raged intermittently and unattended through 1976. American policy-makers, focused as they were on the laborious process of forging bilateral withdrawal agreements, did not pay sufficient heed to developments in Lebanon. To be sure, the United States had maintained a consistent position of several critical aspects of the situation. In particular, the United States had repeatedly declared itself to be dedicated to the preservation of Lebanese territorial integrity and unity.[101] It also endorsed the Constitutional Document drafted by Syria and President Frangieh, concerning the need for some adjustments in the Lebanese political system. In addition, the United States advocated the rehabilitation of the Lebanese Army into a viable instrument for the protection of national security.[102] But these verbal positions did not by any means add up to an active, concrete policy. The absence of policy and active interest was reflected in the fact that during the first six months of the war, no high-level interest was generated, and reports from the consulate accumulated in Washington unheeded. Numerous officials have been quoted as saying that the United States simply had no policy on Lebanon at that time and little interest in devising one:

> Kissinger indeed forgot Lebanon. Nor did he instruct his am-
> bassadors or listen to their information—even those who should
> have been directly involved in his projects . . . . By their own ac-
> counts, official policy makers in Washington stumbled around
> without any feel for the unfolding Lebanese drama.[103]

The absence of a viable policy was reflected in and perhaps exacerbated by two factors, On the one hand, the United States did not
have good relations with the Lebanese president, Suleiman
Frangieh.[104] On the other hand, for all intents and purposes, they had
no ambassador from the beginning of 1976, when Godley left the
country for medical reasons, until 1977. In May, one month after he
had arrived, Ambassador Meloy was assassinated. After that, two
diplomatic envoys served as temporary stopgaps until 1977, when
Ambassador Richard Parker finally took up permanent residence.

That the United States had neither policy nor interest in their
small country remained inconceivable to the Lebanese. They
speculated endlessly on American motives and intentions. Some cir-
culated elaborate theories of CIA plots and grand conspiracy
throughout the country; others remained convinced that the United
States would soon intervene with a major operation, Marines and all.[105]
Ex-President Chamoun, for example, tried to interest the U.S. Charge
d'Affaires in Beirut in a UN or American intervention. The response
he received was noncommittal, essentially that the Lebanese must ex-
tricate themselves from a Lebanese war rather than seeking outside intervention.[106] Waiting for the Americans recalled waiting for Godot.
They could not and would not come; instead, they arranged another
stopgap measure.

American officials viewed the war as an isolated incident that
might pose a threat to all that American efforts had accomplished in
the region. Far worse, it might erupt into a regional war. The single
and overriding American goal for Lebanon until the end of 1975 was
containment. The war was considered a domestic affair; outside intervention should be prevented in order to forestall escalation.[107] By
mid-1976, after an attempt to resolve the conflict itself, the Administration showed signs of changing its position on intervention.
They had decided that only Arab mediation would be effective. Since
Arab mediation appeared to be taking the form of Syrian intervention,
the United States accepted and gradually even welcomed the idea.
King Hussein encouraged the idea, and Special Envoy Brown had expressly concurred.[108]

Thus during 1976, the United States began to support a Syrian intervention in order to forestall a radical takeover.[109] It seemed the only
plausible option, given the United States inability to intervene directly

because of domestic opposition, lack of policy, and lack of interest. A third and significant factor that contributed to the reversal on policy was the official domestic Lebanese support for Syrian intervention.[110] Whether Lebanon would in the long run be better off or not was immaterial. The fact is that the Administration, like the Lebanese government at the time, probably believed that the Syrians would withdraw when they had rectified the situation and that Lebanon *would* benefit. The primary concern was to prevent an escalation into a regional war and to maintain the momentum toward regional peace.

With this in mind, Kissinger gave tacit approval to the Syrian peacekeeping mission and, as is well known, brokered an arrangement with Israel to establish the acceptable limits for Syrian intervention and to lay down a set of rules governing their occupation. These were specified by Israel in March 1976, in a secret document from Foreign Minister Yigal Allon to Kissinger. Thence originated the concept of "red line," a geographical limit beyond which Syrian troops would not be allowed to cross, and a functional limit beyond which Syrian activity would not be allowed to escalate.

## Conclusion

The paradox of 1975–1976 is perhaps the most self-evident of the four: at a time when a small, neutral, friendly country was starting to disintegrate, the United States had neither the power nor the will to act. While this should have been eminently clear to the Lebanese, many insisted on interpreting American inertia either as a deliberate abstention with conspiratorial overtones, or as a temporary aberration that would soon be set straight. And finally, when it did act, the United States legitimized the very situation it had been trying for so long to avoid: regional intervention. Inconsistent representation in the embassy and inadequate policy guidelines contributed quite a bit to the confusion. But a muddling of such proportions could only occur given two basic conditions: first, that the United States had exhausted its superpower steam in another corner of the globe, and second, that Lebanon in isolation mattered little to the United States in any event.

## 1981-1983: THE PARADOX OF COMMITMENT

The years from 1981 to the present have, without a doubt, witnessed, the heaviest American involvement in Lebanon in the history of relations between the two. Yet despite the high level of interaction, communication, and cooperation, the Lebanese and the Americans seem to be misunderstanding each other again. This may, however, be the last waltz. For the ultimate and tragic irony may turn out to be that when the United States did finally commit itself to the extent that the Lebanese had been urging for so long, American bumbling—together with that familiar, blithe Lebanese certainty that the United States would stand by them and produce magic solutions—may have engineered a *de facto* division of Lebanon into Israeli and Syrian spheres of influence. Clearly one hopes that such gloom will prove unwarranted. But the possibility now exists.

While American bumbling has certainly been in evidence over the last two years, it would be inaccurate to pin the blame solely on the United States or any other solo actor for the failure of numerous initiatives. The failure has been a collective one. A myriad of obstacles has been placed in the path of resolution by all parties, whether by error or by design. We will leave the judgment of whether carelessness or calculation was the culprit to the reader's imagination.

The Reagan Administration was elected on a mandate of strength in reaction to Carter's perceived inconsistency and lack of assertiveness. The Iranian revolution and the hostage drama, the Soviet invasion of Afghanistan, and the cacophonous chorus of criticism from European allies all contributed to a resurgence in American determination to strengthen her defenses in the Middle East and elsewhere. The so-called "Nixon Doctrine" of relying on indigenous powers and forces to protect vital American interests had become passe. By early 1981, the Administration had arrived at a broad two-pronged strategy that served as an initial Middle East policy: first, that only American power and initiative could accomplish United States goals, and second, that a common "Soviet threat" might offer a foundation for a new strategic alliance in the Middle East. In line with the first goal, exploration into and eventually negotiations over strategic bases for a new American Rapid Deployment Force (RDF) continued throughout 1981. Secretary of State Haig's first trip to the Middle East in April of 1981 was undertaken primarily in pursuit of the second goal.[111]

During the first months of 1981, many observers noted that the Administration seemed to have no coherent Middle East policy. That was indeed the case with regard to Lebanon and the Arab–Israeli conflict, but not insofar as general vague regional guidelines were concerned. The latter included primarily three broad aims: 1) security of the Middle East—prevention of any Soviet incursion: 2) protection of the oil flow; and 3) "relative stability, or more accurately, the containment of instability which could jeopardize the attainment of the first two aims."[112] Lebanon and the Arab–Israeli conflict fell into the third category, particularly as a sharp dispute between the secretaries of

State and Defense, Haig and Weinberger, precluded the smooth coordination of strategy.[113] Thus a structured and persistent follow-up on the Camp David agreement appeared unlikely, and negotiations over Palestinian autonomy were allowed to follow their own course.

Lebanon clearly qualified as an important area for containment, which was to prove an elusive goal. Events in the Middle East interfered with Administration plans and continued to demonstrate a marked proclivity to do so. The first American involvement rose out of the Syrian missile crisis of April 1981 as Haig was setting out on his first official visit to the area.

## The Syrian Missile Crisis

A Lebanese Forces (LF) attack on the first of April 1981, prompted a Syrian siege of the Christian town of Zahle, deep in the heartland of Syrian-occupied Lebanon. The Syrians were responding to what they perceived as a plan to link up LF militia in the north with Haddad's men in the south via a new road they had planned to construct.[114] Israel's tacit support for the Lebanese Forces now surfaced publicly as Begin vowed not to let his Christian friends be defeated by the Syrians.[115] When Syria began to employ helicopters, Israel shot down two of them on April 28 as a warning. No sooner had it been delivered than the Syrians upped the ante with a warning of their own in the form of SAM-3 missiles near Zahle which they later buttressed with SAM-2s inside their borders. As the episode escalated dramatically, the Reagan Administration sent Philip Habib, a retired American diplomat of Lebanese descent, to resolve the crisis. His dispatch marked the American initiation into Lebanon and set the stage for deeper involvement.

Rather than addressing merely the existence of the missiles and the Syrian–Lebanese Forces dispute in Zahle, Habib began to broaden his efforts and to address his mission to a solution for the overall Lebanese dilemma.[116] Significantly, what Habib ultimately accomplished, with substantial Saudi assistance, was a cease-fire between Israel and the PLO. The original source of the problem—the Syrian missiles—remained, but a cease-fire prevented escalation into a wider Palestinian–Syrian–Israeli confrontation. Thus the mission accomplished an unanticipated set of goals but partially failed in its original task. It also initiated attempts to find a broader solution to the general Lebanese conflict with reference to the regional context.

The Habib mission inaugurated two new trends that would fundamentally alter United States policy in Lebanon over the coming years. The first evolved independently of Habib's efforts but may have significantly affected their outcome and even spawned or contributed to the second. This new dynamic was born on April 28 with the Israeli downing of the two helicopters despite American pleas for restraint, and continued with three rapid-fire developments on May 28, June 7, and July 17. These dates represented, respectively, the Israeli destruction of Syrian SAM-9 missiles in Lebanon as Habib returned to the United States for consultations, an Israeli attack of an Iraqi nuclear reactor, and the massive bombing of PLO headquarters in Beirut. All symbolized a marked Israeli disregard for American considerations and determination to have its own way regardless of cost. Although they took a while to come into full bloom, the summer's tensions ushered in the onset of the lowest nadir in United States–Israeli relations since the founding of the Jewish state.

The breach of trust and divergence in aims may well have shaped the reassessment of the Habib mission from crisis management into an attempt to address broader Lebanese and regional dilemmas. No matter what its sources, the second trend that emerged was a pattern wherein Middle Eastern dynamics caught the Administration by surprise and drew it into the regional vortex further than it originally intended. This was partly a function of Habib's own desire to accelerate a solution to the Lebanese tragedy and perhaps a reaction to Israel's stunning uncooperativeness. But it also resulted from a Reaganesque and indeed generally American phenomenon whereby, caught unprepared the U.S. belatedly attempts to rectify its inadequacy by divulging a pragmatic, comprehensive solution to the whole problem instead of focusing on the piece that originally blew up. This pattern presented a failsafe formula for involving the United States in Lebanon at a faster and unpremeditated rate than it had originally intended. The August 1981 visit of the late President-elect Bashir Gemayel, then head of the Lebanese Forces, signaled a new level of American involvement. It provided a clear indication that the United States did not consider the Lebanese crisis resolved despite the cease-fire, and that it was exploring future options and partnerships. Notably, Gemayel stated in a press conference that he sensed a new level of American commitment and readiness to address the Lebanese crisis in its entirety, with particular emphasis on a Syrian withdrawal.[117] Thus it was apparent, even by August 1981, that the Administration sought a broader solution to Lebanon's dilemma, but most probably no one anticipated the actual scope of future commitments.

## The War of 1982

Attempts to patch up the rift with the Israelis fell apart again after

Israel annexed the Golan Heights. With the assassination of Sadat and Israel's defiance and stubborn independence, the United States found itself temporarily at a loss for strong regional partners except for the Saudis. It focused on holding together the shadow of Camp David by the skin of its teeth, concerned mainly that Israel return Sinai as scheduled.[118] Following that, the Administration heaved a sigh of relief, and, despite a verbal commitment to continuing the autonomy talks, showed little real will to push through any kind of concerted settlement.

The postponement politics simply were not tailored to Middle East realities. Throughout the spring of 1982, all signs pointed to the eventual launching of some kind of Israeli invasion into Lebanon. Perhaps the advent of ministers like Ariel Sharon and Alexander Haig—both bent on destroying the PLO—had made the 1982 campaign an attractive move. Or perhaps the upcoming Lebanese elections augured well for a thrust into the country whose previous president had been elected under Syrian guns. Or perhaps, with the Egyptian deterrent temporarily checkmated, the Israelis figured that they would finish off another military and political opponent, the ever-stronger PLO. Much remains murky, but three things are clear.

1.  When Sharon visited the United States in May 1982, he felt he had received a "go-ahead" from Secretary Haig, whether implicitly or explicitly.[119]
2.  The pretext for the invasion was misleading: the Israeli Ambassador to London, Shlomo Argov, was not shot by the PLO as Israel claimed, but by 2 Iraqis (one of whom was an intelligence officer)[120] and one Jordanian affiliated with Abu Nidal.
3.  The initial phrasing of the war's goals was designed primarily for public consumption. Operation "Peace for Galilee" would have been more accurately entitled, "Operation crush the PLO, transform Jordan, and reconstruct Lebanon."[121]

Whether or not the United States explicitly endorsed the invasion, chances are that it had some advance indication of Israel's plans (witness the American warnings to Israel *not* to invade as early as January 1982),[122] but it was again shocked and unprepared for their magnitude. Haig's resignation on June 25 owed much to his sponsorship of Israel's course of action and the President's own emerging dismay over Israel's tactics, particularly after the siege of Beirut.[123] Once again Ambassador Habib was dispatched for crisis diplomacy, and once again, after innumerable false starts, delays, and inestimable destruction and death, a cease-fire was arranged. The personal presidential commitment embodied in Reagan's phone call to Begin and in various subsequent statements[124] marked an unprecedented level of official attention on Lebanon, albeit again due to regional dynamics.

At the war's end, the Administration had two policy alternatives in the Middle East. The first pertained solely to Lebanon, and it entailed the withdrawal of foreign forces, support for the Lebanese government, and reestablishment of Lebanese sovereignty. The second had broader implications. Like its 1973 predecessor, the war of 1982 had awakened an American administration that had opted for "containment" in pursuit of global strategic aims to the urgency of regional settlement. In this regard, Reagan instructed Shultz in mid-summer to undertake a thorough revision of the United States position on the Arab–Israeli conflict and to produce a long-term plan for movement.

With respect to the first goal, even as early as June 13 Haig had indicated that the United States would link the Israeli withdrawal from Lebanon to the withdrawal of all foreign forces from the shattered country.[125] The first step in the process would be the withdrawal of the PLO. Toward this end, Reagan committed a small force of American Marines (the first since the Vietnam War) to take part in a Multinational Force that would assist the Lebanese Army in the following tasks:

> The Lebanese Armed Forces will assure the departure from Lebanon of the PLO leadership, offices, and combatants, from whatever organization of Beirut in a manner which will:
>   A. Assure the safety of such departing PLO personnel
>   B. Assure the safety of other persons in the Beirut area; and
>   C. Further the restoration of the sovereignty and authority of the Lebanese Government over the Beirut area.[126]

In the first instance of their deployment, the Marines had a clearly defined *mission*, stated above, with a termination point. They would stay no longer than thirty days. If the withdrawal did not proceed smoothly, the mandate would terminate and all MNF personnel would depart immediately. The War Powers Act would not be operable because the Marines would not encounter hostility or engage in combat. They would merely supervise one event in the capacity of neutral peacekeepers.

In a letter to Congress on August 24, 1982, Reagan outlined his understanding of the first goal by stating the Administration's *objectives* in Lebanon to be:

- a permanent cessation of hostilities
- the establishment of a strong, representative central government;

- withdrawal of all foreign forces;
- restoration of control by the Lebanese Government throughout the country; and
- establishment of conditions under which Lebanon no longer can be used as a launching point for attacks against Israel.[127]

The above points constituted, in effect, the complete American policy on Lebanon as of August 1982. It was indeed one of the first times that an American administration had pursued a policy that focused primarily on Lebanon for its own inherent value, and not because it threatened or was threatened by any other regional crisis. Undeniably, however, that sense of Lebanon's value had emerged during an acute regional crisis—and at a period when relations between the United States and Israel were in a dismal state.

Convinced that a long-awaited American shift had arrived, the Lebanese were elated by the nascent Washington focus on Lebanon's intrinsic importance. Clearly, Bashir Gemayel felt convinced that the United States had finally begun to understand Lebanon's centrality, as he saw it. He believed it had made a long-term commitment to Lebanon's survival. Shortly before his death, he said in an interview:

> We are fully satisfied. For the first time, a U.S. President is letting America's friends here feel that they are being supported and that being a part of the free world is not a liability. The efforts of the U.S. to bring back unity and law and order to the country have been wonderful. I never thought the Marines would return [to Lebanon] and be so well-received.[128]

Indeed, much of the exuberance that prevailed in Lebanon at that time—the sense of a new beginning, of a real change, of the end of the tragedy—may have stemmed from a perception in Lebanon among all groups that the Americans finally seemed to be tackling Lebanon's problems with vigor. It was widely believed that, given a strong United States commitment, anything would be possible. The Marines elicited a special respect from all Lebanese, and gratitude for their presence found expression in many ways.[129]

However, the Americans' exclusive concentration on Lebanon did not last long. Two circumstances in particular hastened a shift in focus. The first was a marked American leeriness inherited from the Vietnam era, over military commitments in distant hostile areas. Not even Reagan's strategic posturing could eradicate it from America's consciousness.[130] Fear of getting locked into a distant, violent, and little-understood conflict precipitated an overeager withdrawal of the Marines on September 10, a full 16 days before their mandate was due to expire.

The president announced the pending withdrawal in a speech heralding his new Middle East initiative. The introduction of the Reagan Plan was the second and more critical factor that triggered a digression from a purely Lebanon focus to an Arab–Israeli context. Apparently the timing of the announcement had been imposed on the Administration by the Saudis as a condition for PLO withdrawal,[131] but American shortsightedness may also have played a role. The White House may have been anxious to capitalize on a moment of flux and disarray to present an exciting, major new initiative even before its ink had dried. Reagan said as much himself in his speech:

> It seemed to me that with the agreement in Lebanon, we had an opportunity for a more far-reaching peace effort in the region, and I was determined to seize that moment. In the words of the scripture, the time had come to "follow after the things which make for peace."[132]

Then too, the Israelis may have forced Reagan's hand by mysteriously announcing that the cabinet formally "rejected a U.S. plan for a demilitarized state in the West Bank" on August 29.[133] Whatever motivated the timing, it was far from propitious for Lebanon. It established a formal linkage between the two prongs of the Administration's Middle East policy, opening many golden opportunities for obstruction of one via stagnation in the other.

In effect, what the Administration did was to declare the immediate Lebanese crisis solved when none of its announced goals had been achieved; to define the Marines' mission so specifically that constructive facilitation of the broader Lebanon policy was precluded; to give Syria a chance to regroup, and to extend a free hand in the country to the Israelis with which they could easily block any progress on the Reagan Plan. A case of mistaken identity ensued: the Americans assumed that by arriving at a temporary solution to the war of 1982, they had solved Lebanon's problems. But their timing was critically off. The setting of prior conditions for negotiations by all parties involved did nothing to expedite progress either.

The disastrous series of events that followed is well known. Immediately after the Marines' departure, events heated up and then exploded with President-elect Bashir Gemayel's assassination, Israel's invasion of Beirut, and the massacre of hundreds of Palestinian civilians in the camps. These three developments finished off the Reagan Plan. The opportunity that some analysts had acclaimed at the end of the war had evaporated. The turn of events effectively wed the Administration's Lebanon policy to its Middle East initiative and successfully blurred the lines between the two.

Once again, the Marines arrived in Beirut. But the second MNF had an entirely different mission. Its drawbacks were the opposite of the first mission's over-specificity.[134] The mission was murky and unclear; its duration was unspecified, but linked with the broader Lebanon policy goals of withdrawal of foreign forces, reconciliation and establishment of a strong central government. The MNF's mandate was stated as follows:

> The MNF is to provide an interposition force at agreed locations and thereby provide the MNF presence requested by the Government of Lebanon to assist it and Lebanon's armed forces in the Beirut area. This presence will facilitate the restoration of Lebanese Government sovereignty and authority over the Beirut area and thereby further its efforts to assure the safety of persons in the area and to bring an end to the violence which has tragically recurred.[135]

The Marines were thus sent in as part of a multinational force with no unified command on a vaguely defined, open-ended mission that had no termination date. Furthermore, the nature of the mission as defined did not inherently specify criteria to determine *when* sovereignty and authority over the Beirut area would be considered accomplished. Gradually, the Marines' extended mission came to be defined in the negative: if they *left* Beirut, the government would fall; therefore they had to stay. Theoretically, a mission defined in such terms could last decades.

The parties who were to negotiate predictably set as many obstacles as possible in the way of progress, as no one was in a particularly good position to negotiate on American terms at the end of the summer. Sharon tried to convince Lebanon to opt for a full peace treaty and made threats about the future of south Lebanon should it refuse.[136] The United States concentrated its efforts on forging ties with Lebanon's new president, Amin Gemayel, and discouraging him from deepening ties with Israel. Instead, the United States encouraged Israel and Lebanon to hold talks on something less than a peace treaty, namely an American-conceived and orchestrated withdrawal agreement.

It became quite clear that the Lebanese had thrown themselves fully onto the Americans' ball court when Amin Gemayel arrived in the United States for the first official visit ever paid by a Lebanese president to an American president. Gemayel's remarks on that occasion reflect the depth of the commitment he wished Lebanon to have to the United States:

> American commitment to the sovereignty and territorial integrity
> of a free democracy in Lebanon has been fundamental to our sur-
> vival. The historic U.S.-Lebanon relationship is the cornerstone of
> building the new Lebanon. America's friendship and assistance,
> not only in peacekeeping and peacemaking but also in reconstruc-
> tion, are vital.[137]

The Lebanese had decided to follow the United States lead on the
assumption that only American clout could achieve the withdrawal of
all foreign forces from the country. However, they also apparently
assumed that a presidential commitment was irrevocable, open-ended,
and divorced from potential domestic constraints. They presumed that
the contract between the two had been defined in a fixed manner in the
following terms: the United States would achieve a withdrawal of
foreign forces from Lebanon and the rehabilitation of the Lebanese
Armed Forces in order to give the Gemayel government the clout and
authority it required *before* any large-scale reconciliation initiatives
would be attempted. Similarly, they assumed the United States had
the wherewithal to force a Syrian withdrawal from the country,
because, after all, the United States was a superpower that possessed
so many "cards." Thus the prevalent assumption was that the United
States would be ready to commit much of its political clout, military
personnel, diplomatic credit, and economic assistance to Lebanon on
a long-term basis.

Momentum drained away when it took over a month to obtain an
Israeli–Lebanese agreement to negotiate on withdrawal, another two
months to choose a site for the talks, and an additional two weeks to
determine a mutually acceptable agenda. President Gemayel began
his term with a strong domestic consensus but it began to deteriorate
as negotiations approached the most sensitive issues like normalization of relations with Israel, security arrangements for southern
Lebanon, and the status of Sa'ad Haddad. The negotiations hobbled
along while Syria regrouped its losses through extensive Soviet re-
armament, in addition to consolidating its grip on domestic Lebanese
politicians who might be called upon for favors.

American resolve was badly shaken by the bombing of the United
States Embassy on April 18, 1983. The tragedy signaled a new and
ominous turn of events to come, the first of a series of devastating terrorist attacks on American positions throughout the region. It began
to emerge that, at least in someone's eyes, the United States had lost
its neutrality as an objective peacekeeper and become a party to the
conflict. This was the danger inherent in the Marines' open-ended
mandate: as progress on the Lebanese–Israeli front only limped,

support for the central government of Lebanon might come to be perceived as partisan sponsorship, given the evolution of its mission into a coercive one as noted above. The likelihood of just such an identification increased after the opposition got back on its feet, encouraged by Syria, and began to create additional problems for the president.

Finally American patience ran out, and Secretary Shultz left for the Middle East on April 22. He succeeded in wrapping up the negotiations and concluding a withdrawal agreement between Israel and Lebanon.

The agreement marked a turning point in United States–Lebanese relations. First, it represented another United States-sponsored agreement between Israel and an Arab state, but one of an entirely different ilk than the Egyptian–Israeli peace treaty. Second, it opened the door for a United States–Israeli rapprochment, particularly given the replacement of Sharon by Moshe Arens and the growing Soviet–Syrian axis that suddenly emerged as a major concern. This trend could not bode well for Lebanon whose internal weakness had as yet little to offer in the way of a strategic bulwark against Soviet penetration and who could offer only a partnership in democracy and freedom which translated into a heavy burden on American military and political resources.

Third and most importantly, the conclusion of the Israeli–Lebanese phase of the talks meant the initiation of the Syrian chapter in the process. Both the Lebanese and the Americans had reassured each other that the Syrians would withdraw, but each secretly expected the other to exercise a magical influence to produce the rabbit from the hat. Clearly, a good deal of frustration and mistrust would result from the unforeseen Syrian intransigence. An angry Secretary of State Shultz began to pressure Gemayel for reconciliation talks in accordance with Syrian demands. The Lebanese were taken by surprise, having assumed that their terms—no reconciliation before the withdrawal of foreign forces—had been understood by the United States. This unexpected shift in priorities left the Lebanese feeling betrayed and baffled. National reconciliation talks convened in Geneva but made little headway on the first round.

The new United States–Lebanese relationship began to deteriorate gradually over the summer of 1983. After a unilateral Israeli withdrawal from the Shuf Mountains on September 4 (in effect a violation of the United States-sponsored agreement), hostilities flared and a new stage of intensive conflict began. American advisors training the Lebanese Army tacitly followed LAF units during the battles, and in some cases provided military back-up. On September 7, the Marines returned fire for the first time, signaling an entirely new

phase in the conflict. The Marines had become targets, perceived combatants,[138] and that role became self-fulfilling throughout the fall as the
*U.S.S. New Jersey* began to fire its guns in the Marines' defense. The
continuing trickle of casualties prompted a debate in Congress in
which the issue of the War Powers' Act was circumvented by a resolution on October 12, introducing an eighteen-month limit on the
Marines' presence.

## The October 23 attack: a new phase

On October 23, 1983, a suicide truck bomber destroyed the
Marines' compound in Beirut and caused the largest number of Marine
deaths in one day since World War II. The calamity split open a
domestic debate on the Marines' role in Lebanon and Middle East
policy generally. What was their mission supposed to be? When would
it be completed? How had they become participants rather than
peacekeepers?

Over time, the Administration had progressively defined the mission in different terms. At first, it had been to enable "the Lebanese
Government to resume full sovereignty over its capital—the essential
precondition for extending its control over the entire country.[139] In this
capacity, the Marines would remain at least until the foreign
forces—the Syrians and Israelis—had withdrawn, and possibly longer,
until the government's sovereignty had been re-established. It was
originally envisioned that the task would be accomplished by
December 31, 1982. Later the Lebanese urged the expansion of the
MNF and its role in Lebanon until such time as the Lebanese Army
could be refurbished and declared operative.[140] As the Marines increasingly became entangled in combat situations, Reagan began to term
their presence "essential to the objective of helping restore the territorial integrity, sovereignty, and political independence of
Lebanon."[141] The president later asserted that "the security and
stability of the Beirut area and the successful process of national
reconciliation are essential to the achievement of United States policy
objectives in Lebanon,"[142] thereby shifting emphasis completely from
withdrawal to reconciliation. But the most dramatic statements emerged
after the October 23 bombing, when the president stated:

> Well, the reason they must stay there until the situation is under
> control is quite clear. We have vital interests in Lebanon. And our
> actions in Lebanon are in the cause of world peace.[143]

By defining Lebanon as a "vital interest," the President seemed to be trying not to submit to "international terrorism's" designs, but again to stand proud and grit his teeth after a crisis.

The lack of clarity in the Marines' role and their use for political purposes when diplomacy had not been exhausted place a strain on the United States–Lebanese relationshp by promoting confusion and misunderstanding. Other aspects of United States–Lebanese relations were temporarily eclipsed by the looming questions over the Marines' role. Many Lebanese expressed bitterness and even panic as the United States remained ineffective. The Lebanese Ambassador to the United States reflected this mood when he observed on December 30, 1983 that "when he talks to Congressmen and other officials in Washington,"

> They are only interested in discussing the Marine issue. They don't discuss Lebanon anymore: national reconciliation, strengthening the Central-Government. The issue has become just the Marines, not Lebanon.[144]

We are forced to conclude that, despite all initial indications of a new era of United States–Lebanese relations, the years between 1981–1983 demonstrate that the relationship between the two countries has not broken loose from the constraints that have repeatedly hampered it over the years. To be sure, many aspects have improved, without which such a dramatic rise in the intensity of interaction would have been impossible. But two primary phenomena persist, and their impact may prove to be doubly destructive in the wake of such an intense interlude.

*Miscommunication.*

In the years between 1981 and 1983, misunderstanding between the Lebanese and the United States was neither eradicated nor alleviated. Lebanese misperception about the United States is rooted in two related illusions. First, they assume that Lebanon represents a central point in the world and, ergo, merits priority international consideration. This Lebanese tendency to overestimate the cultural, strategic, and economic centrality of their country to the West is not a unique phenomenon in interstate relations. But the Lebanese have consistently assumed that the United States and other foreign countries would intervene at propitious moments because ultimately they would recognize Lebanon's pivotal role. This tendency has often resulted in policy miscalculations and also inhibited innovative efforts to win international support.

Secondly, a deep belief prevails that, as a superpower, the United States can achieve any end it undertakes. For years, the Lebanese tried to attract American attention and a solid commitment.[145] Once American interest had been attained after extensive and ingenious efforts, the Lebanese assumed that their interests were assured: the United States would stand by them until the country had been reconstructed, the army rebuilt, and the foreign forces withdrawn.

Characteristic overestimations of American will and capability have been portrayed in a number of journalistic accounts, but the mood in Beirut at the end of 1983 was best described by Thomas Friedman of the *New York Times*. He indicated that pessimism in Beirut was attributable to disappointment with the Americans:

> On the one hand, people say they would be lost if the marines left; on the other hand, they cannot understand why America—a superpower—cannot and is not solving their age-old problems. The most unsophisticated believe that it must be due to some kind of American conspiracy against Lebanon. . . .
>
> "I simply cannot accept the fact that Americans can't do anything," said Mr. Tabbara, the architect. "They sent the New Jersey here, and what is it doing? Nothing. We thought it was going to be the genie to provide all our solutions. But nothing is happening. At least in Vietnam you made a war."[146]

Once American support had been obtained, the Lebanese did not move rapidly to resolve the country's internal problems or devise constructive initiatives to capitalize on the American commitment. They showed little interest in the American agenda for a rapid, pragmatic solution. When the U.S. failed to achieve the expected miracles, the Lebanese again expressed bitterness that did not bode well for the future. For example:

> Lebanon's Ambassador to the United States said this week that his government wished the United States Marines had never been sent to Beirut. . . . Rather, Mr. Bouhabib said, the Lebanese now find themselves regretting that they requested United States military assistance in the first place.[147]

For its part, the United States also misunderstood the situation in Lebanon and miscalculated almost from the outset. The Lebanese problem had been inextricably linked to regional dynamics for decades, but the American Administration underestimated the linkage. It had an opportunity at the end of 1982 to approach the situation in isolation and push solely for an internal settlement with all of the diplomatic clout of the United States. Instead, it promptly relinked the Lebanese situation with the regional imbroglio via the announcement of the Reagan Plan. Rather than first seeing through all of its Lebanon objectives, it attempted a jump from the most initial stage of the Lebanon plan into full resolution of the Arab–Israeli conflict. Perspectives differ on which must come first, but without a doubt events have demonstrated the impossibility of addressing both simultaneously.

In a sense, this failure can be traced to a tendency to blur the distinction between at least three roles that the United States has played in the Middle East: crisis manager, "honest broker" or mediator of a peace settlement, and superpower strategist. Reality precludes isolation of these three roles in day-to-day events, but it is imperative that the United States be alert to the requirements of each role and to the need to maintain a separate strategy for each. Thus, for example, a crisis manager should not become involved in negotiations for a peace settlement, a peace plan should not be proffered while a crisis is in the midst of being defused, and American military forces should not be sent in for a crisis and kept in as a bulwark against encroachment on vital interests. Such confusion between roles almost guarantees that crises will emerge in the midst of peace settlement efforts in order to force America to revert to the role of crisis manager. In other words, without a clear mandate, the United States will continue to react to events rather than shaping their course.

Above all, the United States misjudged Lebanon by assuming the two had similar political cultures because both were democracies and free, pluralistic societies. It assumed that the Lebanese government could take decisions and act authoritatively when, in all fairness, Lebanon's hands were tied at a dozen different points. Just as the Lebanese overestimated American capability, the United States underestimated Lebanese helplessness at that juncture of history, and overlooked the role of Lebanon's political culture in its decision-making process. In short, the United States assumed that Lebanon was ripe for quick, pragmatic solutions and accordingly applied a short-term remedy—the Marines. It then grew impatient with the slow and agonizingly complex process of decision-making in Lebanon and showed signs of abandoning the effort barring constructive developments in the near future.[148]

*United States–Lebanese relations in a regional context.*

The second pattern that persisted in the last period was the clear linkage between United States–Lebanese relations and United States relations with other countries in the region. This applied particularly to Israel in 1981–1983. It will be recalled that relations between the United States and Israel began to diverge at precisely the point—April 1981—when Ambassador Habib began to search for broader solutions to the Lebanon crisis. We do not mean to imply by this observation that any plot or conspiracy was afoot; indeed, this was most likely a coincidence. But some general relationship between Israel as a close, strategic ally and Lebanon as a important friend does seem to have existed.

The United States perhaps had more flexibility with respect to Lebanon when Israeli interests faded temporarily from the picture. At the very least, we can posit that Lebanon's claim to primacy as a pro-Western outpost had more credibility when Israel and the United States were at odds. Throughout the end of 1982 and the first half of 1983, the United States appeared ready in the first instance to accept Lebanon's version of the negotiations and to reject Israel's. This did not necessarily mean that Lebanon had *gained* credibility, but only that Israel had temporarily lost it.

After the May 17 agreement, a marked improvement upgraded United States–Israeli relations and Lebanon became, more or less, a black sheep. The most vivid indication of this development occurred in late November of 1983, when, in its superpower capacity once again, the United States established a strategic agreement with Israel to guard against Soviet incursions into the region via Syria. President Gemayel arrived in the United States in December on the heels of Israel's departing prime minister to request alterations in the American-sponsored and -midwived agreement of May 17. Gemayel, on the other hand, was encouraged with a pat on the back and told that the compromise he had squeezed out of participants at his reconciliation talks (a freeze, not a cancellation of the agreement) was not good enough. In the headlines of the *New York Times,* Gemayel got "a pep talk" while Shamir got "a deal."[149]

The conviction that at long last the United States had committed itself to Lebanon because of Lebanon's intrinsic importance was clearly a Lebanese canard. Briefly, for a passing moment perhaps, that had indeed been true. But past experience should have amply demonstrated that the United States acts in response to global, regional, and domestic developments and constraints.

As at other junctures of United States–Lebanese relations, the 1981–1983 period unveiled a number of paradoxes. The first was that American troops were sent to a relatively minor, innocuous country and yet, at the outset of 1984, seemed unable to leave. Instead, they provided a punching bag for would-be assailants to take shots at. The second was that United States peacekeepers became involved as actors in a conflict that was not their own, against their will, and almost without their active consent. That seems to remain a common phenomenon in Lebanon. The third paradox surfaced on the Lebanese side: when they had finally attracted American attention, they seemed to assume that support would be permanently forthcoming.

In a sense, the legacy of 1958 proved counterproductive. The assumption that the Marines could somehow right all that had gone wrong over the previous ten years because they had done so in 1958 was seriously flawed. Instead, sending the Marines on an ill-defined, open-ended mission seemed destined to undermine the very support that the Lebanese had worked so hard to obtain. The stationing of the Marines meant *Congress* would eventually enter the policy process and publicly question the president's strategy, thus restricting the Administration's freedom to maneuver. But most of all, a negatively perceived Marine mission would have repercussions on the American public's perception of Lebanon for quite a while.

The most disheartening paradox of 1981–1983 lay in the fundamental irony that when the United States had finally brought some of its political and military weight to bear on the situation, it actually reaped stagnation in Lebanon. And the Americans were the last resort for the Lebanese as far as foreign weight was concerned. Thus an American withdrawal would spell disaster for the country.[150] For American military and political efforts to reap fruit, the Lebanese will have to apply themselves wholeheartedly and urgently to arriving at an internal consensus while American strength can still remain in the background as a symbol of support for its endeavors.

## CONCLUSION

Much of this chapter has focused on several central questions. The first was whether or not at any point in time the United States ever formulated an explicit "Lebanon policy" because it was treating the country as an intrinsically important, vibrant interest. The answer may have seemed self-evident from the outset. But it has not been self-evident to many Lebanese, and that merits its explicit repetition here: with the exception of a brief moment in 1982–1983, the United States has never dealt with Lebanon on a separate basis from its regional and global interests. At times its actions have been governed by domestic considerations. Generally, however, regional goals have dictated policy on Lebanon. Our aim has been to provide ample evidence that this fact held throughout the history of the relationship. Lebanon has little or no intrinsic significance to the United States except when it enters, or becomes a victim of, regional circumstances. It remains for Lebanese resourcefulness and ingenuity to find ways to capitalize on regional and strategic American interests in order to catch the American eye. But that will not be truly feasible until Lebanon has been reconstructed and brought back to some semblance of normality.

Thus one arrives at the notion that the intensity of the United States–Lebanese relationship in 1982 and 1983 may have been counterproductive for both countries. It is unusual for a superpower to become so entangled in the affairs of a small nation, and unwise for a small nation to place all of its eggs into a superpower's basket. If the endeavor fails, resentment will most likely last for a long time. The United States and Lebanon have had a stable interaction of a lesser scale for years on all levels. One can only hope that potential fallout from an overinvestment will not jeopardize those other important aspects of the relationship.

The second major issue that this chapter has tried to address concerns the formulation of American policy in the Middle East. If Lebanon does not usually elicit any special treatment, then it behooves us to understand what makes broader United States policy tick. On this score, we must conclude that United States policy on the Middle East has all too often been a function of other preoccupations and inappropriate strategies for regional complexity and changeability. Sometimes its determination to fill all roles for all the region's actors has paralyzed policy, in addition to exposing the United States to criticism and resentment. The United States tends to lose track of the fact that it has numerous roles in the Middle East: trouble-shooter, honest broker, and guardian against Soviet incursion. This inability to maintain discrete strategies for each role has frequently led policymakers to address the wrong problem or apply an inappropriate solution. Above all, United States policy has suffered from inconsistency and from a lack of determination to apply itself singlemindedly to the achievement of its goals. A pattern has begun to crystallize wherein an administration spends its first year learning the ropes, replaces its secretary of state by the end of the second year, and remains paralyzed throughout its fourth year by campaign commitments. The continued inconsistency of presidents, secretaries of state, and policies will seriously impede the continuation of a multifaceted role for the United States in the Middle East and elsewhere.

Finally, we have explored various paradoxical aspects of United States–Lebanese relations and discovered many. Most of these paradoxes can be traced to one of three sources: misperceptions and miscommunication that result from the superpower–small state interaction and the misleading cultural similarity between Lebanon and the United States; the assumption that the United States formulates and pursues a policy focused solely on Lebanon and perceives Lebanon as a bulwark of freedom; and, finally, that American policy itself is often ill-suited to regional dynamics or based in one role but directed at a different goal.

Despite the prevalence of paradoxes, however, it seems likely that a close United States–Lebanese relationship will continue. Sometimes it will improve and sometimes deteriorate. In the best of all possible worlds, the Lebanese–American relationship will benefit from its intensive 1982–1983 encounter and strike an appropriate balance between several inappropriate extremes.

## NOTES

1. Kamal S. Salibi, *Crossroads to Civil War: 1958–1976* (New York: Caravan Books, 1976), 15.

2. *Instructions of the Prudential Committee of the American Board of Commissioners for Foreign Missions to the Rev. Levi Parsons and the Rev. Pliny Fisk, Missionaries Designated for Palestine* (Boston, 1819). See A.L. Tibawi, "The Genesis and Early History of the Syrian Protestant College," Part I, *The Middle East Journal* 21 (1957) 1, 2.

3. Henry H. Jessup, *Fifty Three Years in Syria* (New York: Fleming H. Revell Company, 1910), Vol. I, 26.

4. Jessup, Vol I, 38. Eventually, Beirut became one of the few sanctuaries for Protestant missionaries. Jessup reports that by the early 1880's, "Curse followed curse and excommunication followed threatening, until it became difficult for any American to hire a house or buy the necessities of life outside of Beirut. The Maronite Patriarch and the Maronite Emir Bashir ruled Lebanon with a rod of iron, and orders came from Rome to persecute, drive out, and exterminate the accursed Angliz or English as all Protestants were called." (p. 43).

5. Tibawi, Part I, 6, and Jessup, Vol. I, 216. Other accomplishments by 1860 included: a printing press (four million pages annually), four churches, two printed editions of a New Testament in Arabic (the first translation).

6. Tibawi, 5.

7. From an undated printed appeal issued jointly by a U.S. board of trustees and a Syrian board of managers for the college. Quoted in Tibawi, Part I, 13.

8. Jessup reports that of one hundred thousand dollars given for relief in 1860, twenty-five thousand dollars was contributed from the United States. A report to the British Foreign Office from Lord Dufferin described the role of the American missionaries at this time as indispensable: ". . . without their indefatigable exertions, the supplies sent from Christendom could never have been properly distributed, *nor the starvation of thousands of needy prevented.*" Jessup, Vol I, 214. Emphasis in the original.

9. Jessup, Vol I, 301.

10. David C. Gordon, *Lebanon, The Fragmented Nation* (London: Croom Helm, 1980), 180.

11. Adnan Abu-Ghazaleh, "American Missions and Arab Nationalism in 19th century Syria," *The Search*, 1 (Spring, 1980) 2, 135–48; Gordon, 182–3; Michael Hudson, *The Precarious Republic* (New York: Random House, 1968), 40; George Antonius, *The Arab Awakening: The Story of the Arab National Movement* (New York, 1946), 43; Najib E. Saliba, "Emigration from Syria," *Arab Studies Quarterly*, 3 (Winter 1981) 1, 63; Jessup, Vol I, 78.

12. Philip Baram, *The Department of State in the Middle East, 1939–1945* (Philadelphia: University of Pennsylvania Press, 1978), 124.

13. Elie Salem, *Modernization Without Revolution: Lebanon's Experience* (Bloomington: Indiana University Press, 1973), 35.

14. Salibi, 60, 64–5.

15. Gordon, 112.

16. Baram, 125.

17. *Business Week*, March 16, 1969.

18. David L. Sills, ed., *International Encyclopedia of Social Science*, Vol. XII (New York: Collier & Macmillan, 1969), 218.

19. Israel, the only other democracy in the Middle East, has no formal constitution.

20. In Lebanon's case, the system was designed in large part to alleviate Christian fears that *regional* minority status would impinge on their historical *national* majority status in Lebanon. By the same token, the Muslims wanted something in return for formally agreeing to give up claims to majority status within the country despite their regional majority, hence their insistence of Lebanon's Arab "face." For good discussions of the National Pact see Walid Khalidi, *Conflict and Violence in Lebanon* (Cambridge: Harvard University Press, 1978), and Hudson, *inter alia*.

21. Gordon, 111. Also, see Willian Rugh, *The Arab Press* (Syracuse: Syracuse University Press, 1979), esp. Chap. 5

22. John K. Cooley, "The Palestinians," in P. Edward Haley, & Lewis W. Snider, eds., *Lebanon in Crisis* (Syracuse: Syracuse University Press, 1979), notes that "Lebanon had seen nothing in modern history on the scale of the arrival of the Palestinians after 1948, and the even larger numbers of Syrians who began to arrive in the 1960s. By January 1, 1970, when the stage was nearly set for the Jordan civil war and the new migration of the defeated Palestinians fleeing the Hashemite armies, Palestinians and Syrians represented more than three-fourths of the entire foreign population in Lebanon. This population represented in turn, about 23.5 percent of the total resident population, or 564,051 persons. " (pages 22–3).

23. Hudson, 6.

24. See Arnold Hottinger, "The Zu'ama and Parties in the Lebanese Crisis of 1958," *Middle East Journal* 15 (1961), 127–140.

25. Hudson, 8l and 19–21; David R. Smock and Audrey Smock, *The Politics of Pluralism: A Study of Lebanon and Ghana* (New York: Elsevier Scientific Publishing Company, Inc.), 82–89.

26. See Paul A. Jureidini and James M. Price, "Minorities in Partition: The Christians of Lebanon," in R.D. McLaurin, ed., *The Political Life of Minority Groups in the Middle East* (New York: Praeger), 1979, Chapter 7.

27. A.L. Tibawi, *A Modern History of Syria, Including Lebanon and Palestine* (London: St. Martin's Press, 1969), 369.

28. Telegram #142 from U.S. Consul General in Beirut Cornelius Engert to Secretary of State Hull, April 21, 1941, and Kamal Salibi, *A Modern History of Lebanon* (Westport, CT: Greenwood Press, 1965), 186.

29. Stephen Longrigg, *Syria and Lebanon under French Mandate* (London, 1958), 321; Salibi, *A Modern History of Lebanon, 184; Baram, 101 and 131; Tibawi, A Modern History of Syria,* 365; Also see Telegram #449, Engert to Hull, November, 1941.

30. Baram, 59–60.

31. Baram, 90; and Thomas Bryson, *American Diplomatic Relations with the Middle East, 1784–1975: A Survey* (Metuchen, NJ: The Scarecrow Press, 1977), 50–51.

32. Telegram #282, Consul General Gwynn to Secretary of State Hull, August 12, 1942, 2 p.m.

33. Letter from Hamid Bey Frangieh to Engert January 16, 1942, enclosure #1 to Engert's Dispatch #271 of January 31, 1942; letter from Riad as-Solh to General Catroux and copy to Engert, December 20, 1941, enclosure #1 to Dispatch #269 of January 30, 1942; letter from a group calling themselves "the important elements of all classes in the Lebanon," December 23, 1941, to Consul Engert, enclosure #1 to Dispatch #270 from Engert to State Department on January 30, 1942; enclosure #2 of same (dispatch 270) was a resolution adopted at the Maronite Patriarchate on December 25, 1941; Reference to President Naccache in Telegram #135 from Engert to Hull of April 15, 1942, 3 p.m., and #141 of April 20, 1942, 8 p.m.; Reference to President Khouri in Telegram #295 of October 24, 1943, 6 p.m., from Wadsworth to Hull.

34. Letter from Greek Orthodox Archbishop and Metropolitans to U.S. Consul General on January 26, 1942; enclosure to dispatch #340 from U.S. Consul in Beirut to Department of State, April 15, 1942.

35. Walter Browne, *Lebanon's Struggle for Independence, Vol. I* (Salisbury, NC: Documentary Publications, 1977), 136.

36. Telegram from Secretary of State Hull to U.S. Consul General Engert, November 10, 1941.

37. Baram, 105 and 129–133.

38. Secretary of State Hull to Consul Engert, November 13, 1941.

39. Letter from Hamid Bey Frangieh to Consul Engert:

"The Lebanese Government has noted the fact that the American Government has in mind the conclusion of fresh agreements to take the place of the treaty concluded in Paris on April 4, 1924, between the United States and France.

"But pending the conclusion of such fresh agreements and considering the difficulties resulting from the present war conditions, the Lebanese Government would be disposed to assume the obligations deriving from the Paris treaty and to ensure to the United States of America and its nationals the enjoyment and benefit of all rights and advantages which are accorded to them in that treaty. . . .

"The Lebanese Government hopes that if its proposal is accepted there will remain no impediment to the recognition of Lebanese independence by the Government of the United States of America." (January 16, 1942)

Telegram from Engert to Hull, February 6, 1942, 6 p.m.:

"Lebanese Minister of External Affairs [i.e. Frangieh] would be grateful if the Department could express an opinion as to the practicability of his proposal.

"In this connection the President of Syria has just sent a verbal message to me to the effect that the Syrian Government was prepared to make any provisional arrangement we wished to safeguard all American interests until after the war."

40. Letter from U.S. Consul General in Beirut, Engert, to Secretary of State Hull, January 30, 1942, #269. Refers to Riad as-Solh's request to do something about French obstinacy in the insufficient declaration of independence.

41. Telegram #135 from Engert to Hull, April 15, 1942, 3 p.m.; #139 from Engert to Hull, April 18, 1942, 4 p.m.; #141 from Engert to Hull, April 20, 1942; #142 from Engert to Hull, April 21, 1942, 10 a.m.

42. Telegram #280 from Gwynn to Hull, August 12, 1942, noon; and #283 of August 12, 1942, 4 p.m. to wit: "It thus appears that my assumption, as previously expressed, particularly in my 246, July 13, that Spears was responsible for English drive for elections, was wrong. Elucidation as to motives behind this drive must be sought if anywhere in London."

43. Arthur Layton Funk, *The Politics of TORCH* (Wichita, KS: The University Press of Kansas, 1974), 31.

44. Funk, *The Politics of TORCH*, 37. Admiral Darlan, the key man in the French cabinet for the implementation of the operation, was maneuvered out of the French cabinet, so the plan was temporarily shelved.

45. Telegram #135 from Engert to Secretary of State Hull, April 18, 1942.

46. Letter from Engert to Secretary of State Hull, April 20, 1942.

47. Winston S. Churchill, *The Second World War*, Vol. III, *The Grand Alliance* (Boston, Houghton Mifflin 1950), 656.

48. Telegram #139 from Engert to Hull, April 18, 1942.

49. De Gaulle later wrote:

"By the end of July I foresaw that would happen. Although their intentions were carefully concealed from us, it seemed extremely likely to me that the Americans would limit their year's efforts to seizing North Africa, that the British would willingly comply with this plan, that the Allies would employ General Giraud in its accomplishment, that they would exclude me from the operation altogether, and that thereby these preliminary steps to our liberation, auspicious though they were from many points of view, would nevertheless confront us as Frenchmen with inner torments that would raise fresh obstacles to national unity."

Quoted in Funk, 83. See also Telegram #342 from Consul Gwynn to Secretary of State Hull, September 12, 1942.

50. Baram, 60.

51. Baram, 137.

52. Baram, 139.

53. Telegram #304 from Acting Secretary of State Stettinius to Consul Murphy in Algiers (for Consul Wadsworth in Beirut), November 9, 1943.

54. Letter from Alexander Kirk of the American Legation in Beirut to Secretary of State Hull, November 20, 1943:

". . . The Lebanese case is being regarded here as a test of the sincerity of the assurances of the United Nations in respect of the rights of smaller states and that, despite the fact that the United States has no such form of obligation as France and Britain in the matter of Lebanese independence, we are regarded as none the less morally bound in the eyes of the Arab world by virtue of having been the leading and most trusted exponent of the principles of the United Nations . . ."

55. See, for example, Robert A. Divine, *Foreign Policy and U.S. Presidential Elections, 1940–1948* (New York: New Viewpoints, 1974), 121, and the whole account of that election.

56. Telegram #354 from Secretary of State Hull to Murphy in Algiers (also to Beirut), November 12, 1943:

"Unless therefore the French Committee of National Liberation takes prompt steps to restore the duly elected government of the Lebanese Republic and to implement the solemn promises of independence given to the Lebanese people in the name of the French National Committee in 1941, the Government of the United States will be obliged publicly to announce its complete disapproval of the acts of the French authorities in the Lebanese Republic and to take such further steps as may appear appropriate.

"We would take such actions only with the utmost reluctance but we felt that it would be less detrimental to the united war effort than for us by silence to appear to accept a situation which is contrary to the aims and principles for which the liberty-loving nations are fighting."

57. Leila Meo, *Lebanon: Improbable Nation, A Study in Political Development* (Bloomington, Indiana University Press, 1965), 109.

58. Dwight D. Eisenhower, *Waging Peace* (New York: Doubleday, 1963), 177–78.

59. Fahim I. Qubain, *Crisis in Lebanon* (Washington, D.C.: The Middle East Institute, 1961), pp. 127–128; Bryson, 205.

60. Eisenhower to Congress, January 5, 1977.

The definition of International Communism remained murky, as Senator Fulbright discovered when Dulles testified:

> *Senator Fulbright*: Does that history . . .set down a criteria by which you could judge whether a particular country is Communist-dominated? I do not mean one like Russia. I mean borderline cases, such as Syria. Does it give you a guide as to whether or not Syria today is Communist-dominated?
>
> *Secretary Dulles*: I do not think any precise formula is possible. The determination of whether a country is dominated by international communism is a close question in some cases, and the answer is to be found, I think, not in any mathematical rule of thumb. It is determined by a whole complex of actions or lack of action which the government takes in its international and domestic affairs."

Hearings before the Committee on Foreign Relations and the Committee on Armed Services, United States Senate, Eighty-Fifth Congress, First Session, First Session on S.J. Res. 19 and H.J. Res. 117, Part I, Jan. 14, 15, 24, 25, 28, 29, 30, and Feb. 1, 4, 1957, U.S. GPO, Washington, p. 29; quoted in Meo, p. 111–112.

61. Qubain, 41.

62. Khalidi, 38.

63. Salibi, *A Modern History of Lebanon,* 207.

64. J.C. Hurewitz, "Lebanese Democracy in its International Setting," *Middle East Journal* 17 (1963) 5, 501–2.

65. Qubain, 41. cf.: "The rivalry between the two [Nasser and Chamoun] was visible in such simple things as the display of their pictures in public places. Supporters of Sham'un[sic] and Nasir[sic] would display pictures of their respective 'leaders' in prominent places in the towns of Lebanon, and then each would try secretly to tear down the pictures of the other side. This trend became so serious that the government banned all such displays in public places."

66. The opposition had a diverse religious composition, including the Maronite Patriarch and his following. On Independence Day, 1957, the opposition leaders boycotted the official ceremonies and paid respects instead to the Maronite Patriarch. Qubain, 59. See also 44 and 50.

67. Qubain, 42–44.

68. Kamal Salibi, "The Lebanese Crisis in Perspective," *The World Today* 14, 9 (1958) 376.

69. Malcolm Kerr, *The Arab Cold War* (London: Oxford University Press, 1971), 16.

70. Qubain, 61. As President Quwattli of Syria told a Lebanese delegation, "The new republic is the best guarantee of Lebanon's existence. Lebanon is invited to join it whenever she may so desire by merger, or by federation, with the right to maintain her own integrity and special position."

71. Khalidi, 38; Salibi, "The Lebanese Crisis in Perspective," 377–78; Randal, 160–61.

72. The assassination of Nasib al-Matni, a Christian anti-Chamounist journalist, was the incident that triggered the war.

73. Bryson, 205.

74. Qubain, 131; Salibi, *The Modern History of Lebanon*, also refers to a prior request on page 202.

75. "Secretary Dulles News Conference of May 20," *The Department of State Bulletin*, U.S. Government Printing Office, Washington D.C., Vol. 38. No. 989, June 9, 1958, 945.

76. *Middle East Journal*, Chronology Section, June 14, 1958.

77. The Lebanese Foreign Minister, Charles Malik, protested the conclusions vehemently at a lengthy UN session, the details of which are available in Qubain, 181–235. Countries on the other side, Egypt, Syria namely, scoffed at these accusations and termed them fabrications.

78. Qubain, 115.

79. Eisenhower, *Waging Peace*, 269–270.

80. Message from President Eisenhower to Congress, July 15, 1958.

81. Message from President Eisenhower to Congress, July 15, 1958.

82. Qubain, 119.

83. Gordon, 55; Jonathan Randal, *Going All the Way* (New York: Viking Press, 1983), 161.

84. Qubain, 119.

85. Nadav Safran, *From War to War* (Indianapolis, IN: Pegasus, 1969), 115.

86. Meo, 194–7.

87. Robert W. Stookey, "The United States," in Haley and Snider, eds., *Lebanon in Crisis: Participants and Issues*, 227.

88. Qubain, 128.

89. Qubain, 120–121. Although 8 Marines died, only 1 was conflict-related. A conflicting version is given by Gordon, who refers to only 2 Marine deaths in a drowning incident (i.e., no combat-related deaths).

90. Hurewitz, "Lebanese Democracy," 503; Meo, 197–8; Qubain, 239.

91. Willian Quandt, *Decade of Decisions* (Berkeley: University of California Press, 1977), 78, 150.

92. Quandt, 145.

93. Henry Kissinger, *Years of Upheaval* (Boston: Little Brown & Company, 1982), 124. See also Randal, 167. Note also that the domestic situation played a different kind of inhibitory role after Nixon's resignation, when Ford's credibility needed to be proven and Kissinger had some stigma left over from Watergate. Ford tried deliberately to distance himself from the omnipotent secretary, a strategy which inhibited bold, coordinated foreign policy moves (Stookey, 233).

94. David Broder, "Isolationist Sentiment not Blind to Reality," *Washington Post*, March 22, 1975.

95. George C. Herring, *America's Longest War: The United States and Vietnam, 1950–1975* (New York: John Wiley and Sons, 1979), 265.

96. Quandt, 157.

97. Quandt, 162–3. Nadav Safran's elaborately detailed description of Kissinger's shuttles makes this clear. Nadav Safran, *Israel: The Embattled Ally* (Cambridge: Belknap Press, 1978), 414–570. Kissinger himself also reveals as much in that Lebanon only enters into his second volume of memoirs for 3 pages out of over 1200 total, and then he notes nonchalantly:

"I think with sadness of those civilized men who in a turbulent part of the world had fashioned a democratic society based on genuine mutual respect of the religions. Their achievement did not survive. The passions sweeping the area were too powerful to be contained by subtle constitutional arrangements. . . .Before the peace process could run its course, Lebanon was torn apart. Over its prostrate body at this writing all the factions and forces of the Middle East still chase their eternal dreams and act out their perennial nightmares" (p. 789).

The quotation brings alive Kissinger's perception of Lebanon. Clearly, Lebanon was an unfortunate casualty but a dispensable one—and a casualty the United States bore no responsibility for and had little interest in.

98. For elaborate explanations of regional developments in this period see, among others, Walid Khalidi, *Conflict & Violence in Lebanon* (Cambridge, MA: Harvard Center for International Affairs, 1979); Marius Deeb, *The Lebanese Civil War* (New York: Praeger, 1980); "Syrian Foreign Policy-Making," in R.D McLaurin et al., *Middle East Foreign Policy* (New York: Praeger, 1982), 239–302; R.D. McLaurin, "Lebanon and the United States, in Azar et al., *Lebanon and the World in the 1980s* (College Park, MD: University of Maryland, 1983), 87–112; Fouad Ajami, *The Arab Predicament: Arab Political Thought and Practice Since 1967* (Cambridge, England: Cambridge University Press, 1981); and Safran, *Israel*; Salibi, *Crossroads*; and Randal.

99. On the issue of the Eastern Front see, among others, the chapter on Syria in Colin Legum, Daniel Dishon, Haim Shaked, eds. *Middle East Contemporary Survey* vol. I, 1976–1977, The Shiloah Center, Tel Aviv University, 604–21; Itamar Rabinovitch, "The Limits of Military Power: Syria's Role," in Haley and Snider, 55–74; Fouad Moughrabi and Nasser Aruri, eds., "Lebanon: Crisis and Challenge in the Arab World," *Special Report No. 1*, Association of Arab American University Graduates, Detroit, Michigan, January 1977.

Stookey notes that this strategy was first referred to by Syrian Foreign Minister Khaddam on September 9, 1975, and cites *An-Nahar Arab Report* 7 (5) (February 2, 1976): 1, backgrounder (see Haley and Snider, 302).

100. See sources listed in note 98.

101. Stookey, 241.

For example, *inter alia,* note the following entries in *Record of the Arab World: Yearbook of Arab and Israeli Politics,* volumes for years 1969–1973 (entries listed by year): May 27, 1969 (p. 1985); October 10, 1969 (p. 3242); June 8, 1970 (p. 3911); December 29, 1970 (p. 6264); May 3, 1969 (p. 2721); February 4, 1972 (p. 321); September 23, 1972 (p. 347); October 27, 1972 (p. 353). Additional statements for subsequent years can be found in *The State Department Bulletin, inter alia,* September 27, 1976 (p. 401); November 1, 1976 (p. 563); October 25, 1976 (p. 502). These references were continually repeated—perhaps the one constant in the relationship—like meaningless punctuation marks in a text of jibberish.

102. From an American statement of policy upon Sarkis' assumption of the presidency, cited in Stookey, 240–243.

See also the following issues of the *State Department Bulletin*: May 17, 1976 (p. 622); June 28, 1976 (p. 814); August 16, 1976 (p. 237); October 4, 1976 (p. 414) and October 11, 1976 (p. 460).

103. Randal, 171. See also 167. Quandt, 281–284, and Khalidi, 88.

104. Stookey notes that when President Frangieh moved to Jounieh in the thick of the war, the United States did not send an official representative to Jounieh, although the British did. Stookey, 234–5 and 243; Randal, 156–185.

105. Deeb, 49, quotes Chamoun's diary, *Azmat fi Lubnan* (Beirut: Al-Fikr al-Hurr Press, 1077), 72–76, 84, 95; Randal, 158, 168–70, 177, 178–9.

106. Deeb, 49.

107. Stookey, 243; Quandt, 283; Randal, 168, 175–6, 183.

108. Consternation over outside intervention had been a constant factor in American assessments of regional developments and policy. Yet in a press conference in London on April 10, 1976, Kissinger remarked, "It is my impression that the danger

of outside intervention has been reduced" (State Department Bulletin, May 17, 1976, p. 628). This *followed* sporadic unofficial Syrian military intervention. The Syrians were now considered "highly responsible" and seen to be playing a constructive role. See for example Deeb, 9–10, 49, 132; Aruri & Moughrabi, eds., 23; Stookey, 237–9; Randal, 175–6; and Salibi, *Crossroads*, 158.

109. Quandt, 282.

110. Deeb, 7, 11, 39–56, 127–132; Khalidi, 58–65, 70.

111. See for example, John C. Campbell, "The Middle East: A House of Containment Built on Shifting Sands," in *Foreign Affairs*, Vol. 60, No. 3 (1982), 593–628.

112. Campbell, 598.

113. Andrew Knight, "Ronald Reagan's Watershed Year?" in *Foreign Affairs*, Vol. 61, No. 3, (1983) 511–540.

114. Legum, Dishon, and Shaked, eds., *Middle East Contemporary Survey* Vol. V, 1980–1981, 170.

115. Legum, Dishon, and Shaked, 174–5 and 675.

116. McLaurin, "Lebanon and the United States," in Azar et al., 105; Campbell, 613–14.

117. *Newsweek*, August 24, 1981.

118. In his September 1, 1982 speech from Burbank, California, the President noted that the return of Sinai by April 25, 1982 had been his Administration's "first objective under the Camp David Process (*Department of State Bulletin*, September 1982, p. 23). See also Campbell, 611; Knight, 530; and Joseph J. Sisco, "Middle East: Progress or Lost Opportunity?" *Foreign Affairs*, Vol. 61, No. 3 (1983), 618.

119. Zeev Schiff, "Green Light, Lebanon," *Foreign Policy* 50 (Spring 1983), 73–85; Knight, p. 529–530; and FBIS June 17, 1982.

120. *Washington Post*, June 5, 1982 and March 8, 1983.

121. See, *inter alia*, Amos Perlmutter, "Begin's Rhetoric and Sharon's Tactics," *Foreign Affairs*, Vol. 61, No. 2 (Fall 1982), 68. He states that their joint goal was "to crush PLO allies and collaborators on the West Bank, to tighten Israel's grip on the West Bank and eventually force the Palestinians there into Jordan and cripple, if not end, the Palestinian Nationalist movement." See also Khalil Nakhleh and Clifford Wright, *After the Palestine-Israel War: Limits to U.S. and Israeli Policy* (Belmont, MA: Institute of Arab Studies, 1983); and Sisco, 621.

122. Sisco, 620.

This was made clear beyond dispute in an interview that Sharon gave to the Italian journalist Oriana Fallaci. He said,

> I never informed the Americans that I would invade Lebanon. I never spoke with them about plans, timetables, schedules. But during almost one year, that is, since last September (1981), I have been discussing with them the possibility that the operation would take place. I discussed it various times with Alexander Haig when he came to the Middle East; I discussed it with Weinberger when I went to Washington last November, I discussed it repeatedly with Ambassador Habib . . . when I spoke to them about Lebanon I kept warning them, "Don't be caught by surprise if or when we will do it." Or, "If or when we do, don't tell us that you were caught by surprise."

*Washington Post*, August 29, 1982.

123. *Time Magazine*, "A Defiant No to Reagan," September 20, 1982, 30.

124. For example, the President said in a press conference on September 8, 1982, "I'll remain fully and personally engaged in support of the next phase of our diplomacy

in Lebanon." Ambassador Habib followed it up with "I'm particularly gratified that the President is continuing his personal interest in the Lebanese situation. It's going to require continued high-level attention in our government as we pursue the objectives that the President has laid down for us." *Department of State Bulletin,* November 1982, 47.

125. *Washington Post,* June 14, 1982.

126. From the text of the "Departure Plan from Lebanon of PLO leaders, offices, and combatants in Beirut," *Department of State Bulletin,* September 1982, 2.

127. Letter from President Reagan to Congress, August 24, 1982. Reprinted in the *Department of State Bulletin,* September 1982, 8.

128. *Time Magazine,* Interview with Bashir Gemayel, "The Job: Rebuild a Country," September 20, 1982, 31.

129. *Time Magazine,* "Once More into the Breach," October 11, 1982, 24.

130. Sisco, 624.

131. McLaurin, "Lebanon and the United States," in Azar et al., 107.

132. Speech by President Reagan, September 1, 1982, Burbank, California. Reprinted in the *Department of State Bulletin,* September 1982, 23.

133. Wall Street Journal, August 30, 1982.

134. For an excellent analysis see Namoi Joy Weinberger, "Peacekeeping Options in Lebanon," *The Middle East Journal,* Vol. 37, No. 3 (Summer 1983), 341–369.

135. White House Statement, September 23, 1982, reprinted in the *Department of State Bulletin,* November 1982, 50.

136. *New York Times,* September 8, 1982.

137. *Department of State Bulletin,* December 1982, 41–2.

138. *Time Magazine,* "Lebanon Takes its Toll," September 12, 1983, 30–33.

139. Statement by President Reagan, September 20, 1983, *Department of State Bulletin,* November 1982, 49.

140. "Marines' role in Beirut has drastically shifted," *New York Times,* October 25, 1983.

141. Letter from President Reagan to the Congress, October 12, 1983.

142. *New York Times,* October 25, 1983.

143. *Ibid.*

144. "Beirut's envoy doubts value of Marines' role," *New York Times,* December 31, 1983.

145. See Randal, 156–185.

146. "Beirut: City of Despair," *New York Times,* November 11, 1983.

147. "Beirut envoy doubts value of Marines' role," *New York Times,* December 31, 1983.

148. *Time Magazine,* "Mission Impossible," January 9, 1984, 17.

149. *The Week in Review, The New York Times,* December 14, 1983. The headline read: "Visiting Firemen: Gemayel gets a Pep Talk and Shamir gets a Deal."

150. "Beirut, City of Depair," *New York Times,* December 31, 1983.

# INDEX

# A

Abu Iyad, 188
Abu Nidal, 253
Abu Nadir, Fuad, 138, 157
Afghanistan, 250
al-Ahdab, 'Aziz, 96
Algeria, 175, 202
Allon, Yigal, 249
Amal, 10–11, 22, 24, 25, 27, 101, 108–110, 114, 120, 122, 126, 127, 154, 156, 161, 162–204; command council, 194, 195; military capabilities, 180, 187–188; military operations, 109, 188, 192; military training, 187; objectives, 184–187, 189–192, 194; organization, 181–182; social welfare activities, 198; split after Israeli invasion, 10–11, 194–195; and Druze, 199; and Israel, 101, 188, 192–194, 196; and Joint Forces, 182, 184, 187–188, 192; and PLO, 154, 173–174, 179, 182, 184–186, 188, 191–193;

and Syria, 11, 176, 187–188, 191, 194, 201, 202
*Amal* (newspaper), 177, 186, 199
al-Amin, Sheikh Ahmed Shawkey, 202
*al-ansar*, 197;
'Aql, Sa'id, 134;
Arab Deterrent Force, 6;
Arab–Israeli conflict, 3–6, 11, 13, 16, 27–28, 48, 50–51, 58, 62, 69, 71, 81, 84, 87, 89, 97, 122–123, 124, 163, 170, 191, 192–193, 196, 198, 209–210, 212, 216–218, 246, 247, 250–256; 1948–9 war, 5, 81, 209, 268; 1956 war, 209; 1967 war, 5, 50, 81, 86, 87; 1973 war, 170, 246; 1982 war, 6, 11, 13, 16, 17, 27, 28, 58, 62, 69, 71, 81, 96–97, 124, 163, 192–193, 196, 198, 210, 212, 252–256
Arab–Israeli settlement, 6, 28, 33, 145, 212–213, 246–247, 256, 262–263, 274; Reagan Initiative, 6, 16, 33, 145, 212, 256, 263, 274

Arab League, 41, 42, 47, 50, 51, 158, 159, 208, 209
Arab Liberation Front (*Jabhat Arabiyya*) (ALF), 171, 183, 185, 193
Arafat, Yasser, 16, 125, 186, 215
Arens, Moshe, 28, 259
Argov, Shlomo, 253
Arslan, Majid, 13, 22, 112
al-Asad, Kamal, 170, 194, 195, 199, 201, 202
Assad, Hafez, 22, 188, 201, 246, Austria, 43

**B**

Baghdad Pact, 48, 238, 239
Bakhtiar, Shahpur, 176
Bashir, Emir, 267
Begin, Menachem, 21, 23, 251, 254
Beirut, 7, 27, 30, 32, 44, 51, 69, 71, 72, 75, 76–77, 91, 97, 102, 103, 108, 109, 128–130, 134, 147, 153, 161, 166, 167, 174, 181, 182, 185, 193, 224, 241, 242, 252, 253, 254, 256–257, 260, 262, 267
Beqa'a Valley, 6, 7, 11, 15, 16, 17, 18, 23, 44, 51, 74, 75, 76, 97, 154, 155, 156, 163, 165, 166, 181, 193, 194, 195
Berri, Nabih, 22, 27, 108, 126, 161, 179, 180, 183, 187, 189–190, 191, 195–196, 198, 203
Binder, Leonard, 3
Bliss, Daniel, 225
Bouhabib, Abdallah, 262
Boustany, Fuad, 134

Brown, Dean, 248
Burj al-Barajneh, 97

**C**

Cairo Accords, 50, 89, 92, 112, 123, 209
Cambodia, 246
Camp David Accords, 145, 251, 253, 259
Carter, Jimmy, 145, 245, 250
Catroux, Georges, 232
Chamie, Joseph, 163
Chamoun, Camille, 34, 48, 49, 85, 86, 112, 131, 132, 134, 153, 161, 198, 239–243, 248, 271
Chamoun, Dany, 129
Chamran, Mustafa, 178
China, 245, 246
Churchill, Winston, 234
Council of the South (*Majlis al-Junub*), 170, 187, 201

**D**

Darlan, Jean Louis Xavier François, 270
de Gaulle, Charles, 230, 235, 270
Democratic Front for the Liberation of Palestine (DFLP), 93, 125
Deutsch, Karl W., 164–166, 168, 200
al-Din, 'Abbas Badr, 174
Dodge, David, 195
Dulles, John Foster, 238, 241, 242, 271

Hull, Cordell, 233, 235, 236
Huntington, Samuel, 168
Husseini, Hussein, 195
Hussein ibn Ali, Sherif, 111
Hussein, Saddam, 185


**I**

Ibrahim, Muhsin, 125
India, 43, 231
Iran, 25, 30, 40, 58, 152, 155,
    172, 176, 178, 179, 185,
    193, 194, 195, 238, 243,
    250; Revolution, 155, 172,
    176, 178, 179, 194, 250
Iraq, 49, 71, 75, 85, 176, 185,
    186, 193, 209, 217, 231,
    238, 239, 242, 243, 244,
    252
Islamic Amal, 126, 127, 155,
    194
Israel, 4, 6, 8, 9, 10, 11, 13–16,
    18, 19, 20–24, 25, 26–28,
    31, 32, 33, 39, 42, 47, 50,
    51, 52, 58, 62, 63, 65, 66,
    69, 70, 71, 75, 81, 87, 88,
    89, 91, 96, 97, 98, 99, 100,
    101, 103, 105, 106, 109,
    117, 120, 124, 133, 134,
    136, 142, 146, 152, 154,
    155, 156, 163, 170, 172–
    174, 179, 184, 185, 187,
    188, 192, 193, 194, 196,
    197, 198, 208, 210, 212–
    217, 245, 246, 247, 249,
    251–260, 264, 268, 274;
    Agreement of May 17,
    1983, 14, 22, 23, 25, 42,
    63, 71, 106, 214, 257–259,
    264; and Christians, 10, 13,
    14, 15; and Druze, 13–14,
    15, 22, 23, 27, 101, 214;
    and Lebanese Forces, 9,

13–14, 15, 24, 29, 105, 106,
    117, 118, 120, 146, 147,
    152, 153, 155, 156, 216,
    251; and PLO, 50–51, 88–
    89, 91, 170, 251, 252; and
    Sa'ad Haddad, 11, 15, 105,
    192; and Shi'as, 11, 15, 28–
    29, 101, 170, 173–174,
    192–194, 196–197; Mossad,
    28, 196; policy toward
    Lebanon, 21, 22–24, 27–
    28, 39, 51, 58–59, 88, 91,
    103, 210, 214–215, 253,
    257–259, 274; public opi-
    nion re Lebanon, 21, 28,
    214; relationship with Syria,
    6, 11, 14–16, 29, 142, 213,
    216, 217, 249, 251–252,
    256; relations with the U.S.,
    6, 18–19, 21, 28, 142, 245,
    246, 249, 252–253, 255,
    256, 259, 264; 1968 attack
    on Beirut airport, 58, 88, 91;
    1978 invasion of Lebanon,
    172–174; 1982 invasion (see
    Lebanon)
Israel Defense Forces, 8, 13–15,
    16, 21, 22, 23, 28, 31, 34,
    96–97, 133, 193, 196, 197,
    208
Italy, 97


**J**

Jabril, Antoine (Ahmed), 125
Joint Forces (*Quwat Mush-
    tarikah*), 182, 185, 186,
    187, 188, 192
Jordan, 5, 50, 75, 89, 92, 170,
    209, 217, 238, 243, 244,
    246, 253, 268
Jumblatt, Kamal, 13, 31, 112,
    122, 123, 124, 125, 126,
    158, 161

Jumblatt, Walid, 13, 22, 24, 27, 59, 103, 112, 124, 161

**K**

Karame, Rashid, 22, 156
Karim, Nabil, 129
Khaddam, Abdel Halim, 157–158, 177, 273
Khalaf, Salah, 124, 188
al-Khalil, Kazim, 195, 198, 201
al-Khatib, Ahmad, 95–96
Khomeini, Ruhollah, 23, 41, 155, 176, 181
al-Khouri, Marun, 134
al-Khoury, Bishara, 45, 80, 84–85, 232
Khuri, Fuad I., 167, 168, 169
Kissinger, Henry, 245, 246, 248, 249, 272, 273
Kuwait, 49, 157, 175

**L**

Laos, 246
Lebanese Arab Army (LAA), 94–96
Lebanese Forces, 6, 8, 9, 13, 15, 19, 21, 23, 24, 26, 29, 34, 59, 63, 97, 101, 105, 106, 114, 117–161, 216, 251, 252; activities, 117–118, 137–138, 139–151, 160; and Israel, 8–9, 13–14, 15, 24, 26, 29, 105–106, 117, 120, 146, 152, 155–156, 157–158, 216, 251; and Kata'eb, 8–9, 24, 26, 118, 138–139, 147, 149, 151–152, 153; and PLO, 63, 117, 118, 152, 156; and Syria, 63, 117, 118, 251;

command, 8–9, 130–131, 132, 138–139; composition, 117–118, 132–133, 138–139; equipment, 9, 101, 130, 132, 155, 160; Amin Gemayel and, 8, 21, 24, 34, 101, 106, 139, 151–152; Bashir Gemayel and, 8, 19, 26, 59, 63, 101, 106, 118, 119, 130, 139, 144, 156–157, 252; P. Gemayel and, 9, 24; history, 128–132; military operations, 26, 128–132; objectives, 117–118, 133; organization, 9, 118, 132–133, 137–139; training, 9, 130, 132, 146, 155
Lebanese Front, 33, 130, 131, 134–137, 140, 153, 154, 161, 171, 172, 181, 186, 187, 191
Lebanon: Lebanese Armed Forces, 5, 7, 19, 24, 25, 26, 30, 34, 58, 66, 79–114, 117–118, 129, 130, 139–140, 151–156, 159, 161, 174, 177, 181, 186–187, 190, 203, 208, 209, 214, 217, 219, 242–243, 247, 254, 258, 259, 260, 262; and Christians, 79, 80, 83, 84, 88, 90–91, 93, 106, 108, 110, 112, 186, 203; and Druze, 80, 95, 107–108, 112; and Israel, 103, 214; and militias, 92; and Palestinians, 87–89, 91–92, 94, 97, 112, 159, 174; and Shi'as, 80, 83, 90–91, 94, 95, 110, 112, 174; and Sunnis, 80, 81, 83, 84, 86, 90–96, 112; and U.S., 19, 66, 97, 98, 99, 101, 102,

118-119, 120, 153, 198, 257, 258, 259, 260, 261, 264; National Salvation Committee, 198; partition, 23, 30, 64, 66, 135, 136, 200, 216; political change, 6, 11, 30-31, 56-68, 118-119, 121-122, 149-150, 167-168, 181, 189-191, 193-194, 195, 200; political parties: Ba'ath (Iraqi), 125, 126, 171, 201; Ba'ath (Syrian), 126, 171, 201; Independent Nasserite Movement (INM), 112, 124, 125, 126; Kata'eb, 8, 9, 24, 26, 118, 126, 131, 135, 138, 139, 147, 151, 159, 172; Kurdish Democratic Party, 126; Lebanese Communist Party (LCP), 125, 126, 183, 201; National Bloc, 127, 135; National Liberal Party (NLP), 126, 129, 131, 135, 151, 198; National Union Front, 126; Organization for Communist Action in Lebanon (OCA), 125, 126; Popular Nasserite Organization, 126, 185; Progressive Socialist Party, 13, 28, 124, 126; Socialist Action Party, 125, 126; Syrian Social Nationalist Party (SSNP), 24, 34, 87, 125, 126, 172, 201; political system, 4-5, 19-20, 31-32, 39, 41, 43, 44-46, 50, 51-53, 55, 58, 120, 122, 162, 163, 189-191, 227-230; confessionalism, 4-5, 20, 31-32, 41, 43, 45, 58, 189-191,

229; politics (general), 3, 4, 11-12, 29-30, 39, 48-49, 119-120, 229, 263; relations with: Israel, 3, 6, 11, 13-16, 21-23, 24-30, 39, 42, 58, 62, 122, 123, 209-212, 214-217, 257-259; Jordan, 209; PLO, 39, 42, 51, 122-123; Saudi Arabia, 209; Syria, 3-6, 11, 22-23, 29-30, 34, 39, 42, 47-48, 51, 58-60, 62, 63, 92, 122-123, 142, 145, 187-188, 209, 210, 212-217, 271, 274; U.S., 18, 21, 22, 23, 48, 209-210, 212-215, 219-275; social change, 6, 30-31, 49-50, 118-119, 121-122, 163-169, 179-184, 194, 200; society: disintegration, 8-9, 40, 51, 58-59, 64-67, 87, 94, 99, 200; ethnic groups, 4; integration, 8-9, 39-40, 41-42, 46, 200; religious groups: Alawis, 7, 17, 22, 30, 34; Christians, 4-10, 12, 13, 19-21, 24, 26-27, 30, 32, 34, 40-46, 51-53, 59, 70, 79-80, 85, 87-88, 90-91, 93, 101, 106, 108, 118, 119, 121-126, 134-137, 150, 152-156, 161, 216, 224, 228, 239-240, 243, 268; Armenians, 124, 134; Greek Catholics, 10, 13, 26, 134; Greek Orthodox, 10, 26, 45, 121, 122, 125, 134; Maronites, 8, 9, 12, 13, 42-45, 51-52, 59, 80, 87, 93, 101, 118, 122-125, 134-137, 150, 154-156, 216; Druze, 4, 7, 8, 13, 14, 19, 20, 22-24, 26-28, 32,

National Salvation Committee.
See Lebanon.
Nixon, Richard M., 245, 246,
250

O

Organization of Maronite
Monks, 134
Osseiran, 'Adil, 195
Ottoman Empire, 4, 43, 44

P

Pakistan, 238, 243
Pahlavi, Mohammed Reza, 172,
176, 178, 179
Palestine, 5, 43, 123, 124, 225
Palestine Liberation Army, 96
Palestine Liberation Organization, 6, 16, 17, 22–24, 26,
39, 42, 50–52, 58, 63, 70,
87, 89, 92, 93, 97, 112,
117, 118, 122, 123, 125,
182, 184–186, 188, 189,
191, 215, 251–254, 256,
274; Cairo Accords, 50, 89,
92, 112, 123; evacuation
from Beirut, 16, 97, 99;
Melkart Agreement, 92, 209
Palestinian movement, 5, 6, 87,
122–125, 172–174, 179,
180, 190, 193, 274; Palestinians, 5, 6, 8, 11, 12, 16,
17, 23, 33, 47, 58, 74, 75,
81, 87–92, 99, 101, 104,
120–125, 128, 133, 135,
136, 152, 154, 156, 159,
161, 170, 172–174, 179,
180, 184–188, 192, 193,
196, 247, 254, 256, 268;
fighters, 5, 6, 8, 23, 81, 88,

89, 91, 99, 101, 122–124,
128, 133, 136, 152, 159,
170, 172–174, 179, 184–
188, 192, 193; refugees, 5,
16, 47, 81, 87, 120, 136,
172, 256, 268; massacre of,
in refugee camps—See
Sabra, Shatila
pan-Arabism, 48, 49, 84, 85,
112, 121, 239
Parker, Richard T., 248
Persian Gulf, 49, 65, 73, 74
Popular Front for the Liberation
of Palestine (PFLP), 93,
125
Popular Front for the Liberation
of Palestine—General Com-
mand, 125

Q

Qabalan, Abd al-Amr, 195, 196
Qaddafi, Mu'ammar, 41, 54,
175, 176
Qassis, Simon, 102
Quleilat, Ibrahim, 112, 124, 125
Quwwatli, Shukri, 240, 271

R

Ra'd, In'am, 125, 126
Reagan, Ronald, 34, 219, 250,
251, 253–256, 260, 261,
274, 275
Rouquis, Fouad, 129

S

Sa'ada, Abdullah, 125, 126
Sabra, 21, 97, 120, 128
Sadat, Anwar, 62, 253

247, 274; relationship with Israel, 3, 6, 11, 14, 15, 16, 25, 29, 213, 214, 216, 217, 251, 252, 256; relationship with Lebanon, 92, 209, 259, 274

**T**

Tabatabai, Sadiq, 176
Tabbarah, Riad, 164
Tannous, Ibrahim, 102
Tel el-Zaatar, 128–130, 159
terrorism, 51, 64, 65, 70, 195, 219, 258, 260, 261
Tripoli, 6, 7, 16, 17, 30, 34, 44, 70, 76, 93, 96, 106, 161, 215
Troupes du Levant, 81
Troupes Spéciales du Levant, 82, 83
Turkey, 238, 243

**U**

UNIFIL, 176
Union of Soviet Socialist Republics, 42, 48, 63, 65, 66, 90, 112, 209, 237–239, 243–246, 250, 259, 264, 266
United Arab Emirates, 49, 71
United Arab Republic, 49, 85, 241, 242. See also Egypt, Syria
United Kingdom, 43, 45, 54, 55, 111, 230–239, 269, 270, 273
United Nations, 71, 232, 236, 237, 242, 243, 248, 270, 272
United States of America, 6, 7, 18, 19, 21–25, 27–29, 48, 51, 54, 62, 63, 65, 66, 70, 71, 85, 97–99, 101, 102 109, 112, 145, 195, 209, 218–275; American mis-

sionaries, 223–225, 227, 267; and Lebanese Christians, 19, 48, 211; and Lebanese Armed Forces, 19, 66, 71, 97–99, 101, 102, 107, 112, 219, 247, 259; Lebanese Americans, 51, 225, 226; Marines (1958), 242–244, 272; MNF unit, 25, 28, 29, 65, 70, 97, 109, 219, 220, 254, 256– 261, 263, 264; relations with France, 231–237, 270; relations with Israel, 6, 18, 19, 21–24, 25, 27, 28, 211, 246, 247, 251–253, 256, 257, 259; relations with Lebanon, 18–24, 27, 28, 48, 51, 54, 62, 65, 66, 71, 85, 101, 209–213, 219– 274; relations with Saudi Arabia, 18, 253; relations with Syria, 24, 27, 28, 248, 249, 252, 274; relations with United Kingdom, 231–237
*USS New Jersey*, 260, 262

**V**

Vietnam, 245, 246, 254, 262

**W**

Wadsworth, 236
Wazzan, Chafiq, 66, 230
Weinberger, Caspar, 251, 274
World Bank, 71
World War I, 4, 79, 111
World War II, 54, 69, 82, 230–237, 260

**Y**

Ya'qub, Muhammed Shahadeh, 174

# About the Authors

Edward E. Azar is director of the Center for International Development and professor of government and politics at the University of Maryland. He has recently completed AID-sponsored work in Lebanon in which he served as an advisor to the Lebanese government. Born in Lebanon, Dr. Azar is co-author of one book on Lebanon among his many publications. He has contributed to the *Journal of Conflict Resolution, Journal of Palestine Studies, Journal of East and West Studies,* and many others, and is the editor of *International Interactions.*

Paul A. Jureidini is vice president of Abbott Associates, Inc., and a foremost expert on Lebanon who has also advised the Lebanese government. He is a native of Lebanon and a principal Middle East consultant for many public and private sector organizations. Dr. Jureidini is the author or co-author of three Middle East books, one specifically focusing on Lebanon. He has published in such journals as *Middle East Insight, International Interactions, Journal of Palestine Studies,* and *Military Review.*

R. D. McLaurin, senior associate at Abbott Associates, Inc., consults widely on Middle East affairs. Formerly with the Office of the Secretary of Defense, Dr. McLaurin is the author or co-author of six books on the Middle East, one of which in Lebanon-centered. His articles have appeared in *Journal of Palestine Studies, Military Review, Asia-Pacific Defense Forum, Journal of East and West Studies, Institute for Defense Studies and Analysis Journal,* and *International Interactions.*

Augustus Richard Norton, a lieutenant-colonel in the U.S. Army, is on the faculty at West Point. Dr. Norton served for over a year in southern Lebanon with the United States Truce Supervisory Organization. He has published on terrorism as well as the Middle East, and has recently contributed important articles to *The New York Times, The Los Angeles Times, American-Arab Affairs, Armed Forces and Society, Military Review,* and *Middle East Insight,* among others.

Robert J. Pranger is the director of international programs at the American Enterprise Institute for Public Policy Research, where he edits *AEI Foreign Policy and Defense Review,* and is a professional lecturer in Middle East Studies at the Johns Hopkins University School for Advanced International Studies. Prior to joining AEI, Dr. Pranger served as deputy assistant secretary of defense (international security affairs) for the Near East and South Asia. He is the author or co-author of a half-dozen books, most of them dealing with the Middle East.

Kate Shnayerson is a graduate student in Middle Eastern studies at Harvard University and a junior fellow at the Center for International Development, University of Maryland. She is the co-author of one book on Lebanon.

Lewis W. Snider is chairman of the international relations program at Claremont Graduate School. He is author or co-author of several books, two of which focus principally upon Lebanon. Dr. Snider has also contributed to several other books and to *International Interactions, The Middle East Journal,* and other professional journals and newspapers.

Joyce R. Starr is director of the Near East Program, Center for Strategic and International Studies/Georgetown University, where she also serves as overseas representative in the Middle East. Dr. Starr specializes in economic and foreign affairs of the Near East, dividing her time between Washington and the region. At the Center, she is also director of the CSIS Near East Council, which is designed for a corporate membership. Dr. Starr is Middle East editor of *The Washington Quarterly,* publishes in major newspapers, and is a consultant to corporations and organizations. She is the editor of *A Shared Destiny: Near East Regional Cooperation and Development* (Praeger, 1983) and *Challenges in the Middle East: Regional Dynamics and Western Security* (Praeger, 1981).